Library of
Davidson College

*The
Aramaic Origin
of the
Four Gospels*

The Aramaic Origin of the Four Gospels

FRANK ZIMMERMANN

KTAV Publishing House Inc.
New York
1979

© COPYRIGHT 1979
FRANK ZIMMERMAN

Library of Congress Cataloging in Publication Data

Zimmermann, Frank.
 The Aramaic origin of the four Gospels.

 Bibliography: p.
 Includes index.
 1. Bible. N. T. Gospels—Criticism, interpretation, etc. 2. Bible. N. T. Gospels—Language, style, etc. I. Title.
BS2555.2.Z55   226'.06 78–12328
ISBN 0–87068–434–5

MANUFACTURED IN THE UNITED STATES OF AMERICA

To my dearest Rebecca

Table of Contents

Preface	ix
Abbreviations	xiii
Introduction	3
I THE WRITTEN TEXT	25
II THE EVIDENCE FROM MATTHEW	33
III THE EVIDENCE FROM MARK	83
IV THE EVIDENCE FROM LUKE	97
V THE EVIDENCE FROM JOHN	139
VI TEXTS AND DOCTRINES	167
VII LOGIA OF JESUS AND THEIR ARAMAIC SOURCE	177
VIII THE WORLD IS A BRIDGE ... ANOTHER LOGION OF JESUS	189
Appendix I: Aramaisms in Acts	195
Appendix II: The Book of Revelations and its Underlying Document	205
Notes	215
Select Bibliography	219
Indices	
I General Index	225
II Aramaic Words and Forms	228
III Greek Words and Forms	232
IV Hebrew Words and Idioms	234
Arabic — Akkadian — Latin	235
V Versions Cited	236
VI Biblical Passages — Old Testament	238
New Testament	239
VII Index of Authors	241

Preface

NEW TESTAMENT studies have made great strides in the preceding decades. The publication of new manuscripts, the sorting out of their family relationships, the refinement and establishment of a more reliable text, the technique of form criticism, the investigation of rituals, cultural patterns, symbols and sources, the illuminating identity of biblical types and events (typology)—all have contributed in a most enlightening fashion to New Testament advance. In one area, in the field of Aramaic-Greek studies, only a minimal work has been done. The present volume seeks to make a contribution to that branch of New Testament study.

The relation between the Greek text and the underlying Aramaic is of crucial importance, if we wish to go back to the primacy and significance of the Gospel report. Jesus spoke Aramaic, and so did his disciples. The transmission of his sayings and the reports of his activities were in Aramaic. It is imperative to recover, as best one can, the original saying or episode in the Aramaic language wherein it was cast. The Greek Gospels abound in bizarre locutions and unintelligible happenings. This book presents some two hundred new readings as retroversions from Aramaic that clarify many Gospel problems.

The pioneer in this study of Aramaic and Greek relationships was Charles Cutler Torrey (1863–1956). Before and after him have been scholars who have dealt with these problems, either in an incomplete or fragmentized fashion (see the bibliography). His work however fell short of completeness; as a pioneering effort, in the nature of the case, some of his work has to be revised and supplemented. His main contention of translation, however, is undeniably correct.

As the mass of index cards accumulated in the course of this study, I realized that much of the evidence cited from far and wide might be distressing or inaccessible for the student I had in mind. This work is not only intended for the sophisticated scholar, but for a larger group, for those students, oriented to the New Testament, who know their Greek, but less so of Aramaic and Hebrew; and on the other hand, it is intended for those who know Hebrew and Aramaic, but possess a moderate knowledge of the New

Testament and Hellenistic Greek. I have therefore simplified by translating, as a rule, the Hebrew, Aramaic, or Greek, so that the lay public, too, would find its way in the evidence presented in this book. All meanings can be tested by the student in the valuable dictionaries of Liddell and Scott and Arndt and Gingrich for the Greek, J. Levy and M. Jastrow for the Hebrew and Aramaic; J. P. Smith's Syriac Dictionary and C. Brockelmann may be referred to for Syriac and Eastern Aramaic.

Important as it is, much pro and con has been avoided by the following plan. First, the Authorized Version is quoted as the most familiar to all, as well as the most literally translated. The difficulty in the verse is spotlighted for the student by the Greek word or phrase, so that he apprehends at once the problem to be discussed. Second, a short discussion of the usage and syntax of the problematic Greek is given. Third, I have employed modern translations as the Revised Standard Version, the New English Bible, the New American Bible and others that give the best consensus, in the acuity and scholarship of the editors, as to what the verse should mean. This device of citing modern translations serves a double purpose: on the one hand, it points up the difficulty in the verse in short form; and on the other hand, it shows broadly what the verse should mean. The Aramaic is then offered as the resolution of the problematic reading. A final literal translation is offered that supplies the reasonable, and as I believe, the correct explanation, the simple unforced sense from the Aramaic. Much may be argued from the disagreeing translations; I have only stated my findings and conclusions.

While the book is focused on the meaning of crucial passages that have hitherto defied explanation, the investigation provided a number of interesting sidelights. The translation into Greek from Aramaic must have been made from a written record, including the Fourth Gospel. The language was Eastern Aramaic, as the material itself revealed, most strikingly through a comparison of parallel passages. New light is shed on the pristine character of the Eucharist, the Logos, Jesus' attitude towards marriage and divorce, his conception of baptism, Jesus' reason for his own baptism by John, and the purpose of the Transfiguration. The Aramaic hypothesis certifies, moreover, that some 14 logia of Jesus, quoted by the Church Fathers, were very likely original, though outside the canonical Gospels. Appendices with some 15 solutions of difficult verses in Acts, as well as some 8 verses in Revelations give further evidence of their underlying Aramaic documents. The book provides, too, pertinent rabbinic sources, tangential to a number of examples.

Although we have not come to a conclusion about a rationale and constitution of the Gospel text (Kurt Aland), I have followed as standard the E. Nestle-K. Aland edition (25th ed. 1963), and the text of the United Bible Societies (3rd ed. 1968) as well as H. von Soden's edition (see the bibliography), although, judgmentally, I had to be eclectic in the choice of readings. Bruce Metzger's record of the meetings of the UBS committee was an indispensable adjunct in evaluating the manuscriptal material.

Due to the limitations of space, regretfully a number of matters had to be omitted from discussion: the question of the Q material, of the D manuscript, especially in Acts, the chronology and dating of the different sections, of the Petrine and Pauline sources, of evaluating the new finds, as well as the country of origin of the different sources. These studies must be left to the labor of others.

It is with deep gratitude that I thank my dear wife Rebecca who read the manuscript and made valuable suggestions and Ms. Anita Tamari for conscientious editing, and Mr. Bernard Scharfstein of the KTAV Publishing House who handled matters in the launching of this volume.

Abbreviations

Old Testament Books: Gen., Ex., Lev., Num., Deut. (Dt.), Josh., Jud(g)., Sam., Kings, Is., Jer., Ezek., Hos., Joel, Amos, Ob(ad)., Jonah, Mic., Nah., Hab., Zeph., Hag., Zech., Mal., Ps. Prov. Job, Cant., Lam., Eccl., Esth., Dan., Ezr(a), Neh(em)., Chron.

New Testament Books: Mt., Mk., Lk., Jn., Ac., Rom., 1–2 Cor., Gal., Eph., 1–2 Thess., Heb., 1–2 Pet., Rev.

The cited treatises of Mishna and Talmud are as follows:

Ab., Abot; Aboda Zar., Abodah Zarah; Baba Batr., Baba Batra; Bekh., Bekorot; Bera., Berakot; Baba Qam., Baba Qamma; Baba Meṣ., Baba Meṣia; Giṭ., Giṭṭin; Qidd., Qiddushin; Mena., Menaḥot; Midd., Middot; Ned., Nedarim; Sot., Sotah; Yeb., Yebamot. Citations from the Talmud Yerushalmi are preceded by y. or yer.

Other abbreviations are:

ASV	The American Standard Version
RSV	The Revised Standard Version
NASB	The New American Standard Bible: New Testament
NEB	The New English Bible
NAB	The New American Bible
ABUV	The New Testament of Our Lord and Saviour Jesus Christ (John Broadus; alii)
Beck	The New Testament in the Language of Today (William F. Beck)
Gdspd.	The New Testament: an American Translation (Edgar J. Goodspeed)
Knox	The New Testament in the Translation of Monsignor Ronald Knox
Mof.[1]	The Historical New Testament by James Moffatt
Mof.[2]	The New Testament: A New Translation
Mon	The Centenary Translation: The New Testament in Modern English (Helen Bartlett Montgomery).

Nor	The New Testament: A New Translation (Olaf M. Norlie)
Rieu	The Four Gospels (E. V. Rieu)
Rhm	The Emphasized New Testament: A New Translation (J. B. Rotherham)
TCNT	The Twentieth Century New Testament
Wey	The New Testament in Modern Speech (Richard Francis Weymouth) as revised by J. A. Robertson
Wms	The New Testament: A Translation in the Language of the People (Charles B. Williams)
AJSL	American Journal of Semitic Languages and Literature (1884–1941)
HUCA	The Hebrew Union College Annual
JBL	The Journal of Biblical Literature
JQR	The Jewish Quarterly Review
JTS	The Journal of Theological Studies
ZNW	Zeitschrift für die neutestamentliche Wissenschaft und die Kunde des Urchristentums
EB	Encyclopedia Biblica
DCG	Dictionary of Christ and the Gospels
ERE	Encyclopedia of Religion and Ethics

Introduction

JESUS SPOKE Aramaic to his disciples, not Greek. He read his Bible in Hebrew, and probably could speak some Greek and could understand his arraignment before Pilate. His activities, his *logia,* and his preachments were remembered and transmitted by his disciples in the original Aramaic. Yet the reports of his sayings, his actions, his parables, the dialogue between himself and his followers, his miracles and his death, found their form and transmission to us in Greek, and in Greek of a certain character. How, and by what process, were these memorabilia transmuted from Aramaic to Greek, giving way to different versions and different traditions?

Answers to these questions have divided scholars into a number of camps. One group, which originated in the nineteenth century and persists to the present day, contends that the Gospels were written in Greek *ab origine.* They maintain that the strong Semitic character of these documents—some scholars say it is Hebrew, some say Aramaic, while others avoid the issue by the general denomination of Semitic—is circumstantial. The Gospel writers were on intimate terms with Septuagintal Greek, with its Hebraic ideas and phrases, theological terms and language, and the authors must have, at one time or another, breathed the very air of Palestine. More importantly, the Greek of the Gospels, the Hellenistic *koine,* is paralleled by the finds in papyri as shown by the discoveries of Grenfel and Hunt, Thumb, Deissmann, and Moulton and Milligan, to name but a few of the early representatives of this school.[1] Frequently, there are extraordinary parallels to Gospel Greek in the Hellenistic Greek papyri of the first century C.E.—in the writs, receipts, documents, wills, etc. of the common people, found in the dustbins of Egypt. These scholars argue that if we are to speak of Aramaic origins at all, such Aramaic existed only in the minds of the Gospel writers, in concepts, phrases, and coloring, which influenced their writing in Greek. Papias (circa 125 C.E.) relates that Mark became the interpreter of Peter, and it was he who wrote down everything that he remembered (*hermeneutes Petrou genomenos, hosa emnemoneusen akribos egrapsen*). Although the veracity and accuracy of this report is widely questioned,[2] the tradition may serve as an analogous process: The original writing, it is insisted, was done in Greek. Representatives of this view would be A. Jülicher, G. Dalman, E. C. Colwell, A. J. Grieve, Nigel Turner, W. F. Albright. Difficulties in Greek vocabulary, syntax, and usages have been explained, more or less appropriately, through the finds in the papyri.

Nevertheless, of course, there is always Aramaic, the most probable language, persistently evident in the background, prompting another group of scholars to assert that there are some evidences of translations, as well as transmissions of Aramaic locutions, imbedded in the Greek. The statement of Papias again in this connection is quite suggestive, "Matthew, in the Hebrew dialect, compiled the Logia, and each one interpreted them according to his ability" (*Matthaios men oun Hebraidi dialekto ta logia sunegrapsato,* var. *sunetaksato*). The "Hebrew dialect" is well recognized to be Aramaic. The question that now arises is, how much Aramaic is there in the transmitted Gospels? Is it occasionally Aramaic, or are the Gospels largely Aramaic or totally Aramaic? No answer has been forthcoming on this question. Matthew Black has tried to show that the Aramaic manifests itself mostly in dialogue, which therefore gives us largely the *ipsissima verba* of Jesus. The retroversions from Aramaic appearing in mistranslations, and the presence of Aramaic expressions, syntax, and structure show, however, from Black's own work that the substrate Aramaic is not limited to dialogue. The question of how much Aramaic is in the Gospels is still an area to be explored, an essential area, if we wish to get back to the primacy of the Gospel reports and experience.

Another group of scholars, among whom C. C. Torrey was the most vocal and vigorous exponent, comes out flatly with the proposition that the Four Gospels (with the exception of Jn. 21,[3] Lk. 1—2,[4] and the Mk. ending 16.9—20), including Acts up to 15.35, are translated directly from Aramaic, and from a written Aramaic text. This group differs from the previous views which allow scant Aramaic influence, and only occasional evidence of Aramaic *logia* in the background. But here there is an impressive group of scholars, among them Wellhausen, Nestle, Rendel Harris, Schlatter, A. Meyer, Burney, Montgomery, De Zwaan, Wensinck, [perhaps a loose association as they may differ from each other], who maintain that the Gospels are Aramaic documents. A further matter of importance which concerns these scholars is, in what dialect of the Aramaic were the Gospels composed. Was it Judean Aramaic, Galilean, or the so-called Christian Palestinian Aramaic, or was it Samaritan Aramaic, or perhaps the Syriac Aramaic? (There is a considerable number of Syriacisms considered valid by such

INTRODUCTION

scholars as Wellhausen, Burney, Torrey, and Black.) This question of the dialect will be considered in subsequent pages (pp. 22f.).

My own researches have led me to consider Torrey's position valid and convincing that the Gospels as a whole were translated from the Aramaic into Greek. The following discussion supports and expands this thesis with new illustrations and examples. Some scholars have thrown stones at the building Torrey constructed, and have broken some windows (cf. Black, *Aramaic Approach to the Gospels and Acts* 8–9), but the structure stands firm. Torrey's contributions principally, together with those of Wellhausen, Burney, Montgomery and Black, and some 200 new examples of my own, should make the hypothesis of the Aramaic substrate irrefutable. There are now some 500 pieces of evidence. In this connection, by curious contrast, it is remarkable that in many other instances, as in the books of the Apocrypha and Pseudepigrapha, the evidence for the original language of a book may be a mere five or six examples, yet deemed sufficient for an editor to bring in a verdict. Thus in Charles (*The Apocrypha and Pseudepigrapha of the OT*, I, 244), the editor of *Judith*, A. E. Cowley, after offering a number of examples of his contention that Judith goes back to a Hebrew substrate, postulates unequivocally for Hebrew as the original language thereby disregarding the Greek *koine*, in which the Greek Judith is cast. (For other examples see ibid. I pp. 642, 660. and II, pp. 4, 473, 547 where conclusions are based on rather meager, even faulty, evidence.)

There is another hypothesis about the Greek Gospels vis-à-vis the antecedent Aramaic that requires some attention and analysis. Some scholars claim (comp. N. Turner in Peake's Commentary on the Bible[2], 662) that the Gospel writers wrote in Greek while thinking in Aramaic. This viewpoint is quite seductive, and seems unassailable. They argue that like a European who writes a letter in English but thinks in his own language, makes slips in his English, similarly, in the Gospels, the writer could remember the Aramaic tradition but set it down in Greek. In course, he slipped and blundered occasionally in his composition. On the surface, one can hardly dislodge the argument. Indeed, how could you *disprove* that someone thought in Aramaic, but wrote in Greek? Why can't you say moreover that the writer was so saturated with the Greek of the LXX, that he wrote almost naturally in the biblical idiom? This "why can't you say" argument seems persistent and formidable, actually because it is in an elusive frame of reference, where countervailing evidence seemingly cannot touch it or demolish it.

Two exponents of this view are the noted scholars Sir Godfrey R. Driver and Professor W. F. Albright. Driver writes that John "was mentally translating, as he wrote, *logia* that was handed down by tradition and was current in Christian circles in Aramaic, from that language into the Greek in which he was actually composing his Gospel." ("Original Language of the Fourth Gospel" (*Jewish Guardian*, 1923). For this notion of thinking in one language and writing in Greek, comp. too J. Hastings, Dictionary of Christ and the Gospels, I, 131, and R. H. Charles, *Revelation of St. John,* I, cxliii.

The scholar who has argued most forcibly against a written Aramaic text of the Gospels was the late Professor Albright in a number of publications, *From the Stone Age to Christianity,* 2nd ed., pp. 384f. (Anchor ed.), *The Archaeology of Palestine* (1961), pp. 199—203 (Pelican ed.), the lengthiest and most mature presentation of his thesis, and *Commentary on Matthew* (p. clxxv, bot., and clxvi). In the latter he moderates his whole position of unwritten Aramaic sources by stating "[whether] in oral or written form does not really matter." Since, however, this position of unwritten Aramaic sources is shared by other scholars as well, to say nothing of some diehards who deny *in toto* the whole Aramaic substrate, and may continue to be current as an accepted hypothesis without being subject to criticism, it may be of value to examine the main points of Albright's claim. His argument for unwritten Aramaic sources is based upon four premises, with some corollaries, which I cite in his words (*Archaeology,* ut supra, pp. 200f.).

1. "One real difficulty is, however, that we are not fully informed about the possibilities of late Hellenistic Greek in the provinces. There are no literary works written in any contemporary Greek ... The Koine seems to have been used only for conversation or for every day writing on the part of semi-literate persons." This implies that many difficulties will remain unsolved until evidence will be forthcoming from the papyri, if ever.

2. He posits, without adequate circumspection, "The complete absence of contemporary Aramaic literature ..." Albright proceeds to maintain that aside from the biblical Aramaic and that of the Elephantine papyri (the standard Aramaic of the Persian Empire), all other Aramaic such as that of the Judean Aramaic of Onqelos, the Galilean Aramaic of the Palestinian Targum and the Jerusalem Talmud "reflect the speech of the third century C.E. and later." The other Aramaic dialects—the Samaritan, the Babylonian Talmud, Mandean, Syriac, and the Christian Palestinian Aramaic—are all of the second to the fourth centuries C.E. Hence,

3. "Against Torrey's views stand two additional difficulties which are hard to overcome: [a.] none of the dialects sketched above was spoken in Palestine in the time of Christ."

4. Moreover, [b.] "there are no Aramaic literary works extant from the period between the second century B.C.E. and the second or third century C.E., a period of over three hundred years." The hypothesis that Albright advances with regard to Aramaic and its transmutation into Greek, and this is the main thrust of his claim, is that the activities and sayings of Jesus were transmitted in oral form. (This is again an old idea, comp. Hastings, *Dictionary of the Bible*, II, 236—237; A. Wright, *Synopsis of the Gospels* [Notes]), and that the composition was in Greek originally, although there was "a slight shift," as he says, in the transference of Aramaic to Greek.

In order to bolster these views, Albright asserts further that "there was a real eclipse of Aramaic during the Seleucid Empire" (p. 202). Megillat Ta'anit may precede the year 70 C.E. but because of its chronological context, it is safer to date it in the second century C.E. According to him, the story of Aḥiqar, found among the Elephantine papyri, and quite divergent from the Syriac version, is to be explained as being derived from a common source—again through oral transmission, as he postulates. "It seems therefore," he sums up, "[that] there is actually more evidence against the continuity of Aramaic written literature through Hellenistic times.... Other evidence makes it increasingly probable that the Aramaic element in the Gospels comes from the translation of orally transmitted *documents* (?! emphasis mine), that is of orally transmitted Aramaic records of the words and doings of Jesus...." Albright concludes that "Christians may thus continue to read the Greek Gospels without apprehending serious errors in translation (although there were of course many slight changes of meaning in the shift from Aramaic to Greek)" (p. 203).

In *From the Stone Age to Christianity*, Albright takes a generally similar stand, though with some significant differences. He avers that "Judged by the severest standards, it must be said that Torrey has proved a respectable proportion of his examples." Yet on the next page he states that "Although Torrey has demonstrated the existence of a much more important and much more far reaching Aramaic substratum of our Greek Gospels than had been believed previously by any first-class scholar, on the other hand, not a single case of alleged scribal error adduced by Torrey is convincing." Not *one?* Torrey in his *Our Translated Gospels* offered some 130 examples of evidence showing mistranslation of the Aramaic text on the part of the Greek translator, of which some 30 examples have a scribal error of some kind. He limited the number expressly, he says, for the understanding of the general reader, as the purpose was to show via repeated translation that good natural sense appeared where there was non-sense. While some scholars have cavilled at some of the examples, the main contention was brilliantly conceived, and his evidence for the most part holds. In all fairness, it cannot be cavalierly dismissed.

Albright also advances in his book the now familiar argument that there is an absence of any satisfactory examples of Palestinian Aramaic for the period from 50 B.C.E. to 70 C.E., although previously he had believed the span to be over three hundred years. In his *Commentary on Matthew,* these arguments are not repeated, but there is the tacit assumption that the sayings and doings of Jesus were transmitted orally in Aramaic.

Unfortunately, as Albright himself posits it, much of his "case" is put in negative terms. He speaks of the lack of literary Hellenistic Greek in the *koine,* the lack of archeological evidence, and thus, his view is based essentially on "the argument from silence," always faulted as a doubtful procedure. As will be seen in the sequel herein, the other props to the argument are quite thin and invalid.

Thus the characterization that our knowledge of Hellenistic Greek *koine* is imperfect might convey to the student that all studies of NT Greek and Aramaic studies should be suspended until we are as Albright says "fully informed." This is an uncalled-for caveat and sounds like an injunction against debate. A. Deissmann,[5] father of this category of Greek papyrology, thought most decidedly in terms of a Greek translation from the Aramaic.

Incidentally, where the *koine* or another source provided an adequate explanation for a puzzling Greek idiom, although I may have a well-grounded suspicion that the source of the locution is to be found in Aramaic, I did not include such evidence in these pages. If the *koine* was employed for ordinary conversation and the writing of letters, documents, receipts as extant in the Egyptian papyri, the fact is that it *was* the basis for the Septuagint (Thackeray, *Grammar of the OT in Greek,* pp. 20f.) and the language of Polybius (ob. 120 B.C.E.), Diodorus Siculus (140 B.C.E.), Strabo (10 C.E.), Plutarch (90 C.E.) and Josephus. The *koine,* as the renowned Hellenist Thumb averred, is a literary offshoot of the vernacular (Swete, *Introduction to the OT in Greek,*[2] p. 285). The *koine* superceded all the Greek dialects, and took off on its own for a fresh start. The Gospel translators made use of the *koine* very much like the LXX translators made use of their *koine* in translating the Hebrew Bible in their time.

The recent progress in the Greek *koine* studies by investigators, however, is distinctly encouraging, and we are not so completely at sea as one might infer. Undoubtedly parallels from the *koine* may be extensively adduced, but even the scholars who have written our grammars and dictionaries speak most conclusively of Greek translations of Aramaic. J. H. Moulton, in page after page of his *Grammar of New Testament Greek*³ refers to the underlying Aramaic idiom ("Apart from places where he may definitely be translating a Semitic [Aramaic] document etc." I, p. 9 and elsewhere).⁶ So, too, do successive supplementing editors, W. F. Howard (II, pp. 413f.) naturally with exceptions; although in the third volume of the Syntax, prepared by N. Turner he speaks repeatedly of Semitic "influence," Turner apparently hesitated about actual translation (III, 9). This position was challenged by Blass-Debrunner-Funk, *Greek Grammar of the NT*, paragraph 4. In the Greek dictionaries, an Aramaic document is assumed, though with caution (Arndt-Gingrich, *Greek-English Lexicon of the NT*, p. viii) (W. Bauer wrote the Introduction). We may at the very least sum up with Blass-Debrunner-Funk, "Not everything which conforms to Semitic idiom is a Semitism, nor is everything which appears somewhere or sometime in Greek genuine Greek" (p. 4).

As mentioned, Albright regarded as significant the presumed absence of any Aramaic literature contemporary with Jesus and the disciples, and the fact that none of the dialects mentioned by him "was *spoken* (italics mine) in Palestine in the time of Christ" (*Archaeology*, 201). Yet Albright certainly knew but ignored that Aramaic was the language spoken. Did not Jesus speak Aramaic to his disciples? Compare Schürer, *Geschichte*, II, p. 23: "*Der Sprache der jüdischen Bevölkerung in allen hier genannten Gebieten war seit den letzten Jahrhunderten vor Chr. nicht mehr die hebräische, sondern die aramäische,*" following the studies of Zunz, Delitzsch, Kautzsch, Neubauer, Dalman, Meyer, Zahn, and latterly, note Torrey's statement that Aramaic was the principal language of the land (*Our Translated Gospels*, p. ix). It is well known that beginning with the LXX there is ample evidence that the language the translators knew and spoke was Aramaic. For instance, they transliterated the Hebrew term *pesah* in the Pentateuch by its Aramaic form *pasha,* the Hebrew *shekar* "strong drink" by *sikera,* the Hebrew *ger* by *gioras* (Ex. 12.19; Is. 14.1). Parts of the pseudepigraphic Enoch were written in Aramaic (Schürer, ibid, p. 25; Zimmermann, "Bilingual Character of I Enoch," JBL, LX, 1941, p. 159f.). Fragmentary Greek MSS of this period show this characteristic in their transliteration of Aramaic words (Charles, *Apocrypha and Pseudepigrapha*, II, p. 172). Quite a number of books in the Apocrypha and Pseudepigrapha, supposedly written in Greek originally—as was the hypothesis of the leading scholars of the nineteenth century—are now positively known to have been written in Aramaic. (Thus, for example, Nöldeke in 1879 thought that Tobit was written in Greek, but see now R. H. Pfeiffer, *History of NT Times,* pp. 272—273 and the writer's *Book of Tobit,* p. 138.)

At the risk of repetition, the following are transliterations of numerous words in NT showing the Aramaic forms.

abba Mk. 14.36; *(h)akeldamach* Ac. 1.19; *gabbatha* Jn. 19.13; *golgotha* Mt. 27.33; *ephphatha* Mk. 7.34; *korbanas* Mt. 27.6; Jos. JW. II.9.4; *mamonas* Mt. 6.24; *maran atha* I Cor. 6.22; *messias* Jn. 1.41; *pascha* Mt. 26.17; *raka* Mt. 5.22; *satanas* Mt. 16.23; *talitha koumi* Mt. 5.41. To these may be added personal names such as *Kephas, Martha, Tabitha,* as well as the frequent names compounded with *Bar* (son) as *Barabbas, Bartholomaios, Barjesus, Barjonas, Barnabas, Barsabas,* and *Bartimaios*. In passing, the old difficulty of *Boanerges* in Mk. 3.17 may perhaps be explained as *בְּנֵי רְעֵשׁ, defined in the Greek as "sons of thunder" with *re'esh* as a by-form of *ra'ash* (Aramaic!) as *ṭe'em* is a by-form of *ṭa'am* (M. L. Margolis, "The Feminine Ending 'T' in Hebrew," Chicago, 1896). The intrusive ō in "Boanerges" was introduced by a Greek scribe who did not understand this to be a transliterated word in Greek. Unconsciously anticipating the explanation "sons of *thunder*," he thought of the Greek words *boao, boa,* and *boe* all used for great noises such as those of war, wind, and of waves (cf. Liddell-Scott, Greek-English Lexicon⁹) which the scribe mistakenly incorporated into the transliteration. Note Banereges (minus. 70). Aramaic also are the very words of Jesus: *Eloi Eloi lama sabachtanei* (Mk. 15.34) and *talitha koumi* (Mk. 5.41). In addition, Josephus, in mentioning the festivals, designates them by their Aramaic names: *sabbata* Ant. I.1.1.; III.6.6; *pascha* Ant. II, 14.6; III.10.5 and elsewhere; *asartha* Ant. III, 10.6.

Material from Tannaitic sources, especially from 150 B.C.E. to 100 C.E. will be discussed presently.

The truth of the matter is, however, that both Hebrew and Aramaic were functioning coexistently, and in wide areas throughout the Second Commonwealth. The witnesses have some hiatuses in their tacit testimony, but on the whole, the linkage forms a steady and discernible line. The Book of Ezra was written partly in Aramaic and partly translated in Hebrew, Nehemiah in Hebrew partially translated from Aramaic, Chronicles in Hebrew and partially translated from the Aramaic, Daniel in Aramaic and Hebrew, the latter again a translation from Aramaic. (See the writer's *Biblical Books Translated from the Aramaic* for the evidence). At any rate, the proof extends from about 300 B.C.E. to 170 B.C.E. of Daniel. So, too, the Book of Enoch was written in Hebrew and Aramaic (see R. H. Charles, *Apocrypha and Pseudepigrapha,* II, ibid., and Zimmermann, "Bilingual

INTRODUCTION

Character" ut supra, 195ff.). Other books such as Ben Sira and I Maccabees were written in Hebrew during this period.

Aside from the Hebrew Bible and the intertestamental literature, other Tannaitic and pre-Destruction sources beginning with about 150 B.C.E. provide evidence of Aramaic and Hebrew that should not be overlooked. For example, dicta of Yose ben Yo'ezer, ("Early Maccabean," JE, VII: 242) are reported both in Aramaic and Hebrew. Thus in the Mishna 'Eduyot 8.4 there is a statement of Yose העיד (רבי) יוסי בן ויעזר איש צרידה על איל קמצא דכן ועל משקה בית מטבחייא דאינון דכיין ודיקרב במיתא מסתאב וקרו ליה יוסי שריא. "Yose ben Yoezer man of Ṣereda [Rabbi should be omitted, as in some editions, because Yose lived before the Destruction] testified about the *Ayil*-locust that they are clean, and about sluices (of blood and water) issuing from the Temple slaughterhouse that they are clean; and one who touches a corpse is unclean [see Aboda Zara 37b for the explanation of this] and scholars called him 'Yose, the Permitter'." This statement is noteworthy and of prime importance for its Aramaic language, whereas, before and aft, there are 73 Mishnayot that are in Hebrew. The Aramaic tradition must be genuine, as it is inconceivable that all the other Mishnayot in *'Eduyot* should be in Hebrew, and this solely in Aramaic, especially since other statements elsewhere by Yose are in Hebrew, showing once more that Hebrew and Aramaic flourished side by side.

Other passages may be cited in further proof: Ben Yehudah in the Introduction to *Millon Ha-Lashon Ha-Ivrit* (A Complete Dictionary of Ancient and Modern Hebrew, popular ed., 1948); and A. Büchler, *Die Priester und der Cultus*, 1895, trans. into Hebrew *Ha-Kohanim Wa-Abodatam*, 1966 (with some slight additions) cite the Tosefta Sotah 13.4, and Jer. Tal. Sotah 9.24.2 (Krotoschin, 24b, 25a). A prefatory passage has been added in 13.4 as well (Zuckermandel, *Tosefta*, 319):

I. שוב פעם אחת היו יושבין ביבנה, ושמעו בת קול אומרת יש כאן אדם שראוי לרוח הקדש אלא שאין הדור זכאי לכך ונתנו עיניהם בשמואל הקטן וכשמת אמרו עליו הי עניו, הי חסיד, תלמידו של הלל. אף הוא אומר בשעת מיתתו שמעון וישמעאל לחרבא וחברווהי לקטלא ושאר עמא לביזא ועקן סגיאין יהוון אחרי דנא ובלשון ארמית אמרן.

I. [Hebrew] Again, at another time, they were at a session at Yabneh. And they heard an angelic voice saying, "There is a man here who is fit to receive the Holy Spirit, except that this generation is not worthy enough." They turned their eyes to Samuel the Little. When he died, they said, "Alas! Such a man of humility! Alas! Such a man of saintliness! Truly, a disciple of Hillel!" Furthermore, he said at the time of his death, [Aramaic] "*Simon and Ishmael*

will perish by the sword, and their colleagues will be killed; the remaining people will be subject to spoliation, and many troubles will come after this."
He said this in Aramaic (italics mine).

II. יוחנן כהן גדול שמע מבית קודש הקדשים; נצחו טליא דאזלי לאגחא קרבא וכיונו אותה השעה וכיונו שנצחו אותה שעה.

II. [Hebrew] Yoḥanan, the High Priest, heard a voice within the Holiest of Holies, [Aramaic] *"The young men who went to wage war against Antioch have won!"* [Hebrew] They fixed the time, and they pinpointed the hour at which they had won.

III. שמעון הצדיק שמע בטילת עבידתא דאמר סנאה להיתיא להיכלא ונהרג קסגלקס ובטלו גזירותיו ובלשון ארמי שמען

III. [Hebrew] Simon the Just heard a voice, [Aramaic] *"The work* [see S. Zeitlin, *Megillat Ta'anit*, p. 88] *that the enemy sought to bring in the Temple is abolished."* Furthermore [now in Hebrew] " 'K. [reading is presumed to be corrupt for Caius Caligula, assassinated C.E. 41] has been killed, and his decrees are annulled.' What he heard was in the Aramaic language." There are parallel texts that vary unimportantly in the readings. See below.

It is obvious that the first passage is later than the latter two. Samuel the Little belonged to the second generation of Tannaim (C.E. 90—130). and was a contemporary of teachers such as Rabban Gamaliel II and Rabbi Eliezer ben Hyrcanus. The latter incidentally had his *yeshiba* in Lydda. The school bore the Aramaic name of *motheba rabba* "The great Academy," Bek. 5b. The passages, as in so many examples, are distinctive in that both Aramaic and Hebrew are quoted in the same context, showing that the traditional statement in Aramaic is genuine. The texts, themselves emphasize that the statement was made in Aramaic. That the Temple was still standing in II and III demonstrates the pre-Destruction date. (Comp. further, Ben Yehudah, op. cit. 130.)

One should also include the three Epistles sent by Rabban Gamaliel I (so Bacher, JE, s.v. Gamaliel I; J. Derenbourg, *Essai sur l'histoire et la géographie de la Palestine*, 241f.; Graetz, *Geschichte*, IV, 71; Dalman *Grammatik*,[2] S.9 Gamaliel II). The passage runs as follows:

מעשה ברבן גמליאל שהיה יושב על גב מעלה בהר הבית והיה יוחנן הכהן הסופר הלז עומד לפניו ושלש איגרות חתוכות לפניו מונחת אמר לו טול איגרא חדא וכתוב; לאחנא בני גלילאה עלאה ולאחנא בני גלילאה תחתאה שלומכן יסגא. מהודעין אנחנא לכון דזמן ביעורא מטא לאפרושי מעשרא ממעטינא דזיתא. וטול איגרא חדא וכתוב; לאחנא בני דרומא שלומכון יסגא. מהודעין אנחנא לכון דזמן ביעורא מטא לאפרושי מעשרא מעומרי שיבליא. וטול אגרא חדא וכתוב; לאחנא בני גלוותא בבבל ולאחנא בבל ובמדי ולשאר גלוותא בישראל שלומכן יסגא לעלם; מהודעין אנחנא לכון דגוזליא רכיכין

INTRODUCTION   13

ואימריא עריקין (זעירין, דקיקין, ms. var.) וזמנא דאביבא לא מטא ושפרא מילתא
באנפי ובאנפי חברי ואוסיפית על שתא דא יומין תלתין.

(We should read זעירין "small," cf. its parallel רכיכין, or else עריץ "bare" i.e. having no wool. For the variant texts, see Derenbourg, *Essai*, chapter 15 for analysis and discussion; Graetz, *Geschichte der Juden*, IV, 71; A. Büchler, *Die Priester und der Cultus*, 63. The epistolary text, with the variants, is edited by Dalman, *Dialektproben*,² p. 3.) We should translate:

"It happened once that Rabban Gamaliel was sitting on a step leading to the Temple Mount. The kohen Yoḥanan, the well-known scribe, was standing attendance on him and three letters cut to size were lying before him. R. Gamaliel said to him, [Aramaic starts] Take a letter and write: 'To our brothers in Upper Galilee, and to our brothers in Lower Galilee, may your good welfare increase! We proclaim to you that the time of removal has come for setting aside the tithe from the olive stores.' Take another letter and write: 'To our brothers inhabiting the South, may your well-being increase! We wish to advise you that the time of removal has come to put aside/separate the tithe from the wheat sheaves.' Take the third sheet and write: 'To our brothers in Exile in Babylon, and to our brothers in Media, and to the remaining Dispersed of Israel, may your peace increase always! This is to advise you that the doves are tender, and the lambs too small, and crops have not sprouted fully (or, spring has not come in time). The matter has so been deemed appropriate by me and my colleagues that I have intercalated 30 days in this year.'"

The passage instructs in a number of directions. Its date is pre-Destruction, for Rabban Gamaliel, teacher of Paul, was sitting on the steps of the Temple Mount. He spoke to the scribe in Aramaic, and the scribe wrote in Aramaic. Although one of the letters was addressed to Upper and Lower Galilee, where one would expect that the Galilean type of Aramaic would have been employed, it was couched in the recognized Judean (Western Aramaic) dialect. One is drawn irresistibly to the conclusion that the Judean dialect was for correspondence, the Aramaic *koine* for the Judeans throughout the world, even though the different localities may have had their own dialects.

The second significant conclusion that may be derived from the examples cited (and one may see scores of others in the Introduction to Ben Yehuda's Dictionary) is that although the narrative gives the account in Hebrew, filling in the framework and background of the story, the words spoken by Gamaliel, were transmitted precisely as he spoke them. Incidentally, this is probably the same R. Gamaliel who was standing on the Temple Mount (hence pre-Destruction) when someone brought to him the Book of Job in translation (Sefer Iyyob Targum) and he said to the builder "Hide it under a tier of stones!" The Targum is a sign of written creative activity, albeit translation, within two hundred years of 70 C.E..

One may ask, How authentic are these traditions of Hebrew and Aramaic transmission? This intermingling of the texts of both Hebrew and Aramaic, one language closely following on the heels of the other, is confirmed by the practice and tradition, already enunciated by Hillel (80—10 B.C.E.) in a passage ('Eduyot 1.3) puzzling to most commentators, and perhaps even to Hillel himself, concluding that "A man is required to transmit his tradition in the language of his teacher." The passage reads, הלל אומר מלא הין מים שאובין פוסלין המקוה אלא שאדם חייב לומר בלשון רבו. "Hillel said, 'A full *hin* of drawn water disqualifies the purifying bath; but one must transmit the words as he learned from his teacher.'"[7] This injunction, the basis of the Oral Law, is assumed in the Mishna, and of course in the Talmuds throughout, Bera. 47a; Bek. 5a; Shabb. 15a. With some frequency then we find narratives written in Hebrew, but the dialogue is in Aramaic, Sot. 48b; Shabb. 31a, and elsewhere; and contrariwise, the narrative is related in Aramaic, but the dialogue and conversations are reported in Hebrew, Pes. 3b; Bab. Meṣ. 83b and elsewhere. There can hardly be any question that Hebrew and Aramaic flourished side by side before 70 C.E..

The new Bar Kokhba finds by Yigael Yadin and his co-workers confirm what we have been arguing. The discoveries (comp. his *Ha-ḥippusim 'aḥar Bar Kokhba,* Jerusalem, 1971; Eng. ed. *Bar Kokhba,* New York, 1971) categorically are divided into Aramaic, Greek, and Hebrew. As Yadin remarks (p. 24 in the latter edition),

> "The first thing that struck us was that for no apparent reason, some of the letters were written in Aramaic and some in Hebrew. Jews at that period were versed in both languages, yet since most of the letters were in Aramaic, possibly Hebrew had just been lately revived by a Bar Kokhba decree."

In Chapter 10 of Yadin's book, the letters of and by Bar Kokhba are in the proportion of five Aramaic letters, two Hebrew ones, and three Greek ones. In one letter there is the noticeable remark that "the letter was written in Greek as we have no one who knows Hebrew [or Aramaic]" (pp. 130—131), probably a non-Jewish contingent, as Yadin observes, citing Dio Cassius. Other discoveries revealed some 35 documents (one clearly having the date "Year 14 of Hadrian" i.e., 130 C.E.) of which again 3 were in Aramaic, 17 in Greek, and 9 in Greek with subscriptions and signatories in

INTRODUCTION 15

Aramaic or Nabatean, the latter being the famous Babata documents relating to her and her family, property matters, and lawsuits. The previous contention of Ben Yehudah in the Introduction to his dictionary (p. 176f.), and that of M. H. Segal (*Mishnaic Grammar,* p. 16), that the Judeans of the Second Commonwealth were always bilingual is most decidedly confirmed. A good case can be made for the multilingualism of the Judeans in the languages of Aramaic, Hebrew and Greek, although the evidence for this is late. (Comp. the inscription on the cross in Hebrew [i.e., Aramaic], (official) Latin, and Greek, Jn. 19.20 and Segal, op. cit., p. 15.) To be sure, everyone spoke the languages with various degrees of proficiency. The Judeans who had direct contact with the Romans used Latin, the official language of the Roman government; they spoke Aramaic among themselves; and used Greek, and some Latin, when dealing with non-Judeans. Josephus comes to mind in this connection. See below for a further discussion.

The Judeans of the Dispersion who came from their countries to visit Jerusalem and the Temple, and those who came for the Annual Pilgrimages, especially for the Passover celebration, could likewise speak Aramaic and *koine* Greek. (Comp. the instance of Paul who spoke and wrote Greek, yet addressed the congregations in Aramaic, Ac. 21.40; 22.2.)

Thus, from the evidence afforded us, the inroads that Greek made into the Hebrew and Aramaic speech and literature, while considerable, were not overwhelming. (Comp. Neubauer, "The Dialects of Palestine in the time of Christ" in *Studia Biblica,* Oxford, 1885.) The Hebrew and Aramaic idiom, syntax, and vocabulary remained original, consistent, and intact, although Greek words did infiltrate. (See S. Krauss, *Griechische u. Lateinische Worterbuch* and the contributions of S. Lieberman, *Greek in Jewish Palestine.*) Greek words penetrated when new products, commercial terms, or new technical designations in botany or medicine were introduced. Hebrew and Aramaic, the two sister languages, were on a different footing. The Judeans of the Second Commonwealth had a special affinity for Aramaic (compare the early Dt. 26.5 "My ancestor was a wandering *Aramaean*"), and adopted it into the family so that it became native as Hebrew itself. This explains the *forma mixta* of the Mishnaic, Midrashic, and Rabbinic texts, with Greek and Latin as a smaller, ancillary participant in the developmental process.

Albright's arguments that there was no Aramaic literature or Greek provincial *koine* for 300 years, or as his lower figure suggests, between 50 B.C.E. and 70 C.E., and that moreover, Aramaic suffered an eclipse during that period, and that it is impossible to pinpoint the dialect which Jesus spoke to his disciples and followers is contrary to all substantive evidence. Furthermore, the structure of the argument, the fluctuating dates he proposes, the farfetched analogies between the story of Aḥiqar of the Elephantine papyri and the Syriac translation of Aḥiqar which he considers as an example of oral transmission (comp. M. Lidzbarski, "Zum Weisen Achiqar" in *Z.D.M.G.* vol. 48, pp. 671—675 cited by F. C. Conybeare, J. Rendel Harris, and Agnes Smith Lewis in *The Story of Ahikar,* 1913: "The Syriac Legends were a translation *of a book,*" [their emphasis] and especially again in the aforementioned volume, LXXXV of the Introduction, "The Syriac, a translation from some lost original, by the method of literal translation" which is supported by ingenious examples), all this leads us to infer that Albright's conclusions are faulty and arbitrary. It would not be accurate to say moreover that the Aramaic Gospel traditions were transmitted only orally *because* of, or even analogous to, the custom and tradition to transmit the growing body of interpretations of the Torah, and the further developments and amendments in the Oral Law exclusively by word of mouth. Perhaps the oral tradition was kept that way for the most part so as not to harden, and to keep flexible the enactments and interpretations. Together with the oral tradition, written records were kept, if privately, for purposes of memory and accuracy. This substantially is the conclusion of all modern critics[8] and note the principal evidence found in Aboda' Zara' cf. Zeitlin in *Megillat Ta'anit,* p. 2, and n. 2. Megillat Ta'anit, moreover, must be dated before the Destruction for the most part; the second century C.E. (see Albright) was regarded by Dalman as "sinnlos," though some scholars advance the date to Hadrian; but see Zeitlin, op. cit. who says that the last event chronicled is the one that occurred on the 17th day of Adar, 66 C.E. Megillat Ta'anit may very well be cited as one example of Judean Aramaic, at least one century before the Destruction.

Perhaps Josephus, typical of a person with his linguistic proficiency may provide some relevant information. He lived in the first century of the common era, a period characterized by Albright as one in which Aramaic was in eclipse. Josephus' mother tongue was Aramaic. When he first wrote his *Wars* for his coreligionists in Mesopotamia and the Dispersion, it was in that language. His denomination and transliteration of the popular festivals were likewise in Aramaic from the popular speech, although, since he read his Bible in Hebrew, he could have used the biblical terminology of Pesaḥ, Sukkot, Asif, or whatever. He asserts that he served and studied with the three major parties—the Pharisees, the Sadducees, and the Essenes. These studies involved learning all the ramifications of law, custom, and morality, unquestionably in Hebrew, although his etymologies and explanations of Hebrew words are of the most fanciful kind. However, at the request of the Roman emperor, he rewrote all his books in Greek. Here we are indebted to H. St. John Thackeray for a number of relevant discoveries. (Comp. his *Josephus, the Man and the Historian.*) Josephus made use of two amanuenses who divided the work. One, an admirer of Thucydides, embellished Josephus' works with touches and phrases from that author; the other was a lover of poetry, especially of Sophocles, and graced Josephus' style by such flourishes. This of course is atticistic, a fashion of imitating the classical authors and a mark of the period. However, Books 17, 18, and 19 were written by Josephus himself. He confesses to having had to learn Greek laboriously with composition and exercises, and he never was at home in it, neither in writing nor in pronunciation.[9] Moreover, in the composition of his works, apparently following the biblical narrative—especially as it appears in Judges, Samuel, and Kings—he made use of a Greek text to help himself with the choice of words, thus enabling us to recognize his text as pre-Lucianic. This reliance on Greek texts is instructive as to how the Gospel writers similarly performed their task. In Greek Esdras, he followed the Alexandrian text of the LXX. (Comp. Torrey, *Ezra Studies,* and S. Mowinckel, *Stattholderen Nehemias.*) Furthermore, as Thackeray has evidenced, Josephus occasionally departed from the Masoretic text, because he also had at hand and followed a Targum or Aramaic text. This is significant for our perception of how the Gospel translators operated. We may picture Josephus at a writing table. He has before him a Hebrew Bible, a number of Greek versions, and an Aramaic Targum, following them all eclectically, choosing what he wishes from each. Luke could very well be a case in point and a similar compiler.

We may conclude with reasonable certainty that, with varying degrees of proficiency, the average Judean commanded at least three languages. He learned Aramaic as his mother tongue; Hebrew as a second language for the reading of the Torah and the study of Jewish law and custom; and Greek, in a pragmatic fashion, for dealing in matters of commerce and government. Probably Latin was known, too, in a fragmented fashion in government circles.

The language spoken by Jesus and his followers, certainly by Peter and Jesus' brother James, was Galilean Aramaic. We know that Jesus could read Hebrew, as he read the passage from the Haftara in Is. 61.1–2 (Lk. 4.17f.). He probably understood Greek too, as in his conversation with Pilate. Moreover, his Galilean language and accent did not prevent him from being understood either by the crowds who listened to him, or by his many disciples (the discipleship being by no means limited to the Twelve) Lk. 10.1.17. Important as it is to distinguish the different dialects of Aramaic for scientific purposes, it must be understood that although people spoke different dialects they quite understood one another. Otherwise, how could Jesus talk to the people in Jerusalem, or to the woman of Samaria, or the Jerusalem maid speak to Peter, identifying him by his Galilean dialect, or Paul who sat at the feet of Gamaliel in Jerusalem and went to preach to congregations in Syria? The same situation continued through two centuries later when scores of scholars went back and forth from Palestine to Babylon with only the occasional comment on some difference in the language (cf. Baba Qamma Mishna 1). The little synagogue-church at Jerusalem after Jesus' death continued with the traditional pattern of Sabbath assembly. There was a reading of the Torah in Hebrew with the *meturgeman* explaining verse by verse in Aramaic, followed by a reading from the Prophets; next came a Midrashic explanation of a passage or a study session; and then, particularly for the church, a rehearsing of *Testimonia,* adopting Burkitt's phrase, i.e. of proof texts forecasting Jesus as the Messiah (Acts 13.15f.). Lastly, new traditions, as brought by newcomers from different parts of Judea where Jesus had visited or taught, were sifted, discussed, or added, while older traditions, parables, and *logia* were studied and applied. Imperceptibly and subtly, a change took place in the confluence of the traditions. The language changed from Galilean Aramaic to Judean Aramaic, current in the pre-Destruction era.

As primitive Christianity spread to the North, especially in Syria, the Aramaic *koine* (Judean Aramaic) transited to what may be called proto-Syriac. There is nothing extraordinary about this. Since, as postulated above the Galileans and the Judeans understood each other's Aramaic, it was not extraordinary for Paul, born in Tarsus and an Eastern Aramaic speaking Jew (Phil. 3.4ff.), to exert a profound influence (cf. Ac. 22.2; the Pauline sections in the Gospels) with his recounting and exposition of the Gospel stories and doctrines in the proto-Syriac dialect in which he addressed congregations. He had to use Aramaic if he wished to win his Jewish audiences; and he was not the only one. The acts and sayings of Jesus then were shifted from Galilean Aramaic to Judean Aramaic to proto-Syriac.

Evidence for this transformation from one dialect to another is found in the Peshitta, specifically, as P. Kahle assumes, from an old Western Aramaic translation of the Pentateuch transcribed into Eastern Aramaic (Syriac). The Targum to Proverbs is modified Syriac. The Vetus Latina, originally a com-

INTRODUCTION   19

pilation of existing Old Latin translations, was constantly worked upon (Würtheim, *Ahe Text of the Old Testament,* pp. 60, 62). The borrowing of words and phrases, and the modification of the Greek phrasing, as one version took over the style and the vocabulary of the other (the LXX Vatican texts, the Alexandrian, Symmachus, Theodotion, the Lucianic, the Palestinian mixed texts) are well known (ibid., p. 44). Excellent examples of this transferring process of the oral and written traditions from one land to another are exemplified in the Targums. Onqelos, a Palestinian product, received extensive revision on the part of Jewish scholars in Babylonia. The same process transpired, *mutatis mutandis,* with the Halakhic and Aggadic traditions reported in the Talmuds of Jerusalem and Babylonia. (See Albeck, *Mabo La-Talmudim,* Tel Aviv, 1969, p. 143; Y. N. Epstein, *Mebo'ot Lesifrut Ha-Tannaim,* 1957.)

The synagogue-church at Jerusalem was soon dwarfed with the abounding influx of pagans newly converted through the religious enthusiasm and missionary zeal of Paul and his co-workers. Antioch emerged as a strong religious center: "And the disciples were called Christians first in Antioch" (Ac. 11.22). These Greek-speaking converts clamored for their own services in which worship would be in Greek, and the Testimonia and the Gospels be narrated in their own language. The rebellion may have started early (Ac. 6.1f.). Soon translations from Aramaic into Greek appeared. Undoubtedly, the Greek translators were men of repute and masters of Greek, chosen, even commissioned, to perform this demanding task. Yet inevitably many Aramaic words were misunderstood and significant errors occurred in translation. Luke, again, may serve as an example of the points I wish to prove as he made the largest number of mistakes in translating. Torrey found the same larger proportion in his investigations and cases of evidence.

Luke, as a physician, undoubtedly was a man of reputation and standing in the community (cf. M. Rostovzeff, *Social and Economic History of the Hellenistic World,* III, 1598), thought to be a native of Antioch, an educated man with an authoritative command of Greek, his mother tongue. He learned a second language, proto-Syriac, but was not quite at home in it as in Greek. (For further discussion, see the chapter on Luke in this volume.) Probably his travels with Paul commended him to the pagan Hellenistic community as a qualified translator. Although they assumed he would translate competently, Luke shares the same deficiencies of the other Gospel translators, who were not totally familiar with Aramaic (i.e., proto-Syriac), nor expert in its idioms, intricacies, and subtleties. Frequently, too, they limited themselves, as did most Old Testament translators, to translating word for word from the proto-Syriac text in front of them.

The realization that the Gospel writers translated a proto-Syriac—or to speak more accurately now the Eastern Aramaic complex—is imbedded in the very material uncovered. Dalman and Torrey had assumed somewhat arbitrarily that the language must have been Judean Aramaic because the writers lived in Palestine. Other scholars decided on Galilean Aramaic, and yet others on Christian Palestinian Aramaic. This is, however, sheer dogma. Inconsistently, Burney, Torrey, Montgomery, and Black speak frequently of retroversions that are Syriacisms. Thus Burney writes, "There is no reason why such an expression [i.e., in Syriac] may not have been used in Judean Aramaic" in a number, incompatible with the hypothesis set up by them. Such scholars neglected to scrutinize the material they assembled, beclouded as they were by the gratuitous hypothesis that the Aramaic of the Gospels must come only from Palestine.

Luke's *apo mias* (Lk. 14.18) "together," lit. "from one(?)" (and note the feminine) will serve as a case in point. *Apo mias* is Greek mistranslation for the Aramaic *meḥada'* "at once" (Wellhausen). But the truth is that *meḥada'* is found only in Syriac with that preposition and that meaning—never in Palestinian Aramaic. It cannot be equated with *kaḥada', laḥada'* as some authors suppose. It is entirely separate; its provenance then comes not from Palestine but from the North. The material itself constantly supplied the northern locale. The Aramaic written Gospels are a product of the Diaspora of Syria. For other examples, see pp. 25f.

While proto-Syriac was the distinguishing characteristic of the Aramaic substrate of the Gospels, elements in vocabulary, nouns, and verbs common to Babylonian Aramaic are shared with Syriac. (Comp. C. Albeck, *Mabo' la-Mishna,* c. 8 passim; Epstein, *Diqduq,* p. 9.) Although the canon of scholarship is to point out differences and singularities of the Aramaic dialects—and assuredly that investigation is most important—it is equally surprising how much they agree. Thus in the lists of nouns and verbs prepared by Dalman (*Grammatik,* 44f., and for our purposes pp. 48–51), it is surprising how many words are shared in the dialects. Out of the list of 48 words in the Aramaic of the Onqelos Targum, and their counterparts in the Jerusalem Targum, Christian Palestinian Aramaic, and the Samaritan Aramaic, a large number—over 75 percent—share a common meaning and usage.

In passing, Albright's contentions that in the Uzziah inscription לכה התית טמי עוזיה מלך יהודה ולא למפתח "Here were brought the bones of Uzziah,

ziah, King of Judah. Do not open," found on the Mount of Olives by E. L. Sukenik (A. Reifenberg, *Ancient Hebrew Arts,* p. 67) and dated between first century B.C.E. and first century C.E.; that the two words *ṭme* and *haitiyat* or *hethait* are Samaritan (Albright, *From the Stone Age to Christianity,* 385 n.) and that "the percentage of Samaritan words is rather high" are not borne out by the facts. In the first place, *ṭme* is found in Babylonian Aramaic (Ber. 6b; 59a,b; Shabb. 152b; Sanh. 113a; Baba Batra 116a) and in Palestinian Aramaic (Dalman, *Wörterbuch,* 162; Levy, *Chal.* Wört I, 307). Moreover, the fact remains that the inscription was found on Mt. Olives and not in Samaria, and the inscription dealt with the sepulture of a Judahite king, not a Samaritan ruler. *Hethait* might be unusual as the passive in the inscription, but again, it is not necessarily Samaritan—the stone cutter may well have been aware of the passages in Dan. 6.18 and 3.13 and in keeping with the size limitations of the stone, he made use of the *hethait.*

At any rate, out of the Dalman list of 48 words, I have counted 36 Babylonian Aramaic verbs and nouns which share a kinship with the Christian Palestinian Aramaic, the Samaritan Aramaic, or the Jerusalem Targum, either wholly or partially as in the following words: אזל, חצב, חכם, תוב, ארע, טלל, טבע, טעון, טרד, כרי, ינק, מין, אכל, סנדל, עבר, ערבב, חלף, פרזל, פרסם, פשט, צער, כנת, סחא, (קצץ, אריס ("take away" not "lift up"). The term generally used in these pages as Eastern Aramaic is a complex of proto-Syriac and Babylonian Aramaic, the latter of less proportion and influence however.

The lack of archeological evidence for this period—in Greek and Aramaic papyri, or the lack of Aramaic and Hellenistic literature that Albright seems to stress—is not due to an "eclipse" of Aramaic during the Seleucids, or the lack of provincial literary works in the Greek *koine.* Instead, it should be attributed to the fact that most of our finds come from rainless Egypt. Here was found a hoard of Greek papyri (some 20,000 published, and a vast amount yet to be published, cf. "Greek Papyrology," *Oxford Classical Dictionary*), as well as Aramaic papyri from the Elephantine and the Coptic papyri from Chenboskion. It is only a matter of chance that we have the story of Aḥiqar.

Then again archeology has its limitations. It plays a greater or less important role, according to the differences among the archeologists themselves as to dating, identification, character of the finds, language characteristics, etc. With all honor to Albright's integrity, it must be recalled that a number of times he changed his mind with regard to dating. (Cf. for example, his monograph "Biblical Period," vol. I of *The Jews* ed. by L. Finkelstein, pp. 58 n. 53; 62, n. 96; *Stone Age,* pp. 251 n. 74; 270, n. 96.) His oral-tradition argument, citing the oral tradition of the Jewish sages, has point but needs qualification. Tannaitic scholars, while preserving a tradition orally, nevertheless had their own private *written* traditions which eventually became codified in the Mishna. Written documents were always employed. (Comp. H. Strack, *Introduction to the Talmud and Midrash*, p. 12f. for some twelve pieces of evidence.) The Greek Gospels were based upon a written text. The examples given in these pages had been misread rather than misheard. Altogether, the scholars who have dealt with Aramaic-Greek analysis of the Gospels have harvested a rich yield: some 130 pieces of evidence by Torrey, over 25 by Burney, some 20 by Montgomery, the evidence offered by Black and some 200 new examples proposed by myself. Aramaic scholars have demonstrated their case for a written Aramaic document or documents, and additional proof will be supplied in the following pages.

We can now summarize the process whereby the Gospels, originally written in Aramaic, were translated into Greek. When Jesus spoke and taught his disciples in the dialect of the Galilee, his pupils and those immediately associated with him, such as James and Peter, spoke the same dialect and preserved his teachings in it. Although the Galileans pronounced the gutturals in an unclear fashion, and were upbraided for their accent,[10] they were understood by other disciples and auditors, among whom were the disciples of John, who at the death of their master followed Jesus. Jesus was understood by the multitudes who came to listen to him, by the seventy disciples he appointed (Lk. 10.1,17), and by the crowds to whom he preached in the Temple.

However, a subtle change was taking place. The disciples, certainly numbering 120 (Ac. 1.15) inclusive of the apostles (Ac. 1.26) were "translating" in their minds the oral—and perhaps written—traditions into their own dialect, namely the Judean. In this changeover, discrepancies and mistranslations could have taken place and did. (Comp. עפר, עפורא pp. 25f., כחד "deny"and "be ashamed" and some twenty-five other examples in this book's presentation of the differences in discrepant texts of parallel passages.) The transition then from the Galilean to the Judean dialect would mark the first shift in meaning. But there was a second shift in meaning, too.

The largest number of Jews in the Diaspora was undoubtedly in Syria. When the Gospel tradition was transmitted to groups there, particularly in Antioch where the Christians were first denominated as such, another

INTRODUCTION

dialectic transmutation took place. This dialect of Syria in the underlying document of the Gospels may be termed proto-Syriac, to differentiate it from the official Syriac centuries later. Proto-Syriac comprises the larger portion of what might be comprehended as Jewish Eastern Aramaic—which includes the Judean Aramaic that Jews brought with them from their homeland in the form of *Targumim,* which we confidently identify and which contributed to this complex, and much that is common to the Babylonian Talmudic Aramaic, perhaps Mandaic, some persistent Galilean, as well as the predominant dialect of the area in which they found themselves, Syria. The Gospels as they were committed to written form, were written in this nexus of dialects.

The Aramaic Gospels had to be recorded. Certain sections had to be declared authoritative almost immediately because variants and discrepancies had sprung up. Spurious teachings, "false Christs," were emerging. Out of necessity, an elementary and primitive process of editing must have started early, as evident in the Gospel records about marriage and divorce. Alongside the Torah and the Prophets, the leader in the synagogue church had to have a scroll or codex of official character for quoting in order to lend authority to his teaching.

As the church grew, so grew the number of Hellenistic converts who were without a knowledge of Aramaic, and who sat in church at the side or in the back. It was then that a demand rose that the Gospels be translated into Greek so that the neophytes and new worshippers would have a conception of what was taking place at the service. The Aramaic Jewish Christians did not mind. They had the original. Unfortunately, translators were chosen who had a rich Greek vocabulary but who were not so familiar with Aramaic. At all events, the Greek Gospels were translated from the proto-Syriac, the second change following on the Judean Aramaic.

Perhaps now we may dip into a few examples to illustrate the principal themes of this book. First, that there existed a written underlying document in Aramaic and second, that the cast of this Aramaic came from the north of Palestine, the Eastern Aramaic nexus.

Chapter I

The Written Text

THE PURPOSE of this chapter is to show how a number of mistranslations taken from all the Gospels including John, ascend to a written document. It is predominantly the written text that supplies the evidence for translation.

Mt. 25.25 tells of the incident of the third servant, who gives an accounting of the money to his employer. However, instead of transacting some business profitable for his master as he was ordered to do, he took his "talent" and hid it in the ground. The parallel in Lk. 19.20 states that the servant hid it in a napkin (σουδαρίῳ). What is the source of this variant? The difference in the reports undoubtedly goes back to the written Aramaic עפרא "ground, earth" (*terra*, Brockelmann p. 539 b) which was confused with עפורא *sudarium* (ibid., cf. also עפרא "hood." Payne Smith p. 422)—in other words a visual difference. Note that as this is Eastern Aramaic, and implies a consonantal text, it is not likely that ʻafra and ʻafura were confused aurally. ge/ʻafar Mt. 13.5 sc; Lk. 6.49 p.

In Mt. 16.18, wherein Jesus promised Peter that he is to be the rock on which Jesus is to build his church, the verse—a perennial crux—concludes in an enigmatic fashion "And the gates (πύλαι) shall not prevail (κατισχύσουσιν) against it." The noun "gates" with the verb "prevail" is incongruous; we need a personal subject. It is evident that the Aramaic word for "gates"—תרעיא *tărʻyya*—was misread for tārʻayya (from the root *trc*) meaning "attackers, incursors." The meaning of the verse now becomes: the incursors from Hell (meaning Satan and his legions) will not prevail against the Church. (Comp. 1 Peter 3.19.) The translation should be, "The attackers from hell shall not prevail against it."

In Mt. 26.15, and parallels Mk. 14.11 and Lk. 22.5, the differences in the Greek verbs substantially indicate the same Aramaic consonantal text. The Mt. passage reads "They *paid* him (ἔστεσαν) thirty pieces of silver," a quotation essentially from Zach. 1.12. while Mk. 14.11 varies with "And *promised* (ἐπηγγείλαντο) to give him money." A third variant is found in Lk. 22.5 "And *negotiated* to give him money" (συνέθεντο, which properly means "agree, pledge oneself"). It seems quite clear that the misinterpretation of the Aramaic *'aqimu,* 'Aphel of *qum* led to the differences in the renderings. *'Aqim* means "promise," which accounts quite well for the Mk. text. Cf. *'aqim,* or *qayyem* in the pa'el "promise" (Payne Smith, p. 495). The meaning of "agree, pledge oneself" likewise elucidates the text in Lk., and note there the presence of the Syriac translation *waqimu.* As for the Mt. text, cf. associatively *qam* "bargain for" (Jast. p. 1331), Brockelmann *institit (remuneratio)* 652. It most likely had *qayyama/'aqimu* as the Greek in Dan. 6.8.9 (Rhalfs) shows: *istemi* for the Aramaic *qayyama,* and so *istemi/qam* (purely lexically Mk. 3.24.31). The correct translation then would be: "Paid him thirty pieces" (RSV) or "Counted him out thirty pieces" (Gdspd.), not however "covenanted" (AV) or "weighed unto him"(ASV). We may conclude that what seem to be variant readings in the three texts under discussion point to a single Aramaic root, which was interpreted differently by the three Synoptists.

In Mt. 13.55, we have a distinctive Aramaic locution. The people, after wondering about Jesus' wisdom and ability to perform miracles, declare, "Is not this the carpenter's son?" The parallel in Mk. 6.3 reads, "Is he not the carpenter (ὁ τέκτων)?" Matthew implies that Jesus' father Joseph was the carpenter, while Mark asserts that Jesus was the carpenter. (Comp. the remarks of Bauer who in Arndt-Gingrich, Introduction p. xxv is puzzled about the variants.) The underlying Aramaic had the compound *bar naggara,* which idiomatically means a carpenter. Thus in Aboda Zara 50b: נגר ולא בר נגרא i.e., there is no scholar nor son of a scholar (Rashi) i.e., no scholar that can answer that one (literally, no craftsman [carpenter], nor the son of a craftsman [carpenter] that can solve that question). Compare other compounds such as *bar 'amodai* "diver"; *Yehudai bar Yehudai* (Dalman, *Dialektproben,*[2] p. 140) which does not mean "Jew, son of a Jew," but simply "Jew! Jew!" Similarly *Yisrael* is the same as *ben Yisrael* in Hebrew; *bar hilkan* means "a reporter of halakhot"; *bar levai,* a Levite; and *tabbaha* and *bar tabbaha* "a butcher." Lévy, *Chal. Wört.,* I, 111; Jast., 189. Probably, *bar naggara* was interpreted correctly and idiomatically as "carpenter" by Mark, but Matthew misunderstood the compound rendered word for word "son of the carpenter." Their original texts, however, were identical. Joseph hardly enters into the characterization—Jesus was the carpenter.

There are four interrelated passages based on a single Aramaic word which nevertheless led to different interpretations in the Greek. Mt. 10.33 reads, "But whosoever shall *deny* (ἀρνήσηταί) me before men, him will I also *deny* before my Father." Similarly Lk. 12.9 *deny* (ἀρνησάμενος, ἀπαρνηθήσεται). However Lk. 9.26 has the different version, "For whosoever shall be *ashamed* of me (ἐπαισχυνθῇ) and of my words, of him shall the Son of Man be ashamed" (ἐπαισχυνθήσεται). Mk. 8.38 likewise has "ashamed," "Whosoever therefore shall be ashamed of me (*epaischunthe*) and of my words in this adulterous and sinful generation, of him also the Son of Man shall be ashamed" (*epaischunthesetai*). While it would seem a little unusual for the Son of Man to be "ashamed" of the one who was "ashamed" of Jesus and his words upon earth, the question of "shame" does play a role in the resurrection. Cf. Y. Kil. IX, 31b "When [at the resurrection] I stand among the righteous, we [I] will not be ashamed, and if we [I] stand among the wicked, we will not be ashamed" and the late talmudic passage (b. Qidd. 81a), "Better that you shame Amram in this world than you shame him (תיכספו מני/ה)) [note the preposition] in the next" (Soncino trans.), or perhaps "you be ashamed of me." In the explanation of the NT passages, it seems likely that the root כחד was misunderstood. One translator, bilingual in Hebrew and Aramaic thought of *kḥd* in the sense of "deny," as in Job 10.6, "I did not deny the words of the Holy One," while another translator thought of *kḥd* in the sense of "shame," found noticeably in Eastern Aramaic only. (Comp. Payne Smith, p. 212; Brock. p. 324.)

Under the heading of Aramaic locutions, one that the Greek translator missed appears in Mt. 18.23; 22.2 where the passage reads, "Therefore is the kingdom of heaven likened unto a certain king ... " The Greek reads however ἀνθρώπῳ βασιλεῖ "to a man, to a king", and so Rhm, although the locution is odd. Other modern translations render simply, "compared to a king" (Mof.,[1] Mof.,[2] RSV, Mon, Gdspd); "like a king" (NAB), omitting "a man." An objection could be raised that the textual milieu does not describe a royal court. The expression, however, has an Aramaic provenance גבר מלכא which the Greek translated word by word, as *naggara* and *bar naggara* ut supra, a familiar enough procedure. For the Aramaic locution, compare Dalman, *Dialektproben,* p. 20 *Babylonian Aramaic* גברא דמלכא b. Meṣ. 86a. Note the contrast, Dalman ibid, with גבר הדיוט on the next line meaning "an ordinary lay person." Literally translated גבר מלכא means "man of the king" i.e., an adherent of the king, king's officer. Compare the English "king's man," Webster's International Dictionary,[3] 1245, and the Ptolemaic and Seleucid coteries "the king's friends" (W. Tarn and G.T. Griffith *Hellenic Civilization,*[3] 1953, pp. 57—58).

A mistake in the reading, too, is found in the passage in Lk. 11.42 which runs, "But woe unto you, Pharisees! for ye tithe mint and rue and all manner of herbs, and pass over judgment and the love of God; these ought ye have done, and not to leave the other undone." It will be noticed that "judgment" and "love of God" are coupled in an unusual fashion. Then again, it is possible to pass over the Law (better "pass by," the translation is too literal for ועברין על דינא—cf. the Peshitta, i.e., "violate the law of, trespass"; *krisin* here bears more closely the sense of "law" in this context ["Hebraistic," Plummer]). However, to "pass by, pass over" the "love of God" is incongruous. Mt. 23.23, in a more expository fashion, perhaps glossing over the difficulty, reads, "You have neglected the weightier matters of the law (i.e., not *ḥumrei dina* in this passage but יקירא "the precious things" of the law, a mistranslation), justice (*krisin*) and mercy and faith." The latter two words are an expansion and interpretation of "love of God." That is to say, in the aforementioned context of Lk., the proper reading was obscured by a wrong vocalization. The word חובא "duty, responsibility" was misread as *ḥubba* rt. *ḥbb* "love," the Aramaic consonants nearly identical. The Lk. passage bears the meaning: You have trespassed justice and duty towards God (objective genetive). These are the precious things, the ethical elements inherent in the law. Observe that *ḥobah* and *ḥubba* would not have been confused aurally.

A peculiar passage, to cite one example from the Fourth Gospel hitherto unexplained satisfactorily, is found at Jn. 8.48: "Then answered the Jews and said unto him, 'Say ye not well that thou art a Samaritan, and hast a devil?'" Why the Jews should characterize Jesus as a Samaritan, when everyone knew he was not, or to take "Samaritan" as a personal attribute in a pejorative sense is unparalleled, though the ill-feeling between the Jews and Samaritans as peoples (Neh. 3.34; Ezra 4.12; Ben Sira 50.25f.) is well known. The Greek translator misread his text, reading a Resh for a Daleth. He read שמרי *shāmrai* "Samaritan" instead of שמדי *shamdai* "devil, demon." The forms are found variously as *shamdan, shamdai, 'eshmodai*.[11] The derivation is not to be taken as the Persian *aeshma daeva* as two words (so R. H. Pfeiffer, *History of New Testament Times,* p. 271, and see his note; however, see the writer's Book of *Tobit,* Index, Asmodeus) now disavowed by Persian scholars (cf. Kohut, *Aruch Completum,* Suppl. p. 70) but is to be taken from *shmd* (L. Ginzberg, Art. *Asmodeus* in JE). I do not share the view that it means "The cursed one," but rather "The destroyer," the later development of the *malak ha-mashḥit* (cf. also *malake ḥabbala*). Striking is the combination of שמדון שידא *shamdon shidda* Gen. Rabba sec. 36, in Theodor's edition, p. 335. "Shamdon the devil," as in the Johannine passage, has *shomron* in a number of variant readings (cf. Theodor's apparatus, ibid.) Now, the passage in John should be more fittingly translated: Are you the devil himself, or do you have a demon?" The repetition is not redundant. (Cf. partially Rev. 12.9; 20.2 [Diabolos, Satanas].)

A difference in parallel texts occurs in another instance indicating an Aramaic source. A problem word in the Gospels is *skandalizo* with its noun *skandalon*. The verb classically (Liddell and Scott, s.v.) means (1) to cause to stumble and (2) to give offense to or spread scandal about anyone. The noun carries the meaning of "trap, snare," with the added significance of "stumbling-block, offense, scandal." Since the words appear in peculiar phrases and circumstances in the Gospels, extended and ad hoc meanings are assigned to the verb, as "cause to sin," in the passive *skandalizesthai en tini* "be repelled by someone, take offense at someone" as, in the instance of Jesus, wherein by refusing to believe in him, or by becoming apostate from him, a person falls into sin; *skandalon* not only means "trap" but carries the overtone of "temptation to sin, enticement" to apostasy or false belief. The many nuances of the words cannot be summarized here. The reader is referred to the excellent exhaustive article by Gustav Stählin in *Theological Dictionary of the New Testament* by Kittel, Friedrich, Bromiley, VII, 339f. and the literature cited there. The overtones, implications, and inferences offered there, however, are more of a testimony to the acuteness and scholarship of the writers than to the simple meaning of the text. Translation limits ingenuity. The AV sticks to the meaning of "offense"—from the Latin *offensio* meaning "stumbling-block." The LXX employs the Greek mostly for *moqesh* "trap" and *mikhshol* "stumbling-block."

There are a number of passages, however, where the cited meanings of *skandalizo* do not apply, or are forced with considerable difficulty. Thus, in Mt. 18.4 (parallels in Mk. 9.42; Lk. 17.2). Jesus called a young child to him, and set him in the midst of the disciples and said, "whosoever shall humble himself as this little child, the same is greatest in the Kingdom of Heaven." Then v. 6 continues, "But whoso shall *offend* one of these little ones which believe in me, it would be better for him that a millstone were hanged about his neck..." In what manner one "offends" ($\sigma\kappa\alpha\nu\delta\alpha\lambda i\sigma\eta$) these "little ones" is difficult to portray. It cannot be that these "little ones" are the neophytes who have been recently admitted into the church, for as Allen remarks, the passages can be taken to deal only with real children (*Matthew*, p. 96). In parallel situations, for example, where people had brought children to be blessed by Jesus, and the disciples had rebuked the people for so doing, Jesus had taken a child, and setting him amongst them, said in effect that if one does not become like a little child one cannot enter the Kingdom of

Heaven. Thus, there is no question that real children are present and not "neophytes." It is striking, that the disciples rebuked the people for bringing the children (Mt. 19.14f.; Mk. 10.13: Lk. 18.15). It is further striking that Jesus, apparently in remonstrance to their action, declared in Mt. 18.10, "Take heed that ye *despise* (καταφρονήσητε) not one of these little ones. For I say unto you...." The difficulty in the previous verse "offend one of the little ones" (Mt. 18.6) persists. The NAB in feeling the difficulty translates "disedifying them" and Moffat reads: "is a hindrance to..." What I propose to show is that the text requires some sense of "despising, scorning, making light of" and this tenor is shown in v. 10: "take heed ye do not despise one of these little ones..."

A standard equivalent of *skandalizein* in LXX is the root kšl/tql, common to Hebrew and Aramaic, meaning "stumble, falter." The Greek translator evidently confused the roots *tql* and *qll* on a number of occasions. This comes from his misapprehension of the grammatical form. For instance, אתקל might be understood by him as coming from the rt. *tql* "stumble, fall" or the apocopated form as his grammar would allow him from *qll*. Mutatis mutandis, as found in targumic texts, other apocopated formations from *tql*, a plural and singular (cf. Levy, *Chald. Wört.*, p. 551) are found. The form *qll* in the Itpe. Itpa. is found in the sense of *contemptus est* (Brockelmann, p. 652, and Payne Smith in *Thesaurus Syriacus*, II, 3615) *meqalal* meaning *levis, vilis, contemptus, 'etqalal/levis factus est, spretus est*, Arabic *taqalla;* the Syrian 'aphal with *al* means likewise *sprevit, contempsit* (Gal. 5.26), synonym *besar*. Compare further Dalman, *Wörterbuch*, p. 362 for further forms of *qll*, and indeed found frequently in Babylonian Aramaic in the sense of "deride, scorn." Compare also Jastrow, who according to their respective forms treats some occurrences as קיל (p. 1359) and others as קלל (p. 1378), both under the 'Aph'el. Our verse therefore in Mt. 18.6 and parallels should read, "But whoso shall make *light* of these little ones" which would correspond very well to the verse in 18.10 "Take heed that ye *despise* not one of these little ones...." The Aramaic form is passive, but could tolerably carry the well-known connotation of a reflexive as part of its function. Thus what is active or stative in the Hebrew text of MT כשל would be rendered in Aramaic in the passive/reflexive form, and vice versa. Compare MT and Targums, specifically for *tql* in Hos. 14.2; Is. 3.8; 63.13; Ps. 109.24. Therefore an expression such as אתקלו בה means not "they were offended in him" but "they derided him," very much like '*aqallu beh* in the Aph'el.

Similarly, see the passage in Mt. 13.57. After the people had heard Jesus in the synagogue, and had wondered where he had acquired such wisdom, they say, "Is not this the carpenter's son? Is not his mother called Mary?... - And his sisters, are they not all with us?..." Verse 57 should now be translated in the continuity not "And they were offended in him," but *"And they made light of him."* The sequel shows that this interpretation is correct: Jesus said unto them, "A prophet is not without *honor,* save in his own country."

Jesus was very sensitive about his honor and to any humiliation projected upon him. This was part of the Jewish psychological climate. Thus MT mentions *bōsh,* "to shame," some 160 times, to say nothing about the synonyms of *ḥerpah, kelima,* and the root *baza.* The theme of humiliation runs like a scarlet thread through Tobit: "It is better that I die rather than live for I have heard false reproaches" (3.6); Sarah, his daughter, prays: "Take me from the world that I hear no more reproach" (3.13).

The noun *skandalon* "snare, trap" must convey something of that sense in the verb *skandalizein* as Allen sought to vouch for in his *Gospel According to St. Mark* (1915, pp. 199—202), though queried by Stählin in his article *skandalon* in Kittel-Friedrich-Bromiley, p. 341. Nevertheless, the Aramaic in the passage in Mt. 17.27 gives the only proper sense. The narrative describes that the exactors of tribute came to Peter and asked whether his master had paid tribute. Jesus declared that only strangers pay tribute, and "Then are the children free. Notwithstanding, lest we should offend them (σκανδαλίσωμεν) go thou to the sea, and cast a hook, and take up the fish that first cometh up...." The word "offend," with regard to the payment of taxes, is not appropriate here. The translations that render the passage reveal the almost insoluble difficulty when we are confined merely to the Greek. ASV translates conventionally, "Lest we cause them to stumble"; Wms: "that we may not influence them to do anything wrong"; TCNT "that we may not shock them"—all inapposite, it seems to me, and psychologically awry in the situation where Jesus and Peter are under duress to pay the tax. The Aramaic equivalent נתקל, which was mistranslated here by the Greek, has the special meaning of "be caught, ensnared." (Compare Jast., 1691; Levy, *Chald. Wört.,* 551, in particular Ps. 9.17 [נוקש] Prov. 12.13, Targ. מתקל בישא, Pesh. מתחד and comp. the noun *tiqla* "trap"). Our verse now should be read as "Lest we be caught, be arrested, fetch the money and give it to them for me and thee" the only appropriate and pointed meaning to the verse.

One instance in which the root *tql* was mistaken as a noun for a verb is found in Mt. 13.41, where the text reads, "The Son of Man shall send forth his angels, and they shall gather out of his kingdom all *things* that offend (πάντα τὰ σκάνδαλα) and them which do iniquity." The contrast between "things" and "persons," which are paired off oddly, has been a source of puzzlement to commentators. As Arndt-Gingrich remark (s.v. *skandalon,* 760), "Nevertheless the fact that Mt. continues with καὶ τοὺς ποιοῦντας τὴν ἀνομίαν would require us *to take* task. *to mean persons*" (italics mine). Similarly, other translators as Moffatt,[2] "All who are hindrances," Beck "All who lead others to do wrong," and NAB "All who draw others to apostasy." These renderings fly in the face of the stubborn neuter plural. Others translate with the exigency of the text, "All that hinders" (TCNT), "All causes of sin" (Wey, RSV; Gdspd.).

The underlying Aramaic, however, is the source of the difficulty. The translator misinterpreted the form מתקלין which he considered to be a noun, plural of *matkela* "stumbling block" (Levy, *Chald. Wört.,* I, 83; II 551; Dalman, *Wörterb.,* 248, 425; Jast. 864, 1691). He should have regarded the form as *matkelin,* 'Aph'el of *tql*—"persons who cause others to stumble." The consonants would have been identical. The translation of the verse should obviously be: "and the angels shall gather out of his kingdom all those who cause others to stumble, and those who do evil."

As of now, we have witnessed some characteristics of a translator. He has not, to use the language of today, vowelized properly; we have seen that he has confused one root for another; he mistook a Daleth for a Resh; he was not familiar with Aramaic locutions; he was shaky in his syntax, mistaking a noun for a verb; he mistranslated in pursuing a wrong definition and interpretation; he rendered word for word though the whole verse makes for non-sense. We have seen, then, some samples of misconstruction of an Aramaic text that the translator had before him. More evidence, specialized and detailed gospel by gospel, will now be presented.

Chapter II

The Evidence from Matthew

THE PROOF that Mt. served as the original for translation comes through diverse avenues. Evidence shows that the Greek translator mistook one Aramaic root for another—characteristic of one who had Aramaic as an acquired second language; he kept in mind some stock Greek translations for Aramaic words which led him into awkward, frequently erroneous wooden equations. He misapprehended small idiomatic particles, the cause of much grief to translators universally. Because Aramaic was a second language to him, as will be seen, he often failed to perceive the nuance in a word or expression, and this led him astray with the sequence of the verse. Interesting too are the various features of Aramaic rhetoric, specifically wordplays, that come through in the retroversion from the Greek, a distinct trait of Semitic languages generally, and no less in Aramaic. (Compare I. M. Casanowicz, "Paronomasia in the Old Testament," JBL, 1893, 105ff.; H. Reckendorf, *Über Paronomasie in den Semitischen Sprachen;* D. Yellin, *Ḥiqre Miqra;* M. Black, *Aramaic Approach.*)

In addition to wordplays, there are other rhetorical devices such as alliteration, assonance, the devices called by the Arabs *talḥin* and *tawriyyat* (D. Yellin *Ḥiqre Miqra'*, I, 17) put to good use by R. Gordis (*The Book of God and Man*, pp. 167, 196, 347, 357), and the plethorizing of similar consonants as Black has shown. Aramaic syntax, especially the *peʻil* with the dative, as a functioning construction for the passive, manifests itself in the Greek with some disastrous results. The translator also misunderstood the fluctuating chronology in the Aramaic participle, and consequently distorted the time sense for the passage. Then, of course, because the text lacked the vocalic signs, the translator misvocalized words. It is noteworthy too that the translator blundered in identifying and distinguishing the determinate and indeterminate status of the noun in Aramaic, a matter of consequence in other translated books. (Compare the writer's *Biblical Books Translated from the Aramaic,* pp. 10, 11, 13; and *Inner World of Qohelet,* 104.) On the *talḥin,* see pp. 37, 101, 118, 124, 143, 158, *infra.*

A passage in Mt. 18.24 contains a parable in which a master summoned his servant to settle accounts with him. The servant owed the lord, according to the text, 10,000 talents (μυρίων ταλάντων)—a talent being worth (so Huck, 1936) about 1,000 dollars; hence, the servant would owe his master 10 million dollars. As the servant could not pay, the master decided that the servant, with his wife and children, should be sold to pay the debt. The servant begged for mercy and patience, promising that he would pay everything. The master released him compassionately, and forgave the debt. However, the same servant refused, in turn, to extend forgiveness of a debt of a trifling sum to a fellow servant. When the master was informed of the servant's rapacity and cruelty, he countermanded his own indulgence, and remanded the servant to prison until he should pay the debt.

A number of questions assail the reader. In what manner does a servant come into possession of 10 million dollars which he owes to his master? Granted that the master may have compassion, would he forgive 10 million dollars in debt? Interesting and suggestive is a variant *pollon,* "many" (cf. Von Soden's edition of the NT, II, v. 24 in the apparatus, p. 67), which brings the reading within the realm of possibility, and which furnishes the clue for solving the difficulty. The translator misvocalized the form רבו, det. רבותא (cf. the Pesh.; Payne Smith, p. 526; Brock. 707, especially in the other nominal formations) rendering "10,000" instead of רבותא *rabbutha* (Payne Smith ibid.; Jennings, *Dictionary,* 200, Brock. 706), meaning in this context "large amount, considerable sum." The passage now carries the meaning that the servant owed the master *much money,* but the amount is not specified. This makes the story tolerably acceptable to the reader. This variant reading "much" would provide a separate locution and tradition. The consonants in Aramaic would have been the same.

Within the same episode, and in the category of confusion of roots, an interesting example occurs at Mt. 18.34. The master had condemned the wicked servant to the torturers (βασανισταῖς) till he should have paid his debt. A number of translations take exception to the word "torturers" and translate instead "jailor," so RSV, with the footnote "Gk. torturers," Gdspd., Moff. Under the circumstances, "jailors" would be the more natural word. The Greek word, *basanistes,* and its associates *basanizo* "torment," and *basanismos* "torture, torment" indicate the fundamental meaning, as indeed assumed by other translators (AV, NAB, NEB). The meaning "jailor" is the ad hoc meaning assigned to *basanistes* in the text, as the single instance for this passages as given by Liddell and Scott in their *Greek and English Lexicon*.⁹ Torture was introduced under Herod, but it is not in accordance with Rabbinic law. A retroversion to Aramaic shows the source of the difficulty and the solution. In Aramaic, a byform of אסר appears as יסר. The latter verb signifies both "tie, put on, bind," and "torture" (Jast. p. 582, Levy, *Chald. Wörterb.* I. p. 340; cf. the noun ייסורא "bonds, chain," and "torture" Jast. p. 582; Levy, ibid.). Note the confusion between the two readings in Jast. (p. 582) in a number of examples. The word is found in Talmudic Babylonian Aramaic: B. Meṣ. 84b, 85a; Ber. 60a. Probably the form in Aramaic was *yissurin* "chains, prison," but was misinterpreted as *yissurin* "tortures," which the Greek translator personified as "torturers." Variantly, the form may have been איסורין Levy, *Chal. Wört.*, I, pp. 25, 51. The instinct of translators to render "jailors" is quite correct for an ad hoc interpretation, except as we have seen the basis for the literally correct translation goes back to the Aramaic, mistranslated.

Another instance of the confusion of meanings due to misunderstanding in the same root is found in Mt. 24.13. In one of his last exhortations to his disciples, Jesus, foretelling the great apocalyptic events of wars, rumors of wars, famines, pestilences, and earthquakes, says that the disciples will be given to the authorities to "be afflicted, and [they] shall kill you" (24.9). However, v. 13 ends with the consoling words "But he that shall *endure* ($\dot{\upsilon}\pi o\mu\epsilon\iota\nu\alpha s$) to the end, the same shall be saved." The finish seems limp and disappointing. The verse from one view is a banality; certainly, if one endures to the end, he will be saved. But how is one to endure to the end (v. 9 "They shall kill you!"), if Christian life under the Romans was in constant jeopardy, and persecution and murder were in ordinary course (vv. 21–22)?

Now one of the features of eschatological religion, extended to the believer, is the *hope* that the suppression of the religion, and the persecution of the believers, will be eradicated, and the triumph of the new world will emerge in glory. Compare Hos. 12.7 "And in your God put your unfailing trust" (*qawwe l*) (Mof.); Dan. 12.12 *'ashre hamehakke,* Theod. *hupomeno* as in our Mt. passage "Fortunate the man who waits and lives to see ... "; Hab. 2.3 "For there is still a vision for the appointed time. At the destined hour, it will come in breathless haste, it will not fail; if it delays, wait for it ... " (NEB); and compare, as a confirming phrase, the Targum in a free translation to Is. 42.22 ויסבר לסופא "And he will hope to/for the end." It now becomes clear that the sense of the passage in Mt. (and the parallels in Mk. 13.13, as well as in Lk. 21. 19, which has other elements to be treated separately), should read, literally, "And he who hopes to the very end will be saved." His hope alone will justify his salvation. (Cf. Rom. 8.24 "We are saved by hope" [Pesh. *sabarta*]; Heb. 6.11 "Full assurances of hope unto the end" [*sabarchon*].) It follows then that the translator confused two meanings (1) *sebar* סבר "hope, wait for" and the *pai'el* סיבר *saibar* "endure." The latter form is Syriac; Jewish Aramaic, and Christian Palestinian Aramaic is dialectically *sobar*. A similar confusion of forms is extant elsewhere, and will be discussed separately. The translation should run, "He who has hope to the end will be saved."

There are a number of passages that require a complete reconstruction because of the compounded misunderstandings of the translator. A familiar text is found in Mt. 6.22:

> The light of the body is the eye; if thine eye be single (ἁπλοῦς), thy whole body shall be full of light. But if thine eye be evil, thy whole body shall be full of darkness. If therefore the light that is in thee be darkness, how great is that darkness!

A number of scholars have offered improvements to this verse. H. J. Cadbury in his article "The Single Eye" (*Harvard Theological Review*, 1954, pp. 69–74) interpreted the phrase "If therefore thine eye be single" to mean "if your eye is generous," like the Hebrew *'ayin ṭobah*. Torrey, assuming *haplous* to be the equivalent of Aramaic *shlem* translated, "If then your eye is sound....," then antithetically, "But if your eye is diseased. ..." However, he failed to catch the symbolic significance of *'ayin ṭabah* ... *'ayin bisha* (Hebrew would be *'ayin ra'ah* or *ṣarah*) i.e., a generous eye, a covetous eye; and so Mof.[2] acutely, "So if your Eye is generous.... but if your Eye is selfish [but in his *Historical New Testament,* the E is not capitalized]. The present writer cannot follow Nor: "But if you have poor eyesight"; Gdspd: "sound...unsound"; RSV: "Sound...not sound"; NAB: "good...bad."

The passage is skillfully contrived. It can be interpreted on a physical and spiritual level. An examination of the passage leaves no doubt that through *talḥin*—that is beyond the usual sense—there are overtones with other nuances in certain words, which bring out the full force of the passage.

In the first place, the expressions "a good eye" and "a bad eye," as used frequently in Mishnaic and Talmudic writings, in both Hebrew and Aramaic, are largely employed in a symbolic sense. (Compare Abot 2.13.14 [Taylor's ed.]; in Aramaic עינא טבא b. Pes. 88a; עינא בישא Levy, NH Wört., III, 640; עינו צרה b. Abot 5.13 i.e., niggardly about his own money.)

Then again in the Mt. passage the word "body" (σῶμά) is a mistranslation. It is not body but "soul," Hebrew and Aramaic *nefesh*. The generous eye is a light to the inner soul, not *body*. (Compare Prov. 20.27 "The soul of a man is like a light from God.") If the eye be generous, open, benevolent, your whole soul is lighted, radiant. By contrast, the body cannot be illuminated.

If, on the other hand, your eye be "niggardly," mean, stinting, grudging, then your soul will be dark. The Aramaic word *hashika* (חשיכא) "darkened" carries the overtone of *hasika* "witholding, grudging," i.e., the Arabic *talhin*. Possibly, there was a misreading, *Sin* for *Shin*. The passage now should be translated:

The light of the soul is the eye;
If therefore thine eye be generous,
Your whole soul shall be full of light.
But if your eye be grudging,
Your whole soul shall be full of darkness.

If the *talhin* be assumed as a factor in the remaining clause, the text will carry the following overtones:

If the light in you be lacking (*hasik*) how great is that lack!
If the light in you be darkened (*hashika*), how great is that darkness (*hashoka*)
If the light in thee is lacking, how great is that darkness!
If the light in thee is dark, how great is that lack!

Added to this meaning of *hasik* "lack" may be the sense of "withhold" as well as "diminished" (Jast. p. 488), which would be a further dimension to the *talhin* in the verse.

Another passage that requires extended examination is Mt. 21.9. Jesus was entering Jerusalem, "And the multitudes that went before, and that followed cried, saying, 'Hosanna to the son of David' (ὡσαννὰ τῷ υἱῷ Δαυιδ); 'Blessed is he that cometh in the name of the Lord. Hosanna in the highest'" (ὡσαννὰ ἐν τοῖς ὑψίστοις). Mk. 11.9 varies with, "Hosanna; blessed is he that cometh in the name of the Lord. Hosanna in the highest." For the latter phrase, Luke 19.38, has "Glory (*doksa*) in the highest."

There are a number of difficulties with the Mt. passage. (1) What does Hosanna mean? (2) Since the word was used in and out of the Temple in liturgical use during the Festival of Booths, what does Hosanna signify at the *Passover* entry of Jesus into Jerusalem? (3) What is the syntax of "Hosanna *to* the son of David" in the dative case? (4) If we translate "Save the son of David" (Torrey: Save the king!), what are we to make of the second Hosanna phrase "Save in the highest," unparalleled as a Hebrew or Aramaic phrase? Were we to translate "Save now, O God, blessed be in the name of the Lord the one who comes" (Dalman; cf. Moff. in Ps. 118.26 "In the Eternal's name, blessed is this one who enters"), then Dalman denies any Messianic associations. Furthermore, the idea that Hosanna acquired a meaning similar to "Hail!" is unsupported and a gratuitous assumption.

It becomes obvious that Hosanna is a transliteration not of a Greek word but of an Aramaic one, which was not recognized by the Greek translator. Note the Semitic suffix -an(n)a. There are variants as in D *ossana,* Jerome *osanna;* Pesh., Syr. Curet., Syr. Sin. אושענא. In the Aramaic text, the expression appeared as חוסנא לבר דוד *husna,* Hebrew *hosen* "power" and is to be translated following Dn. 2.37; 4.27, BDB, 1093 "(royal) power to the son of David!" The *Ḥet,* a weak guttural, was easily reduced to *Aleph.* (Compare אסנא, חסנא "granary, storehouse," Jast. 95a.) Perhaps the Greek reading originally was *osana* with short ŏ and note the Syrian אושענא with the short vowel (note the Aleph again). For this confusion or substitution of ou/o and ou/ŏ/ō see Hatch-Redpath, *Concordance,* III, 124—125; Blass-Debrunner-Funk, par. 30; 28, 35. This expression "Power to the son of David" could very well be the battle cry or revolutionary slogan of the restless elements in the capital, Jerusalem.

The second phrase "Hosanna in the highest" (Greek plural) is a reflection of the Aramaic *ḥusna bimromayya* (Jerome has *brama*), again a shout and hail, probably from religious elements "Power through God!" The Beth is the Beth Instrumenti. Hebrew *marom* Aramaic *meroma* "heights, heavens" is by metonomy another name for God. (Compare Job 16.16, Is. 38.14 which is used today in Israel for "I swear by God." See R. Alcalay, *Hebrew-English Dictionary,* 1496.) *Meroma, meromayya* would have been employed substitutively to avoid the tabooed pronunciation not only of the Tetragrammaton but *Adonai* as well (Lev. 24.11). According to this reading of *ḥusna* "power," the arrival of Jesus in Jerusalem was a signal for outpouring of all parties to hail him as king (Mk. 11.10), one group thinking him the earthly king from the Davidic line, or in fact the Messiah, and another group that wanted no earthly king but a theocracy alone with God as ruler. (See S. Zeitlin, *Rise and Fall of the Judean State.*) Note that *doksa* "glory" of Lk.

THE EVIDENCE FROM MATTHEW

could easily be a free rendering of *ḥusna* as *doksa* contains the concept of power, might, Arndt-Gingrich, 202.

The substrate Aramaic supplies a satisfying reconstruction to the passage in Mt. 12.43f. (parallels Lk. 11.24f.). The text reads,

> When the unclean spirit is gone out of a man, he walketh through dry places [ἀνύδρον τόπων i.e., *ḥorbata* "ruins," a mistranslation, see p. 46] seeking rest, and finds none. Then he says, "I will return unto my house from whence I came out"; and when he is come he findeth it empty (σχολάζοντα), swept (σεσαρωμένον), and garnished (κεκοσμημένον). Then goeth he, and taketh with himself seven other spirits more wicked than himself, and they enter in and dwell there.

This is certainly a weird picture: "The original meaning of the passage is very hard to see" (Montefiore). It cannot mean that the evil spirit "At its return, is pleased to find that its dwelling has (at its previous expulsion) been swept and garnished, as if it had only been sent away for the sake of a spring cleaning!" (Wellhausen quoted by Montefiore, *The Synoptic Gospels*, II, 633). Nor can the passage be interpreted in a sort of half jocular, half ironical vein which is "very peculiar" as Montefiore admits.

The truth is that the expulsion of a demon from the body was of crucial importance, and there was always the danger that he would return with "seven other devils more wicked than himself,"—the seizures and the paroxysms would even be more violent than before. The evil spirit found his abode (the man) "empty." No attempt had been made, that is, to stabilize himself through repentance, prayer, or "good works" so as to prevent the evil spirit from re-entering.

The underlying Aramaic contributes in clarifying the peculiar puzzling expression "house... empty, swept, and garnished." The term "house" apparently misled the translator to think sequentially of how a house is "swept" and tidied up. The word *baitha* means not only "house" but "abode" (BDB, 109a), and naturally refers to the human body. Bearing that meaning in mind, the Greek translator misconstrued the succeeding Aramaic words completely: They ran סריק חמים ומצטבי (*seriq, ḥamim wemeẓtebe*). (Compare the Peshitta, which has however *wamẓabat* "adorn, set in order" a secondary root of *ẓbi* "find pleasure in, desire," so Nöldeke *Syriac Grammar*, par. 58, n. 1.) The translator took *seriq*, correctly, to mean "empty"; *ḥamim*, however he understood (carrying the mental image of house) as "swept" (the word is used for sweeping a house, Payn. Sm. p. 145; Brock. p.

238). It would have been more appropriate to have interpreted the word as "warm." The last word *wemeẓtebe* he confused with *wamẓabat*—a misapprehension of the root. He should have translated "desirable, agreeable," not as AV's "garnished" or the modern "adorned." We have now a harmonious relationship of all the verbs, and an acceptable picture of what the evil spirit is doing. After roaming around among the ruins, the evil spirit returns to the man, his previous habitation, and finds him *vacant, warm,* and *desirable.*

Mt. 23.25 exhibits a confused metaphor again, and it is the Greek translator who is responsible for the confusion. The passage reads, "Woe to you, scribes and Pharisees, hypocrites! For ye make clean the outside of the cup, and of the platter, but within, they are full of extortion (ἁρπαγῆς) and excess (ἀκρασίας)." Clearly, the inside of the cup and platter, cannot be filled with "extortion" and "excess," whatever these words mean. Variants to the latter reading are *akatharsias* "uncleanliness," vg. sy^s (*ṭenufta*), sa, bo (Nestle and Huck's sigla), though the reading may seem to come in as a correction and hence may be secondary. Lk. 11.39, in the parallel passage, reads *ponerias* "wickedness," seemingly a mixed figure again. Note the sequence Mt. 23.26, "First cleanse the inside of the cup. . . . that the outside also may be clean." The translator clearly had on his mind the objectionable Pharisees who were filled, as he thought, with extortion and excess. The Aramaic writer was more subtle. He wrote *ṭenufta wezahama* "impurity and foulness," characteristics of the unwashed pot. (Compare for the first reading in Burkitt, 138 cited above, and note the expression in Y. Ab. Zar. II, 14c "It is like drinking out of an offensive, foul cup," rt. *zaham*.) However, he was able to convey the expression to the reader (*talḥin*) and imply the overtone of "sin," which *ṭnf* means. Cf. Brockelmann (p. 136), *iniquitas, peccator fuit;* and in the nominal form not only *iniquitas,* but *zohama* "foulness, impurity," and also having the sense of "sin", (Jast. p. 384). The Greek translator, however, picked up only "extortion" and "excess" which distorts the comparison and the figure.

The Greek Mt.'s treatment of the root *peras* "break," (Jast., p. 1232) is an interesting example of the way Matthew translates. Mt. 15.37, in the episode of the loaves and fishes, reads, "And they did all eat and were filled; and they took of the broken [meat], τῶν κλασμάτων, that was left seven baskets full." We understand that the broken [meat], or "fragments" were the broken pieces of *maṣa,* the unleavened bread, made with but flour and water, thinly rolled, and baked in a fire for about 15 minutes, as the Bedouin are accustomed to do to this day. The Greek translator saw the Aramaic word *perista,* or pl. *perisata*) פריסתא (Brock. p. 600; Payn. Sm. p. 460), which means "morsels of bread," and translated it too literally into "that which is broken up" (cf. Mt. 14.19) and hence a mistranslation. To make sense and point in the episode, he should have rendered with the more encompassing and meaningful "morsels of bread." *Perista* usually is combined with *laḥma* "bread," Hebrew, *perusat leḥem*, but may very well stand by itself. (Compare P. Smith, p. 460; Jast., p. 1221.) Elsewhere in parallels, Mt. 14.20; Mk. 6.43; 8.8, and Lk. 9.17, the rendering should be likewise "morsels of bread." Again, we see how the Greek translator rendered too literally, misinterpreted the idiom, and took *perista* as if it were a passive participle formation.

A puzzling problem is solved via the Aramaic in the injunction given to the disciples in Mt. 16.6 where Jesus said to them, "Take heed and beware of the *leaven* (ἀπο τῆς ζύμης) of the Pharisees and the Sadducees." The disciples imagined that his statement referred to the fact that they had not brought bread along with them. Jesus reproved them for their lack of faith. "Then understood they how he bade them not beware of the leaven of bread, but of the doctrine (τῆς διδαχῆς) of the Pharisees and Sadducees" (Mt. 16.12). Mk. 8.14–21 does not state explicitly that the loaves mean "doctrine," but only insofar as v. 14 states that the disciples forgot to bring bread. Lk. 12.1, whether earlier or later, preserves the simpler form of the statement, "In the meantime, when there gathered together an innumerable multitude of people, inasmuch as they trode upon one another, he began to say unto his disciples, 'First of all (see below p. 42), beware of the leaven of the Pharisees, which is hypocrisy'," with no explanation again of what leaven should mean. The question is, what is meant by "leaven," and how is it related to "teaching" (doctrine)? Moreover, why is it in some fashion "hypocrisy"?

One of the principal criticisms that Jesus levelled against the Pharisees was that they lay on the people with a heavy hand, "the weightier matters of the Law"—piling upon them without letup law upon law and detail upon detail. (Compare Mt. 23.4; Lk. 11.46, "You load men with burdens hard to bear, and you yourselves touch not the burdens with one of your fingers.") Presumably, the Aramaic word that Jesus had in mind and articulated was the Aramaic word *ḥamira* (associated with the Hebrew cognate *ḥomer*) meaning "weighty, strict, stringent," the Aramaic feminine adjective (neuter) taking over the function of a noun, as in the phrase *min ḥamirata deRab* "one of Rab's strict regulations" (Y. Ab. Zar. II, 41d Jast. p. 477 for examples). The disciples, according to the version in Mt., misinterpreted the Aramaic word *ḥamira* "legal severity" to mean "leavened bread, bread"

Jast. 477, sub. II, חמירא (cf. its Hebrew parallel *homeẓ*), and consequently confused Jesus' meaning. Jesus upbraided them for their lack of understanding: Do ye not understand...? (v. 9); How is it that ye do not understand...? (v. 11).

We have other instances where the disciples misunderstood Jesus' words. Thus, see their misunderstanding of the Aramaic *demak* signifying (1) sleep and (2) die (p. 147, 158). As mentioned, however, the original *ḥamirta/ḥamirata* seems to have partially occurred with the correct explanation, "the leaven of the Pharisees *which is hypocrisy*" in Lk. 12.1 (cf. Plummer, *Luke,* a.l., which had the germ of the correct interpretation. Translate: "Beware of the legal severities of the Pharisees, for that is hypocrisy"). The *didache* "teaching" in Mt. 16.12 is the blanket explanatory term for *ḥamirata* "legal severities."

Incidentally, in the Lk. passage just cited (12.1), there is a problematic word πρῶτον "first" which juts out peculiarly in position and meaning in the verse. The conventional procedure is to keep the word outside the direct quotation "He began to say unto his disciples first of all, 'Beware ye of the leaven' (i.e. legal severities as above) etc.; others, as early as Tyndale, put the word in the discourse; "First of all beware of the leaven..." (and so Torrey, *The Four Gospels,* p. 147, though Plummer, p. 317, thinks it makes for "poor sense." Montefiore (II, p. 952) regards the concourse of the throngs as inexplicable, and that *proton* was added to "smoothe over the difficulty." The word *proton* should be elucidated from another point of view. It represents the Aramaic *min de-resha'* מן דרישא meaning not only "first, from the first" but also "again." (Syriac; Babylonian Talmudic, Payn. Sm., p. 540; Brock. p. 728 sub e; Jast. p. 1478; L. Ginzberg, *Geonica,* II, Index.) The word was mistranslated "first of all" whereas the correct rendering should be "again." The reason for Jesus' saying "again" comes from the fact that he mentioned the legal severities of the Pharisees some seven verses before (11.46); actually, the whole drift of the discourse is against the "lawyers" through the rest of the chapter to v. 54., as Lk. constituted the account. The translation should now read, "He began to say to his disciples, '*Again* beware of the severities...'" This does not begin a new discourse, but is a continuation of his previous teaching, beginning Lk. 11.46 and continuing through 12.12.

The root טמן was misunderstood by the Greek translator in one instance. He apparently did not know that the word occasionally has the sense of "insert, immerse, plunge." This meaning is evidenced in such passages as Prov. 19.24 "The sluggard plunges (*ṭmn*) his hand in the dish..." (NEB).

Moffatt: drops his hand; similarly Prov. 26.15. Likewise in Talmudic Hebrew as in "What is it like? Like a child who had his finger immersed/plunged *ṭmn* in honey..." Ned. 45a; "The seller must not immerse (*ṭmn*) his weights in salt" (so as to weight them), Baba Meṣ. 61b; Baba Batra 89b. Note now the text in Mt. 13.33 (parallel Lk. 13.21) which reads, "Another parable spoke he unto them, 'The kingdom of heaven is like unto leaven, which a woman took and hid (ἐνέκρυψεν) in three measures of meal, till the whole was leavened.'" The woman did not *hide* the leaven; she put in leaven with the measures of meal. The Greek translator took *ṭmn* in the more usual sense of "hide." He should have translated with "insert, immerse." While the Aramaic verb was most likely *ṭmn,* compare טמר, a dialectal variant of טמן for *krupto* (and compounds) in p s c Phil in Mt. 13.33 and Lk. 13.21, there is the possibility that the verb טמע "hide, sink" may have been employed. Note its use as in the following phrase, "Who is an עיסה widow? One who had had mixed (*ṭmʽ*) in her a priestly strain, but of doubtful priestly legitimacy," Ket. 14a. 'Isah means "dough," and note its use with *ṭmʽ*, a good parallel to the Marcan passage. The NT passage should however now be translated, "... leaven which a woman took and inserted in three measures of meal."

When the translator has fixed in his mind a standard, even inflexible, Aramaic-Greek lexical equation for certain words, and he follows that pattern more or less consistently, he tends to end up with mistranslations. Thus, for example, the Greek word *doron* "gift" as a translation of the Aramaic *qurbana,* meaning both "sacrifice" and "gift," is wrongly rendered in a verse wherein "sacrifice" is the only correct translation. So the leper, in Mt. 8.3f., who by the touch of Jesus is immediately cleansed is told to go his way; "Show thyself to the priest, and offer the gift (δῶρον) that Moses commanded for a testimony to them." The ordinances about leprosy, to which Jesus referred, are found in Lev. 14.2–32. The passage relating to our problem, and the requirement for sacrifice in the cleansing of the leper are in 14.4f.

> The priest shall command to take for him that is to be cleansed two living clean birds, and cedarwood, and scarlet and hyssop. (6) And the priest shall command to *kill* one of the birds in an earthen vessel over running water; (6) He shall take the living bird with the cedarwood, and the scarlet stuff, and the hyssop, and dip them and the living bird in the blood of the bird that was *killed* over the running water; (7) And he shall sprinkle seven times upon him who is to be cleansed of leprosy, then he shall pronounce him clean.... After

the leper shall have bathed himself, and shave all his hair, he shall take two he-lambs, fine flour, and oil, and the priest takes the he-lamb for a guilt-offering; (13) And he shall *kill* the he-lamb in the place where they kill the sin-offering and the burnt-offering.... (14) And the priest shall take of the blood of the guilt-offering....

The passage furthermore makes provision for one who is poor, perhaps indeed for the masses of the poor (whom Jesus had in mind),

(21) But if he is poor and cannot afford so much, then he shall take one male lamb for a guilt-offering to be waved to make atonement for him, and a tenth of fine flour mixed with oil for a cereal offering, and a log of oil; (22) Also two turtledoves, or two young pigeons, such as he can afford, the one shall be a sin-offering, and the other a burnt-offering... (24) And the priest shall take the lamb... (25) And he shall *kill* the lamb of the guilt-offering... (30) And he shall offer of the turtledoves or young pigeons such as he can afford, (31) One for a sin-offering and the other for a burnt-offering; and the priest shall make atonement before the Lord.

It must be clear from the quoted passages that the sine qua non for the cleansing of the leper is a *sacrifice* of an animal or a bird. Blood is required, so that it be sprinkled upon the leper to cleanse him. The *minḥa*, or the intermingled oil and fine flour, is only a concomitant of the central sacrifice of the lamb, the oil perhaps being used to cure disease, and more importantly to ward off evil demons. (Compare Mk. 6.13; James 5.14.) The commentator Rashi in referring to b. Men. 91 pointedly explains that the fine flour mingled with oil is required, as the sin-offering and the guilt-offering of a leper requires libations (*hata'to wa-'ashamo shel mezor‘a ṭe‘unim nesakim*). The ruling actually is based directly on the Mishna, b. Men. 90b.

We may conclude that sacrifice, even for the most poverty stricken, required the killing of a lamb (Lev. 14.25), a turtledove, or a pigeon for a sin-offering to make atonement (ibid. 29). It follows now that *qurbana* must mean "sacrifice," and certainly cannot be translated as "gift." The libations, the flour mixed with oil, are an integral part of the sacrifice. Translate: "... offer the sacrifice that Moses commanded..."

The well-known problem with the transliterated word *korban,* omitted in Mt. 15.5 "But ye say, Whosoever shall say to his father or his mother, 'It is a *gift* by whatsoever thou mightest be profited by me'" but expressly put in by Mk. 7.11, "If a man shall say to his father or mother, '*Korban,* that is to say a *gift* by whatsoever thou mightest profited by me'" finds its resolution once more through the Aramaic word *qurban*. In these two passages the word was mistranslated as "gift." Usage seems to indicate (Nedarim 1.4, cited by Levy, NH *Wörterbuch*, IV, p. 371, that *qo/urban* implies "I take an oath" (by the life or existence of sacrifices on the altar). As Levy puts it, האומר קרבן שאני אוכל לך אסור, ר' יהודה מתיר *Wenn Jem. sagt, ein Korban soll das sein, was ich etwa von dem Deinigen essen sollte, so darf er nichts von dem Seinigen essen. R. Juda erlaubt es, weil qorban ohne vorges. Bet bedeutet: Ein Schwur beim Leben des Korban. Das. 3.2f. und sehr oft* nadar beqorban, *er gelobte mit Korban.* A parallel is found in Josephus, *Against Apion*, 4, par. 167 (Loeb Classics) where he states that Theophrastus claimed that the laws of the Tyrians prohibit the use of foreign oaths, and in enumerating, he includes among others the *oath* called "Korban" (*kai ton kaloumenon orkon korban katarith mei*). *Qorban* as "oath" simply follows along a linguistic pattern of האלהים (Sabb. 145a), המעון (Ket. 27b), העבודה (Yebam. 32b), "By God! By the life of the Temple! By the life of the Temple service!" The oath presumes that the Temple, and the divine worship, and so indeed the *qorban* "sacrifice" would last eternally as sancta.

Of course, in other texts, *qurbana* has the alternate meaning of "gift," both in Syriac and Talmudic Aramaic. Thus Josephus goes on to say in the previously quoted statement, that, interpreting specifically from the Hebrew, it means "God's gift." (Compare, however, Thackeray's note, p. 230.) Furthermore, in another passage (*Ant.* 4.73), Josephus states that the Nazirites call *korban* that which translated in Greek has the meaning of "gift." Associatively, *korbanas* in Mt. 27.6, meaning "treasury," is obviously an extension of the sense of "gifts," and probably was called by its full title *bet qurbana* "place of gifts." (Compare the Peshitta.) To sum up, the NT Greek translator did not know or bear in mind that *qorban* may have the three meanings of "gift, sacrifice," *and* "oath."

On a number of occasions, the translator misjudged the meaning of *ḥurba*. As this word has a number of meanings, this led to some confusion. *Ḥurba* (masc.) may mean (1) heat, dryness, rt. I *ḥrb* and (2) *ḥurba* (fem.) "desolation, waste, desert," rt. II *ḥrb* "waste, ruin." It also can be read as a noun meaning "ruins, deserted building(s)," as *ḥurba dedabra* (Ket. 13b), a ruined building standing in the field; *ḥorba 'aḥat meḥurbot Yerushalaim* (Heb.) "one of the ruins of Jerusalem" (Levy, NH *Wört.*, II 105; Jast. 430). The Gospels mention that Jesus would "go into a desert apart" (Mt. 14.13; Mk. 6.32; Lk. 4.42). While in most instances "desert place" would serve adequately, if not competently, in some translations the renditions are awry.

Thus Lk. 9.10 reads, "And he took them (the apostles), and went aside privately into a desert place belonging to the city called Bethsaida." The translation follows the texts of the Alexandrinus, codex Ephraemi, the "Ferrar Group," the *koine* ["Byzantine"] text and W (so-called Freer Logion). See Huck, Proleg. X. Some scholars regard the Greek text as problematic. Thus Plummer (243) regards the text as conflate. UBS omits "desert place." Torrey thought that *polin* has been mistranslated, and that *qeritha* means "open country"; however, he departs too radically from the Greek. The Aramaic could contribute to solving the difficulty. While it is possible to say that a city borders on the desert (Jn. 11.54), it seems strange to say that a desert (*res communes*) belonged to the city. Actually, the episode intends to convey that Jesus and the disciples went to *ruins* that belonged to the city, where they could be alone. Compare such expressions as *ḥurba demata* "the ruins of the city" b. Ket. 13b; *kotel ḥurba* "wall of a ruined building" b. Baba Bat. 20a. B. Bera. 3a has the interesting story of R. Yose, who was travelling, and "entered a ruin, one of the ruins of Jerusalem to pray" (cf. Jesus and his disciples). Elijah, who was there, asked him, "Why did you go into the *ḥurba?*" and he said, "To pray." Elijah then enjoined him not to pray in a ruin. Our Rabbis taught: There are three reasons why one must not go into a *ḥurba*; because of suspicion (of sexual license), because of falling debris (*mappolet*, see p. 59—60), and because of demons." In Lk. 9.10 obviously *ḥurba* was mistranslated as "desert" for "ruins."

On the other hand, *ḥurba* was translated too literally in Mt. 12.43 (parall. Lk. 11.24) when the demon is described as going through dry places ($\delta\iota'$ $\dot{\alpha}\nu\dot{\upsilon}\delta\rho\omega\nu$ $\tau\acute{o}\pi\omega\nu$) seeking rest. We know that demons inhabit ruins (as above; cf. Thompson, *Devils and Evil Spirits of Babylonia*, p. 139, "O Evil Demon, hie thee to the ruins" (cited by Allen, *Matthew*, p. 141). It is apparent that the Greek translator thought of *ḥurbata* as "dry places," whereas he should have translated "He walked through ruins, seeking rest."

There is a peculiar phrase employed by Mt. who says that, as punishment, the wicked will be cast into "outer darkness" ($\tau\grave{o}$ $\sigma\kappa\acute{o}\tau o\varsigma$ $\tau\grave{o}$ $\dot{\epsilon}\xi\acute{\omega}\tau\epsilon\rho o\nu$; 8.12; 22.13; 25.30). It usually is presumed the wicked will be bound in prison (cf. b. Shabb. 152b, quoted by Allen, p. 265), and there is no doubt that the wicked will be cast into darkness (Allen, p. 78). What, however, is the "*outer* darkness"?

The normal procedure with imprisonment of the malefactor was to place him in a dungeon, "I have sent for thy prisoners from the dungeon" (Zech. 9.11); "prisoner to the dungeon" (Is. 24.22). From this lead, it should be clear that in all the cited instances in Mt., the translator misread his text. He read *bara'* "outside" instead of *bera* "dungeon." Syriac spells *bira* without the Yud. For a similar confusion of the same words, see p. 49. The Aramaic probably ran *leḥashoka debera* "to the darkness of the dungeon," this being the usual description.

Mt. 11.24 reads, "But I say unto you, that it shall be more tolerable for the land of Sodom (*ge/ereṣ* in the LXX) in the day of judgment than for thee." Of course, Sodom is not a "land," it is a city (cf. Gen. 19.1; Ez. 16.53). Note the upbraiding of the *"cities"* (11.20)—specified to be Chorazin, Bethsaida, and Capernaum—and the comparison with Tyre and Sidon, all cities. The Aramaic reads: *medinat sedom* which in the forefront of the translator's mind appeared to be *medina* as "land," but also, despite the strictures of Torrey ("Notes on the Aramaic Part of Daniel" p. 259f. in *Transactions of the Connecticut Academy* etc. xv, July 1909) means "city" in proto-Syriac and Eastern Aramaic (Payn. Sm. p. 252; especially Brock. p. 145). We accordingly should rectify the conventional translation with: the city of Sodom. I am anticipated now by S. Lachs, *JQR* April, 1977, who however does not distinguish between *medina* as Hebrew or Aramaic.

The following mistranslations, simple errors, illuminate the further translator's inadequate comprehension of his text, and his imperfect knowledge of Aramaic. Mt. 5.25 reads, "Agree with (really אתרעי "be reconciled") thine adversary quickly ("adversary" i.e., your opponent in the law [Aramaic: *be'el dinak*] while thou art on the *way*(?); Greek, *en to hodo*), lest at any time the adversary deliver thee to the judge. . . . and thou be cast into prison."

It would be most unusual, as the verse implies, to meet with one's opponent on the way (Allen, *Matthew*, p. 49 questions: "to judgment?"; RSV, throwing caution to the winds, "to the court"). My suggestion is that most likely the Aramaic read: *behalka'* (Hebrew *halakhah*), "in the law, on the legal point," which the Greek translator read as *behalka'* "on the way" (Payn. Sm. p. 104; Jast. p. 353). The translation should now read, "Be reconciled with your opponent quickly, before you are [come together] with him about a legal ruling," Aramaic *'ad ant behalka/behilketa 'immeh*. Note that *halaka* is pronouncedly Jewish Babylonian Aramaic though found naturally in Jewish Palestinian Aramaic (derived, one may surmise, from Akkadian *elku* "custom"). There is a trace of this in Syriac—*halek dina* meaning "the sentence is pronounced," or "carried out" (Payn Sm. p. 104). For other observations on this verse, see p. 113. In addition, the word *'ad* in the

Mt. passage in the underlying *Aramaic*, which the Greeks interpreted as "while," should have been translated in its other usage as "before" (Dalman, *Wörterb.*, p. 292).

One would expect *bedina* as the characteristic, more inclusive term; *halka/hilka*, refers to a legal ruling or a legal decision. In this context the word is most pertinent—one is going to court with regard to a question of the law, of what the ruling in the law may be. The term would correspond to the later *halakhah pesuqah* "legal decision." This must be now the correct interpretation, because otherwise the manner in which it is described presumes the guilt or malfeasance of the defendant, "lest at any time the adversary deliver thee to the judge." Why should we assume that you as defendant will lose your case and your opponent hand you over to the judge? Perhaps to the contrary, you may win your suit? The point about the behest is that it involves two principles of the later articulated Talmudic maxims of acting more ethically, on a higher level, than adhering to the strict letter of the law. A later Talmudic formula phrased it as לפנים משורת הדין—one should not act severely, according to the letter of the law, but beyond what the law requires; and act also according to the principle of פשרה, "compromise." (Compare Bera. 45b; Bab. Meṣia 30b; Sanh. 6a; Mekilta Yitro, ed. Epstein-Melamed and S. Federbush, *Ha-musar we-ha-mishpat beyisrael*, Ch. 5.[12])

A puzzling text is found in Mt. 11.19. The verses preceding it consist of Jesus' defense of John's behavior. V.18 portrays John as an ascetic, "neither eating or drinking, and they say, 'He hath a devil.' The son of man [i.e., *hahu bar nasha*, Aramaic idiom meaning 'I'] came eating and drinking, and they say, 'A man gluttonous, and a wine bibber, a friend of publicans and sinners.'" The verse (11.19) which we have to analyze, sums up mysteriously with the conclusion, "But wisdom is justified of her children" (καὶ ἐδικαιώθη ἡ σοφία ἀπὸ πάντων τῶν τέκνων αὐτῆς). The AV accords with C,K,D,Th(eta), Latin, Sy[sc] (cf. Nestle's ed. a.l.). As editor, however, he prints *apo ton ergon autes* "by her works" which makes for passable sense, the *teknon* reading of Mt. being due supposedly to the harmonization with the *teknon* reading in Lk. 7.35. (See the resolution of the committee, Kurt Aland, M. Black, Bruce Metzger, and Allen Wilkgren, as editors of UBS, Metzger, p. 30.) But is this not *ignotum per ignotius?* How is one to explain the reading *teknon* in the other parallel, Lk. 7.35? All in all, *teknon* appears to be the more original, although the more difficult reading. As such, it is to be preferred, and, if possible, explained. *Ergon* seems to be a correction, introduced in order to make sense out of the verse, and so "works" replaced "children." Moreover, *ergon* is not earlier than the fourth century (Allen, *Matthew*, p. 118; Plummer, *Luke*, p. 209). Incidentally, the assumption made by some scholars that an unpointed עבדיה was misread (Lagarde, Zahn, Klostermann) has been correctly challenged by Eb. Nestle and Lagrange on the basis that *teknon* is never used for *'abda* (Metzger, p. 30). The frame of reference is Aramaic but from a different direction. The Greek translator read *toladata*, root *yld*, meaning "children" whereas he should read it by its other meaning "the events to come." Aramaic *tolda'*, like the Hebrew *toladah*, means "children, progeny, generation" and also "history, events to follow." (Compare Onqelos Gen. 2.4; 5.1.) This is implicit in the verb *yld*, as producing events, (Prov. 27.1) and the explanation of BDB, 410a "an account of man and his descendants=history." The usage of *toladah* as "result, consequences, future events" in later Hebrew is well known (Ben Yehuda, *Thesaurus*, s.v. *toladah*, p. 7688f.). Our passage in Mt. and Lk. should now be translated: "Wisdom will be justified by the events that follow."

The translator erred in Mt. 22.14 where the text reads, "For many may be called but few are chosen" ($\dot{\epsilon}\kappa\lambda\epsilon\kappa\tau o\iota$). There is first of all a literary question to be discussed as to where the verse properly belongs, whether at the end of Mt. 20.16, or as a conclusion to Mt. 22.14. The editors of the Greek text of UBS (apparently in accord with Nestle) disregard the evidence of C, D, W, et al., vg., sy[cs] and completely replace the verse borrowed from 19.30 "Thus the last shall be first and the first shall be last," omitting our passage at 20.16. Allen (*Matthew*, p. 215) furthermore observes "It is almost impossible to give the words any meaning in this connection (sc. 20.16). They are genuine in 22.14." However, at 22.14 he says, "Vv. 1—14 do not seem to suit this connection" (p. 236). The truth, as I see it, is that the concluding words are most fitting at 20.16. In 22.14, by contrast, it was thought that "*many* are called" referred to the remaining people at the wedding party. "*Few* are chosen" however would be misapplied and incongruous to the members at the feast, because only *one* wedding guest was ejected. Nor can "few" refer to the wedding guest in a general way either since he was the only one ejected, and cast into prison (*lehashoka de bera, bera* as above p. 47). "Chosen" is not appropriate for the one who was thrown out.

When we review the same episode in ch. 20, we learn that many workers were called to do paid work in the vineyard. Some, who were hired last, and who worked but an hour, were paid the same wage as the other laborers. The workers grumbled about the obvious injustice. The employer declared that he had a right to apportion his money as he saw fit. Jesus added, as a conclusion, "Many are called but few collect their due wages." The Greek translator thought of the Aramaic verb *gaba'* in the sense of the Eastern Aramaic "choose." But he should have rendered with the more pertinent meaning of *gaba'* as "collect"—sums of money, tribute, taxes, charities, and the like (n. pl. *gebayata* "collection of alms etc." Payn. Sm. pp. 58, 59; Brock. p. 100; Jast. pp. 205f.). The brief proverb "Many are called but few collect" sounds like it is borrowed from the business world and signifies: Many are called for work, but only a few collect fully for work done.

The Aramaic likewise clarifies a difficulty in Mt. 25.21.23. For the two servants who had commerced successfully with their master's money, the reward came in the promise that each servant would be "ruler over many things." The master ended the statement with "Enter thou into the joy (εἰς τὴν χαρὰν) of thy lord." The word "joy" in the text combined with "enter" is incomprehensible, and scholars propose that *chara,* "joy," should have the sense of "festive dinner, banquet," with the qualification of "perhaps" in the remark of Arndt-Gingrich (p. 884, but Mof.[2] reads "feast" in his translation). Dalman (*Words of Jesus,* p. 117) supposed that either *simḥa* or the Aramaic *ḥedwa* must mean in Mt. 25.21 and 23 "joy connected with a festival, wedding feast," with which one may agree in principle. However, there is no "joy of wedding" in this instance; the nuance, and the situation of master and slave, is different; it is simply "merrymaking." The Aramaic word in question would have been בסמא *besama* (Pay. Sm., p. 49; Brock. p. 80) meaning "pleasure, enjoyment, *feasting*"; עבד בסמא "he made a banquet." In effect, the translator chose the word "joy" mistakenly instead of the more natural "feast, merrymaking."

In commenting about the character and activity of John, his predecessor, that he was like Elijah and a "prophet," Jesus said to the crowds following him, "What went ye out to the wilderness to see? A reed shaken by the wind?" (κάλαμον ὑπὸ ἀνέμου σαλευόμενον.) "But what went ye out to see? A man clothed in soft raiment? Behold they that wear soft clothing are in king's houses. But what went ye out to see? A prophet? Yea, I say unto you, and more than a prophet" (Mt. 11.7–9).

Here Jesus remarks on the motives that prompt crowds to gather. If a king, or a wealthy person passes through the town, with an entourage and showy luxurious clothes, people will crowd the thoroughfares to gawk as he passes by. If a prophet comes to town, people will want to see him, observe his miracles of healing or hear him. But now, in v.7, will the townspeople

THE EVIDENCE FROM MATTHEW

really go to the wilderness to see "a reed shaken by the wind?" Why, furthermore, will they go that far, "to the wilderness?"

It is the Aramaic that restores the proper figure, the parallelism, and the significant relevance. The translator saw in his text קניא מתזע ברוחא, *qanya mitza' beruḥa*. He misvocalized. He took *qanya* to be a "reed," and with this interpretation considered *ruḥa* to be "wind." The correct reading, with the same consonants is "A zealot shaken by the spirit." Crowds would gather to see fanatics seized with spasms, possessed with religious frenzy and zeal, who "speak with other tongues" (Ac. 2.4), and roll naked on the ground in ecstasy (1 Sam. 19.24). Persons who possessed or were possessed by such zeal went to the wilderness, their most comfortable refuge, to escape supervision and harassment of governments. (Compare the instances of Moses, Elijah, John, and Jesus). For קני as "reed" and קני *qannai* as "zealot," compare Jast. 1392; Dalman, *Wörterb.*, p. 675. Syriac has only the nominal formation *qene'ta*, Brock., p. 675.) We should now translate our phrase: "Or as one frenzied/agitated by a spirit."

A verse in Mt. 8.22, with a similar parallel in Lk. 9.60, contains both a wordplay and a misvocalization. After one of the would-be disciples said to Jesus, "Lord, suffer me first to go and bury my father," Jesus said to him, "Follow me; and let the dead bury the dead." Commentators suppose (cf. note a.l. in the NAB; Allen, *Matthew*, p. 82) that the dead who "bury" are spiritually dead themselves, and the call to follow Jesus might sometimes necessitate the abandonment of human relations. The difficulties about this perplexing interpretation are apparent. The verb for bringing a body to burial is, in Hebrew, *hebi* (2 Chron. 28.27; 2 Kings 23.30), or *yabal* in the Hof'al (Job 10.19; 21.32). Aramaic uses the term *'ata'* in the Aph'el as in the Targums to the Kings and Chron. passages above (Payn. Sm., p. 32). *Qabar*, both Hebrew and Aramaic, is the most suitable word. It is likely that the Aramaic text reads שבוק למיתיא למיתיא, *Shebuk l'maithayya lemithayya*, modernly translated, "Let the buriers (undertakers) bury the dead." The translator, because of the succession of the same letters, and apparently the same words to him, vowellized *mithayya* in both places making for impossible sense. Of course, he missed the wordplay as well. The consonants were identical.

In the incident where Jesus comes to John at the Jordan to be baptized by him, the latter forbade him, saying, "I have need to be baptized of thee; and thou comest to me?" Mt. 3.15 continues, "And Jesus answering said unto him, 'Suffer it to be so, now; for thus it becometh us to fulfill all righteousness.'" (οὕτως γὰρ πρέπον ἐστὶν ἡμῖν πληρῶσαι πᾶσαν δικαιοσύνην.) It is evident that there are a number of questions to be resolved. First, since *dikaisune* means righteousness, or an act of righteousness, in what way is the immersion in the Jordan to be considered an act of "righteousness"? Second, there was no demand in Jewish law for a ritual immersion except when one has been defiled, as through contact with a dead body, or *pollutio noctis,* and also in more stringent regulations with regard to priestly rites. Immersion in Judaism is not a sine qua non for the forgiveness of sins. In Christian doctrine (1 Cor. 1.13—16; Ac. 22.16; Gospel acc. to the Hebrews; in Jerome, Against Pelagius III, 2, cited by Huck) baptism assumes its significant place, unless we assume that the later baptism was retrojected to Jesus. Finally, in what manner was immersion an act fulfilling *all* (?) (πᾶσαν) righteousness?

Before proceeding to discuss these questions, and to show the relevance of the Aramaic to the difficulties in the verse, a short digression may be inserted here to define the Aramaic *zakuta'* in this connection. The reader may refer to S. Schechter (*Some Aspects of Rabbinic Theology*) whose work did not cover the whole subject; these remarks are only supplemental.

Dikaisune is almost a standard reproduction of *ṣedek, ṣedaka* in the LXX; Aramaic *zakuta'* "righteousness," is an almost universal synonym of *ṣedaka* in the Targums and Peshitta. (Compare MT. and Onqelos in Gen. 15.6; 30.33; Dt. 6.25; 9.4—6; 24.13; 33.21; MT. and the Peshitta Jer. 51.10; Ez. 18.20; in the LXX Ps. 72.(Heb. 73)13 [lexically and so Mic. 6.11.] In Jewish theology, the Hebrew *zakut* acquired another meaning and concept as "merit," conventionally rendered. Thus, during his life, a wicked man accumulates, adding one sin to another, a grievous balance of "demerits" (*kaf ḥobah;* Shabb. 32a). If not cancelled or annulled this will prevent him from entering the world to come (*'alma d'ate*). According to one view, his repentance will repeal his fate, if enough good deeds be accumulated (b. Yoma 86b). One can imagine a situation where sins and merits are evenly divided (Shabb. ibid.; b. Qidd. 39b; 40b). A man's good deed for another has the power to add to his account a "merit" for righteousness, and thus "credits" accumulate. The more a man could muster these *zakwatha,* the more could he account himself fortunate. The *ṣaddik* naturally has many merits. Sometimes, in the grip of a great calamity, whether individual or national, regardless of how many "merits" he has acquired, they may be completely exhausted. Hence the ordinary man and the *ṣaddik* as well have to depend on what is known as *zakut 'abot* "merits of the fathers"—either their own fathers or the Patriarchs—for salvation. (Compare b. Bera. 27b; Y. Bera.

THE EVIDENCE FROM MATTHEW   53

7a.) However, as one cannot know how many "merits" he has stored up, nor indeed their "value," it behooves a man to acquire as many *zakuyot* as possible.

The Greek *pleromai* has its counterpart in Aramaic as *shelam* "fulfill, complete, perfect." As discussed above, the religious Judean desired to be replete as possible with "merits." Compare the instance recorded in Y. Bera. 4c of one who seeks to pray, should first garb himself in a tallit and tefillin (phylacteries) and then pray, so that he take upon himself "the yoke of heaven," משלם, replete, complete with the commandments. Compare the commentary *Penei Moshe* to the passage. Compare this with the parallel passage in Bera. 15a "He who wishes to take upon himself the 'yoke of heaven' in as *complete* a fashion as possible (shelemah), he should take time (or, turn aside 'for natural functions' Rashi), to wash his hands, put on his phylacteries, recite the Shema, and then pray."

In the light of the above information, the verse in Mt. should bear the sense, "It is good to be replete with as many merits as possible." The translator erred in translating *zakwatha* "merits" as *zakutha* "righteousness." Probably the Aramaic text ran *shefar lan lemishlam kol zakwatha* — שפר לן למשלם כל זכותא. *Shelam* (and idem *mala'* as a stative verb) can bear the passive meaning "be filled with, be complete with." *Kol zakwatha* is of course accusative. (Compare Davidson, *Hebrew Syntax*,[3] p. 112; Margolis, *Grammar,* par. 61.) The translator took the verb as transitive. Our text therefore bears the significance that Jesus thought that to be baptized, and this before he knew or started his ministry, would make him complete with all (Hebrew-Aramaic for "every kind of"), or additional, merits.

A confusion and a misunderstanding of the root שוי/שוא misled the translator in another instance. The passage Mt. 22.39 requires some preliminary analysis, because the Aramaic itself offers a solution to a hitherto unresolved problem. Someone had asked Jesus the question, "Master, which is the great commandment in the law?" Jesus replied, "Thou shalt love the Lord, thy God with all thy heart, and with all thy soul, and with all thy mind (διανοία)" (Mt. 22.36—37). The parallel passage in Mk. reads, "With all your heart, and with all your soul, and with all your mind, and with all your strength." Lk. has the order, "With all your heart, and with all your soul, and with all your strength, and with all your mind" (Lk. 10.27). If we follow the original statement in Dt. 6.5, "And thou shalt love the Lord thy God with all thy heart, and with all thy soul, and with all thy might," it follows that (1) we have a surplus phrase in "with all your mind"; (2) The position of the phrase in the verse is uncertain as indicated in the different order in Mk. and Lk.; and (3) the phrase is obviously a gloss (and so Torrey) as the balanced verse in Dt. shows, and as the Septuagint attests. The question now to be considered is, where does the phrase "with all your mind" come from?

Quite early, the verse lent itself to Midrashic explication. An early tannaitic tradition has it (compare the Sifre to the passage, Mishna Bera. 9.5; Tg. Jon. to Dt. 6.5) that the reason *lebabka* in the Dt. passage is written with two Bets is that one should serve God with two "hearts," that is, with two minds, two natures (cf. 1 Kgs. 3.9 *leb shome'a* "an understanding mind" in this sense), with the *yezer ha-tob* and the *yezer ha-ra'*, with both the good and evil inclinations. There is some searching also about *nefesh* (further in the Sifre). In our terms, does nefesh mean (1) body, (2) soul, (3) mind or (4) desire (Dt. 12.20; 1.26; Ps. 10.3)?

Someone neatly put a gloss into the Aramaic, originally in Mk., in the underlying text between "heart" and "soul," defining heart with "mind," i.e., רעינא as the Pesh. has it here as a translation. But the Aramaic gloss defeated itself, as it could be interpreted as an explanation, fore and aft, both for *lebab* and *nefesh*, because *ra'ayana* itself means both thought and desire. (Cf. Jastrow, P. 1487; Brock., p. 738; Payn. Sm., p. 545.) The Greek translator properly selected *mind* exclusively, not "desire." The gloss moreover was recognized, being placed after the genuine text in Lk. It had been a practice similarly from pre-Masoretic days to place variants (or glosses) at the end of the verse, sometimes at the caesura (*'etnahta*), sometimes side by side. (Compare Zimmermann, "The Perpetuation of Variants in the Masoretic Text," *JQR*, vol. 44, 1944, pp. 259f.) The explanation of the variant comes through via the Aramaic.

We continue with Mt. 22.38–39, "This [And thou shalt love, etc.] is the first and great commandment. (39) And the second is like unto it, 'Thou shalt love thy neighbor as thyself.'" The first question is, if the *safra*, the one learned in the Torah, asked for the *one* great commandment, why does Jesus respond with two? The second question is, how is the second commandment "like unto it" ($\dot{o}\mu o i\alpha$ $\alpha \dot{v}\tau \tilde{\eta}$)? In what sense is the first commandment similar to the second?

It must be obvious that Jesus did not wish to limit himself to one verse. The first verse affirms the loyal obligation of man to God, to love Him with heart and soul, while the second speaks of man's duty to his neighbor. A man cannot fulfill his religious obligation with but one. The commandments are correlative. If one loves God, he should love his neighbor, and the converse is equally valid, demanding, and true. The word "is like," however, has been mistranslated. The text should have run, "The second has the same value (or worth, or importance) as the first." The Aramaic probably ran *wedatren deshawe leh*. The root שוה, שוא means "like" but also "of worth, of value, valid" (Payn. Sm., p. 562; Brock., p. 758; Jast., p. 1532). Jesus implies that both verses are equally indispensable for the religion of man, and are on a par with one another.

In another example, the differences in the textual transmission in Mt. 23.27 and Lk. 11.44 exhibit their divergences through the primary Aramaic source. The diatribe against the Pharisees reads, "Woe unto you scribes and Pharisees, hypocrites! For ye are like unto whited sepulchres (τάφοις κεκονιαμένοις i.e., whitewashed graves), which indeed appear beautiful outward, but are within full of dead men's bones, and of all uncleanness." Lk. 11.44 varies with "For ye are graves which appear not" (μνημεῖα τὰ ἄδηλα, literally, graves that are not seen). We learn from talmudic records with regard to graves (Baba Kama 69a) that they were marked with lime, the white color (*simana dehiwwar*) intended to simulate the white of a corpse's bones. The lime was immersed in water and spread around (*denihawwar tefe*) so it could be seen from a distance (Maimonides). The passage in Mt. probably ran *qibrin mehawwerin* "whitened graves." Lk. however, gentile and Syrian, confused the roots I *ḥ(w)r* "see" and II *ḥ(w)r* "white," or perhaps read the form *hairin* (Payn. Sm., p. 13; Brock., p. 222; some "Targumic" texts of Prov. have the form, which copyists altered as presumably they did not understand the root, in 23.32; 17.24, with a further possibility of Qidd. 39a, Jast., p. 439). The form would be the participle active plural used impersonally for the passive, to be translated as "graves that are seen." This, however, created a difficulty. For if the graves were seen, then how could people be unaware of them and walk over them? A correction was in order. Lk. probably introduced *ouk* "not" into the text to make sense. Since a variant explained is no variant, the text in Mt. is most likely original.

A comparison of the texts in Mk. 16.8 and Mt. 28.8. shows that the differences between them stem from a misreading in the Aramaic. The text of Mk. reads, "And they went out quickly, and fled from the sepulchre; for they trembled and were amazed (εἶχον γὰρ αὐτὰς τρόμος καὶ ἔκστασις; lit. for trembling and fear [see below] possessed them); neither said they to any man; for they were afraid." The passage in Mt. runs, "And they departed from the sepulchre with fear and great *joy* (μετὰ φόβου καὶ χαρᾶς μεγάλης)." An attempt is made to explain the divergencies in the texts in that the two Marys were at first filled with fear, but afterwards were filled with joy by the message of the angel (H. B. Swete, *The Gospel of St. Mark,* ad. loc.). Nevertheless, "fear" and "joy" pair off oddly, especially as we have in the earlier tradition of Mk. "trembling" and *ekstasis*. This Greek word in the LXX and other Greek translations is primarily employed for "fear" (cf. Hesychius *phobos*), and so is used for *zewaʻah, ḥaradah, shammah, saʻar, timmahon,* as well as *tardemah* in the secondary sense of "trance," which is not relevant to our text. Mk.'s reading "fear and trembling," as in English, is the most natural phrase. Where, then, did Mt.'s reading "joy" originate? It would be quite possible that בועתא "rejoicing" and ביעותא "fright" were confused with one another. Note how similar forms are as found in Aramaic texts—e.g. ביעתא "rejoicing," בעותא "fright," as well as Syriac בועתא rt. בעת "fear." Dalman, *Wörterb.*, p. 51, registers ביעותא "Schrecken" and ביעתא "Freude." (See also Jast., p. 164 and Levy, *Chäld. Wört.,* p. 85.) The objection may be raised that the misreading of "rejoicing" for "fear" in the Targums of Jonathan, is based upon a root found only in Jewish Palestinian Aramaic, but not in Eastern Aramaic or Babylonian Aramaic. The translator of Mt., who, I presume, lived in Syria, may very well have known the Palestinian Targums from synagogal readings of the Torah and its concomitant translation into "traditional" Aramaic by the meturgeman, and therefore thought he saw the root for "rejoicing."

Discrepant texts in Mt., Mk., and Lk. likewise betray themselves, as in the instance of Mt. 17.5 which reads, "This is my beloved son, in whom I am well pleased (*en ho eudokesa*)"; Mk. 9.7 "This is my beloved son" without, however, "with whom I am well pleased"; Lk. 9.35 "This is my son, my chosen (*eklelegmenos*: text is according to p⁴⁵ ⁷⁵ א B L et al., incorporated in the UBS text as a most probable reading; see Metzger, p. 148). In the parallel texts, Mt. 3.17; Mk. 1.11; Lk. 3.22, the reading is uniformly "This is my beloved son with whom (thee, Mk. and Lk.) I am well pleased." The reading of Lk.'s "my chosen," disconsonant with the other readings of Mt. and Mk., to say nothing of his own reading in the parallel passage, is interesting. Where did *eklelegmenos* originate? The Aramaic argument would assert that אתרעית, usually translated "I am well pleased," would be the source. However, אתרעי has the important meaning of "choose." Note that this Aramaic root is employed for בחר "choose" in the pentateuchal Onqelos some 32 times, statistically more than רצה and חפץ, and is obviously a significant variant meaning, actually a more pointed signification in the context than the looser "I am well pleased." At any rate, Lk.'s "chosen" is another variant translation of אתרעי, the Aramaic text (cf. Jast., p. 1486).

THE EVIDENCE FROM MATTHEW 57

There are a number of other passages, which are parallel to one another, but deviant in their wording. These require some reconstruction. It is interesting to note how the Aramaic reconstruction makes some fruitful suggestions. The first passage, Mt. 5.15, reads, "Neither do men light a candle, and put it under a bushel (*modion*), but on a candlestick; and it giveth light unto all that are in the house." Mk. varies with an addition (4.21), "And he said unto them, 'Is a candle brought to be put under a bushel, or under a bed (μόδιον, κλίνην)? And not to set on a candlestick'?" On the other hand, Lk. 11.33 reads, "No man when he lighteth a candle, putteth it in a secret place (κρύπτην), nor under a bushel (μόδιον), but on a candlestick...." This reading in Lk. is contradicted by another passage in Lk. 8.16 which reads, "No man, when he hath lighted a candle covereth it with a vessel (σκεύει), or putteth it under a bed (κλίνης), but setteth it on a candlestick..." In short, Mt. has "under a bushel"; Mk., "bushel, bed"; Lk. in 11.33, "cellar, bushel"; and in 8.16, "vessel, bed." By canons of criticism, Mt. has the simple unglossed original reading. It had not סאתא, as the Peshitta translates, nor מודיא (cf. Burkitt on the passage) which simply reproduces *modion*, but the rarer word מאנא. Brock. (p. 373, #7) defined as *medimnus*, i.e., a bushel containing six Greek modii (Lewis and Short, *Latin Dictionary*, p. 1122), although there seems to be some variation (Payn. Sm., p. 256) on this. Probably *modion* in the Greek was a simplifying term (compare J. Jeremias in his *Abba*, p. 101 "unbestimmt"). At any rate, this מאנא was the source of much confusion. In Lk. 8.16 the word was interpreted as במנא, במאנא "vessel." But Lk. 11.33 had a different tradition, or his copy read בכמנא "in secret" *locus occultus* (Brock., p. 331). The word עריסא, (compare furthermore with the Hebrew עריסה meaning a "kneading trough," Jast., p. 1117, 1121), was taken to mean "bed" in Mk. 4.21 and Lk. 8.16 and was so mistranslated. This latter reading "kneading trough" had been made by other scholars as well, and undoubtedly is the basis for the translation in NEB "meal-tub." The Aramaic retroversion seems to supply a satisfying explanation of the variants which have not received any proper explanation hitherto.

A nuance by definition ("shade of difference") cannot properly be called "mistranslation," yet occasionally this slight variation in meaning may assume the disproportion and distortion of a real mistranslation. This is detected most markedly in synonyms, where one word may be used for another, yet in context, it may not legitimately be so employed. A case in point would be the passage in Mt. 8.32, where the Gadarene swine went over the cliff, and "perished in the waters" (ἀπέθανον). Mk. 5.13 reads,

"And were *choked* in the sea" (ἐπνίγοντο), and similarly, Lk. 8.33 uses the verb "choked." I have no doubt that the swine, when they fell in the waters, were "choked," but it is peculiar for a writer to describe their drowning that way (more naturally Mt.). The Aramaic root *ḥanaq* most frequently signifies "choke," and thus the translations by Mark and Luke followed the usual meaning of the Aramaic word. However, in the Eastern Aramaic *ḥanaq* means not only "strangle, hang," but also "drown, be overwhelmed by waves, be submerged in water," the only appropriate meaning here. (Compare Brock., pp. 244–45; Payn. Sm., p. 149.)

A similar case, where the unsuitable nuance or perhaps an outright mistranslation may be presumed, is found at Mt. 22.5 where a man, a king (see on this expression p. 27) invited people to attend the wedding of his son. V. 5 continues, "But they not caring went away." Probably "neglecting" (the invitation) would seem the proper translation (cf. Allen, *Matthew*, a. l.). On the other hand, the rendering of Lk. 14.18 "But they all with one consent began to make excuse (καὶ ἤρξαντο ἀπὸ μιᾶς πάντες παραιτεῖσθαι) indicates that two roots—שאל "ask" and שלא "neglect"—were confused. The Etpe'el of *she'el* (compare with the Syriac in the Mt. passage) means to "make excuse" (Payn. Sm. p.554; Brock., p. 749a). It can easily be seen that אשתלי and איתשיל as found in the literature (compare Epstein, *Diqduq*, pp. 72, 98), in their naked forms, appear quite similar to one another, and certainly in the plural, מתשלין (Dalman, *Grammar*, p. 306) and משתילין could easily have been confounded. Between the Mt. and Mk. readings, however, the preferment of the one lection over another is difficult.

The word *argos* means "idle, careless," corresponding for our purposes to the Aramaic *bṭl* (cf. the Greek-Aramaic equation at Ezr. 4.24, in Hebrew and Greek at Qoh. 12.3). The word *bṭl*, however, does not only mean "cease" but transitively means "make null and void, repeal." It is employed idiomatically with "words," as in *debarim beṭelim* (b. *Giṭṭin* 32b; *'Aboda Zara* 16b; *Yoma* 77a). The word *bṭl* has the additional sense of "belittle, disparage, treat another in a deprecating fashion as if he were of no account" (cf. Ben Yehudah, s.v., 515f.). This meaning now elucidates the passage in Mt. 12.36 where the text reads, "But I say unto you that every idle word (ἀργὸν) that man shall speak, they shall give account thereof in the day of judgment." This condemnation, based upon the conventional rendering, seems unduly harsh. If one should utter an idle or careless word, should he be judged by, or held accountable for the word (literally: every word, a Hebrew/Aramaic idiom) spoken idly? The Aramaic word was *baṭla* or *mebaṭla,* and this is what Jesus, who was always sensitive to deprecation or humiliation, articulated. The Aramaic word, however, bears the meaning of "disparaging, belittling, render something worthless" (comp. Alcalay, *Hebrew-English Dictionary*, p. 219 "despise, belittle," Dalman, s.v. "nichtig, wertlos, leer," and Arabic *baṭala* Hava, *Arabic-English Dictionary*, p. 37 "be reduced to nothing, render a thing worthless"). Modern Hebrew biṭṭel 'et ha-ish means "He made the man of no account, reduced him to nothing." (Cf. the synonymous *req* signifying (1) "empty" and (2) "worthless.") The noun *baṭlan*, which at one time signified a man who did not need work, and could supervise with others the town's affairs and its needs, pejoratively became one earning good natured contempt. (Compare the noun *baṭalah*, Jast., p. 158.) The sensitive Jesus, who felt keenly the inhospitable reception to his teachings in Chorazin, Capernaum, and other localities, declares, for this occasion, that anyone who offends another by a belittling, humiliating word will have to account for this in the next world. This is of a piece with the statement in Abot 3.15 that he who exposes his fellowman to shame in public has no portion in the world to come; and the statement that he who puts his neighbor to shame in public is considered as if he had shed blood (b. Bab. Mes. 58b). However, here the Greek translator took the word *bṭl* in its usual, common meaning of "idle, vain."

Again in Mt. 23.23, the failure to discern the shade of meaning in the Aramaic failed to give the finer distinction to the verse. The verse runs, "Ye pay tithe of mint, and anise and cumin, and have omitted (Aramaic really *shabkin*, "abandoned") the weightier matters (τὰ βαρύτερα) of the law, judgment (κρίσιν would be the Hebrew *mishpaṭ*, hence "justice," ASV rightly "justice") and mercy and faith" (Aramaic *haimenutha* "truth, honesty," actually a mistranslation and similarly RSV probably with Mi. 6.8 in mind). Undoubtedly the "weightier" matters signify the more precious matters of law, justice, mercy, and honesty. The Aramaic read *yakiratha* (and so the Peshitta) which, indeed, means "heavy weighty matters" but, more appositely, the precious things of the law (cf. Hebrew *yaqar* "precious" Prov. 6.26; Jer. 15.19; Ps. 116.15). The passage now reads, "Ye have abandoned the precious things of the Torah: justice, and mercy, and honesty."

To this group, of nuances unsuitable in context, may belong the instance of Mt. 7.27 where the storm of rains, floods, and winds bring down the house, "And it fell; and great was the fall of it" (ἡ πτῶσις αὐτῆς). Lk. 6.49 offers the variant "and the ruin (τὸ ῥῆγμα) of that house was great." For another reference to these sections (Mt. 7.24—27 and Lk. 6.47—49 see p. 46). It is obvious that the Aramaic *mappulteh*, and so the Peshitta in both verses, was in the original text. In Mt., however, the translator rendered according to the one meaning of *mappulteh*, "fall, collapse," rt. *nefal*, but in Lk. the translator associated the meaning with "ruin." For the Mt. employment of "fall, collapse," cf. Ber. 3a, cited previously "You must not enter a ruined building for prayer, *mipnei ha-mappolet*, because it may fall in," and for Lk.'s usage, see Payn. Sm., p. 291.

The text in Mt. 18.26 contained an Aramaic word that the Greek translator again misunderstood. The passage runs, "The servant therefore fell down and worshipped him ($\pi\rho\sigma\epsilon\kappa\upsilon\nu\epsilon\iota$) saying, 'Lord, have patience with me, and I will pay thee all.'" The passage deals with the 10,000 talents for which the servant was in default. (On this extraordinarily large debt see p. 34.) *Proskunesis* almost always is a religious act, hence the AV "worshipped." However, in a similar situation three verses later (v. 29), the fellow servant "fell down at his feet and *besought* him ($\pi\alpha\rho\epsilon\kappa\acute{\alpha}\lambda\epsilon\iota$)," the Greek term repeated in v. 32., where the master uses it in describing the petition of the first servant. It follows that the word "worshipped" in the very first instance is incongruous, and the Aramaic בעי was misunderstood in that connection. Although it has the meaning of "worship, pray, implore" (cf. Dan. 6.14 ba'ei be'utheh literally praying his prayers," the cogn. acc.), a more fundamental meaning is "ask, *beg*," the required meaning in v. 26. *Proskuneo* has the sense of "pray"/"bow down." (Compare Jn. 4.23—26 and note the equation of Ex. 11.8 *proskunesousi/hishtaḥawe*, Targ. *be'ei*; Is. 44.15 *wayisgod lamo/be'a' minneh*). Translate "fell down and begged him."

The root תמה also presented difficulties to the translator. In Mt. 19.24 we learn of Jesus' statement that it is easier for a camel to go through the eye of a needle than for a rich man ($\pi\lambda o\acute{u}\sigma\iota o\varsigma$) to enter the kingdom of God. V. 25 continues, "When his disciples heard of it, they were exceedingly amazed ($\dot{\epsilon}\xi\epsilon\pi\lambda\acute{\eta}\sigma\sigma o\nu\tau o$) saying, 'Who can be saved'?" While *temah* means primarily "wonder," it also harbors the sense of "be alarmed, be disturbed" (for *ekplesso/tmah*, cf. Lk. 2.48; Mk. 1.22; 11.18). Thus the Peshitta, for example, will employ *temah* for *shamem*, Ps. 40.16, *ḥarad* Gen. 42.28 and in Onqelos Deut. 28.28 *sha'ammuth/timmahon*; and so *ekstasis* of the LXX for *ḥaradah*, Gen. 27.33, 2 Kings 4.13; Ez. 26.16 and its use for *timmahon* Dt. 28.20; Zach. 12.4. From the nature of the question that the disciples posed, "Who then can be saved?" it follows that they were not amazed so much, but perturbed, or alarmed about themselves that they would not be saved. In addition, the preceding verse speaks of a special case of "the rich man." The question now arises, why should the disciples be worried about the rich man who could not enter the kingdom of God? They themselves were not rich,

THE EVIDENCE FROM MATTHEW

but poor folk, fishermen, etc. and the circumstance hardly applied to them. Upon analysis, the term "rich man" is incorrect. The Aramaic did not have on this occasion the usual *'atir* but מיתר *meyattar* "one who has abundance of things, who has more than he needs," who has excess baggage, so to speak, which will prevent him from entering the kingdom of God. The translator rendered *meyattar* as "rich" (cf. *yitrah* "riches, affluence," BDB, 52a; Akkadian *atâru* "reichlicher werden," Ges.-Buhl,[17] p. 328). Now everything falls into place. If a man is not rich, but has more than he needs, and therefore cannot enter the Kingdom of God, the disciples had reason to worry. Jesus parries by saying that with God all is possible. This still is vague, and leaves the disciples unsatisfied and disturbed that they may not enter the kingdom. Peter presses him, "Behold, we have forsaken all, and followed thee; what shall we have?" (v. 27). Jesus replies that those who have left houses and lands and family for him, shall receive a hundredfold, and also will inherit everlasting life. Peter's question and Jesus' replies confirm the point and correctness given here to Jesus' declaration that anyone who has a surplus, or more than he needs, cannot enter the kingdom of God. Implicitly, Peter and the disciples having nothing and "forsaken all" will gain the kingdom.

There is a nicety in Mt. 27.19 which the translator failed to recognize in the root חש. Pilate's wife requests him not to harm Jesus in any way. The verse runs, "Have thou nothing to do with that just man (an Aramaic expression לא לך ולצדיקא הוא (Μηδὲν σοὶ καὶ τῷ δικαίῳ ἐκείνῳ); for I have suffered many things (πολλὰ γὰρ ἔπαθον) this day in a dream because of him." In Aramaic, חש usually means "suffer" (pain), as in the expression "one who has a pain in his head (*hash berosho*) should study the Torah"; but it also means "being apprehensive" (Jast., p. 441). Now since Pilate's wife had a dream which served in ancient times as a forecast of events to come, it was not suffering that she experienced from the dream, but *apprehension*. The same psychology is manifested in Julius Caesar, Act II, 1.80 where Calpurnia, Caesar's wife, has frightening dreams of Caesar being murdered and is referred to in such words and phrases as, "And these does she apply for warnings and portents, and evils imminent...." Repeated again, "Yet now they frighten me... call it my fear...." Then she is reproved, "How foolish do your fears seem now...." Translate Mt. 27.19: "I apprehended much this day through my dream *about* him בחלמי בה"—cf. the Peshitta—not *"because* of him."

In the Sermon on the Mount, it is difficult to decide whether at Mt. 5.3 "Blessed are the poor in spirit" is more original than the parallel at Lk. 6.20

"Blessed are ye poor" (*ptochoi*). Allen (*Matthew*, p. 39) assumes that "poor in spirit" is probably a later amplification, so as to have readers avoid thinking that "poor" means materially deprived, and ridden by poverty. It is striking, however, that the origin of "poor in spirit" is an Aramaic locution מכיכי רוחא; the translator, rendering too literally, did not catch its true gist. *Makkike ruḥa* can mean literally "poor in spirit." It really signifies those who are without hope, dispirited—*depressed in spirit* would serve as a good translation. *Mekak*, and its by-form *muk*, means literally "poor" but also "humble, cast down, *downcast*" (and for the phrase, cf. Targ. Is. 57.15; idem 66.2; Prov. 18.14; Ps. 34.19).

A word that is a snare to the Greek translators is φθόνος, usually translated "envy," so the AV and Gdspd. (Allen, *Matthew*, p. 290), though modern translations, are patently dissatisfied with the rendering. Compare Mt. 27.18 where the various renderings are "were jealous," Rieu; "out of spite," NEB; "through sheer malice" Phi; "jealousy," NAB. At the parallel Mk. 15.10, again the translations vary: AV, ASV read "envy," Wey, "sheer spite," Rieu, NAB, "jealous, jealousy." Whatever the impelling motives were in handing over Jesus to the Roman authorities, it could hardly be "envy" that aroused the priests, and the rulers and the people (?) to bring Jesus to Pilate, nor because of "envy" of Jesus' reputation (Swete, *Mark*, p. 371). Nor do the other words used in the various translations at Mt. 27.18, as "spite," "jealousy," "malice," represent the real motives that spurred Jesus' arraignment. The motivation must be sought from another viewpoint. Jesus not only advocated an examination and renewal of Jewish ethical ideas and a reversal and change in Jewish law, but he manifestly was a political danger to the state. Overtly, Jesus was considered a king, and this was the charge inscribed as the reason in the titulus on the cross. Actually, as modern scholars have advanced, he was a political revolutionary (cf. S. G. F. Brandon, *Jesus and the Zealots*).

The underlying Aramaic word that caused the inapposite Greek translation was קנאה which usually was rendered "envy." It might have been translated more fittingly as "zeal, zealousness," or the modern "religious fanaticism." For this meaning, cf. Sanh. 9.6 (81b) הקנאין פוגעין בו, "zealous persons (like Phineas) strike at him when he is caught in the act" (Jastrow). There is more to this, however, than fanaticism. The biblical sense of *qina'ah* is not only "ardor, zeal, jealousy," but "anger." (Compare first its parallel in MT: with *ḥemah*, Ez. 5.13; with *'ebrah*, ibid. 38.19; with *'af*, Dt. 29.19; with *ka'as*, Jb. 5.2; and interpreted by BDB as "ardor of anger"

THE EVIDENCE FROM MATTHEW 63

(888b); in the Hif'il "provoke to jealous anger" Dt. 32.16; Ps. 78.58 and for our thesis, more importantly, "anger, indignation" in Eastern Aramaic, Payn. Sm., p. 509.) In short, *qina'ah* cannot be translated by a single word; "angry zeal" would be appropriate. The translation should not, however, be "envy." For the mistranslation elsewhere of this root see p. 51.

The root שדי (with its synonym רמי) admits of many meanings, primarily "throw, cast." An associated meaning bears the signification of "lay down, set down," which, in different circumstances, and in another context, becomes a bit grotesque. It is idiomatic to say that if one saw "a great snake lying in the road," the term *shedi* (passive participle), is proper. It becomes improper to say (Mt. 15.30) "And great multitudes came unto him, having with them those that were lame, blind, dumb, maimed and many others, and cast them down (ἔρριψαν) at Jesus' feet, and he healed them." The text does not show consideration or gentleness on the part of the people who wished to help—they would hardly cast down the afflicted—though NEB still translates literally, "They threw (!) them at his feet." Other renderings such as "laid them," Gdspd., NAB, Torrey; or "put them down," TCNT; are the only correct translations. For ῥίπτω = שדא, compare Mt. 27.5 Peshitta, Mt. 15.30 s p c render with רמא. The improper rendition "throw at his feet" is too literal a translation.

Conversely, the passage in Mt. 9.36 requires more probing, because the root *shedi* may not be the apposite verb, though the Greek verb is the same. The text reads, "But when he saw the multitude, he was moved with compassion on them, because they fainted and were scattered abroad (ἐσκυλμένοι καὶ ἐρριμμένοι) as sheep having no shepherd." The first Greek verb means "worried, troubled," but *rhipto* extant as the perfect passive participle in the text is defined conjecturally as "helpless, dejected." The translations vary widely: "distressed and scattered," ASV; "torn and thrown down," Rhm; "mangled and thrown to the ground," Ber.; "distracted and dejected," Wey; "bewildered and dejected," Gdspd.; "harassed and helpless," RSV, NEB; "lying prostrate from exhaustion," NAB. The expression of course is biblical (Num. 27.17; Ez. 34.5f.; Zech. 10.2). On *rhipto*, see Allen (*Matthew*, p. 99) and Arndt-Gingrich p. 744, where a parallel is cited from the literature about animals lying on the ground. What the people or the sheep were doing remains problematical. Here, an interesting error (?) in the printed texts of the Peshitta serves as a clue for the correct reading . The Peshitta reads דלאין הוו ושרין. What probably took place is this: the Greek translator read *shedi* (שדי) which he took as "cast down," misreading the

Daleth for Resh. The original reading was שרי "let loose, rambling, without direction" (compare Targ. Yeru. Num. 27.17). This fits in well with the sequel "Like a sheep without a shepherd"—the shepherd keeps the sheep together and prevents them from wandering off. For this meaning, see Payn. Sm. (p. 595f.) and Jast. (p. 1630)—"untie the camels," let them loose. The confusion between *shedi/sheri* is found elsewhere, 'targ.' Prov. 13.12, and compare the Peshitta there, as well as the Peshitta passage cited above. The translation should be: they were listless and adrift.

Another word that is a source of confusion to the translator is the Aramaic קבל. The word has a number of significations among which are: (1) receive, (2) welcome, and (3) listen. The equation of שמע/קבל is found more than a hundred times in the Onqelos Targum to the Pentateuch. (Compare E. Brederek, *Konkordanz zum Targum Onqelos*, 1906). Additional significations are (4) complain against, protest (5) take (as used by Onqelos in the Pentateuch some 16 times for Hebrew לקח—Gen. 4.11; 14.24, 27.36, etc. Brederek, ibid., p. 61 and in the Peshitta, 2 Chron. 19.7, and Jennings, p. 187), (6) assume guilt (Lev. 19.8,17; 20.17 Num. 14.34; 18.32), and (7) accept.

It is evident that in the various meanings of *qabbel* there are nuances, that at first blush seem only slight, but, if placed in a wrong context, these nuances will appear disjointed. Hence it is apparent that the translator made use of one meaning instead of the more pertinent one, and the rendering comes through awry.

Thus in the following passages where *dechomai* is the verb, for example, Mt. 11.14 where Jesus advances a *novum* in identifying John the Baptist as Elijah: "If you will receive it, this is Elias," we should translate, "If you will accept it (this idea), this is Elias." Note the use of קבל and the lexical equating in the Peshitta for *dechomai* in Mt. 10.40; 18.5; Lk. 18.17, and elsewhere. In the passage where "they on the rock are they that receive (*dechontai*) the word with joy," both Mt. 13.20 and Mk. 4.16 employ the more simple *lambanein* "take, receive." The underlying *qabbel* in Mt. and Mk. in p s, and probably the original Aramaic text, indicates that the translation should be "welcome." It is obvious that Mt., Mk., and Lk. give different nuances to *qabbel*.

In one instance, however, there seems to be a genuine mistranslation of *qabbel*. Jesus had forecast his passion to the disciples. Mt. 16.22 (parallel Mk. 8.32) continues, "And Peter *took* him (*proslabomenos*), and began to rebuke him, saying, 'Be it far from thee, Lord: this shall not be unto thee.'" The expression "took him" is peculiar. A more explicit meaning is attempted by a number of translations in assuming, as they indeed render

THE EVIDENCE FROM MATTHEW

"took him aside," and so Rhm, Wms, Nor, Beck, Mon, NAB, Gdsp.; "took him by the arm" NEB; RSV and Mof. retain "took him" of the AV. The many-faceted *qabbel* (perhaps II *qabbel,* a secondary root, as suggested by Jast. 1309, but not considered as such, by Brock.; Payn. Sm., s.v.) is the source of the difficulty. The Aramaic ran וקבליה פטרוס "And Peter protested to him, remonstrated with him, charged him." Usually, *qabbel* is constructed with *'al,* but the preposition fuses with the suffix, as in Qidd. 59a . . . אזיל זירא לר׳ קבליה. "R. G. went and complained against him to R. Z.: R. Z. (in turn) went and complained (קבליה) against him to R. Y." (See Jast., p. 1309; Levy NH *Wört.,* IV, p. 236; idem, *Chal. Wört.,* p. 340.) Note in the passage the synonymous verb in the sequel "rebuke." Translate: "And Peter protested to him, and began to rebuke him."

Another word that proved ambiguous to the Greek translator is קם meaning (1) rise and (2) stand. Hebrew distinguishes between קם "rise" and עמד "stand." In one instance, the Aramaic קם was misunderstood. Mt. 12.41 reads, "The men of Nineveh shall rise in judgment with this generation, and shall condemn it." The Greek reads ἀναστήσονται ἐν τῇ κρίσει, literally, "will rise in the judgment," see Liddell and Scott,[9] p. 144 (*graece,* of a law court, *rise*). "Rise" or "stand" may not make too great a difference, but it is instructive that the Hebrew expression is עמד בדין (cf. b. Yeb. 29b; Ketub. 42a; b, where nine examples appear in that folio), Bab. Batr. 106b; Bab. Meṣ. 15a, and not קם בדין. This means that the Greek translator thought that קם בדינא means "rise in judgment." The correlative Hebrew idiom tells us that the phrase should have been translated as "stand in judgment."

Another failure to comprehend the nuance involved occurs in the well-known episode of the king who invited people of the town to come to his son's marriage. They made light of the invitation and would not come. The king sent his servants to importune them. "And the remnant took his servants, and entreated them spitefully, and slew them" (Mt. 22.6 ἀπέκτειναν). "The details are out of line, and harmony with the story itself" as John Marsh says in his *Commentary on Matthew,* Peake,[2] 791. This is an overplay, out of character both with the marriage and the invitation, and obviously inappropriate—it is hardly likely that the citizens slew the servants. Probably מחא or חבל, both meaning to give blows, but also to kill, Brock. *necavit,* for example, *ḥabal nafsheh* "he killed himself." We should translate: "they treated them shamefully, and with blows."

The category of the smaller particles in the Aramaic—prepositions, conjunctions, demonstrative and relative pronouns, and adverbs—notable evidence and an array of examples of misunderstanding and mistranslation on the part of the Greek translator, has been demonstrated in the work of Burney, *Aramaic Origin,* 66f.; Torrey, *Four Gospels,* 64f. and elsewhere); Black (*Aramaic Approach,* Chapter V). There are additionally two instances that may be included that may be of significance in the whole construction of the passages.

The wise man, in Mt. 7.24, built his home upon the rock (ἐπὶ τὴν πέτραν), and because of the foundation, the elements could not overturn it (v. 26). In contrast, the foolish man imprudently built his home upon the sand (ἐπὶ τὴν ἄμμον); storms came and overturned it. This raises a number of questions. First, not every man, wise or not, can build his home conveniently upon a large (even) rock when he wants to. If a city dweller acquires a parcel of land, side by side with his neighbor—as the returning exiles did in Jerusalem (compare Neh. 3)—there may or may not be the large appropriate rock to build on. Palestine certainly is a rocky terrain but the rocks are not that many or suitable that a man could pick and choose the rocky foundation on which to build his house. Lk. probably had these questions in mind. Uniquely for Lk., as he describes it, the wise man first had to "dig deep" (Lk. 6.48), and only then "laid the foundation on a rock." According to Lk., the imprudent man built his house "without a foundation" and "upon the earth." The source of the difficulty in Mt. 7.24 was probably בנא בכיפא, which should be translated "He built *with* rock." As for the improvident man בנא בחלא "He built with sand." The point of the comparison now is that if a man builds his house with rock, that is, mostly with rock, cemented with clay and dried in the sun, the house will not be easily thrown down. But if he builds wholly with sand (or clay), the first onrush of water and storm, will collapse the house. Though *epi* means largely "on," it may represent the preposition *b* as in the Syriac translation (p s c) for Greek dative in Mt. 4.4; p s Mk. 11.18; Lk. 5.9; *epi* with the genetive p s Mt. 24.17; s Mt. 24.3. In Hebrew *epi*/b Gen. 4.12.14; 6.5a;6. Is. 19.2 and elsewhere.

Mt. 25.1 peculiarly starts, "*Then (tote)* shall the kingdom of heaven be likened unto ten virgins, which took their lamps, and went forth to meet the bridegroom." There is no connection between this and the preceding first episode (about the faithful and wise servant, who carries out the behests of his master), and with the succeeding third episode, which tells of the wicked servant who suffers degradation and punishment. What is the significance of the word "then" which would appear to be a resumption, and a further advance and continuation of the previous episode?

Actually, the three episodes of Mt. 24.45 f. (Who is a faithful and wise servant), the episode of the Ten Virgins Mt. 25.1f., and Mt. 25.14 (the man who travels to a far country, and entrusts his servants with varying sums of money) are interrelated and bear a common theme. Each one deals with the negligence and the dereliction, of the inefficient, slothful servant who does not have the interest of the master at heart. In the first instance, there is the servant "who eats and drinks with the drunken" (24.49). In the second instance, five maidservants (not "virgins") had not prepared oil for their lamps (25.3). In the last example, the servant who had not invested money to make a profit, was called "a wicked and slothful servant" (25.26) by his master. If so, the initial word "then" is inappote, and hardly to be explained as "At the period of Christ's coming" as Allen avers. The word that began the parable was בכן, Syriac וכן, (Broc., p. 333), the simple *ken* being the Syriac for "afterwards," as in Rom. 11.35. (Compare *bekhen* at the beginning of the parable in the edition of the *Palestinian Syriac Lectionary of the Gospels* of A. S. Lewis and D. S. Gibson: Dalman, *Dialektproben*,[2] p. 40.) It does not mean "therefore" (so Dalman *deshalb*) but "accordingly." (Compare further, Gen. 4.15; 30.15; Ex. 6.6; Num. 16.19; 20.12; 25.12.) In the latter cases, *bekhen* is a rendering of לכן meaning, as BDB puts it "According to such conditions" (p. 486); Gesenius-Buhl,[17] p. 351 similarly, and with other examples in Levy, *Chal. Wört.*, I, 369. In short, *bekhen* is a functional transitional word which previously appeared in the Aramaic underlying text to smooth the introduction of the second parable of the wise and foolish virgins. This interpretation is seemingly confirmed in the third episode which begins with *hosper gar anthropos* "Indeed just as a man travelling into a far country ..." The three episodes are contrived to follow one another, with transitory functional adverbs. *Tote* as "then," introducing the foolish virgins parable is a mistranslation of וכן/בכן, and should have been translated as "And so;" "accordingly"; "in similar conditions"; "in similar circumstances."

In the reappearance of Jesus to the disciples after the resurrection, Mt. 28. 16—17 relates that they went to a mountain in Galilee where Jesus arranged to meet with them. When they saw him, they worshipped him. V. 17 concludes with the astonishing statement "... but some *doubted*" (ἐδίστασαν). This doubt, however, blights the climax of the awesome scene, and the reading "doubted" seems suspicious. The Peshitta provides a clue *'etpalag* "be doubtful" from which Torrey derives the extended meaning that they took leave of their senses. For the correct interpretation, we need to supply another meaning to *p'lag* "be paralyzed." This is indicated by the noun *palga'* meaning "paralysis" as in the expression *k'ib palga'*, lit. a stroke on one side, hemiplegia; generally a stroke (Payn. Sm. 477), apoplexy

(Brock. 570), epilepsy (Jennings 174); as an equivalent of *paralutikos*, Mt. 4.24 c, similarly Arabic faliğ, and Pes. 111b (correct Jastrow, p. 1176). So, too, the puzzling verse in Ps. 55.10 should be translated, "Destroy, O God, paralyze (*palag*) their tongue!" not the insipid "divide." Accordingly, the Mt. verse above should convey the sense that when they saw him, they worshipped him; indeed, some were paralyzed, meaning figuratively they lapsed into immobility and a state of shock. Comp. our English expression "paralyzed with fear." Note also that "but" is a mistranslation of beram which has the meaning of both "but" and "indeed," Dalman, Aram.-Neuheb. Wort. p. 62. We should translate "Indeed, some were stunned (with awe)."

There are a number of examples where there is a misunderstanding of the Aramaic *pe'il* form (passive) with the dative of agent. There is some controversy because of the parallel in the similar structure of and function of the Greek passive with the dative of agent. Thus, Lk. 23.15 "And, lo, nothing worthy of death is done *unto* him" where obviously Pilate means nothing worthy of death has been done by him (Jesus), and therefore he should be released. Though Wellhausen (*Einleitung,*[2] p. 18) claimed this as an example of an Aramaism, Moulton-Howard (p. 459) presented enough examples in the Greek to justify Aramaic rejection. Black (pp. 66–67) however to the contrary discounts the Greek usage.

A number of other examples should be considered. In Mt. 5.8 we read in the Beatitudes, "Blessed are the pure in heart, for they shall see God." The phrase "to see God" is an impossibility on a number of counts. (1) No one, in the theology of the period would write or teach that one literally would see God, even if in the words of one writer "the higher religious life were intended." There always is a qualifying, interpretative word such as *panim, penei, lifnei* Aramaic *qedam,* before Yahweh's name to avoid anthropomorphism. (2) The passage in Ex. 24.10 "And they saw the God of Israel. ... and they saw God and they ate and drank" (v.11), belonging to the earlier documents of the Pentateuch, is reproduced by the LXX (third century B.C.E.) as "They saw the *place* where the God of Israel stood," and in v.11 "And the chosen ones of Israel ... appeared (or were seen) in the *place* of God." One is also reminded of the word *yera'eh* (Dt. 16.16) as vowellized later by the Masoretes, and compare Montgomery (p. 25), "It was impossible in the later theology to think of a human seeing the Lord Himself. And the process of alleviating the difficulty had already begun in the Masoretic text, most manuscripts of which have substituted 'Adonai' for 'YHWH,' which latter however is still found in some hundred manuscripts."

THE EVIDENCE FROM MATTHEW

"The pure in heart," (Mt. 5.8)—those who are not, and cannot be perceived by the outside world as being the pure in heart—will nevertheless be noticed by God himself. (Compare 1 Sam. 16.7 "Not as a man sees does God see, because man judges by appearances, but God looks into the heart.") The passage ran דחזין לאלהא which the translator read as דְּחָזַיִן לְאלָהָא for דַּחֲזַיִן לֵאלָהָא. We should translate: "Happy are those who are pure in heart for they will be seen by God." The participle has the flexibility of functioning in the past, present, or future tense. (Cf. Margolis, *Grammar*, par. 58.) The identical consonants made for the easy misreading.

This type of construction, the Aramaic participle with the dative of agent, is found also underlying passages such as Mt. 27.57 and 13.52.

There are a number of examples of misvocalization, another indication of a written underlying consonantal text. Mt. 10.27 reads, "What I tell you (λέγω) in the darkness, say ye in the light." The parallel passage in Lk. 12.3 runs, "therefore whatsoever ye have spoken (εἴπατε) in darkness shall be heard in the light." Doubtless the change in the Greek to the plural (*eipate*) by Luke was made by him to harmonize with the previous verse, wherein Jesus was speaking to his disciples. Adhering without deviation to the text extant, there was possibly a misreading of אמרית "I said" and אמריתון "You have said." Most likely, however, the confusion originally consisted of אמרית "I said" and אמרית "You said" (singular distributively). In the latter part of the same passage a difference in parallel texts ascends to a slight consonantal misreading. In one text, the reading is, "And what ye hear in the ear (εἰς τὸ οὖς), that preach ye upon the housetops." The parallel passage in Lk. 12.3 runs, "And that which ye have spoken in the ear in closets (ἐν τοῖς ταμείοις, in inner rooms, in private rooms) shall be proclaimed upon the housetops." The word "closets," lacking in the Mt. text, looks very much like a gloss, in the Lk. text. Where did this gloss originate? Very likely, the Aramaic text offered a variant reading. One text read באדנא "in the ear," and another read באדרונא "in the inner room," employed regularly for *ḥeder* in the Targs.[5]. (Compare Levy, *Chal. Wört.*, p. 12.) According to Levy the word is extant in Syriac and Babylonian Aramaic. Luke probably incorporated the reading from the margin as part of his text, a familiar process.

Again, in Mt. 3.4, with the parallel text in Mk. 1.6, a misvocalization took place in the substrate Aramaic. The first passage reads, "And the same John (*autos* = *hu* used in Aramaic with names; cf. this writer's *Inner World of Qohelet*, p. 100) had his raiment (ἔνδυμα) of camel's hair," while Mk. 1.6 reads, "And John was clothed (ἐνδεδυμένος) with camel's hair." Hence, there is a differentiation between the noun in Mt. and the verb in Lk. Undoubtedly the differences stem from the vocalization of לבש לה, the one reading לבש לה or לבוש "he had raiment" (Payn. Sm. pp. 234—235) and the Marcan lection לביש לה "he was dressed."

The famous verse in Mt. 5.13 (and parallel in Lk. 14.34) runs, "Ye are the salt of the earth; but if the salt have lost its savor, ($\mu\omega\rho\alpha\nu\theta\hat{\eta}$), wherewith shall it be salted?" The Greek verb really means "be foolish," and so indeed the Syriac c adds תפכה ותשטא (Burkitt, I, 20). How does salt become "foolish"? We should translate "become tasteless," Rhm, or "become insipid," Mof. Some aid can be obtained from the Talmudic passage in Bekh. 8b, wherein, among a series of conundrums by the Athenian wise men as put to R. Joshua b. Hananya, the text runs, מילחא כי סרי במאי מלחי לה אמר להו בסילתא דכודנתא ומי איכא סילתא לכודנתא ומילחא מי סרי. "Salt, when it becomes insipid (literally, turns bad), in what manner can it be made to be salty again?" (He said to them), "With the after-birth of a mule." (They asked), "But does a mule have an afterbirth?" (He answered), "Does salt turn insipid?" It is clear from the NT passage that salt changes in character, say, if it is used to salt fish wherein it acquires a fishy taste and smell, and cannot be used again in the cooking of a soup, for example. Although this salt does not lose its acrid taste, it cannot be reused for a different purpose; it is "cast out, thrown away." There are a different set of circumstances between R. Joshua's observation and the NT passage. To R. Joshua salt, in its pristine condition, cannot lose its salty essence. The NT passage assumes that the salt had been used for some seasoning purpose, and cannot be used again. The question now is, how in the NT passage, did the salt become translated as "foolish"?

The Bekhorot passage supplies a clue with the term סרי or better with its fuller by-form סרח (the roots are interchanged variantly in Mss., cf. biblically Trg. Joel, 2.20, Levy, *Chal. Wört.*, 190) which means "be foolish" and also "be smelly, be stinking." סרי is used, for example, when wine and honey are mixed, and then upon decaying, turn rancid. Similarly when rice and millet are mixed, they are excluded from the laws of leaven, not because they are unfit for Passover use, but because they come to a state of spoilage (סירחון).

We are now in a position to understand the NT passage "If salt becomes spoiled (after usage), wherewith can it be seasoned again? It is therefore good for nothing, but to be cast out, etc." The Greek translator misunderstood סרח/סרי as "foolish" and mistranslated. He should have rendered, "If salt becomes spoiled (putrid)"—the rest of the verse, appropriately, would be—"How shall it gain its saltiness again?" It may be added that while this interpretation may serve, the illumination of the Bekhorot passage provides an interpretation that yields a more cogent sense. The first Bekhorot query is, if salt becomes smelly, how can you use it for seasoning? It is possible then that the NT passage was misread as ואיכנא מליחין לה, that is, the active participle was misread. The word לה in the expression represents a dativus ethicus. We should now render: "if salt becomes foul, how can one salt things with it?" Incidentally, further on, the expression of "you are the salt of the earth" is meaningless. The mistranslation came about because salt is found in the earth. The Aramaic expression was מילחא דארעא "You are the salt of the *world*," meant to preserve the inhabitants of the world from corruption. It also could be pointedly "You are the salt of our *land*," to preserve the inhabitants of Palestine from immorality and corruption. The Aramaic word means (1) earth, (2) land, and (3) world, with the second preeminently as the conventional designation of Palestine.

A striking instance of misvocalization which engendered a mistranslation may be seen at Mt. 6.19 which reads, "Lay not up for yourselves treasures upon earth, where moth and rust doth corrupt (ὅπου σὴς καὶ βρῶσις ἀφανίζει), and where thieves break through and steal," or literally, where moth and rust remove. Arndt-Gingrich (p. 147) recognize that "moth" and "rust" are paired off inappositely: "It is not likely that a hendiadys is present here." *Brosis*, of course, means "food."

Jennings (*Dictionary*, 21) has called attention to the fact that 'ākhlā of the Peshitta means "weevil." Rust would be *ios*, and *akhla* would be the same as האוכל = הגזם (locust or weevil) as in Mal. 3.11, or as Bar Bahlul says, "That which devours wheat." What the commentators have missed is that the text was misvocalized or misread as 'u/'okhla "food" whereas the translator should have read 'akkala "the eater," Tg. Jud. 14.14 or ākhlā, the participle employed as a substantive meaning "moth, weevil, maggot" (Payn. Sm. p. 15; Brock. p. 17). Translate therefore; "Nor moth nor weevil rot away." While *aphanizo* means "to destroy" (used of animals, see Arndt-Gingrich for references) and so the Peshitta here *meḥablin*, more likely with reference to moths and weevils the word was מסרחין, cf. the equation of the Greek and Syriac Phil in Mt. 6.16.19, or the by-form מסרין, and the Peshitta to James 5.2 "Your riches are corrupted (Peshitta: corrupted and rotten (*seri*), and your garments moth-eaten."

A number of syntactical matters may be looked at. In the statement at Mt. 21.32 "For John came to you in a way of righteousness and ye believed him not," the translation should have read as an objective genetive "with a way *for* righteousness". "In" (ἐν) is for the familiar "with" as often in NT Greek. In Mt. 17.10–12 we have an unrecognized quotation, "And his disciples asked him, saying, 'Why then say the scribes that Elias must first come?'" (v.11) "And Jesus answered and said unto them, 'Elias truly shall first come, and restore all things. (v.12) But I say unto you, 'That Elias is come already, and they knew him not.'" It is manifest that v.11 is problematic, and contradicts v. 12. Torrey assumes that v. 11 should be taken as a question. Some improvement is evidently needed, since the whole dialogue seems repetitious. The source of the difficulty lies in the fact that v. 11 is a quotation, but unrecognized. Quotations are not signalized by marks as in modern writing, and the reader must be alert to the circumstance that he is confronted by a quotation. (See R. Gordis, "Quotations as a Literary Usage in Biblical, Oriental and Rabbinic Literature," *HUCA,* XXII, 1949, and the same scholar's *The Book of God and Man,* chap. XIII, "The Use of Quotations in Job.") Our passage then should carry the import of a question "(People say) Elias indeed shall first come ... But I say unto you, 'Elias has come. ...'"

Mt. 2.2.9 speaks of the Magi who had seen the star of the new born Savior "in the east" (ἐν τῇ ἀνατολῇ). It has been observed, however, that the Magi could not have used the phrase "in the east" and should have used the customary "our country"; critics further point out that *anatole* is singular here, but plural in the preceding verse (Allen, *Matthew,* p. 12). Some translations have acutely deduced that "in the east" meant at the star's rising, and so Wey "For we saw his star when it rose," or NEB "We have observed the rising of his star," similarly NAB. Most likely, however, the Aramaic word במדנחה should have been considered as a verbal noun, "in its shining," not "east"; כוכבא moreover means not only "star," but as I prefer to consider it, "planet," used for Mercury, and with attributive determinants for Venus; כוכבא דשביט = comet (Jastrow, p. 619). Jupiter and Saturn were in conjunction in 7 B.C.E. (Peake,[2] p. 771). Astrologers, while concerned with stars, were concerned more with planets that had influence on human destiny. (Compare further Shabb. 156a "He who was born under Mercury.") That folio contains other names of planets. See articles on Astrology and Astronomy, in JE, II, and in Morris Jastrow, Jr. *Civilization of Babylonia and Assyria,* p. 261; and particularly George Foucart's article in ERE, IX, 782, sub *Personification* "As a general rule, we notice the preeminence of comets over fixed stars, in their normal aspect, that of planets over the constellations, that of the moon over the sun. ... " In sum, the Magi, as the verse should be interpreted, saw the planet rise—or shine more brightly—when Jesus was born.

THE EVIDENCE FROM MATTHEW

A puzzling statement is found in Mt. 26.54; actually it is a misinterpretation of a small particle taken by the translator interrogatively, but which should have been understood as a conjunction. The passage, at the arrest of Jesus where he declares to the Roman officer that he could summon legions of angels to his aid to thwart Roman misdeeds, describes nevertheless in the next verse how Jesus retracts and then says, "But how (*pos*) then shall the Scriptures be fulfilled, that thus (*outos*) it must be?" The verse is very awkward. Allen translates: How then should the Scriptures be fulfilled that thus it must happen? (p. 281) Others: "How then could the Bible be true when it says this must happen?" (Beck.); "But in that case how would the scriptures be fulfilled, which say that this must be?" TCNT. It must be evident, however, that the sense of the passage should be: "As the scriptures have to be fulfilled, so must it come to pass." In short, two words were mistaken for one another, or unconsciously exchanged as they were quite similar in הכנא . . . היכנא (Syriac would be איכנא; the spelling however in Babylonian Aramaic varies considerably, Cf. Levy, *Chal. Wört.*, p. 197; and further Dalman, *Grammatik* p. 220 who registers איכדין, היכדין and הכין, אכין.) The translator accordingly took the words misrendered as a question. The position of the particle at the beginning of the sentence probably misled him. We should translate "As the scriptures must be fulfilled, so it must be." Cf. *'aikhana/hosper* in the Peshitta Mt. 13.40; 20.28; 24.27, and for *pos 'aikhana* Mt. 12.4; 22.12.43.45; Mk. 2.26; *outos/hākhana* Mt. 1.18; 2.5; Mk. 7.18.

For another example of a misunderstanding of Aramaic syntax, we may look at Mt. 27.4. The sequence previously describes Judas' remorse at having betrayed Jesus, and Judas seeking to return the thirty pieces of silver to the priests and elders, saying, "I have sinned in that I have betrayed the innocent blood." Then v. 4 continues, "What is that to us? See thou to that." The verse evidences its difficulty by the additional two words that AV supplies to make sense. The Greek reads, τί πρὸς ἡμᾶς; σὺ ὄψει, literally translated, the verse runs, "What to us? Thou shalt see." The verse appears disjointed and awkward. Then, again, *opsei* being in the future (explained by some as an imperative, Moulton, *Grammar*, II, 258) what is it that Judas will see? The various translations depart widely from the text. RV, Gdspd. "What is that to us? See to it yourself"; NAB, "What is that to us? It is your affair" and Mof. adds, "And not ours." The fact of the matter is that the Greek translator misconstrued the underlying Aramaic. By retroverting the Greek literally, the passage runs לן מא חזי לך. The translator wrongly divided the phrase into two parts. Perhaps the text variantly may have read (cf. Syriac s) לן מא לן חזי לך. Translate: "What is it to us what is seen by you!" לך is an ethical dative on the analogy of מה לי ולך (Jud. 11.12 and elsewhere). The phrase should be taken as a complete sentence. The verb חזי was interpreted as an active participle. It should have been taken as a passive; חזי לך may be explained as "What is it to us what you see for yourself (Dativus commodi)." The translator missed the brachylogy of the Aramaic.

A Greek construction has puzzled scholars in Mt. 26.45; Mk. 14.41, "And he cometh the third time and saith unto them, 'Sleep on now' (καθεύδετε τὸ λοιπὸν; literally, sleep now, or sleep in the future, or sleep hereafter; see the various translations below); 'it is enough (ἀπέχει); the hour is come'..." I give the fuller text as given by Mk., Mt. omits τὸ and ἀπέχει. The questions that scholars have dealt with are: (1) What is the sense of *to loipon,* and how does it suit the context? (2) What is the explanation of the impersonal *apechei* which in its varied meanings has the signification of "receive in full"; "have back"; (intrans.) "be distant"; (midd.) "abstain from, avoid, keep free" (from something), (impers.) perhaps = "it is enough," or "the account is settled," the latter as an explanation given specifically for the present passage? Cf. NEB and note. Translations are completely at loggerheads about the meaning of the passage, "Sleep on the remaining time and take you rest" ABUV; "Sleep and take your rest hereafter" Knox (a different syntax); "Are you still sleeping and taking your rest?" Gdspd.; "So you sleep and rest? It is enough" Mof.[1]; "Still asleep? Still resting? No more of that!" Mof.[2]; "Still sleeping? Still taking your ease? Enough!" NEB (with the footnote that the Greek is obscure and that a possible meaning is "The money has been paid, the account is settled.") Similarly NAB, with *apachei* as "It will have to do."

Loipos means "remaining." As a substantive, pl. masc. "the others," neutr. pl. "the other things, the rest," in adv. use of time "from now on, in the future, henceforth" (Arndt-Gingrich, p. 481). According to these lexicographers, our present text "is variously interpreted, may mean, 'You are still sleeping!' or 'do you intend to sleep on and on?' Also possible 'Meanwhile, you are sleeping! You are sleeping in the meantime?'"

If we look to the Aramaic, it appears that the Greek translator misread his text. *loipos* is lexically יתר (compare its equation in MT and the LXX Jos. 13.27; 1 Kings 11.41; 14.29 and elsewhere), and in the Mk. text he should have read יתיר "more" (Payn. Sm., p. 199; Jast., p. 604); moreover, the Aramaic in back of *apachei* is סגי "much, very much, greatly." Cf. Num. 16.3 *echeto humin* = *rab lakhem* = targumm. *sagi,* and so the Vulg. in the Mk. passage *sufficit* "enough." The Aramaic of Mt. 26.45 probably formed two

THE EVIDENCE FROM MATTHEW

clauses, and is to be taken as a question, since declaratives and interrogative sentences cannot be easily distinguished in Aramaic,

דמכין אנתון יתיר
וניחין אנתון סגי

which we may translate literally "Do you sleep the *more?* Do you rest so much?" The Gk. translator put a stop before *sagi* and so distorted the parallelism of the members, and imparted to *sagi* the impersonality of "It is enough." Translate a little more freely, "Are you still sleeping? Must you rest so much?" It is possible however that both clauses should be treated as declarative, "You are sleeping too much; and you are resting too long!"

The translator misconstrued the syntax in another verse, and mispointed his text as well. In Mt. 12.33 the passage reads, "Either make the tree good (Ἢ ποιήσατε τὸ δένδρον καλὸν) and the fruit good; or else make the tree corrupt (σαπρὸν literally, rotten) and his fruit corrupt; for the tree is known by its fruit"; elsewhere the correct meaning of the verse comes through in an approximate parallel passage, "Every sound tree bears good fruit, but the bad tree bears evil fruit" Mt. 7.17. The difficulties in our present verse are evident; *poiesate* in the imperative is incomprehensible. *You* cannot, on command, make the tree good, nor its fruit good. The obvious sense should be something in the order of "If the tree is a good one, it will have good fruits." For discussion and explanation we may easily restore the Aramaic as follows: עבד אילנא טב ופירין טבין. The translator mispointed his text עבד as an imperative; he should have understood the word as a participle עבד. He did not know that the idiomatic עבד טב means "prosper, fare well." Compare Jastrow, p. 1035, and such expressions with 'abad "How art thou? How does the field fare? How are the oxen? The land is doing well (crops promise to be good). The land is not doing well." The verse therefore bears this significance, and so indeed translate, "If the tree fares well, then the fruits will be good; if the tree fares ill, then the fruits will be bad." A tree, accordingly, will be known to be good or bad by the fruits it bears. Compare with the translation of Phi "For you can tell a tree at once by its fruits."

The Waw expresses consequence as the Arabic *fa, then* BDB 255. The conditional *if* may be dispensed with in idiomatic Aramaic. Thus, אדלי יומא אדלי קצירא "When, if, the day is at the height, the sick man is relieved" (Jast., p. 310); "If there is pestilence in the city (דבר בעיר) don't walk in the middle of the street," etc., Bab. Qam. 60b.

There are a few texts that are even more problematic, wherein a careful reconstruction restores the natural sense. The section in Mt. 18.23, previously discussed, deals with the master who forgives his debtor servant, who in turn is unrelenting to a fellow servant; the master, hearing of the servant's cruelty, reverses himself and consigns the miscreant servant to the jailors. V. 35 ends the parable with a rather disjointed admonishment ("muddled" Montefiore), "Thus also my heavenly Father will do to you unless you forgive each other his brother from your hearts" (my translation). AV translates freely and adds "their trespasses." As Allen remarks (p. 201), "The details of the parable do not seem altogether consistent... The story has quite probably been adapted by the editor to suit the context." Nevertheless, Allen concludes that the main point is "that an unmerciful disposition will meet with the divine wrath." Hardly. It may be good theology, but cannot be derived from the text. Montefiore explains, "The king is God, who has to forgive man far more than man has to forgive his neighbor. But unless man forgives his neighbor, God will not forgive him." He could have added the parallel: "Be like unto him. As He is gracious and merciful, so be thou gracious and merciful," Shabb. 133b. However that may be, his symbolic explanation is far afield from the text.

As I see it, the concluding passage in Mt. omitted two seemingly similar words, which by their omission, annulled the point of the moral. The passage read in the Aramaic הכנא יעבד לכון אבי דבשמיא אין לא תשבקון אנש לאחוהי לחובה מן חובא דבלבכון. The translator failed to understand that the two words are different: חובא is "sin"; חובא or חבא according to the masoretic system (rt. *ḥbb*), is "love." The passage therefore originally ran, "Thus will my father in Heaven do to you unless ye forgive each man his brother for his *sin,* from the *love* in your hearts." The translator could not comprehend the meaning because he thought that both words were to be vocalized as חובא "sin." This reconstruction, and the restoration of the two words as essential to the text is based upon the realization that the whole parable is a wordplay on *ḥoba,* "debt" that the servants owed (vv. 30, 32, 34) and on *ḥubba* (vv. 27, 33)—love, compassion, and charity.

Mt. 24.45f. exemplifies the "good and faithful servant" (its syntax is discussed on p. 129). The servant, upon the promotion given by his master, becomes a "steward." V. 48 considers the alternative "But if that evil servant (ὁ κακὸς δοῦλος ἐκεῖνος) shall say in his heart, 'My lord delayeth his coming... and shall begin to smite his fellow-servants....'"

The difficulty with this sequence is that we are unprepared for the "wicked" servant. How did the servant suddenly become "wicked"? The Greek translation indicates that a misconstruction of the Aramaic syntax took place. The Aramaic ran ואין דין עבדא בישא יסבר בלבה which should be rendered, "If the servant thinks evil in his heart...." The translator thought of בישא as modifying עבדא, hence "his wicked servant." He should have construed בישא as a noun, object of "should think." Note that in this section the translator was also miscued in his syntax at v. 25.1 (see p. 67) and at 24.51 "will divide him and his portion" for which see Torrey, *The Four Gospels,* p. 55 and note.

A distinctive feature of Semitic languages, including Hebrew and Aramaic, is the frequent occurrence of wordplays in the texts. Some appear by design, others quite artlessly, as a characteristic of biblical poetry, of prophetic discourse, and of prose.

Evidence for this rhetorical device is given for the Gospels by Black, *Aramaic Approach,* chap. 6, where he adduces examples of parallelisms of lines and clauses, alliteration, and assonance and paronomasia, although with regard to the latter he states that alliteration, assonance and wordplay are "practically confined to sayings of Jesus, the speeches of the Baptist, and the early chapters of Luke" (p. 142). This is not quite the case, however. There are enough examples of wordplay, to show (see below) that they come from all sections. Incidentally, the evidence to be presented here is specifically for wordplays, the marked feature of Aramaic, as they include in themselves much that is alliteration, assonance, and a plethora of similar consonants, dentals, labials, gutturals and sibilants. The disclosure of wordplays obviously is further indication of Aramaic written records.

Thus Mt. 2.11, the Magi "presented unto him gifts," אקריבן לה קורבנין; קורבנין "gifts" as in Syriac (Eastern Aramaic again) and adopted probably in Hebrew, e.g., קרבנות מלכים "gifts of kings to the Temple" (Jast. p. 1411). Mt. 2.12: the Magi return home "by another way," באורחא אחרינא. Mt. 3.9: "Abraham to our father," אברהם לאבא (*patera echomen ton Abraam*); Mt. 4.3: "Command these stones be made bread" (literally, loaves), Gk. *artoi* = כיפתא ... ריפתא. Alternate forms may be in the determinate plural; Mt. 5.28: "But I say unto you that whosoever looketh on a woman to *lust* after her hath *committed adultery* with her already in his heart." There is a wordplay on "desire (רגג) ... commit adultery (גר)." Mt. 5.29 "And if your right *eye* offend thee, pluck it out, and cast it from thee; for it is profitable (*sumphorei* "expedient") that one of your members should perish, and not thy whole body should be cast into hell." There is an implied wordplay in "eye." "Profitable" here is פקח (cf. Peshitta); actually, פקח means "open one's eyes," Gen. 3.7 and Levy, *Chal. Wört.,* II, p. 283. Mt. 6.24, "No man can serve two masters; for either he will hate the one, and love the other; or else he will *hold* to the *one* and despise the other יאחד לחדא *'antechomai'*/אחז Dt.

78 THE ARAMAIC ORIGIN OF THE FOUR GOSPELS

32.41; Mt. 7.9—10: "Or what man is there of you, whom if his son ask *bread*, will he give him a *stone?* Or if he ask a *fish,* will he give him a *serpent?*" The wordplay is evident in the words ריפתא ... כיפתא (ut supra). Also *fish* and *serpent* form the wordplay נונא ... חנינא. Like the Hebrew תנין (*serpent*, Ex. 7.9; 10.4; Dt. 32.33; Ps. 91.13) so the Aramaic חנינא while meaning a large monster is also used for serpent as in Shabb. 150a "Nebuchadnezzar rode on a male lion, and tied a serpent around his head." Tangential to this passage in Mt. is the noteworthy parallel in Lk. 11.11—12, where there are not only differences in the readings, but in addition we have extended wordplays, "If a son shall ask bread of any of you that is a father, will he give him a stone? Or if he ask for a fish will he for a fish give him a serpent? Or if he shall *ask* an *egg,* will he offer him a *scorpion?*" Ask ... egg plays on בעי (ask) and ביעתא (egg); offer ... scorpion forms the wordplay on אקרב (offer) and עקרבא (scorpion). Likewise, Mt. 7.13: "And broad is the way leading to destruction," probably רויחא אורחא; Mt. 17.27 "That take, and give unto them for me and thee" סביה והביה חלפי וחלפך (cf. Burkitt, I, p. 101); Mt. 15.27, "The dogs eat of the crumbs that fall from their masters' table" פרתותא דנפלין מפתורא.

The famous phrase "Burden and heat of the day" occurs at Mt. 20.12 in back of which is the paronomasia of יוקרא ... ויקדיה (*to baros tes hemeras kai ton kausona*). *kausona*=heat (see M. L. Margolis, *kaiein,* ZAW, 26, 1906, p. 85f.; *kaisthai/yaqad* Is. 10.16[1]; *kausis/moqed* and so Aquila) *yaqad* is used figuratively with envy, love, faith, etc. (Payn. Sm. p. 195), and used with (late) *zoni yaqidta* "torrid zone." The Aramaic suggests the translation "The heaviness and blaze of the day." Mt. 25.18 "But he that received one (talent) went and *digged* in the earth, and *hid* his lord's money," חפר ... חפי; Mt. 23.4, "For they bind heavy burdens and grievous to be borne, and lay on men's shoulders; but they themselves will not move (lit. *are not willing to*) with one of *their fingers,*" בצבעוהן לא צבין. Mt. 24.5: "For men shall come in my name saying, 'I am Christ'; and shall *deceive many,*" ושגיאין ישגין; Mt. 27.6: "And the chief priests took the silver pieces, and said, 'It is not lawful for to put them into the treasury, because it is the *price* of *blood.*" The wordplay is evident in דמי דמא. Actually, there is a mistranslation involved as well. While דמין means "price," it should have been rendered as "money," and the phrase should have conveyed the meaning of *blood money.* Compare the popular expression דמים תרתי משמע (based on Meg. 14b, Rashi differently) "*damim* has two meanings," i.e., blood and money.

Interesting is a possibility that John the Baptist, who ate locusts and wild honey in the wilderness may have eaten יוחנא one of the few locusts

THE EVIDENCE FROM MATTHEW

recognized to be "clean" for eating. Compare with Ḥullin 65a, which lists four kinds of edible locusts as derived from the Pentateuch. Popular names are provided for some of them as the *zipporeth keramim*, the Jerusalem *yoḥana*, the *arṣubia*, and the *razbonith*. (For some tentative identifications of these species of locusts, see Lewysohn, *Zoologie des Talmuds*, p. 286ff, cited in the Soncino Ḥullin p. 352, and compare further Kohut, *Aruch*, IV, p. 118a. There are variations on these names of locusts. Vide R. Rabbinovicz, *Variae Lectiones* on Ḥullin, p. 37. About the eating of locusts whether live or dead, see S. Lieberman, *Texts and Studies*, p. 193.) Moreover, the name John, Greek "Ιωάννης, is certainly not יוחנן, but most likely, following the Greek, יוחני (see further). The form יוחנא is the usual for a male (Kohut, ibid, p. 176). The curtailed form in -a for -an is a well recognized phenomenon where the Nun falls away (as in מגדון מגדו, 1 Chron. 8.36, 2 Chron. 25.1) and especially with regard to Yoḥanan, abbreviated from the latter to Yonas, Yonan, in some ten equivalents in the LXX, both in the uncials A and B, and so יוחנה, יוחנא Ḥullin 133a; Ab. Zar. 16b מר יוחני, (see Jast. p. 568 for further references). As the Greek transliterations suggest יוחנא, the Aramaic form, with the *shewa* near the accent, was reduced from יוחנא in turn from יוחנן. In view of this, then, יוחנא... יוחנא/יוחני, i.e., the circumstances that John ate the ritually clean locusts would form a wordplay. יוחנן and יוחנא are confused in the Mss. of the Talmud, Rabbinovicz, op. cit., ibid, p. 37.

Two other examples of paronomasia may be added. Mt. 12.11 reads, "And he said unto them, 'What man shall be among you, that shall have one sheep (*a* sheep, חד ערבא), and if it fall into a pit on the Sabbath day, will he not lay hold on it, and lift it out?'" The wordplay would be חברא (pit) and ערבא (sheep), cf. the Peshitta. The parallel in Lk. 14.5 has different animals "ass or an ox" which forms a different wordplay חברא... חמרא. Mt. 13.44, "The kingdom of heaven is like unto a *treasure hidden* in a field...." The words played upon are מטמרתא מטמרא. The root means "hide," and the noun "treasure"; perhaps alternately טומעיא, cf. Job 3.21 ויחפרהו ממטמונים, and the Targ.

The presence of Aramaic locutions in Mt. (and in the other Gospels as will be shown) is further proof of Aramaic origin, and of relevance for evaluation. Dalman, in his *Words of Jesus* has shown the numerous parallels in the rabbinic literature, and demonstrated how Hebrew and Aramaic saturate the Gospel literature. One wonders how, after all the examples are set forth, and with Dalman's own reconstructions in the Aramaic (and sometimes in Hebrew) that he arrived at the non-sequitur and the illogicality that the Gospels were not translated, but were transmitted, in some kind of "mould" (his word), to the Evangelists.

The Gospel translators, as Jewish Christians and Christians, were naturally immersed in the biblical idiom from their knowledge of the Greek LXX. The translations abound with biblical phrases. This cannot be argued for, however, with regard to *non-biblical* phrases, native to the Aramaic idiom.

In Mt. 16.28, for example, the text runs, "Verily I say unto you, 'There be some standing here, which shall not taste of death (*geusontai thanatou*) until they see the son of man coming in his kingdom.'" The expression "tasting death" may occur both in Hebrew and Aramaic, but Hebrew in the light of the plethora of Aramaic examples presented throughout is not to be considered here. Thus in Aramaic, "He who wishes to taste the taste of death (טעמא דמיתותא), let him put on his shoes and sleep" (Yoma 78b). Similarly Mk. 9.1; Lk. 9.27; Jn. 8.52.

The translator failed to understand the Aramaic idiom in Mt. 19.3. The passage runs, "The Pharisees also came unto him, tempting him (lit. testing him) and saying unto him, 'Is it lawful for a man to put away his wife for every cause (*kata pasan aitian*)?'" While עלא (cf. the Peshitta) means "cause," it has the more pungent meaning of "fault" in this connection, in Dan. 6.5 meaning there "ground for accusation," BDB, p. 1106; and here similarly the Aramaic locution means "for any fault" or "pretext." For the construction, see Lev. 4.2; 19.23; 1 Kings 8.37b; and BDB, p. 482. This controversy about divorcing a wife is based upon Dt. 24.1, a controversy (whether one should emphasize the word ערות or the word דבר in the Deut. passage) in which the schools of Hillel and Shammai were at odds, the former claiming that a man may divorce a wife for any reason (דבר) even if she burned his pottage (הקדיחה תבשילו) as they put it, while the school of Shammai would limit divorce only on the ground of ערות, sexual misconduct (b. Giṭṭin 90a and Sifre on the biblical passage). This controversy must have been brewing for a long period, as we may gather from the fact that Ezra (cf. Ezra 9.2.14; Neh. 13.26) initiated divorces from the foreign wives. The question put to Jesus was asked from the viewpoint of Bet Hillel. The translation should run, "Is it lawful for a man to divorce his wife for any fault?"

The well known passages in the Beatitudes (Mt. 6.13 and Lk. 11.4) as well as other passages where "temptation" (*peirasmos*) is mentioned (Mt. 26.41; Mk. 14.38; Lk. 8.13; 22.28.40.46); usually with the conventional translation of "Enter not into temptation" appears in Bera. 60b אל תביאנו

לידי נסיון "Put us not to the test," the prayer now incorporated in the Jewish Prayer Book. The testing, or better the ordeal, in and of itself, is not only painful and harrowing to the ordinary man, but even for one who is a saint, for, as the Rabbis tell it, God "tested" Abraham (Abot 5.3), and it is a sign of distinction that Abraham was steadfast in the "test" (i.e., anent Isaac's sacrifice). Compare further "Until the time of Mordecai, no one, put through the ordeal (נסיונא would be the Aramaic form for "ordeal") of crucifixion was rescued (ולא אתנסי)," Targ. II, Esther 3.14; see Levy, *Chal. Wort.* II, pp. 114–115 for other examples. The NT Aramaic probably was לא נעל לידי נסיונא. Torrey's translation that the phrase should mean "Let us not fail in the test," that על means "go down" as in מעלי שמשא "setting of the sun" is unexampled and unidiomatic.

An unrecognized Aramaic locution may be seen too in Mt. 26.9 where the text reads, "But I say unto you, 'I will not drink henceforth of the vine until I drink new (*kainon*) in my Father's kingdom." As Allen remarks (*Matthew*, p. 277), why *new?* The word מחדש (cf. *de novo*) may mean "again." Compare its use in modern Hebrew "newly, afresh, over again" (R. Alcalay, *Complete Hebrew-English Dictionary,* 1963, p. 718); and partially with the Akkadian where the adverb *eššiš* and with *a-na* the *eššutu* "newly" as *a-na ĕssut azbat* "I took again in possession"; in Eastern Aramaic the form would be חדיתאית "newly" (Payn. Sm., p. 129; Brock., p. 217 *de nuo*). Translate: Until I drink it *again*..."

A new light is shed on the expression in Mt. 5.18 which reads, "For verily I say unto you, 'Till heaven and earth pass, one jot or one tittle ($\iota\hat{\omega}\tau\alpha$ $\dot{\epsilon}\nu$ $\ddot{\eta}$ $\mu\iota\alpha$ $\kappa\epsilon\rho\alpha\iota\alpha$) lit. one iota or one stroke (of a letter) shall in no wise pass from the law, till all will be fulfilled.'". *keraia* is employed for קרן in the LXX and means "horn, corner," and hence may mean "tip" (of a letter). Since the word occurs in combination with the word iota (Yod), we recognize it as the idiomatic expression קוצה של יוד b. Men. 29a (read קוצו של יוד; Rashi, Tosafot and Ms. Munich) admittedly Hebrew, not found in Aramaic. Compare, however, קוצתא "a curl, ringlet" Payn. Sm. 497. The translation may be "the foot of the Yod" (so Rashi; the Tosafot, "the top") Men. 29a. The expression is reported in the name of the quasi-Tanna Rab. The term תג does not apply here (contrast Strack-Billerbeck a.l.) as the Yod does not have a crownlet in the authoritative synagogal Sefer Torah. (Cf. Men. 29b and compare plate #19 in E. Würtheim, *Text of the Old Testament,* trans. P. R. Ackroyd, p. 121.) The underlying Aramaic was something like לא יוד ולא קוצָה/קוצה. We should translate, "Neither a Yod, nor a particle of it." An apposite parallel to the idea of the Mt. verse is found in Ex. R. sec. 6: "Solomon and a thousand like him shall pass away, but not a particle (קוצה) of thee (i.e., the Torah) will I allow to be blotted out".

There is finally a series of texts that disagree with one another. Mt. 17.20 reads, "If you have faith as a grain of mustard seed, you will say to this mountain (*orei*), 'Move hence to yonder place' and it will move, and nothing will be impossible to you." Mt. 21.21 after the withering of the fig tree, states, "If you have faith and mercy and never doubt, you will not only do what has been done to the fig tree (*sukes*), but even if you say to this mountain, 'Be taken and cast into the sea' it will be done." Mk. 11.22f., "Truly I say unto you, whoever says to this mountain, 'Be taken up etc.'" Lk. 17.6 varies with, "If you had faith as a grain of a mustard seed, you could say to this sycamine tree (*sukamino*) 'Be rooted up and be planted in the sea' and it would obey you."

There are two kinds of figs: the *ficus carica* corresponding to the Hebrew תאנה "fig tree," the more delectable, and preferred kind, and the fig of the sycamore inferior to the above, called *ficus sycomorus* I. Löw, *Aramaeische Pflanzennamen*, p. 332. The *sukaminos* is equated by Liddell and Scott with *morea* "mulberry tree" (p. 1670), and is cited by them in the Lk. passage 17.6. *sukmoros* is considered to be the same as *morea* or *moron* (Latin, *morus, morum* = *moron*, and therefore supposed to mean "foolish"). The Mt. "fig tree" and the Lk. "sycamine tree" were misread one for the other, and hence the discrepancy: תאנתא i.e., the contracted form תתא (cf. I. Löw, *Aramaeische Pflanzennamen*, pp. 335, 338) and תותא Löw, ibid, 335, 338 "mulberry." "Mountain" remains problematical, but it may be altogether separate from the "fig tree" in the parable.

Chapter III

The Evidence from Mark

THE EVIDENCE from Mark is less than that of Matthew, Luke or John. Perhaps this is to be expected; the proportion of chapters is Mark 16; Matthew 28; Luke 24; John 21. The Marcan examples for the underlying Aramaic are impressive, nevertheless. The examples exhibit the same characteristics of a translator found in the other Gospels writers.

The translator confused roots on a number of occasions. Thus Mk. 3.3 records the instructions of Jesus to the man with the withered hand, "Stand forth," literally, "*Rise* into the midst" (ἔγειρε εἰς τὸ μέσον). How does one "rise" into the midst? Apparently in Lk. 6.8 there is a recognition of the difficulty where the verse reads "Rise up and stand forth in the midst. And he rose and stood forth." It is evident that the expression in Mk. should read simply, "*Stand* in the midst (or center)." The Aramaic קם means both (1) rise and (2) stand, as opposed to the Hebrew which employs two words—קם "rise," and עמד "stand." The Greek translator should have rendered with (2) rather than (1). See the writer's *Biblical Books Translated From the Aramaic,* p. 112 for examples in the Hebrew Bible translations for similar misinterpretations of *qum,* and supra p. 65. For the equation of *egeiro/qam,* compare Mt. 9.5; Mk. 3.3; 12.26 (Peshitta).

Mk. 5.7 contains another example of confusion of the roots אסר "bind, jail" and יסר "torture." Undoubtedly this misunderstanding comes about in the different forms wherein the Alef is replaced by Yod, e.g., Tg. Esther, II.1.3 אייסר "bind" and compare Dalman, *Gramma.,* p. 300. יסר evolved as a secondary form to mean "bind" side by side with אסר. Compare Levy, *Chal. Wört.,* I, p. 340 and the noun ייסורא meaning (1) binding and (2) torture, and Jast., p. 583. In a number of passages it would seem that the translator mistook one for the other. For example, Mk. 5.2 mentions the man in the tomb, who had an unclean spirit; upon seeing Jesus the man exclaimed, "What have I to do with thee, Jesus, thou son of the Most High God? I adjure thee, by God, that thou torment me not" (v. 7). The evil spirits (v. 12) speak through the unfortunate man's mouth. Spirits cannot be physically tortured, but they are apprehensive of being tied down and bound. For this binding, the term *'asar* is used regularly in incantations against evil spirits. (Compare J. A. Montgomery, *Aramaic Incantation Texts from Nippur,* pp. 282, 290, and especially p. 52.) Translate: "I adjure you not to bind me," and similarly for the parallel passages in Mt. 8.29 and Lk. 8.28. For a similar confusion of the same roots, see p. 35.

Two roots are confused again in the text at Mk. 6.20 where the difficult passage reads, "For Herod feared (ἐφοβεῖτο) John, knowing that he was a just man and holy, and observed him (συνετήρει); and when he heard him, he did many things[?], and heard him gladly." I follow the more difficult reading "was in distress" ἠπόρει/ἐποίει "he did," of Nestle, H. B. Swete, and UBS, Metzger *A Textual Commentary on the Greek New Testament,* p. 89. Of two parts of the verse we may be reasonably certain—the first and last. But the רישא is contradicted by the סיפא; the first part "Herod feared John" runs counter to the last part "Herod heard him gladly." The middle section cannot be construed satisfactorily because it is a "tangle of confused thoughts and purposes which lead to no definite course of action" (Swete, *Gospel According to St. Mark,* p. 124). We know that Herod was hostile; he sought to kill John (vv. 16—17); at the same time he was fearful (v.16) and so v.20. The verse can be explained consistently, from the perspective of Herod's hate and fear, as follows:

1. "observed him." One of the meanings of the Greek *sunterei* is "watch one's opportunity" (Liddell and Scott, p. 1727). Thus Lk. 14.1 "watched him" נטר; Dan. 7.28; נצר LXX, Sym Jb. 27.18; *ntr* also means "watch with hostility" Lev. 19.18 "You shall not avenge or bear a grudge"; used also in the sense of "spy" e.g., "They watched and found Daniel making petition" Payn. Sm., p. 337, and cf. our expression "This will bear watching." Hence our expression ונטר לה "he watched for an opportunity" or alternately "He was on the watch for him, kept him under surveillance." The usual translations miss this nuance completely when they render the text as it stands, "kept him safe," ASV; "preserved him," ABUV; "so he protected John (!)" Mof.; "kept him in custody."

2. "He did many things" should be abandoned for "He was much disturbed" as suggested above by UBS, and similarly Gdspd. The Aramaic expression probably was ועק לה. See Gen. 32.7, where the language generally is similar to our present verse "And Jacob was greatly afraid and distressed; *aporeo*/צר, and 1 Sam. 30.6 "David was greatly distressed."

3. "And he heard him *gladly*" (ἡδέως) is impossible in the context. The translator misread or misinterpreted the form בִּיעֲתָא (var. form בּוּעֲתָא) "rejoice" (Jast., p. 147, 164 as in Trgg. texts) for בִּיעוּתָא "fear"; other forms are בּוּעֲתָא (sic) "terror" (Payn. Sm., p. 38; Brock., p. 85); בִּיעוּתָא "fright" Is. 21.4 and בִּיעֲתָא "joy" Dalman, *Wörterb*, p. 51. It is evident that the Greek translator should have translated "He heard him with fear" or as equally possible "He heard of him, about him, with fear" in both instances in the verse.

The objection may be raised however that בּוּע "rejoice" and its nominal formations are not found in Syriac or Eastern Aramaic but only in the Jewish Aramaic of Palestine. (Compare Levy, *Chald. Wört.*, p. 85; Dalman, *Wörterb.*, pp. 48, 51.) The objection may be of some moment, but it is not too serious. The word appears to be found in the Targs. of Jonathan of Is. Ps. Minor Prophets (Levy, ibid., p. 85;) about a dozen times, and there can be no reasonable doubt that Aramaic translations as such were heard in the synagogues, and were therefore known to the Jews of Syria, who may have brought such Targs. with them. This error of "joy" for "fear" seems to occur again (see p. 56).

Our whole passage would now bear the translation, "For Herod was afraid of John, knowing that he was a man holy and just; but kept him under surveillance; and when he heard about him, was much disturbed and heard reports of him with apprehension." The reader will see that the verse harmonizes well in all its members.

The same confusion with the same words occurs in Mt. 28.8; the parallel in Mk. 16.8 gives the correct clue (see p. 56). In Lk. 24.41 we have a somewhat similar circumstance where "the disciples disbelieved for joy" (?), Greek *charas*. This is a strange collocation, and could hardly be "joy" implying belief as contrasted with "disbelief," a *contradictio in adjecto*. V. 37 furthermore declares that they were "startled and frightened," and supposed that they saw a spirit. Jesus, trying to convince them that it was he who was appearing to them said "Why are ye troubled, and why do doubts arise in your heart?" (v.38) Arndt-Gingrich, 185.

The root בעא, and the noun בעותא "question," were most likely the source of the confusion with the noun בועתא "joy." The disciples disbelieved not because of "joy" but because of the *questions* that arose in their minds—a natural consequence. Perhaps, too, the reading "joy" may have been tendentious, as later readers may have been astonished that these disciples did not recognize Jesus right away, and disbelieved because of the doubts they had. The disciples should have recognized him and rejoiced. Be this supposition as it may, the verse should now read, "And while they were still disbelieving, because of their doubt and they wondered, he said to them. ..." Note the sequence of (now) the proper synonymous words, disbelief, doubt, and wonder.

Aside from the confusion of roots and forms, the Mk. translator made outright mistakes in his rendering. Beginning with Mk. 9.18 there is a description by a father regarding his son, "And wheresoever he [the spirit] taketh him, he [the spirit] *teareth* him (ῥήσσει): and he [the son] foameth and gnasheth with his teeth. ..." V. 20 continues, "And they brought him unto him: and when he saw him, straightway the spirit tare him (συνεσπάραξεν), and he fell on the ground, he wallowed foaming". V. 26 reads in further sequence "And crying out, and much convulsing him (*sparaksas*). ..."

There is something of a problem about the meaning of the Greek verb *sparasso*, the fundamental meaning of which is "tear, rend," e.g., dogs tearing flesh from the bones; "rend asunder, pull to pieces"; and this is the basis of the AV translation "a tearing asunder." There is also the derived sense of "convulse" picked by Arndt-Gingrich to explain our NT passages and hence applied to the convulsion of an evil spirit. However in *susparasso* in Lk. 9.42 the explanation adhered to by Liddell-Scott is "tear" (p. 1733).

For a spirit to "tear" a boy is unnatural and indeed incomprehensible, yet the reading strikes one as being decidedly original and genuine. The Aramaic seems to supply the key to the difficulty. The Hebrew and Aramaic root טרף means fundamentally "tear," but has many varied senses, "cast with force, knock, strike against; throw away, reject, eject"; also "chop, beat, mix" and especially, for our investigation "unbalance the mind, put one in spasms", e.g., "a dove came and *rolled* before him *in spasms*" Sanh. 95a; also with דעה/לב "be confused, bewildered," e.g., "His mind became confused" (with drinking) (Jast., p. 556; Payn. Sm., p. 182b).

In the Mk. verse discussed above, טרף in the pe'al means "make one demented, throw into a paroxysm." Accordingly, in v. 18 we should translate "seized him and made him mad"; in v. 20 "The spirit made him deranged"; v. 26 "Drove him out of his mind with seizures."

The proof for the underlying טרף in the Aramaic document becomes confirmed in the variation and discrepancies of the parallel texts. In Mk. 1.26 the text runs, "And when the unclean spirit had torn him (*sparaksan*), and cried out with a loud voice, he came out of him." However, in the parallel passage in Lk. 4.35 the passage runs differently, "And when the devil had thrown him (ῥίψαν) in the midst, he came out of him, and hurt him not."

From the preceding texts, Mk. 1.26; 9.18. 20.26 we should have expected something like "had torn him" i.e., טרף made him mad. The Lk. passage however ascends to the same טרף except that Mk. interpreted the word to mean "had torn him" while Lk. interpreted the word as "throw." Compare Ḥullin 3.3 טרפה בכתל, "He threw the bird at the wall." The Aramaic again shows how the discrepant Greek texts arose.

Mk. 4.5 (parallels Mt. 13.5; Lk. 8.6 shortened the verse) provides another mistranslation as well as a confusion of roots. The text reads, "And some fell on stony ground ($\pi\epsilon\tau\rho\hat{\omega}\delta\epsilon\varsigma$ "in the rocky places") where it had not much earth; and immediately it sprang up ($\epsilon\xi\alpha\nu\epsilon\tau\epsilon\iota\lambda\epsilon\nu$), because it had no depth (v. 6); and when the sun rose, it was scorched; and because it had no root, it withered away." The whole march and structure of the verse sets forth how the seed did not grow, but withered because of the sun. I suspect the puzzling phrase "immediately sprang up"; it should, in more likely consonance, read "it withered away," in agreement with the rest of the verse. And so the Syriac, interestingly; see Burkitt on the passage, and immediately below. If the seed fell upon a stony rock (so the Syriac, and Lk. 8.6 *epi ten petran*), it certainly would not spring up. The translator confused roots, I שוח meaning "spring up, flourish," used of "sprouting crops, seeds" (Payn. Sm. p. 564; Brock. p. 763); and II שוח, the appropriate word, meaning "be consumed, waste away." While this root is employed primarily in the sense of "melt," it has derivative, secondary meanings of "waste, consume" (Brock., p. 763; Payn. Smith, p. 564, 2) Jewish Aramaic (Levy, *Chald. Wört.*, II, 459, a, b). The verse now becomes harmonious in all its parts, "And some fell on a rocky place where it had not much soil, and immediately it *withered* away because (!) it did not have much depth of earth. And when the sun was up, it was scorched etc." More importantly, it is interesting that two of the older Syriac versions, c and s, translate, "And because it had no moisture, it failed and withered" (not sprang up). Compare Burkitt, I, p. 289 (ביץ ויבש). Apparently, because "sprang up" occurs again in v. 7 and v. 8 the Greek translator proleptically, with his eye off the sequence, rendered likewise "sprang up" instead of "withered."

The Aramaic root *yetar* found in Mk. 4.19 was misunderstood. The AV text runs, "And the cares of this world, and the deceitfulness of riches, and the lusts of other things ($\alpha i \; \pi\epsilon\rho i \; \tau \grave{\alpha} \; \lambda o\iota\pi \grave{\alpha} \; \epsilon\pi\iota\theta\upsilon\mu\iota\alpha\iota$ lit. desires for the rest of things) entering in, choke the word, and it becometh unfruitful." This expression, "desires for the rest of things," is recognized as being peculiar to Mk. (Swete, *Mark*, p. 80). In addition, it seems vague and indefinite after the specifics of worldly cares and deceitful riches; what are "the rest of the things"? Moreover, Lk. 8.14 in a parallel passage offers a variant reading *hedonai tou biou* "pleasures of life." Apparently the Aramaic was רגתא דיתירותא *rigtha* or *regitha/epithumia* as an equation is found in p s c Jn. 8.44, p Lk. 22.15, as well as *rag/epithumeo* p s c Mt. 5.28 and *yetar* and its compound ut supra. The Greek translator misapprehended the Aramaic word as "the remaining things" whereas he should have made the verse more specific by rendering the "desire for abundant things, superfluous things, luxuries" (Payn. Sm., pp. 199–200; Brock., p. 313) which would form the natural complement to desires for "deceitful riches." The variant in Lk. remains a bit problematic. It may be, however, that דחיותא "of life"/דיתירותא "superfluous things" was a misreading of one word for the other on the part of Lk.

An interesting reading in Mk. 6.21 indicates that the Mk. translator knew the word Galilee, as the name of the district, but did not understand גלילא, in its basic meaning, as a general term for "district, region." The text runs, "And when a convenient day was come, that Herod on his birthday made a supper to his lords, high captains, and chief estates of Galilee (literally, the chief men of Galilee, καὶ τοῖς πρώτοις τῆς Γαλιλαίας)." It is strange that Galilee should be singled out specifically, because besides the Galilee, this Herod (cf. EB, II, 2030) had control of the district of Peraea, Jos., *Ant.*, XVII, and 8.1. The Mishna divides Jewish Palestine into Judea, Galilee, Peraea (compare G. A. Smith, *Historical Geography of the Holy Land*, chs. 20–21; E. Schürer, *Gesch.*, II, 1.2). The *magistanes*, who were the highest civil dignitaries, and the *chiliarchi*, the chief military officers (Rev. 6.15), corresponding to the *Tribuni militum*, the commanders of a Roman cohort, are just generalized and unspecified as to any province unless we assume that "Galilee" covers the district of Paraea as well (unlikely), to say nothing of the towns of Machaerus, Pella, Philadelphia, Gerasa, and Gadara "the metropolis of Peraea" (Jos., *Wars*, IV, 7.3). In the light of these contravening facts, I am inclined to regard גלילא as a mistranslation of "Galilee" (Brock., p. 45). We should render, "Made a supper for his courtiers, and the chiliarchs, and the chiefs of the districts." The Aramaic probably ran, רישי גלילא. For the sense of both "district" and "Galilee" see Jast., p. 249. In addition, note Lk. 23.5 where Syriac c has גלילא s has גלילא (Galilee!). Similar variants are found at Mt. 26.69; Mk. 14.70. Burkitt remarks on this I, pp. 405, 407.

The description of Jesus walking on the waters (so for the nonce) is most simply portrayed in Mk. 6.45–52. Jesus had told his disciples to get into the boat to precede him; when he had taken leave of them, he went into the hills to pray (v. 46). Evening came, the boat went out to sea, and he was left alone on land (v. 46). As the disciples in the boat were hard pressed by the wind, he came to them walking, v. 48, on the sea ($\epsilon\pi\grave{\iota}\ \tau\hat{\eta}\ \theta\alpha\lambda\acute{\alpha}\sigma\sigma\eta\varsigma$), and wished to go by them. They thought it was a spirit, v. 49, and were frightened—they may have thought that Jesus was the נחשול "storm-spirit", the word's original meaning "storm" (Jast. p. 897). Jesus allayed their fears and the wind died down.

In *Origins of Christianity,* p. 77, F. C. Conybeare, rationalist and demythologizer, questioned this "walking on the sea," and emended the Greek $\pi\alpha\rho\acute{\alpha}$ for $\epsilon\pi\acute{\iota}$ to mean that Jesus was walking on the sea shore. The question is correctly put. The Greek text receives an arbitrary, even radical emendation on his part, however. The answer should have been given on the simpler basis of the Aramaic על ימא, but the expression is ambiguous. It may mean "on the sea" or "on the sea shore," 2 Sam. 17.11: "Like the sand on the sea shore" and elsewhere. Similarly, as an indication how the phrase if literally translated could mislead, על הבאר does not mean "(Jacob) sat on the well" but "by the well." The Aramaic expression similarly means "On/at the sea shore." Probably the story received amplification, expansion, and editing to make it a miracle and even more pronouncedly so with the rescue of Peter, Mt. 14.

There are two other divergent texts that receive clarification through resorting to Aramaic. Where Jesus bids the crowds farewell in Mk. 6.36, the word employed is *apotaksamenos,* best translated by the RSV as "He took leave of them," which Mt. 14.23 recounts more abruptly as *apolusas* "He dismissed them." Actually, both verbs refer to the Aramaic פטר which in the 'Aph'el means "dismiss". For example, That they should *dismiss (ptr)* the school children at the fourth hour of the day, (during the summer heat), Num. R. sect 12, or "take leave" as in Tanḥuma Bereshit 13, "They took leave of him in the evening ... In the morning, they again took leave of him" (מפטרי Jast., p. 1158).

A verse in Mk. 9.17f. requires two corrections which the Aramaic furnishes as a solution, one in syntax, and one in proper definition. The text reads, "And one of the multitude answered and said, 'Master, I have brought unto thee, my son, which hath a dumb spirit" ($\check{\epsilon}\chi o\nu\tau\alpha\ \pi\nu\epsilon\hat{\upsilon}\mu\alpha\ \check{\alpha}\lambda\alpha\lambda o\nu$) lit. having a spirit that does not speak. Obviously, it was not the spirit that was dumb, but the son. Swete, *Mark,* p. 197 maintains that the effect produced upon the demoniac is transferred (?) in thought to the demon. But this would strike one as a lame explanation. When we revert to the Aramaic (see below) the difficulty is resolved. First it should be recalled that the Semitic languages are much more elastic and loose in construction, so much so that the relative pronoun, for example, need not refer to the noun preceding. Thus in the phrase "the man who" there can be no question that "who" refers to "man." This is not quite so absolute in Aramaic or Hebrew. (Compare A. B. Ehrlich, *Miqra Ki-pheschuto*, I, pp. 320 top, 323; II, pp. 96–98; Burney, *Aramaic Origin*, p. 110; Lk. 6.22.23. For the expression, "he teareth him" in the verse, see p. 87).

V. 25, in the same continuous episode, relates furthermore that Jesus "rebuked the foul spirit, saying unto him, 'Thou dumb and deaf spirit (τὸ ἄλαλον καὶ κωφὸν πνεῦμα) I charge thee, come out of him.'" As commentators have remarked (Swete, *Mark,* p. 201), "deaf" is a new feature in the case. Perhaps the difficulty may be resolved by surmising that we may have a doublet. *Originally* the text read חרש which has the meaning of both (1) deaf and (2) dumb. Compare BDB, p. 361, and the ruling of the Mishna Ter. 1.19 "The ḥeresh of which the scholars speak (in a legal sense) means everywhere 'deaf and dumb.'" Since then ḥeresh could be ambiguous, a glossator wished to narrow down the meaning that the child was dumb but not deaf, and therefore added דלא ממלל. The Aramaic of our text ran איתית לותך ברי דאית לה רוחא דחרש דלא ממלל. The translation should be, "I have brought my son to you, who has a demon, who is deaf, who does not speak." The successive "who"s are all relative to and modifying the "son." The repetition of *de* confused the translator.

Mk. 10.30 contains a puzzling, difficult phrase. There was an interchange between Jesus and his disciples, wherein Jesus had described how difficult it was to be saved. The disciples were disturbed, "Who then can be saved?... We have left all and followed you." Jesus replied, "Verily I say unto you, there is no man who hath left house (i.e. household), or brethren, or sisters, or father or mother or wife, or lands for my sakes or the Gospel's" (v. 29). "But he shall receive a hundredfold now, in this time, houses, and brethren, and sisters, and mothers and children, and lands, with persecutions (μετὰ διωγμῶν); and in the world to come eternal life." With *persecutions?* Were all these promised fortunes to be accompanied by persecutions? One might consider that the phrase is a satirical gloss or perhaps that of a disillusioned reader, familiar with Christian martyrdom, but the Mss. strongly support the phrase. Behind the Greek is the Aramaic רדף (cf. the Peshitta and the Syriac equation of *dioko/redaf* in Mt. 5.10; 10.23; Lk. 21.12; Jn. 5.16; 15.20) meaning generally "pursue," but also bearing the connotation and nuance of "strive after." Thus in such passages as Dt. 16.20 "Justice, justice thou shalt pursue," or Ps. 34.15 "Seek peace and pursue it", the translation should be "strive after/pursue" for the better nuance since justice and peace are conceptualized, invisible and elusive, and "pursue" does not suit as a verb; similarly for mercy, Prov. 21.21; judgment or justice, Ps. 119.84; foulness, ibid., v. 150 (cf. Jast., p. 1453; A. B. Ehrlich, *Randglossen,* II, p. 199). Probably the Aramaic text read עם רדיפיא which the translator naturally considered to mean "persecutions." The word *redifayya* however is brachyology for "other things that people strive for," i.e., lands, cattle and sheep, slaves, money and the like. Figuratively, in later Hebrew, *rdf* is used for ambition, for rulership, desire for rich food, sexual passion, etc. (cf. E. Ben Yehudah, s.v. vol. 13, 6455 b). The context now makes sense with that meaning. The translator should have rendered a little more loosely perhaps in the sense "All things like such, all things that follow through with this, other strivings."

In Mk. 14.30 Jesus prophecies to Peter "That this day, even in this night, before the cock crow twice (*dis*), thou shalt deny me thrice." In v. 68 Peter made the denial and the cock crowed. At the third denial, v. 72 states, "And the second time (ἐκ δευτέρου) the cock crew." There is some question about the cock crowing twice. In the parallel accounts, Mt. 26.34; Lk. 22.34; Jn. 13.38, there is only the simple statement "and immediately the cock crew." Torrey, in notes to his *The Four Gospels* on Mk. 14.72, and Metzger, *Textual Commentary,* pp. 114, 116, have serious reservations about the repeated crowing in vv. 68 and 72. I would propose that the trouble stems from the source at v. 30. The Aramaic there reads קדם דקרא תרנגלא דתנינא "Before the cock crows *again*." The difficulty arose from the mistranslation of דתנינא which the Greek mistranslated as "twice" (the start of the chain of confusion in the subsequent verses) instead of *again*. The number of times the cock would crow is irrelevant. What the passage means is that before the cock would crow once again to herald the dawn, Peter will have denied Jesus thrice.

A passage that has puzzled scholars is Mk. 11.38. The sons of Zebedee, James and John, had asked whether they would be able to sit to the right and to the left of Jesus in his "glory." V. 38 continues, "But Jesus said unto them, 'Ye know not what ye ask; can ye drink of the cup that I drink of? and be baptized with the baptism that I be baptized with?'" The parallel in Mt. 20.22 poses the same question, but omits the baptism question, "Are you able to drink the cup that I am to drink?" and so the Nestle text. His apparatus supplies the verse about baptism but it is weakly supported in the Mss.

What is the baptism that Jesus refers to? And if he were to be "baptized," why would this baptism be so painful or onerous that the sons of

Zebedee would not be able to bear it? Swete thought (*Mark*, p. 237) that the royal baths of Herod are referred to, although it seems much more likely that the metaphorical use of the baptism is common in the later Greek. Swete's citation from Is. 21.4 need not be considered, and the other example, from Jos. *Wars*, 4.1.37 is only partially satisfying. The article in Arndt-Gingrich (p. 131) is much more pointed and full, but assumes for the passage gratuitously that Jesus would be aware of his martyrdom. Behind the Greek is the Aramaic עמד (1) dive, plunge, sink, set (of the sun), (2) baptize (cf. Baby. Talm. Aramaic אמודי (בר) "diver." Levy, *Neuhebr. Wört.*, I., p. 94 and Syriac, Brock., p. 529). The first part of v. 38 "the drinking of the cup" is a biblical figure, especially of "drinking the cup of staggering," i.e., the benumbing cup Ps. 60.5; Is. 51.17. In the second part the translator was manifestly influenced by the *baptisma* of the later decades (Acts 8; I Cor. and elsewhere) and of course, by the baptisms themselves current so prominently in the Gospels. There is a nuance here that the translator missed. It would have been much more in keeping with the alternate and more fundamental meaning of עמד to translate, "Can you *plunge* in where I will be plunged?" (For *'amad* as "plunge," comp. Payn. Sm., p. 416, "He plunged in the depth of the sea"; Brock. p. 529 *se mersit, immersit*. For the passage at Lk. 12.49—50, where *baptizein* is also employed but again with a different connotation, see p. 122).

There is both a mistranslation and misvocalization at Mk. 5.10, where the mad man of the tombs, possessed of devils, importuned Jesus that he not send him "away out of the country"(ἔξω τῆς χώρας). Lk. 8.31, phrasing it a bit differently, has the demons begging Jesus not to "command them to go out into the deep," literally, the abyss (ἄβυσσον). It has been proposed that the divergence comes from a misunderstanding of the Aramaic ארע, supposedly to mean (1) land and (2) abyss. (Compare *Dictionary of Christ and the Gospels*, II, p. 130.) But *'ara'* meaning actually "underneath" is unsupported for the definition of "the abyss." Others take the view that the Aramaic תחומא and תהומא were confounded with one another. This is improbable as *tehum* is but rarely used for "land," and always in a standard fashion for גבול "boundary." I suggest: ברא, the standard Aramaic equivalent of שדה "field," that is, the open country as opposed to the city, BDB, p. 961 under f., was confused with, and misread as ברא (in Syriac written defectively without Yudh: *bira*), the Pit, likewise "abyss" being figurative (comp. ירכתי בור, בור תחתיות, יורדי בור) for "destruction, death" as in Ps. 55.24 BDB, p. 92b. ברא and בירא could easily be misread for one another.

There is another passage in this category of confusion of roots and consequent mistranslation evident in Mk. 4.30, where the passage reads, "And he said, 'Whereunto shall we liken the kingdom of God? Or (literally) by what parable may we place it?'" (ἐν τίνι αὐτὴν παραβολῇ θῶμεν). This is a most peculiar way to say "How shall we place it?" for which other Ms. groups, specifically the miniscules 1-118-131-209 examined by Kirsopp Lake and designated by Nestle by Gk. L(lamda) (cf. his *Introduction to Novum Testamentum Graece,* p. 69*) offer as an alternate reading (*parabalomen auten*) i.e., "With what comparison shall we *compare* it?" Actually, this is the only way of expressing the thought, "How shall we compare the Kingdom of God?" How is the more difficult reading to be explained? It is the Aramaic that points to and relieves the difficulty. The word I שוא means ("place, put") and II שוא "liken, compare." It should be obvious that the translator confused the two. He should have rendered with the sense of "compare" exactly as Lk. 13.18. The whole verse now carries the parallel in its two members:

How may we liken the kingdom of God,
And with what comparison should we compare it?

There is one Marcan passage which has hitherto remained an enigma to commentators but which may be resolved through retroversion to Aramaic. The passage runs as follows: "For the Pharisees, and all the Jews, except they wash their hands with the fist (*pugme:* so the text with Swete, Nestle; the AV renders "carefully" based upon *pukna,* so א w.vg (syᵖ) in the apparatus in Nestle; UBS with Nestle prints *pugme*) eat not, holding the tradition of the elders" (Mk. 7.3). The solutions offered for this problematic text have not been regarded as satisfactory. As summarized by Swete, *pugme* "with the fist" cannot mean "up to the elbow" as interpreted by Mediaeval Greek scholars, nor "up to the wrist" as explained by Lightfoot and Edersheim; *pukna,* "carefully," as a more easy reading may be a gloss borrowed from Lk. 5.33 perhaps not "often" but "scrupulously," cf. Ps. בטילאית "scrupulously," if it is not a corruption altogether, cf. *pukme* of D. Nor is Swete's interpretation satisfactory, even if it explains that "with the fist" means with the hands held with clenched fingers while the attendant pours water over them (2 Kings 3.11. This text should not be given as proof by some writers, as the pouring of water on the hands of Elijah by Elisha, simply means being in service to Elijah as a special follower. Comp. Pritchard, *Ancient Near Eastern Texts,* 446a as an early custom of this, though the editor considers this a libation on the tomb). At any rate, the washing of the hands with clenched fists would be unsatisfactory in Jewish legal procedure, as the inner part of the fist would remain untouched by water.

The word for "fist" in the Hebrew Bible is dubious. The conventional word אגרוף is questioned by the current dictionaries: Gesenius-Buhl[17] *unsicheres Wort;* Koehler and Baumgartner, "broom, shovel, rake" (p. 10). BDB (p. 172), accept the LXX *pugme* "fist," but notes that Onqelos renders with כורמיזא supposedly to mean "staff, club." BDB, apparently following Levy (*Chal. Wört.,* I, p. 389) who indeed defines the word as *Schleuder* "sling," *Wurfwaffe* (something hurled as a weapon) and so Siegfried-Stade. Jast. p. 625 however, reads "fist." Sa'adyah, quoted by Ibn Ezra, simply defines it as "something hard"; Ibn Janaḥ, "something that wounds or breaks" but not "fist." At any rate, because of the lack of its cognate in Semitic languages, and the uncertainty of philologists, the word אגרוף cannot be employed in any reconstruction of the underlying Aramaic to the verse in Mk. under discussion.

In Aramaic, the word ידא "hand" has the meaning likewise of "fist" (Payn. Sm., p. 186, and cf. e.g., the expression אגונ׳סטא דבאידא "pugilists"). To formulate a basis for discussion, let us reconstruct the Aramaic of our Mk. text which ran שייגין אידא באידא באידא. The translator understood well enough to translate the first two words "They wash their hands." The next two words he did not recognize at all, supposing that one, באידא, was thoughtlessly repeated in his Ms., and so he tacitly eliminated one of the words from his translation. The other אידא was just as puzzling—he had just rendered "They washed their *hands*"; now what in the world was the next באידא "with the hand" supposed to mean? To wash the hands with the hand makes no sense. He, *faute de mieux,* hit upon the idea that, since באידא could mean "with the fist" perhaps the sentence could mean that the Jews wash their hands vigorously with the fist, which is not only absurd, but unsupported by anything that we know of Jewish law. Contrast Swete a.l.

Incidentally, it is not generally recognized that in Hebrew, too, the word יד means "fist." A key verse that would confirm this meaning is in Num. 35.21 where the text reads, "Or in enmity smote him with his *hand* that he died; he that smote him shall surely be put to death: he is a murderer...." Now the one who attacked the other did not do so by slapping him to death; he used his fist and murdered him. This would be the only interpretation possible. Other examples of יד as "fist" would be found at 2 Sam. 23.21, "He snatched the javelin from the grasp (fist) of the Egyptian"; other examples may be cited from 1 Sam. 17.57; Num. 22.23; Is. 5.25; of course, yad as "power" is well recognized. In many instances we would translate more idiomatically with "grasp" which in English is simply more sophisticated than "fist."

The expression אידא באידא, also באידא באידא, is an idiomatic Eastern Aramaic expression which lends itself to a number of definitions. Hebrew has the reduplicative יד על יד (Jast., p. 564). Of course, it may literally mean "hand with hand, hand in hand" and the sense would be that the Jews wash their hands, one hand with the other. The expression also bears the general sense of "one after the other, in order, successively, singly," (cf. Payn. Sm., p. 186; Brock., p. 295. Pesh. s in our passage simplifies with חדא חדא.) Then the passage would carry the signification of washing one hand and then the other. Such scrupulosity would be in character with other idiomatic expressions of washing the hands, e.g., משי ידין "rub, hence to wash and dry," esp. one's hands before and after meals. (Jast., p. 851) and semantically comparable to the other roots as שזג (Palestinian/Galilean Aramaic) and סחי fundamentally "to wipe, cleanse," employed for the washing of the body, the hands and feet. It is quite admissible that the variation found as בטילאית mentioned above may be a variation to our text, wherein one translator cut loose from the text and telescoped the whole sense by rendering "carefully." We should, however, translate the text, "For the Pharisees, and all the Jews, except they wash their hands rubbing one hand with the other, do not eat at all."

A number of wordplays may be noticed. In Mk. 5.33 where the ill woman "told him all the truth" (*aletheian*), and in v. 34, where Jesus in turn says to her, "Thy faith (*pistis*) hath made thee whole" there is a play on the Aramaic הימנותא meaning both "faith" and "truth." Compare the Greek-Syriac equation in Ac. 16.1 (*pistos*), and for *'emet* in Ps. 57.11; see Brock., p. 75.

Moreover in Mk. 11.24 there seems to be a wordplay of the root בעי which means both (1) ask for, desire and (2) pray. The passage reads, "Therefore I say unto you, 'What things soever ye desire (*proseuchesthe*), when ye pray (*aiteisthe*), believe that ye receive them, and ye shall have them.'" Note, first of all, not only the wordplay, but that the AV quite adroitly transposed "desire" and "pray." Matter-of-factly, the Greek reads literally "when ye pray and ask." This impresses one as a mistranslation because the Aramaic probably read כלא די תבעון כד בעין "Everything that you ask for while praying" was mixed up by the translator who confused in meaning the first בעי with the second.

In the passage at Mk. 7.13 "through your tradition which ye have delivered" there is a wordplay on "tradition" and "delivered," literally, handed down אשלמתא אשלמתן.

Note, however, in this latter passage that the translator, rendering word for word, missed the time-sense in the sequence of the verse. Jesus, accusing the Pharisees of distorting their tradition, says, "Making the word of God of none effect through your tradition which ye have delivered (*paredokate*)." Retrovertedly, the Aramaic ran אשלמתא דאשלמתן. Although the verb form is the aorist—and so indeed did the Greek translator render—the translation is askew in its temporal sequence. It is not the tradition that you handed down (Montefiore: "The tense is odd"), but which you do hand down now. The Greek translator did not understand that in Eastern Aramaic the perfect "has often for us the appearance of a Present" (Nöldeke, *Syr. Gramm.* par. 256), or "of actions continually repeated" (ibid, par. 258). The same result would be achieved, Nöldeke goes on to say, if *hawa* with the participle following הויתון דמשלמין (ibid par. 261) would be employed. Accordingly the verse should be translated, "the tradition that you hand on."

Chapter IV

The Evidence from Luke

BEFORE CONSIDERING and evaluating the material from Lk., and the data for the Aramaic evidenced from the Greek translation, it will be necessary to examine a special problem at the beginning of Lk., sections 1.5—2.52. The language in these chapters is considered to be starkly Hebraistic, indeed with the added speculation that they must have been translated from a Semitic original (Wellhausen, *Einleitung*,[2] 26f.; Nestle, ZNW, pp. vii, 26of.; Spitta, ZNW, p. vi.293; refs. by Mof. ILNT, p. 267). Hebrew is argued for specifically by Torrey and R. A. Aytoun (JTS, pp. 18, 274f.); or these sections may have been, as other scholars assert, freely composed archaistically in Greek by Luke himself (Mof., ibid); or may have been originally Aramaic, and then translated—so hypothesized by Mof., p. 267 bottom and Plummer, *Luke,* p. 7. To what degree Luke was a compiler of traditions and sources, "how much he freely composed, and how much he selected," is not our function to enter into at this juncture. The problem that we wish to deal with is, were these two chapters originally written in "Palestinian Jewish-Christian Greek," in Hebrew, or in Aramaic?

Chapters 1 and 2 give a very strong impression of underlying Hebrew. The Greek phrases translate easily into Hebrew, and one could conclude that Hebrew was the language from which Luke was translating. Of course, the suspicion arose that the Greek was largely imitative of the LXX (Plummer, *Introduction,* pp. 1—11), but no less prominent was the thought that the translator could still skillfully make use of the same Greek phrases in translating from the Aramaic. I had indeed looked for the telltale signs of mistranslation from the putative Hebrew, and found none. In contrast, examples of Aramaic appeared which could not be, in their differentia from the Hebrew, anything but Aramaic. Other things puzzled: The Magnificat and the Prayer of Zacharias could have been originally in Hebrew only, as are all prayers in Jewish tradition with two or three minor exceptions (see the writer's *Biblical Books Translated From the Aramaic,* p. 76 and Mof. op.

cit., p. 271, n.1). In summary, studies yielded the following conclusion with the evidence to follow presently: the narrative portions in ch. 1.5—2.52 were translated in a skillful Greek biblical idiom from the Aramaic; the biblical idiom becomes less strongly marked when more current historical matters are dealt with (ch. 3); as prayers, the Magnificat (1.46—55) and the Prayer of Zacharias (267—79) were composed or adapted from a Hebrew source. The main concern here, proof for the *narrational* sections of Lk. 1—2 from the Aramaic, is evident from the following examples.

First, there is a difficult passage in Lk. 1.17 which reads, "And he [John] shall go before him in the spirit and power of Elijah, to turn the hearts of the fathers to the children, and the disobedient to the wisdom of the just; to make ready a people *prepared* for the Lord" (ἐτοιμάσαι κυρίῳ λαὸν κατεσκευασμένον). The phrase is tautological; if John is to make ready a people for the Lord, how is it that they are already made ready, *prepared?* The different translations, with their paraphrases, sense the difficulty, "Make ready for the Lord a people prepared (?)" RSV; "To prepare a people that shall be fit for the Lord," NEB; "Perfectly ready for the Lord" Gdspd; "To prepare for the Lord a people well-disposed" NAB; "To make a people ready and prepared for the Lord," Mof.[2] It is apparent that there is a wide diversity of opinion about the syntax, the crucial *kateskeuasmenon* Peshitta גמירא, and the precise meaning of the latter part of the verse.

The retroversion to Aramaic, following partially the Peshitta, illuminates the source of the difficulty לתקנא לאלהא עמא גמירא "To prepare" (actually "to better, restore anew, improve"; תקן may comprehend all these meanings, Jast., p. 1691) or "to restore for the Lord a people *lost*" or "now being lost," the peʻil gemira' like the paʻul in Hebrew may express potential action. (Compare Ehrlich, *Randglossen*, IV, p. 236.) The translator who misunderstood *gemar* elsewhere, see p. 109 with the remarks on Lk. 6.40, thought the Aramaic to mean "complete, perfect," more freely "prepared." Compare with the synonym קן, and the way the Syriac translation uses the word תקן, to render *kataskeuazo* in Mt. 11.10; Lk. 7.27 and *katartizo,* Lk. 6.40; and furthermore, note how the Greek employs the same two Greek words in Mt. 21.6 and in the present passage (Lk. 1.17). The verse now applies with particular force to the special mission of John that, like Elijah, he is to restore to the Lord a people relapsing into sin and ruin. The translator therefore should have defined גמירא as "coming to an end, deteriorating, being *lost.*" He should have translated "to restore to the Lord a people about to be lost."

THE EVIDENCE FROM LUKE

Lk. 1.24—25 reads, "And after those days, his wife Elisabeth conceived and hid herself (περιέκρυβεν ἑαυτήν) five months, saying 'Thus hath the Lord dealt with me in the days wherein he looked on me, to take away my reproach among men.'" It is both difficult to understand, and peculiar to say, that Elisabeth, after her wish for a child reached fulfillment and satisfaction, should *hide* herself. Why should Elisabeth go into seclusion? "Her motive can only be conjectured" (Plummer, p. 19). Again, it was the Aramaic that was misunderstood. The translator had before him the word אתכסית (*'etkasyat;* there are variable forms; the one projected here is Eastern Aramaic). The translator thought of the reflexive to mean "she hid herself." However, the Etpe'el carries the meaning of "she adorned herself (also with royal clothes)." (Compare Gen. Onq. 24.65; Targ. Is. 3.7; Jon. 3.6.7; 1 Kings 11.29; and compare כיסויא "clothes", Targ. Esther II 6.10.) The first verse now becomes clear: Elisabeth, after her longed-for pregnancy had come to pass, adorned herself (daily) for five months, to make known and to glory in her pregnancy—an unusual practice, as she had to do domestic work. She now had the pride of the expectant Judean mother, who, especially in the case of the barren Elisabeth, was to find joy in the birth of a child. The adornment for five months is specified, because her pregnancy, then, was manifest to all, and the adornment became incongruous, and perhaps awkward.

The second verse, 25, was equally distorted by the Greek translator, owing to his misunderstanding of the particle in ביומיא "for the days" not "in." The particle *b* should have been translated "for" as in Dt. 19.21 "A life for a life, eye for eye," and other examples in BDB, p. 90. Moreover, the cryptic expression "For thus hath the Lord dealt with me" (πεποίηκεν) refers specifically to the *adornment;* although she has adorned herself, she naturally ascribes this new privilege of adornment to God's mercy and grace in place of the days that he looked upon her with indifference or disapproval (a biblical idiom, BDB, p. 908, sec. 6 and somewhat similarly Ps. 92.12), and now He has removed her reproach from among men. The translation would now yield a very satisfying sense "Thus hath the Lord done for me for the days that he looked upon me—to remove my reproach from among men." Note that the word "conceived" התעברת, and "take away" (reproach) אעבר, as well as "dealt" (with me) עבד form wordplays.

Further along in the chapter, a third example of an underlying Aramaic idiom is evident at Lk. 1.35 which runs, "The angel answered and said unto her, 'The holy ghost shall come upon thee, and the power of the Highest shall overshadow thee (ἐπισκιάσει); therefore that holy thing (ἅγιον) (!)

which shall be born of thee shall be called the son of God.'" The fact that *hagion* is neuter is remarkable.

The idea that the "power" of God shall overshadow Mary is a little difficult to imagine, with all the other miraculous notions associated with the whole nativity event despite what Arndt-Gingrich, 298 compares this with in such passages as Mt. 17.5; Mk. 9.7, and others. A "cloud," can overshadow (Mt. 17.5), but not "might" or "power." In the OT it is the רוח ייי (the later *ruaḥ ha-qodesh*) that "rests" upon the recipient; in the expressions describing it, various verbs are employed—היה על Num. 24.2; Jud. 3.10; 11.29; or the early צלח על Jud. 14.6; 19.15; 1 Sam. 10.6, and in the "Messianic" passage, such as Is. 7.2; 61.1; 63.14—but never "overshadow." The substrate Aramaic supplies the proper and satisfying solution. The Eastern Aramaic root גנן with its by-form גני has the fundamental meaning of "inhabit" (Brock., p. 123); in addition, it has the sense of "cover, protect," and significantly "lie down upon, rest on," (Payn. Sm., p. 73) and especially with reference to the spirit (Brock., p. 123), both in the verb and the noun (Payn. Sm., ibid). Its by-form or associate "often said of the Holy Spirit" גנן, גנא has the same connotation of "lie down (on)." The second meaning of גנן is "overshadow," and note the use of אגן for both *episkiazo* in the present Lk. passage, and *skenoo* in Jn. 1.14 as well as the synonyms טלל/*skia* Mt. 4.16; Lk. 1.79; /*skene* Lk. 9.33; 16.9; *episkiazo* Lk. 9.34 in the pa'el, 'aph'el idem Mk. 9.7; Mt. 17.5. The inevitable conclusion seems to be that the translator took the inappropriate meaning of גנן, "overshadow," instead of "rest upon." Translate "The power of the Most High shall rest upon thee." Comp. Mic. 3.8.

The awkwardness of the phrase, "The holy thing that shall be born of thee shall be called the son of God" (διὸ καὶ τὸ γεννώμενον ἅγιον κληθήσεται υἱὸς θεοῦ) has been explained by Proksch, *Theological Dictionary of the NT*, I, p. 101, to mean that "*hagion* here belongs to the subject for the predicate is *huios theou;* but the expression *to gennomenon hagion* is to be explained by the supranatural origin of the new life, which is called *huios theou* because of its origin . . . not grounded in the Messianic office of Christ but in his origin." *hagion* as neuter still remains difficult, although Blass, Debrunner-Funk, par. 138 allow that "The neuter is sometimes used with reference to persons, if it is not the individuals but the general quality that is to be emphasized." Perhaps the substratal Aramaic may offer the proper solution. It ran דהוא יליד קודשא יתקרי בר אלהא where יליד קודשא may mean "born of the Holy One" (for a parallel construction, cf. Job. 14.1). קודשא and קדש are names for God, see the writer's article "A

Suggested Source for Some of the Substitute Names for Yahweh" in *Studies in Jewish Bibliography*, in honor of I. Edward Kiev, p. 587f. On the other hand, *hagion*, as neuter, may represent the abstract קודשא "holiness" (compare Schleusner, *Lexicon*, I, p. 21 e f g). "Born of holiness" means simply that the birth has been announced by the Angel like the birth of Samson, Jud. 13. The translator did not recognize יליד קודשא as a customary construct. The Aramaic substrate composed the couplet with the vague ambiguous design of *talḥins* and wordplays, as if leaving it for the reader to puzzle out and resolve. The passage may mean:
(1) For he, born of holiness, shall be called a divine being (בר אלהא).
(2) For he, born of God, shall be called son of God.
The Jewish Christian who wrote this may or may not have left his statement deliberately ambiguous. The Greek translator, however, combined (1) "holiness" and (2) "son of God," fundamentally a misunderstanding. On *bar 'elaha'*, as "angelic being, divine being," and further remarks on this verse and the interrelated v.32, see p. 126f.

The proof for the Aramaic unfolds in another verse in Lk. 1.39 which reads, "And Mary rose in those days and went into the hill country with haste ($\mu\epsilon\tau\grave{\alpha}$ $\sigma\pi o \upsilon \delta\hat{\eta}s$) into a city of Judah (a mistranslation, pointed out by Torrey, *Our Translated Gospels*, p. 84: read ליהוד מדינתא Ezr. 5.8, "to the province of Judea"), and entered into the house of Zacharias, and saluted Elisabeth." No explanation is given why Mary should go "in haste"; in fact, the "haste" is contradicted by the vague expression at the beginning of the verse "in those days." We should expect something like "with concern, with solicitude," in view of Elisabeth's pregnancy, and matter-of-factly, the Syriac translates בבטליאותא "with care, concern," similarly Phil יציפותא, "with care." There is, however, a third possible reading: From the impression given by Luke, we learn that Mary was retiring and modest (1.29). The possibility exists that while the root בהל means in biblical and Jewish Aramaic both "hurry, be concerned with," but in Eastern Aramaic signifies "be quiet" (but cf., too, בהלתא Pesh. / בהילו "quickly", Ezr. 4.23), the sense of the root may have not been understood. Among the three choices before us, "in haste," "with concern," and "quietly," the received text seems the less probable. The trustworthy variant evidence from the Peshitta "with concern," and the alternate "quietly," (perhaps even "secretly," an extended meaning, cf. Mt. 1.19 where the Cur. has מטישאית / בהילאית "secretly" [Jennings, p. 33; Brock., p. 61]) are the two readings for our probable choice. In the ascending order of probability, then, the textus receptus is questionable; "with concern" is preferable; "quietly" seems most apposite. This confusion of meanings of

בהל as "haste" and "quiet" could be another example of words with contrasting meanings. See R. Gordis, "Studies in Hebrew Roots of Contrasted Meanings," *JQR*, vol. 27, 1936.

A fifth example for the Aramaic Lk. 1–2 may be seen in 1.78 which reads, "[Remission of sins comes] through the tender mercy of our God; whereby the dayspring (ἀνατολή, literally, the shining one) from on high hath visited us, to give light to them that sit in darkness." In the context here *anatole* is a bit difficult to interpret. It may mean (1) "that which grows" as a bud, or sprout, or (2) a shining. On the whole, editors and translators favor "shining" and so "When the day shall dawn upon us from on high," RSV, and similarly Arndt-Gingrich "dawn from heaven," "the Sunrise from on high shall visit us," NASB; "a dawning," Knox, similarly Gdspd; a new day " ... will break on us," Wey; "The morning sun will rise upon us," NEB; " ... he, the Dayspring, shall visit us," NAB. By contrast, A. Jacoby, ZNW, 20, 1921 maintains and translates as "sprout, or scion of God." Doubtlessly, *anatole* means "shining," and here the Greek translator is rendering the Aramaic צמח meaning "shine." Now it is known that צמח *ṣemaḥ* is a name for the Messiah as implied in the Hebrew Bible, and in the LXX by translating *ṣemaḥ* by *anatole* in three passages, Jer. 23.5; Zech. 3.8; 6.12 and continued and confirmed by rabbinic Judaism as a name for the Messiah (cf. Targ. Is. 4.2 where *ṣemaḥ* is given in the Aramaic as משיחא), it follows that the Lk. text through *anatole* intends the Messiah. So Strack-Billerbeck a.l. As the LXX translates the verb *ṣamaḥ* by *epilampse* "shall shine" (Is. 4.2), following the meaning of the Aramaic צמח "shine," it follows that this is what was in the Lk. text, but the translator rendered it too literally as "The shining one." The exigency of the text demanded that he boldly translate "the Messiah." Note the personalized sequel *visited*. The rendering of *ṣemaḥ* as "the shining one" is a mistranslation.

Interestingly there seems to be a bifurcation in the interpretation of *ṣemaḥ*. (1) In the biblical writings, *ṣemaḥ* means an "offshoot" of the Davidic line, as the hoped for redeemer of his people (Is. 11.1f. *neṣer, ḥoter*) and note *ṣemaḥ*'s rendering by the Targ. as *mesiḥa* (Jer. 33.15). Note too as parallel names for the Messiah the very late *yinnon*, "grow," Strack-Billerbeck, I, p. 65; also אפרים "sprout," very late, which has nothing to do with Meshiaḥ ben Ephrayim. (2) With the Greek translators, *ṣemaḥ* acquired, via the Aramaic, the sense of "The Shining One" as a name for the Messiah (Is. 4.2 LXX and comp. the Targ. as well). This double tradition including "The Shining One" is confirmed by another parallel name in Tannaitic literature Mish. Nazir 9.5 as נהוראי "The shining one," although the name is common for a number of late amoraic teachers. Compare Strack-Billerbeck, ibid., p. 67; J. Klausner, *Ha-ra'ayon ha-meshiḥi be-yisrael*³ (The Messianic Concept in Israel), p. 289. Note the remark of a Nahorai about the Messiah in b. Sanhedrin 97a.

These five examples, with corroborative wordplays, should suffice to show that Lk. chaps. 1–2—with the exception of the prayers—were translated from an underlying document in the Aramaic. These introductory chapters would make them a piece with the rest of Lk. originally in Aramaic as the forthcoming examples will demonstrate. As a physician, recognized through his function as a man of standing (Julius Caesar gave Roman citizenship for example to all the doctors in Rome) Luke knew Greek well as his use of the language shows; but he knew less Aramaic, even though he lived in Syria. As mentioned, his errors in translation are more numerous and more surprising than any of the other Gospel writers. His grasp of Aramaic is discerned in his confounding roots and forms. Thus, there seems to be a confusion of roots in Lk. 3.8, paralleled in Mk. 3.8. The Lk. text runs, "Bring forth therefore fruits worthy of repentance (ἀξίους τῆς μετανοίας), and begin not to say within yourselves 'We have Abraham to our father' for I say unto you that 'God is able of these stones to raise up children unto Abraham.'" The evidence that this verse is translated from Aramaic is also offered by other scholars, who have noticed that the phrase "begin not to say" is the Aramaic locution *sheri* plus the verb, and is a stereotyped expression meaning simply "Do not say." The translator rendered too literally "Do not begin." Compare Torrey, *Our Translated Gospels*, p. 305, on the verse in Lk. 3.23 "Jesus began to be thirty years of age, etc."; and then the wordplays "Abraham" and a "father," "stones" and "children" as evidence of Aramaic אבנין/בנין; אב/אברהם. (See pp. 77, 125).

Commentators have been troubled by the phrase "fruits worthy of repentance." The RSV translates, "That befits repentance," and so Mon. similarly Moff.; NASB renders, "In keeping with your repentance"; TCNT, "Let your lives prove your repentance"; NEB, "Prove your repentance by the fruit it bears"; Arndt-Gingrich "Fruits in keeping with your repentance," (p. 77). It is clear that *aksios* is difficult and perplexing. While *aksios* can very well mean "worthy," as found in numerous combinations as "worthy of love," "worthy of praise," "worthy of sanctification," "worthy of God," etc., (Arndt-Gingrich, ibid.), "worthy of repentance" is not quite the interpretation required in this context. In Aramaic, as in Hebrew, there are two roots I שוא, II שוא, the first having the signification of "be worthy, equal, alike" and the second having the sense of "place, set, put" (BDB, p. 1000; Levy,

Chal. Wört., p. 463; Jast., p. 1533; Payn. Sm., p. 562 and Brock., p. 760, however, think of only a single root, with a plethora of meanings). Amidst so many meanings of the verb, the translator probably chose the wrong meaning—the second *shwa'*, "set, place," was the appropriate one. The meaning of the verse should be: Do such deeds that lead to, or are directed toward repentance. The Aramaic probably ran עבדו פירין דשוין לתיובתא. It is possible too that the verb may have been passive, as passive formations with שוא are frequent. The translation then literally would be: Produce fruits that are set for (i.e., directed toward) repentance. For the elusive, and varied meanings of the Aramaic *shewa*, compare Jast. p. 1533; this root has been misinterpreted elsewhere (see pp. 55, 93).

Attention should be given to the root קבל (see p. 64), a source of uncertainty in a number of instances because it has at least four distinct meanings in Lk.: (1) receive, accept, (2) welcome, (3) hear, (4) complain, rebuke (Payn. Sm., p. 487; Jast., p. 1309). For the third meaning (hear), Onqelos employs *qebal* some fifty-five times for *shama'*. (See Ch. J. Kosawski, *Ozar Ha-Targum*, I, p. 428f.) Note that Jastrow assumes three roots; in his discussion (p. 1309b), this outstanding lexicographer confused Roman numerals III, IV, and II on that page, so that the mistakes of Luke need not surprise us. *Dechomai* means receive, take, welcome, in Hellenistic Greek; nevertheless, a comparison of parallel texts indicates that we are dealing with the root קבל which was mistranslated. Thus Lk. 10.16, "He that heareth ($\dot{\alpha}\kappa o\acute{u}\omega\nu$) you heareth me; and he that despiseth you, despiseth me; and he that despiseth me, despiseth him that sent me." The parallel in Mt. 10.40 shows the required sense "He that receiveth ($\delta\epsilon\chi\acute{o}\mu\epsilon\nu o\varsigma$) you receiveth me," i.e., קבל was interpreted by Mt. as "receive" but by Lk. as "hear." Even more precisely, this Mt. verse should run, "He that welcomes you, welcomes me." The Lk. passage, on the other hand, should read, "He that welcomes me," not "heareth." Note the proper contrast to "welcome" in the "despiseth" that follows.

There is another instance where Lk. as translator did not accurately differentiate two roots, or rather mistook the grammatical form because both the roots took on a similar form. The text in 18.7 reads, "And shall not God avenge his own elect, which cry day and night unto him, *though he bear long with them?*" And v. 8 continues, "I tell you that he will avenge them speedily." The end of v. 7 disrupts the continuity between the first part of the verse, and the sequel in v. 8, and therefore sounds suspect in the context. The Greek reads, $\kappa\alpha\grave{\iota}\ \mu\alpha\kappa\rho o\theta\upsilon\mu\epsilon\hat{\iota}\ \dot{\epsilon}\pi'\ \alpha\dot{\upsilon}\tau o\hat{\iota}\varsigma$, literally, "be longsuffering over them." It is generally conceded that this clause, as an implicit explana-

THE EVIDENCE FROM LUKE

tion of the unjust judge and the widow in the parable, "gives rise to great difficulties ... and the original connection of the parable (vv. 2—5), with the explanation (6—8) is not undisputed" (Horst in *Theological Dictionary in the New Testament,* IV, 381). In the main, there are three difficulties: (1) what is the construction of *makrothumei*?(2) what is its meaning? and (3) what is the syntax and meaning of *ep' autois*? To solve the difficulty, Plummer, *Luke,* p. 414, gave the meaning of "be slow, be backward, tarry" to *makrothumei*; this, however, does not solve the difficulty of the abrupt turn in the sequence of the thought.

We cannot take *makrothumei* out of its sense and its usual standard equivalent of האריך אפים, Aramaic אגר רוחא root נגר, also used elliptically, "to be longsuffering, patient" (Payn. Sm., p. 328; Brock., p. 415; Levy, *Chal. Wört.,* II, p. 91). The translator, however, was mistaken. He thought he saw the familiar מגר רוחה and assumed that the root was נגר. He should have taken it from the root גרא which has a similar grammatical form. The expression מגרי רוחה means "to stir up his spirit, arouse his spirit." The roots of גר, גרי, גרגר, (a reduplicated form) are interrelated (observation of Payn. Sm., p. 77, s.v. גרג meaning "stir, provoke, stimulate" Levy, *Chal. Wört.,* pp. 154, 156). Thus the Aramaic would clear up the difficulties in the verse. The Aramaic probably ran ומגרי רוחה עליהון. The verse should be translated, "And will not God execute justice for his chosen ones who call to him day and night, and stir *His spirit on their account*? I tell you He will execute justice for them at once." גרה is used, in later Hebrew, for the rousing of laughter, sexual passion, ability to speak (Ben Yehudah, II, p. 836). There is the possibility that ער (Hag. 1.14) and גר are cognates, Arabic ġr. cf. Tur-Sinai in Ben Yehudah, IX, 6387; 'r is used idiomatically with רוח. עליהון regarded as a difficulty in the Greek, means "for them, on their account," and refers to the elect who cry to Him. For "faith" in the next verse, really "persistence, endurance," see p. 158.

The word מלתא, commonly translated as "word, matter," is quite rich in other meanings and associations. Thus in the phrase מלתא דקסמין, Targ. Yer. Num. 31.8 "a matter of sorcery, of witchcraft" is the full expression for *miltha'* alone, meaning "magic, sorcery," e.g., אמרה איהי מלתא "She spoke a word" (cast a magic spell). Parenthetically, *miltha'* ramifies in other meanings pejoratively as Ta'an. 21b כי הוה עביד מילתא "When the surgeon bled a person"; מלתא בישא—pollution Y. Yeb.II, 3d. The word is used especially in incantations. See Montgomery, *Aramaic Incantation Texts,* p. 85, and the texts at 6.12; 12.9; 34.5; 38.6. We have an instance of this מלתא as "magic" in Lk. 4.36, where the parallel text confirms the reading. After Jesus had driven out the unclean spirit from the demoniac, the text continues, "And they were all amazed, and spoke among themselves, saying, 'What a word (*logos*) is this!' For with authority and power, he commandeth the unclean spirits, and they come out." It will be understood readily that the people did not say, "What a *word* is this!" but rather in admiration "What *magic* is this!" The translator did not catch the meaning of *miltha'* for the verse. The phrase, moreover, "with authority" (*en eksousia*), is inappropriate. The retroversion בטעמא means "by command" (see infra).

The parallel passage in Mk. 1.27 reads differently. "What thing is this? What new doctrine is this?" Whether this is an expansion of Lk. or whether, as is more probable, Lk. contracted Mk., need not be discussed for the moment. Perhaps Mk. has a doublet; *miltha'* can mean "thing" (cf. Heb. *dabar*). Apparently, though, the word *miltha'* was interpreted differently, understood on the one hand by Lk. as "word," while Mk.'s translator thought of *miltha'* as *didache* meaning "doctrine, teaching." *Miltha'* as "teaching" is represented frequently in rabbinic literature. Compare ר' פ' אמר בה מילתא which means that "The Rabbi made a statement, pronounced a verdict, made a new teaching on the subject." See further discussion of *miltha'*, p. 105.

Commentators have found difficulty with the syntax of the Greek which reads διδαχὴ καινὴ κατ' ἐξουσίαν, καί τοῖς πνεύμασι τοῖς ἀκαθάρτοις ἐπιτάσσει κτλ. Conventionally translated "For with authority commandeth he even the unclean spirits, and they do obey him." I suggest, "What is this? A new teaching by *command*?" The word *ta'ama* as above. There is an implicit play on words herein. *ta'ama* as employed in rabbinic literature frequently means "biblical support, biblical authority." Thus, the Gemara, on initiating discussion on a ruling laid down in the Mishna, will begin it by asking *mai ta'ama* "What is the biblical supportive verse for this law?" Like legalists the world over, they always looked for a precedent. In the aforementioned verse in Mk., the people are "amazed" that a new teaching has come forth by Jesus' own command—a new teaching in which he had not implored the help of God (Num. 12.13; Deut. 32.39) or his angels to expel the demon. (For the appeal to superhuman powers for this aid, see Montgomery, op. cit. p. 115, last paragraph, and #5,7,8 as examples.) This was for the people the new *miltha'*. Jesus effected the expulsion and cure on his own. The same Aramaic word *miltha'* was the source of the difference between the texts of Mk. and Lk.

The root אחד has a number of significations (1) grasp, (2) seize, (3) catch, (4) include. It is employed by the Peshitta for the simplex *kleio* in Mt. 6.6

and Lk. 11.7, and the compound *apokleio* in Lk. 13.25. In the Targs., אחד, for the discussion at hand, is employed in such locutions as Job 18.9 יתאחד בתקלא "be caught in a net"; Lam. 4.20 אתחד במצד "caught in a snare," Levy, *Chal. Wört.*, I, 19. The passage in Lk. 5.6 describes a fruitless night of fishing; when, at the behest of Jesus, the disciples had let down the nets once more, the text reads "And when this was done, they inclosed (συνέκλεισαν) a great multitude of fishes; and their net brake." It is obvious that we should translate with Rieu "They netted an enormous catch of fish" or "They caught" NAB, although TCNT keeps "enclosed" and so Mof., HNT, RSTV, Torrey. Unquestionably, it was a catch of fish (so in v. 9) that they hauled in, but the translator of Lk., fixed upon the wrong meaning of אחד "enclosed" by translating with excessive literalness.

This misunderstanding of אחד is found in another instance in Lk. 20.20 where the passage runs, "And they watched him and sent forth spies, which should feign themselves just men, that they might take hold of his words (ἵνα ἐπιλάβωνται αὐτοῦ λόγου, literally, that they might seize his word) that so they might deliver him unto the authority and power of the governor." Similarly, in v. 26, "And they could not take hold of his words (literally, again, they were not able to seize his word (ut supra) before the people." In the parallel texts to this passage, Mt. 22.15 has "entangle" (παγιδεύσωσιν), Mk. 12.13 "catch" (ἀγρεύσωσιν). The last two translations express exactly what we require, and indeed in modern translations this is the meaning: in Lk. 20.20.26 "catch" NASB; RSV "take hold" but in v. 26 "catch," and so NEB for the latter verse. Arndt-Gingrich define, figuratively, "catch someone in something," although this is the only passage cited for this. It seems probable, again, that the source of the divergencies was the misapprehension of this root אחד. Lk. translated too literally "take hold" as he did ut supra, but Mt. and Mk. understood the other significations that אחד has.

One word that seemed to be a pitfall to the translators of both Lk. and Mt. is the Hebrew-Aramaic חיותא, the basic root with multifaceted meanings. Lk. 12.22 reads (with parallels in Mt. 6.25) "And he said unto his disciples, 'Therefore I say unto you, Take no thought for your life (τῇ ψυχῇ) what ye shall eat; neither for the body what ye shall put on. The life is more than meat, and the body is more than raiment'" (v. 23). With his ascetic strain, Jesus enjoins his followers to give up the satisfactions of the flesh and to trust to God's providence Mt. 6.31, Lk. 12.29 and elsewhere. The objection to "life" in v. 22 may be that when a man is concerned about what he is to eat, it is not "life" that he is thinking of. "Life" is not quite the correct translation of *psuche*. This kind of "life" has to be of a piece with and a parallel to the body, as necessary as the clothes one wears. Although in the Greek, *psuche* and *soma* are paired off well enough, "life" is not coupled pertinently with "body." While נפש as the standard retroversion of *psuche* means in this instance "seat of the appetites, particularly of hunger" (cf. Ps. 107.9 *nefesh re'eiba*, Pr. 27.7; with noun or verb *saba'* "satisfy" Is. 56.11; Je. 50.19 and see BDB for other examples), it is still not "appetite" that would be appropriate for the verse. The proper word would be the Aramaic חיותא, which like the Greek *bios* means both "life" and "living, livelihood," and so, associatively, Latin *vita* and *victus;* this חיותא was the source of mistranslation in the verse, "livelihood, *nourishment, sustenance*" instead of "life." In addition, note the wordplay in v. 23. The word is found in Syriac in the sense of "life" (Brock., p. 229; Payn. Sm., p. 140); although lacking the sense of "nourishment," which is found in Babyl. Talmud. Aramaic (Levy, *Chäl. Wört.,* I, p. 253; idem, *Neuheb. u. Chald.,* II, 42; Jast. p. 452). The same root—though with a different nominal form—with the meaning of "nourishment, victuals" *is* found in Syriac (Payn. Sm. 264; Schultess, *Lexicon,* 62). Translation will bring out the vigor, the new meaning of the verse and the wordplay on חיותא: Don't worry about your nourishment, חיותא, about what you shall eat; nor for the body what you should put on. For living (חיותא) is more than food, and the body more than clothes.

A puzzling verse that does not allow for a single explanation is Lk. 6.24. We read, "But woe unto you who are rich! For ye have received your consolation" ($\pi\alpha\rho\acute{\alpha}\kappa\lambda\eta\sigma\iota\nu$). The Greek word is difficult to retrovert, because it allows for a number of meanings (1) encouragement, exhortation (2) appeal, request (3) comfort, consolation. Compare Arndt-Gingrich, p. 623, who give exegetically the sense of our verse as "of comforting circumstances, events," etc., Acts 15.31, to which, however, Foakes Jackson and Kirsopp Lake, *Beginnings of Christianity* (IV, p. 82) offer the alternatives of "exhortation," Jerome, *consolatione,* perhaps altogether suspect in view of the following verse. It may be possible that the translation here is in the sense of Old English *"comfort,"* i.e., "consolation" Eastern Aramaic נוחמא. This Aramaic word means (1) consolation and (2) resurrection. On the basis of this, the clause might be translated, "You have had your *resurrection!*" similarly Torrey, "heaven." Still, the word does not quite fit the circumstances.

Paraklesis, the Greek word in question, perhaps would best be taken in the sense of "What one asks for, petition, request" and would correspond to the Aramaic בעותכון (cf. Burkitt, p. 276). The sense then would be, "You rich! You've gotten what you wanted." While this reading could serve competently, and perhaps we should let the matter rest there, an alternative should be considered. בעותכן as "desire, want, prayer" does not plumb the depth of the verse's pertinence. It lacks a certain spurn for the rich. Compare Lk. 16.23 where the rich man is in torments, and ibid 18.25 where the rich man can no more enter the kingdom of God than can a camel go through the eye of a needle. בעותכן could very well be a corruption of בועתכן "your joy, your delight" (see p. 56, 85), and this sense has been correctly perceived by Tey who translates "For they have had their happiness down here"! We should translate similarly, "Woe unto you who are rich! You have gotten your delights."

In Lk. 6.40 we read, "The disciple is not above his master; but everyone that is perfect ($\kappa\alpha\tau\eta\rho\tau\iota\sigma\mu\acute{e}\nu o\varsigma$, literally, having been perfected) shall be as his master." The Greek verb means basically "mend, restore, make complete," with the extended meaning in our verse "fully trained," literally, having been complete, as the perfect passive indicates, and so in classical Greek (Liddell and Scott, p. 910). The Greek form, however, shows that the translator read גמיר in the verse (cf. *gemar* in the Peshitta and the Syriac Sinaitic), as the passive participle in Aramaic. However, while passive in form גמיר may be active in meaning. גמירי "they learned," Margolis, glossary, 99; par. 58k; Levy, *Chäl. Wört.*, I, p. 146; Jast., p. 255; Kohut, II, p. 312. The meaning of the verse should be changed to "But everyone who learns may be as his teacher."

The Aramaic likewise clarifies a problem in Lk. 11.19. The charge against Jesus was, not that he was casting out devils at all, but through Beelzebub "the chief of the devils" as others had accused him (vv.15, 16). V. 19 continues, "And if I by Beelzebub cast out devils, (note שדי שידין, wordplay), by whom do your sons ($o i\ v i o i\ \dot{v}\mu\hat{\omega}\nu$) cast them out? Therefore shall they be your judges." The question arises, how do *sons* enter into the situation? And were there not some "fathers" who cast out demons as well? The existence of demons here, from OT (Deut. 32.17; Is. 34.14) to NT (Lk. 8.2; Mk. 16.9; Mt. 12.45) was not questioned. Although the popular Judean religion believed in demons and evil spirits, people constantly sought out exorcisers to expel them, and resorted to anyone who seemed to possess such capabilities. The solution to the difficulty in the text lies in the fact that the translator misread his Aramaic. The passage read in Aramaic ואין אנא בבעל דבבא שדי אנא שידיא, בניכון במנא מפקין אנתון, מטול הנא אנון נהוון לכון דיניא. "And if I through Beelzebub (really בעל דבבא the Enemy, Mt. 13.28 i.e., Satan, as discovered by others misread as בעל דבבא i.e., "Lord of Flies," see EB, I,

515[13]) cast out demons, then *among you,* how are they cast out? Consequently, those actions themselves will judge you."

First, the translator misread ביניכון "among you" as בניכון "Your sons." In this recovered reading, Jesus throws off the criticism levelled against him. "If you say I expel by Satan, then how do you cast him out? If you do cast him out, those actions themselves expose you to judgment." Second, the impersonal אנון refers to the unmentioned but implied expelling actions. For the idea that actions may judge a person compare מעשיה מוכיחין עליה "its manufacture proves what it is," (the way the bread is made evidences the type of bread it is). Ber. Rabbah 16.6 מעשי מודיעין אותי "My actions make me known" and note variant in Theodor-Albeck, I, p. 146 (cf. further Qoh. Rab. 10.14; Sifre 1.7; Yalqut Shimoni on Josh. 1.4).

The translator of Lk. also mistook the sense of the root שלם in the following verse (11.21) "When a strong man, armed, keepeth his palace, his goods are in peace" (ἐν εἰρήνῃ). The goods are in *peace*? The NEB, though free, gives the correct sense of the passage "The possessions are safe," Gdspd, NAB, Mof.[2] "undisturbed," at any rate, not as the RSV "In peace." The translator, falling back on the root meaning, considered either בשלמא, or בשלימותא as having the definition of "peace." What is required is that the "goods should be whole, unbroken, unimpaired" i.e., בשלימותא. Compare the Targ. שלימותא "fullness, integrity" and the adj. שלים (Jast., p. 1584; Brock., p. 782a; Payn. Sm., p. 582). We should translate therefore, "His possessions are intact."

Chapter 3 of Lk. contains a genealogy commencing with Jesus, and ascending, in transposed order, through David and Abraham to Adam. The last verse (38) of this reversed genealogical line reads, "Which was the son of Enos, which was the son of Seth, which was the son of Adam, which was the son of God (*Adam tou theou*)." To say that Adam was the son of God is a most astounding statement: In the first place, Adam was never called the son of God. Then, again, the idea that Adam was the son of God would conflict most disturbingly with the beliefs of the Jewish Christians who would read the book. For to them, only Jesus was the son of God. Adam was indeed thought of as a semi-divine being; God consulted angels about Adam's creation, and he was created in God's "image"; he was extremely handsome, and a divine radiance suffused his countenance. He was not, however, the son of God. The first one to use the expression "original man" or "heavenly man" was Philo, who combined ideas of Midrash, philosophy, Plato, and the Sages. The original Adam was believed to be created primordially in heaven, the second Adam, corruptible, upon earth. Paul, in this connection, did not depend upon Philo. With Philo, the original man is an idea, with Paul it is the personality of Jesus. Philo identifies Adam as the original man; Paul regards the original man as the second Adam (main passage; 1 Cor. 15.45—50). Influences from Alexandrinian circles of course must not be ruled out. (See L. Ginzberg, art. "Adam Kadmon," JE, I, p. 182.) In short, in NT, Adam is *contrasted* with Christ (compare ERE I, 86).

It is furthermore doubtful fantasy to assert that Luke added the words "Adam son of God" (Torrey) or to believe, as does Plummer, that it was inserted by Luke for Gentile readers to show the divine common origin of all mankind by declaring that Adam was the son of God. This simply would be contraindicated by the "Adam" in Genesis which states that God created Adam. Montefiore's explanation that the whole idea of the sonship of God was in Lk.'s time in a state of flux is unsupported.

The usual formulation to describe the step-by-step father and son lineal descent is given in the Bible as A. son of B. son of C. Later variations are sons of A; B. his son, C. his son. D. his son, etc. (1 Chron. c.5,6,7, et passim). In the passage of Lk., the Greek translator did not understand his text again. The Aramaic was probably ברא לאלהא, the latter a passive participle with the dative of agent (see Payn. Sm., p. 55 for the form) which should be translated "Adam created by God". The translator, after translating "son of" in the previous verses some seventy-two times, lapsed when he came to the very last one. He confused of course ברא "son" with ברא "was created." Alternatively, the forms may have been בריה דאלהא (Jast., p. 193 "creature, creation of God") misread as בריה דאלהא "son of God."

In the following exposition, Aramaic too offers a confirmatory reading of what the original may have intended. In Lk. 12.25 (and comp. parallel Mt. 6.27) the text reads, "And which of you by taking thought ($\mu\epsilon\rho\iota\mu\nu\hat{\omega}\nu$ more literally means 'being anxious') can add to his stature ($\dot{\eta}\lambda\iota\kappa\iota\alpha\nu$) one cubit ($\pi\hat{\eta}\chi\upsilon\nu$)?" The objections raised by Plummer (*Luke*, p. 326) are quite pertinent. People are not "anxious" to add to their height, to say nothing of the monstrosity of adding a cubit (by definition, from the length of the elbow to the tip of the third finger). One must take the view that *helikia* must mean "age"(Heb. 9.11; Jn. 9.21.23) and not "stature" (19.3), and that *pechus* means "span," as one would say "span of life." (Compare "Weights and Measures" in J. Hastings, *Dictionary of the Bible*, p. 909b and followed by Arndt-Gingrich, p. 662, Gdspd. "add a single hour to his life," NAB: "a moment to his life span" perhaps a bit free.) RSV however, keeps to "add a cubit to his span of life" with a footnote, "or to his stature"; NEB "add a foot to his height" with a note "a day to his life" as an alternate reading; Mof.¹ "an ell to his stature; Mof.² "an ell to his height."

With this *crux criticorum* in mind, the Aramaic may serve to show how the difficulty arose, and what the original reading was, although, as above, some students of the text have guessed at the partial solution. With some variable verbal forms, the Aramaic probably ran: מן הוא מנכון כד יצף משכח למוספו/לאוספו על קומתא קומא. The translation, in the light of discussion, will be given below. קומתא is the problem word, and its root is seemingly mentioned twice in the verse, and hence led to a confusion on the part of the translator. As the text stands, there are two meanings, and the words are homonyms, with an evident wordplay as well, with two different lexicographical listings. The first (masculine) has the meaning of "rising, standing," but also "a measure, about a fathom, the width of the outstretched arms," Payn. Sm., p. 495, employed for *orguia* Acts 27.28 (there used for "fathom"); in our verse *pechus* is "cubit," Peshitta אמתא.

The second קומא (feminine!) is employed for *helikia* in the sense of "age," Jn. 9.21, specifically for a man's age. This second קומא has likewise the sense of "a measure of height," but also "time of life." Thus, the three קומתא דסבא, דעלימא, דטליא are "Times of boyhood, of youth, of old age"; קומתא משמליתא refers to "fullgrowth" i.e., age of 25 years, Payn. Sm. p. 274. The translator made a mistake on two counts. The feminine קומא, "age," he understood as a feminine form well enough, but he mistranslated it as "stature" (Brock., p. 653; Payn. Sm., p. 495), when he should have taken it as "age, time." The other קומא which he erroneously translated as if it were masculine "ell, cubit," he should have rendered as a feminine with the same sense of "age." The translation, with the characteristic wordplay, would shape up as, "Can you, by worrying, add on time to your age?"

There is one passage that one commentator at least has had difficulty with, and for which, the Aramaic seems to fingerpost the proper solution. "Fear not, little flock (τὸ μικρὸν ποίμνιον)," the text in Lk. 12.32 reads, "for it is your Father's pleasure to give you the kingdom." The expression "little flock" is unparalleled in NT, and is out of place and out of time. For the construction of the Greek nominative in place of the vocative, see Blass-Debrunner-Funk, par. 147, where they state "The arthrous Semitic vocative is being reproduced by the Greek nominative with the article." V. 32 is not found as a parallel in Mt. A. Loisy (*Les Évangilles Synoptiques*, I, p. 620, [1907]), has argued that "The little flock that had riches to distribute to the poor is not the small group of poor persons (*le groupe très peu fortuné*) who accompanied Jesus in his ministry, but the later Jewish community before whom the redactor puts forward his ideal of renouncement" (cited from C. G. Montefiore, *The Synoptic Gospels*, II, p. 956). Loisy evidently considered the passage as anachronistic; codex Bezae omits 32. The fact is however that Lk. may very well have found this verse in his Aramaic source. It bears evidence of mistranslation.

The tenor of the whole discourse may be summed up in the words of the passage, "And seek ye not what ye shall eat, nor what ye shall drink (v.29); sell what ye have and give alms. ... " This is a stern demand, and Peter is troubled by it, "Then Peter said unto him, 'Lord, speaketh thou this parable unto us, or even to all,'" (v. 41) meaning "Do we share this burden alone, or will this demand be shared by all?" To give away one's wealth and property would be a formidable prospect and a serious sacrifice.

The inappropriate expression "little flock" at this early stage is actually based upon a mistranslation, "Fear not this slight decree." The Aramaic probably read גזרא קליל, the adjective employed need not be determined according to frequent usage, and so the translator misunderstood it as an adjective instead of an adverb. The noun he assumed to mean "flock." (For this meaning, cf. Brock., p. 112; Jast., p. 232; Payn. Sm., p. 68 and the lexical equation here in the Syriac of p s c.) The actual admonishment of Jesus is of a different sort—Jesus exhorts his followers that giving up possessions and property is but "little" to dread as against the rewarding prospect of coming into the kingdom of God. גזרא was mistaken as "flock"; it should have been translated as "decree." (Cf. op. cit. of Brock., Payn. Sm.; Jast. ut supra.) We should render, "Fear little this decree, for your Father has chosen (= רעי see p. 56) you to give you the kingdom." Note, in the next verse, the play upon גזרא and גזא דלא "treasure that does not fail in heaven."

A complicated passage, partially discussed in another connection (p. 47), has a difficulty unique to Lk., which is cleared up if the Aramaic be resorted to. Lk. 12.58 reads, "When thou goest with thine adversary (בעל דינך "your opponent in the law") to the magistrate in the way (mistranslation for הלכתא "a court ruling, see p. 47) give diligence (δὸs ἐργασίαν, supposedly meaning "give pains, make an effort") that thou mayest be delivered from him, lest he drag (κατασύρῃ literally, take by force, more intensive than *suro*) thee to the judge, and the judge deliver thee to the officer, and the officer cast thee into prison." *ergasia* basically means "work, business" (s *'abda*), then "practice, profit, gain"; Liddell and Scott think of a Latinism *"da operam ut ... "* for this passage, as does Plummer; Arndt-

Gingrich "Give pains that ... ," similarly Rh, "take pains." It must be confessed however, that "give pains" remains somewhat peculiar and extravagant in the context. What now has the Aramaic to offer by way of solution? Retroversion secures for us תגרותא "merchandise, barter, trade, business" employed as a rendering for *emporia* in Mt. 22.5 in the Syriac of s p c; for *emporion* Jn. 2.16 s, and in the verb for the synonymous *pragmateuomai* Lk. 19.13 p; and *diapragmateuomai* Lk. 19.15 p s c. *ergasia* is employed in the LXX for *mela'ka, po'al, ma'ase*, etc. It appears that the Greek translator misread his text on three counts:

    1. He should have read תגרתא "quarrel, complaint, law case," Yeb. 100a "I used to decide the men's case (תיגרא) first, now I decide the women's case first"; and in the "Targ." to Prov. 15.18; 26.20.

    2. He misvocalized תגרותא "business," whence his *ergasia* "business," instead of תגרתא.

    3. He misunderstood the Lamed as a sign of the accusative instead of its prepositional function. The locution means "give in to the complaint, yield to the quarrel." Intuitively the Syriac hit almost on the required meaning: Hab tagrutha "give terms" (Jennings, p. 233) is the sense to be given to the locution. This would seem to be in keeping with the tenor and sense of Mt. 5.25 "Make friends quickly with your accuser."

The second part of this verse likewise contains a problematic word. There is first of all, the question as to why you should be *dragged* before the judge? If you are meeting your opponent at law for a legal decision (not "in the way," this has been discussed above, p. 47), since the case is not yet decided, why are you taken by force before the judge? This is what the verse reads, "... lest he drag you (*katasure*) to the judge." Some Mss. smooth over the difficulty by reading "condemn you," D, it. syr. s c (Nestle). This would be satisfactory except that the Mss. are in a minority, and for the support of the reading the Mss. cited are late; moreover, the reading "condemn" looks like an intentional correction of "drag." Peshitta's "bring" is free. The reading of Syriac Ph נגד, however, is most suggestive, and supplies creditably the original reading. The equation of *katasuro/ngd* is found elsewhere in the simplex *suro/ngd* in Jn. 21.8. While the word means "conduct, drag," the Aramaic word frequently but not exclusively, cf. Targ. Cant. 7.5 ולמנגד מן די יתחייב בדינא לנגדא, has the meaning of "flog, beat with stripes, cudgel," Payn. Sm., p. 327. The Aramaic in all likelihood ran למא ינגד לך לדינא "Lest one flog you to torture you." Flogging a suspect was a common procedure of the Roman courts (in the colonies). (Compare Saul Lieberman, "Roman

Legal Institutions in Early Rabbinics and in the Acta Martyrum," *JQR*, 1944, 35, pp. 12, 14.) "The suspending and torturing was performed publicly, in front of the *bema* of the judge." See further, ibid, p. 15, n. 97: "The Hebrew *din* often means 'to torture.'" See Tos. San. XII, 434[18]; Ber. Rabb, XI[5], ed. Theodor-Albeck, p. 943; similarly, in the Talmud of Palestine, Ber. II 5c נסביה ודניה ואודי is to be translated, "He had him seized, tortured him, and (then) he confessed." (All the above by Prof. Lieberman.) In the light of this information, it now appears that the translator read לְדִינָא for לְדַיָּנָא. He misread proleptically in the light of the succeeding readings of "judge" which have their legitimate place. We should now translate the whole passage, "When thou goest with thine opponent-at-law to the magistrate for a legal ruling (ut supra, p. 47, 113), give into the complaint lest you be flogged for torture, and the judge deliver thee to the officer, and the officer throw you into prison." The step-by-step procedure in the reconstructed passage makes for a harmonious concord in all the parts.

In the episode reported in Lk. 14, a man has prepared a great supper, and his friends sought excuses not to come. The man then sent his servant to invite persons from "the streets and lanes of the city" (v. 21), and still the party hall was not filled. The servant was sent again to invite still others, and the passage states that the master instructed the servant to go out "into the highways and hedges (φραγμούς) and to compel them to come in, that my house may be filled." A peculiarity of this verse is that the servant is to seek out persons from *hedges* which does not couple well with "highways." As in English, we would expect "highways and by-ways," not "hedges." It is far-fetched to explain that one would seek vagabonds among the hedges, who were supposedly accustomed to live there (Arndt-Gingrich). In Aramaic the retroversion would be סיגא *seyaga* (compare the equation of *seyaga/phragmos* in Mt. 21.33; Mk. 12.1 and the present passage in p s c). What most likely took place was that סגיא, *sugya,* (root *segi* "walk") "a walk, path" was confused or misread as *seyaga* "hedge." *Sugya* is Babylonian Talmudic Aramaic, and these words, *seyaga* and *sugya* could easily have been confused (see Jast., pp. 961 and 978 for further evidences of confusions in MSS). Translate, "among the roads and walks."

In another parable, as is reported in Lk. 16, a householder demanded an accounting from his steward, as it was bruited about that the steward was mismanaging the owner's affairs. The steward was in danger of being deposed. To conceal his fraud, the steward called in his owner's debtors, and "Said unto the first, How much owest thou unto my lord?" V. 6 continues,

"And he said, 'An hundred measures of oil." And he said unto him, 'Take thy bill, and sit down quickly, and write fifty.'" The Greek reads καθίσας ταχέως γράψον πεντήκοντα, literally, sitting quickly write fifty. While it is of minor importance how *tacheos* should be taken syntactically, whether fore or aft, there is a shortfall in the story, in that the steward does not explain how or why, however willing the debtor be to reduce by a wide margin his indebtedness, that he should write in his own hand without surprise this kind of fraudulent reduction so benefitting him. The Aramaic elucidates matters. It read כד יתב סב כתביך בפריע כתוב חמשין which we may translate, "Take your papers (so Greek) and sit; in *discharge of the debt* write fifty." The translator misunderstood the syntax; he misunderstood (confusing roots) בפריע as "quickly" (cf. Dalman, *Aram.-Neuheb. Wörterb.*, pp. 333, 336) instead of the pregnant construction בפריע "payment of debt" = פורענא דחובא, used absolutely (Payn. Sm., p. 439; Brock., p. 603 med. pag.; Levy, *Neuheb. u. Chal. Wört.*, IV, p. 130 and note פריעא, Jast., p. 1235 et seq). Although בפריע "quickly" is absent in Syriac, however, in the Syriac Palestinian dialect and Samaritan, Schultess, *Lexicon*, p. 163 it is found. According to the restored Aramaic reading, the steward falsified the papers with the connivance of the debtors. The deceitful character of the steward was intimated at the beginning of the parable. The master "commended the unjust steward because he had done wisely" (v. 8); actually, the master was distracted from his original suspicion, gulled by seeing the paid bills in front of him.

A noteworthy mistranslation, too, is found in Lk. 17.12 which reads, "And as he entered into a certain village, there met him ten men that were lepers, which stood far off (πόρρωθεν)." Since Jesus talked with them (v. 14), they could not have been quite so far off. The underlying Aramaic ran מרחקין "unclean," as the translator thought it to be as if רחיקין "from afar." רחק is the Pa'el means "make unclean." Compare its usage for תעב, נדה, גאל, פגל, מאס in the Targs. (Levy, *Chal. Wört.*, II, pp. 418–419a). The further proof that "unclean" is to be assumed in the verse is evidenced in v. 14, "As they went they were *cleansed*." Incidentally, the Aramaic in v. 12 probably ran דקמו רחיקין where idiomatically קם loses much of its meaning as "stand" and simply means "were" (Jast., p. 1331), much in the same usage as the Talmudic and Mandaic קאי, an auxiliary verb, almost otiose.

In the story of the Prodigal Son (Lk. 15) there is a charge made by the older brother, as a reproach to his father, when the younger brother returned, "As soon as this thy son was come, which hath devoured thy living with harlots (μετὰ πορνῶν) thou hast killed for him the fatted calf" (v. 30).

Now the older brother, in coming from the field, as it is described, had not yet met up with the younger brother, so a question arises, how did he know that the younger brother had spent the family patrimony "with harlots"? True, according to v. 13, the young man had gone through the money "with riotous living," literally, living in a prodigal fashion, *zon asotos* = כד חיא בזלילותא (*asotia/zollel* Prov. 28.7). The solution to the contradiction between vv.13 and 30 is to be found in the substrate Aramaic בזלילותא which means "with luxury, prodigality" in keeping with the sense of v. 13. The Greek translator unfortunately had his mind elsewhere and saw or misread בזלילתא—fem., pl., emph.—as "loose women" (Payn. Sm., p. 116; Brock., p. 197, *meretrix*, vb. Pa'el *ad lasciviam induxit*.) Compare semantically Latin *ganeo* "glutton" and *ganea* "brothel." Both passages, vv. 13 and v. 30, should be translated [living] "in an expensive style." Interesting in an associative semantic development is the word טעיתא, pl., which means both "wild, wayward actions" and collaterally "harlots" (Babl. Talm. Aramaic, Jast., pp. 542, 543).

The extraordinary difficulty in Lk. 21.5, if resort be made to the substrate Aramaic, is again easily elucidated. The text reads in substance, "And some spoke of the temple, how it was adorned with goodly stones and gifts" (λίθοις καλοῖς καὶ ἀναθήμασιν). The peculiarity of the phrase lies in the fact that "beautiful stones, and gifts" are coupled incongruously. Then in the next verse, Jesus, while ominously forecasting that "there should not be left one stone upon another," makes no mention of the "gifts." Torrey proposed קורבנין/רברבין. The parallel in Mk. 13.1 is too loose and aberrant to be of help. It is clear that a phrase such as "beautiful and large stones"—the stones used in building of the Temple were enormous (Plummer, p. 477)—would be an appropriate reading. The Aramaic probably read: כיפתא שפירתא ואיקרתא. The translator was quite aware of the gifts that pagan rulers would send to the Temple (2 Macc. 3.2–7; Jos. B.J. v.5.4 and the "gifts of kings" mentioned in the Mishna Ned. 2.5, and so he rendered איקרתא with its Aramaic meaning of "gifts," and the Aramaic word has that meaning, Payn. Sm., p. 14; Brock., pp. 307, 308a; Jennings, p. 20). However, he should have translated with its other meaning that יקר has, viz. "heavy." Translate, "Adorned with beautiful and heavy stones." This certainly makes for the appropriate sense.

After Jesus admonished his followers not to falter, though they be reviled and betrayed by kith and kin, he continues in Lk. 21.19, "In your patience, possess ye your souls," ἐν τῇ ὑπομενῇ ὑμῶν κτήσεσθε τὰς ψυχὰς ὑμῶν, literally, "in your endurance you will acquire your souls." The verse is complicated by a number of definitions and interpretations. *hupomene* may mean "endurance" of suffering (Plummer, p. 480; Arndt-Gingrich, p. 854 the same). Latin Mss. differ with (1) *patientia* (2) *tolerantia* (3) *sufferentia*. Then again *ktesesthe* may mean (1) *possedebitis* (Vulgate) or with other Latin texts *adquiretis*. The modern translations on the whole take *hupomene* to be "endurance," so Rhm, Knox, RSV; "By standing firm, "NEB; "Hold out stedfast," Mof.² *psuchas* is rendered by "lives," Rhm, RSV, NEB ("true life"), but "souls" by Mof.¹ and Knox. The NAB translates, "By pertinent endurance you will save your lives." While *hupomene*, as well as the verb has, in the main, the meaning of endurance, we may note that in the LXX *hupomene* is mostly rendered as a translation for "hope, expectation," Hebrew תקוה, and mostly for the form קוה (twenty-six times), יחל (seven times) חכה (forty-four times) but not once for "endure." "Endurance" is Stoic, "hope" is Gospel. Perhaps the terms that should have been used here should have been *elpizo* and *elpis*, "hope." (Compare Acts 2.26; 24.15; Romans 4.18; 8.24 "We are saved by hope" and v. 25, I Cor. 13.7 and of course in OT Ps. 27.14 and elsewhere.) The Aramaic word in our Lk. passage was בסברתא which has both the meaning of "hope" and "endurance," and it is the former that is to be preferred. Note also the *talḥin* or implied overtone of "gospel," a meaning which סברתא also has.

Moreover, since *ktesesthe* is the future indicative (but really imperative), and hence the lexical equivalent of תקנון, it is on the doubtful side whether "Possess/acquire your souls" is the correct reading. We should read with different vocalization תקנו, imp. of תקן "prepare." The Aramaic, in short, ran בסברתא תקנו לנפשכון and we should translate, "Prepare your lives in hope," i.e., order your lives with hope, very much like Romans 8.24 (in the Syriac בסברא הו חיין) "We are saved by hope." See further the remarks on "Those who hope to the end will be saved," p. 35, 161. (In the similar passages of Mk. 13.13 and Mt. 10.22; 24.13 the translation should be "He who hopes to the end will be saved.") The reconstruction of the Lk. passage, however, shows that it is independent of the Mk. and Mt. texts.

We may notice another misapprehension of the underlying Aramaic text in Lk. 8.18 where the text reads, "Take heed therefore (βλέπετε) how ye hear." The word *blepein* means "see," or more accurately "look at with attention," corresponding in the LXX to הביט for the most part (Hatch-Redpath) and the translation of this should literally be "See what you hear." Mof¹, RSV, and NAB translate "Take heed"; Mof.² and Gdspd. "Take care" which are nearer to the mark as far as the interpretation of the Greek may go. The Aramaic probably had אדיק which means to "look at with

THE EVIDENCE FROM LUKE

attention" (Jast., p. 287) and also "be exact, be careful" and compare its use in the Peshitta הביטו Lam. 4.16. It is obvious that the translator mistakenly rendered with "look" instead of "be careful." A good translation of the verse would then be, borrowing from Mof[2] and Gdspd., "Be careful how you listen," or "Attend to what you hear," it being understood that our translation ascends to a misunderstanding of the Aramaic (compare Levy, *Chal. Wört.*, p. 173; Jast. ibid). חר in Syriac likewise is a good synonymous alternative. Note how *blepein* and compounds are translated by חר in Jn. 13.22; Mt. 14.19; Lk. 9.16, Mk. 6.41 and frequently. But חר is so specifically Syriac that I prefer דק, as it is common to Syriac, Jewish Aramaic, Babylonian Talmudic Aramaic and Christian-Palestinian Aramaic (Brock., p. 146; T. Nöldeke, *Mand. Gramm.*, p. 251. *Theoreo*, a good synonym of *blepo*, is used by the Peshitta for דק, Jn. 20.12, p s and Mk. 12.41).

There also seems to have been a misapprehension of the underlying Aramaic text at Lk. 22.44 which runs, "And being in an agony, he prayed more earnestly, and his sweat was, as it were, great drops of blood (ὡσεὶ θρόμβοι αἵματος) falling down to the ground." This verse, as well as the preceding v. 42, do not find universal support in the Mss. Some omit, others transpose after Mt. 26.39. However, a goodly number include the verses, see the apparatus in UBS for the listing of the details. Syr. s retains; Syr. c omits. Plummer, *Luke,* p. 509 regards them as authentic, even if not in place in the Lk. narrative. Gdspd. does not translate the verses altogether; Mof.[1] puts them in parentheses; Mof.[2] translates without comment. NEB translates with a footnote "some witnesses omit." In his ILNT,[3] p. 275, Moffatt regards the verses as a legendary insertion "... probably a non-Lucan fragment of genuine tradition which has floated in to this section of the gospel...." Harnack defends the passage as original, Mof. ibid, p. 225, n.

Whether the passage be genuine or not, it existed already in the underlying Aramaic. There is a question of the sweat being like "drops of blood," which Plummer (*Luke,* p. 510) explains "the drops of sweat *in some way* (italics ours) resembled drops of blood." The translator, however, misread his Aramaic text, being in empathy with the tragic event to follow. While it can be understood that in the heat of the day or under great emotional stress, one may perspire so heavily as to drip the perspiration on to the ground, still, there will be no blood. Now the original Aramaic ran דועתה איך נוטפתא דמיא "His sweat was like drops of *water* falling to the ground." The translator, his emotions welling up within him, saw or thought he saw דמיא as if it were (ד)דמא, "of blood." Unconsciously, he may have dramatized in anticipation of the impending tragic sequel.

In this category of mistranslation, the text at Lk. 6.1 may prove interesting. The passage reads, "And it came to pass on the second Sabbath after the first (ἐν σαββάτῳ δευτεροπρώτῳ) that he went through the cornfields; and his disciples plucked the ears of corn, and did eat, rubbing them in their hands." The Greek *deuteroproto* "second after the first" has been a puzzle for centuries. Jerome did not know what it meant. The evidence is divided, with its retention in *most* of the uncials and cursives, omitted by *Aleph*, B, L, and a half dozen other good cursives. Its very persistence despite obscurity and its uniqueness argues for its genuineness (Scrivener, Tischendorf). Other Mss. divide the word *deutero proto,* others *deutero proton;* see the apparatus in UBS. No Sabbath, however, is known by this name. Arndt-Gingrich (p. 176) quote Epiphanius who defined *deuteroproton* as *deuteron sabb. meta to proton* "the second Sabbath after the first." Here again the underlying Aramaic would make an enlightening contribution. The Aramaic ran originally, והוא ביומא דשבתא דתנינא מדרישא. The translation would be, "And it was on the second Sabbath, *again*, that he went through the cornfields...." The translator construed his text to make a pause after בשבתא; דתנינא he took as construed with מדרישא, with the sense of "second of the first," for which he combined or manufactured the *deuteroproton* of the Greek text. Actually דתנינא modifies יומא דשבתא "the second Sabbath day"; מדרישא means "again." See Payn. Sm., p. 540, Brock., p. 728; and comp. for this error elsewhere, Zimmermann, *Biblical Books*, p. 89 and see p. 42 in this volume. The "second Sabbath" is "the next Sabbath" as Knox renders. One question that springs to mind is, what is the first Sabbath that is implied here? One may advance the explanation that if we follow the material as paralleled in Synoptic Gospels, Mk. 1.21—28, Lk. 4.31, in Mt. in 7.28f., the Sabbath would be that one wherein there was the first challenge to Jesus' individual way to cure people. The charge against him was his disavowal of precedent, "What is this teaching?" See the discussion on this verse on p. 105, 106. He did not invoke the mercy of God, nor offer any prayers, but effected the miraculous cure on his own authority (Lk. 4.36), a challenge to *dogma*. The next challenge to *authority* would be the plucking of the ears of wheat on the Sabbath, a violation of the Halakhah as in the present passage. This apparently was the first public transgression of the Law. There is the additional possibility that since there are four episodes of healing on the Sabbath day—a violation mentioned in Lk. 6.6; 13.10f. 14.3—one of these episodes did not find its right place, in that the occurrence of 6.6 should be placed before 6.1, and this would further resolve the problem of "On the second Sabbath again..." i.e., dealing with another instance of healing on the Sabbath. The Aramaic, then serves as a good explanation of the puzzling *deuteroproton,* and restores the reasonable sequence of the Sabbaths.

Several Aramaic locutions found in the text of Lk. 21.29—30, also presents a number of mistranslations. The verse reads, "And he spoke to them a parable, 'Behold the fig tree, and all the trees (ἴδετε τὴν συκῆν καὶ πάντα τὰ δένδρα); when they now shoot forth (προβάλωσιν), ye see and know of your own selves (βλέποντες) that summer is now nigh at hand.'" The expression "see the fig tree and all the trees" is awkward. Apparently Luke as the Greek translator apparently considered the Aramaic אתבין, Hebrew התבונן, as a simple "look at," Dan. 8.5, whereas he should have translated it "discern, distinguish." Cf. the basic בין "between"; Levy, *Chald. Wört.,* I, p. 93; Payn. Sm., p. 38. It is quite possible, too, that the ordinary Aramaic *haza* "see" has the sense of "distinguish." Compare the Hebrew *ra'ah* BDB, p. 907e and Mal. 3.18; and Payn. Sm., p. 136 for *haza* "perceive, consider, notice." While the Greek *oida* means more than "see," secondarily "know," it does not seem to have the meaning required here. The Hebrew-Aramaic root is found in Ps., Prov. Job, with the sense of "look at, distinguish, consider." Moreover, תאינתא was mistakenly read as a singular instead of a plural, as the consonants were the same, and this plural reading would make for greater consistency in the verse. Furthermore, the following verse with the plural "When they burst (into leaf)" shows clearly that "fig trees"— plural—was intended. Translate: "See the difference between the fig trees and all other trees."

Commentators (Plummer a.l.) have difficulty with *prosbalosin* as it is without an accusative, and to relieve the difficulty, we are advised to supply "leaves," and see parallels in Mt. 24.32 and Mk. 13.28. The Aramaic, however, in the 'Aph'el (Hebrew Hiph'il, idem) may be stative, describing a condition, and hence not necessarily taking a direct object. The Aramaic probably was מא דמפריעין or כד מפריעין "When they blossom forth." Cf. the Peshitta rendition here. The Greek translator renders literally the Aramaic in front of him and therefore failed to put in "leaves," required by the sense.

There are a number of passages that require a closer and more detailed examination. The first reads (Lk. 22.25), "And he said unto them, 'The kings of the Gentiles exercise lordship over them, and they that exercise authority upon them (ἐξουσιάζοντες αὐτῶν), are called benefactors'" (εὐεργέται), literally, doers of good. The passage contains the following difficulties: If the kings of the Gentiles exercise lordship, then "over them" in the passage refers syntactically to the preceding Gentile peoples; consequently, "they that exercise authority upon them" in the sequence is puzzling and incomprehensible, and at the best, making for dubious sense. The parallel passages, Mt. 20.25; Mk. 10.42 "And they that are great exercise authority upon them," do not clarify except that the "kings" and the "great" exercise authority. The use of "benefactors" in Lk. seems to be a surplusage. The underlying Aramaic in Lk. pertinently clears up the difficulties—it ran: מלכי עממיא שלטין עליהון, ושליטיא דשלטין עליהון מתקרין עבדין טבין. The translation would read, "The kings of the Gentiles rule over them, and the governors that rule with them (literally, at their side i.e., at the side of the kings) are called 'good ministers' (literally, servants)." However,

    a. The translator of the Aramaic rendered too literally. The translation of שליטיא in contrast to the "kings" is "governors," not those "who exercise authority."

    b. עליהון was misinterpreted "on them" instead of "beside them," a well-known use. (Compare BDB, p. 755, second column.)

    c. The translator missed his cue at עבדין טבין. He saw or thought he read עבדין טבון "doers of good, those who do benefices," Targ. Ps. 14.2; Ex. 34.6 (Onq.); Es. Targ. II, 8.13, whereas he should have read עבדין טבין "good ministers." טבין and טבון are frequently confused with each other in the Targums. Cf. Sperber's edition, vol. I, 303, apparatus. The noun 'abda does not mean "slave, servant" in this connection but those who are in service with the king, his ministers, courtiers, even chiefs of the military. Compare with the familiar עבדי דוד, עבדי שלמה who are commanders, nobles and princes in their own right.

The whole meaning of the passage now is in full contrast to the verse that follows. Gentile rulers have the great men, the princes and ministers, rule with them, but this is not the case with the disciples as the following verse demonstrates. "But ye shall not be so; but he that is greatest among you, let him be as the younger (זעירא is mistranslated; read 'least'); and he that is chief, as he doth serve."

Another text requiring closer examination deals with the interpretation of "baptism" and its original significance. Reference has been made to Mk. 10.38f. (p. 92). It is to be noted, however, that because of the different psychological situation and the frame of circumstances in the narrative of Mk., the verb in question was עמד, "plunge," which the context internally demands. In the present parallel text of Lk. 12.49—50 the verb is טבל. The passage reads, "I have come to send fire on the earth; what will I, if it be already kindled! But I have a baptism to be baptized with (*baptisma de echei baptisthenai*); and how I am straitened till it be accomplished!" The conclu-

THE EVIDENCE FROM LUKE 123

sion of the first verse should be translated on the basis of Aramaic, "How I wish it were already kindled!" and so Torrey, *Our Translated Gospels,* and his justification for this rendering in note p. 36. The second verse "a baptism to be baptized with" is incomprehensible *in this context.* Then again, if it is an ordeal that he must undergo, why is it a "baptism"? And why is he distressed "until it be accomplished"? Tangentially, Jn. 4.2 asserts that Jesus did not baptize. Moreover, in the verse, the locution "be baptized *with*" is puzzling.

In the circumstances described in Lk., *baptizein* is Greek for the Aramaic טבל. The latter bears the usual meaning of "immerse, dip," as in a liquid such as water, or in the blood as in the sacrificial cult (Lev. 4.9; 9.9). In Judaism there is no immersion for the washing away of sins (contrast Acts 22.16 and elsewhere in NT), nor for the repentance of sin. Immersion is largely for a cleansing of the body (i.e., because of contamination by a dead body, or *pollutio noctis*), and not for the repentance of sins, as Josephus expressly states (Ant. 18.5.2) "For the washing would be acceptable to him, if they made use of it, not in order to the putting away of some sins, but for the purification of the body" (note that this is said as if in a side reflection on John's teaching). Immersion is required, too, for vessels, pots, etc. to remove anything of defilement and to qualify them for use. (The author of article "Baptism" in Hastings' *Dictionary of the Apostolic Church* has peculiar notions about Jews "sprinkling" themselves before eating, and washing themselves before "breakfast" 129a).

By extended and associative meaning טבל has also the sense of "cleaning, purifying." Thus the name טבליהו "God has dipped, purified," BDB, p. 371, and quite relevant to our passage טבל בנורא—"purifying by fire"—is regarded in the talmudic discussion (Sanh. 39a) as more effective than immersion in water. אדרבה עיקר טבילותא בנורא הוא, "On the contrary, real cleansing is in fire," and on the same page "Wherewith did he purify (טבל) himself (after contact with a dead body)?" Answer, בנורא טביל "He did it by means of fire." Incidentally, this is the point of John's remark, that while he has purified the people by means of water (Mt. 3.11), the one coming after him will *cleanse* ("baptize") with *fire* thus with a truer, greater cleansing process. טבל then is the correct Aramaic retroverted word for our passage in Lk.

Accordingly our section should bear the rendering, "I came to send fire on the land (ארעא the land of Palestine, not "earth"), and how I wish it were already kindled! I have a *cleansing* to do, and how impatient am I till it be completed!" The Aramaic read טבילותא לאטבלא. The translator should have read the word as aph'el (a common formation for טבל, Jast., p. 517) and not the Itpe'el apocopated reflexive, making for the peculiar "be baptized *with*." Translate "I have a cleansing to make."

The evidence of an underlying Aramaic document not only manifests itself through mistranslations and miscomprehensions of shades of meaning, but likewise through plays on words, through *talḥin,* through overtones that the word conveys, through implications of meaning beyond the word(s) in the text. (See R. Gordis, *Book of God and Man,* pp. 167, 196, 347; Zimmermann, *Biblical Books,* p. 62). Further evidence of the underlying Aramaic is found in alliterations and in locutions peculiar in Greek, but whose natural idiom is Aramaic. These phenomena are again supportive of the underlying thesis of this book that the Greek we possess rests on a written Aramaic document, specifically, in our present considerations in Lk. Some examples follow.

In Lk. 4.1 (and parallels) "[Jesus] was led by the Spirit in the desert" represents the Aramaic אדבר ברוחא במדברא, wordplay.

In Lk. 4.3, where the first temptation occurs "Command this stone that it be made bread," a paronomasia occurs in כיפתא ... ריפתא, "stone" and "bread," cited before; the Aramaic words being Babylonian Talmudic Aramaic, Jast., pp. 634, 1476.

In Lk. 5.3, "And he sat down, and *taught* the people out of the *ship*" forms a wordplay אילפא and אלף.

Lk. 7.12, "Now when he came nigh to the gate of the city, behold there was a dead man carried out, the only son of his mother ..." There are three wordplays "city," מתא, (Eastern Aramaic, Babylonian Talmudic, Payn. Sm., p. 311 in the plural for Syriac usage, Jast., p. 859) and מייתין מיתא "bringing along a dead man." Compare v. 14 "and they that bare him, stood still." See p. 51 re שבוק למיתיא למיתיא.

Lk. 8.8, "He who has ears to hear, let him hear." There is a wordplay on למשמע ... ישמע, similarly Lk. 14.35. The second word however does not mean "hear." It means "understand," as in "an understanding heart," 1 Kgs 3.9; Zech. 7.12.

Lk. 10.20, "Your names are written (literally, enrolled) in heaven," שמהתכון רשימין בשמיא, a collocation of *shin,* and *mem.*

Lk. 11.5, "Friend ..., lend me three loaves ..." alliterative רחמי ... לחמין. For the plural of *leḥem,* compare Y. Ḥag. III, p. 79d. The words, aside from the interchange of *l m n r* vocables, were assonant as well.

Noteworthy is Lk. 11.11 (the parallel passages have been dealt with earlier, p. 78) which deviates from Mt. 7.9f.; however, in going its own way

THE EVIDENCE FROM LUKE 125

with additions, the Lucan passage shows with the accretions an underlying Aramaic text. Aside from עקרב . . . אקרב, תנינא . . . נונא, בעא . . . ביעא, note also the play on "father" and "stone" אבא . . . אבנא, a slighter one in ברא . . . כיפתא.

Lk. 11.42 *"Pass over judgment* and the love of God (on this see p. 28). . . . these ought ye to *have done,"* obviously an alliterative play on עברין . . . עבדין.

Lk. 12.21 "layeth up treasure" is the alliteration of סאם לה סימתא.

In Lk. 12.46, we have phenomena which may be interpreted in a number of ways. The text reads, "The lord of that servant will come in a day, that he looketh not for him, and at an hour that he is not aware, and will cut him in sunder, and will appoint his portion with the unbelievers" (μετὰ τῶν ἀπίστων θήσει). While the whole section, v. 42f., is patently a *mashal,* it seems strange nevertheless that the wicked servant is deposed, and he and his "portion" are to be cast with "unbelievers." That such is the fate of the wicked would be the obvious deduction. "Unbelievers," however, steps out of character with the rest of the parable. The Aramaic probably ran דלא מהימנין which the translator thought to be the usual "unbelievers." He should have conveyed the thought that he and his destiny will be cast and deposed with the non-stewards i.e., with the other slaves or, with a different interpretation "with those not to be trusted." Most likely, however, we have a *talḥin* here, with the conventional translation reversed: the rendering should be "non-stewards" with the overtone of meaning "unbeliever." For הימנותא, meaning both "faith" and "stewardship," Payn. Sm., p. 103 ("office"), מהימן "eunuch," ibid., p. 255; Brock., p. 175. The word is mistranslated with some frequency, see below p. 158, 161, and Zimmermann, *Biblical Books,* p. 111.

Lk. 16.3, "My lord taketh away from me the stewardship; I cannot dig; to beg I am ashamed." There is a wordplay on חפר "dig" and חפר "be ashamed," Payn. Sm., p. 154; Jast., p. 493. In Lk. 18.31—32 "will be fufilled . . . will be delivered up" is a wordplay משלמין . . . משתלם.

Lk. 22.10 "There shall a man meet you bearing a pitcher of water . . . " There is a paronomasia on the words גברא "man" and גרבא "pitcher," Payn. Sm., p. 77; Jast., p. 263.

Lk. 21.2 ארמלתא . . . ארמית, wordplay, "The widow threw (coins)" Greek, *ballousan.* In Lk. 23.35 לאחרניא אחי יחי נפשה "Others he saved alive; let him save himself alive."

In a different category, Greek Lk. betrays its translation from Aramaic through Aramaic idioms and locutions. Such expressions have been explained on the basis of the Semitic influence of the LXX or from the result of having a person who thinks in Hebrew or Aramaic, but writes Greek. The object of this book is to show that "thinking in Aramaic but writing in Greek" is without basis. Some examples in Lk. have been commented upon, but only with tangential parallels (cf. Strack-Billerbeck, on Lk. 1.32, p. 100 our passage to be discussed), and they did not reach the unavoidable conclusion that there was an Aramaic document under the Greek. Thus the text reads, "He shall be great, (μέγας) and shall be called the son of the Highest" (καὶ υἱὸς ὑψίστου κληθήσεται). In this preliminary context of the annunciation to Mary, the denomination of Jesus as "the son of the Highest" is incongruous. For in the passages v. 31 and v. 33, fore and aft, no intimation is given as yet of the divine attributes of Jesus. If he is the son of God, *arguendo,* then the parallel statement *ante* "He shall be called "great" falls decidedly short. The promise is that he shall ascend the throne of David, which is to last forever, to be indeed the Messiah, and bring redemption to Israel from foreign yoke, and that is all; cf. b. Bera. 34b. And proleptically even in v. 35 "son of God" may be explained as בן אלהים = בר אלהא "an angelic being, a divine person." Compare Job 1.6; 2.1, translated there appositely by "angels," Mof.; "heavenly beings" in the American translation (J. M. Powis Smith); "members of the court of heaven" NEB, not to be rendered "sons of God," RSV, NAB and hence in v. 35 בר אלהא should be interpreted as "heavenly being, divine being." In our present text, too, בר עילאה and בן עליון (Ps. 82.6), (and see Strack-Bill., *Luke,* p. 100), simply means "a divine being" very much like the later Hebrew בן עליה, which, too, simply means "a saintly being" who enjoys the divine presence in the hereafter, b. Succa 45b; Rashi ad loc.; and Sanh. 97b. The translation of our phrase should run, "a saintly man, a godlike person," not "son of the Most High." Incidentally, v. 35 is contradicted by 3.22, where Jesus is, after the baptism, called God's beloved son, and undoubtedly the reading originally was *huios mou ei su; ego semeron gegenneka se* ("You are my son; this day I have given birth to you"), Mof., ILNT, p. 100. While it is true that 1.34f. is called into question by a number of scholars (Harnack, Resch, Usener: Mof. ibid, p. 269) I would say that it seems authentic enough, for, even if vv. 34-—35 are an insertion, the mistranslations from the Aramaic show that the insertion was already present in the original Aramaic. This is further indicated by the fact that the misreading "he shall be called 'great'" (*megas*) fails to convey the uniqueness and distinction that Jesus was to achieve, because *megas* is too generalized—anyone may be "great"—and the same is said of Lk. 1.15. The Aramaic for "great" was רבא which also means "teacher," and the outstanding characteristic of Jesus' ministry is that he taught the people by means of parables and sayings, and the multitudes called him "Teacher" and "Rabbi." The translator chose the wrong meaning at this point, and translated *rabba* as "great." Our whole verse now has the meaning:

He shall be a Teacher,
And shall be called a divine being.

An expression indigenous to Aramaic, but which the Greek translator did not recognize, is evident in the text of Lk. 10.6. First there is the injunction, "And into whatever house ye enter, first say, 'Peace be to this house.'" Then v. 6, "And if the son of peace (υἱὸς εἰρήνης) be there, your peace shall rest upon it; if not, it shall turn to you again." The intent of the phrase "son of peace" can be discerned with fair approximation. It apparently means "one who has a peaceful disposition, who has a tendency to peace" or as some of the modern translations have it, "And if a man of peace is there" RSV, NASB; "If there is anyone there who loves peace" Gdspd.; "men of good will" Knox.

Nevertheless "son of peace" is an unparalleled locution except in Aramaic where בר שלמותא which means "one of the same mind, one of the same conviction" i.e., one who is a kindred spirit (compare Payn. Sm. pp. 54, 581–582); note too that *shlm* (pp. 581f) has the signification of "to follow, be a follower of, adhere to, especially with regard to doctrine, (Brock., p. 92). The translator misunderstood the idiom. We should translate, "And if a kindred spirit be there . . ." i.e., a follower, a fellow-Christian. Observe the wordplay of שלמא "peace" and שלמותא throughout the passage.

Mention was made in connection with Mt. 3.15 that the word *zakuta* "merit"—not "righteousness"—was the proper translation of δικαιοσύνη in that context. Another example of this misunderstanding is found in Lk. 10.29 which reads, "But he willing to justify (*dikaiosai*) himself, said unto Jesus, 'And who is my neighbor?'" In asking Jesus what he should do to inherit eternal life, Jesus in reply to the student of the Torah (not "lawyer" AV, but *sofer,* or *safra,* the earlier term for the later *ḥakam, ḥakamim*) said that one should love God (Deut. 6.5) and that one should love one's neighbor as oneself (Lev. 19.18). Then the man asked Jesus in effect, what is meant by "neighbor"? The term "justify himself" then is not the proper word. There was no need to "justify" himself; for Jesus had already told him (v. 28) "Thou hast answered right." The modern translators point up the difficulty; "vindicate himself," NEB; "desiring to put himself in the right," Mof.[1] Bas; "anxious to make an excuse for himself," Mof.[2]; "determined to acquit himself of reproach," Amp. These renderings miss the point; there is no contention or issue involved; the student is asking earnestly for a definition. How can he extend his love for his neighbor in even a more large and encompassing fashion? Jesus tells the story of the good Samaritan. The students actually sought to know how, by loving his neighbor, he could accumulate more "merits" *zakwatha*, for himself, not "justification." Lk. had mistakenly translated *zakutha*, probably in one of the verbal forms, to mean "justify" instead of "merit"(see p. 52).

Among the Aramaic locutions one may also cite Lk. 12.8 "Whoever shall confess me before men" (*homologese en emoi*), literally, whoever confesses in me, which is a reflection of the Aramaic usage . . . ב אודי "admit something, acknowledge" followed by the preposition (Jast., p. 564). The NT expression in Lk. 4.13 *achri kairou* "until a time" is undoubtedly a literal (mis)translation of the Aramaic *ad zimna* "for a while." See p. 200.

Lk. 24.16 likewise has an Aramaic idiom which the translator failed to recognize. After the resurrection, Jesus joined Cleopas and his companion on their way to Emmaus; they had been discussing the events in Jerusalem, and the verse continues, "But their eyes were holden (ἐκρατοῦντο hold, take) that they should not know him." What is meant by "their eyes were held"? Modern translations have their difficulties. "Their eyes continued to be held that they should not recognize him even for an instant," Mon.; this is too free a translation; at any rate, how did their eyes continue to be *held* when they were conversing and reasoning together? (as in previous verse); "But something held their eyes from seeing who it was," NEB. This translation comes close to the intended meaning. Torrey, assuming an Aramaic antecedent, translates "shut," אחד. There is however a Hebrew (also Aramaic) idiom אחז את העינים "fix one's eyes" (by an optical delusion). In Hebrew, compare אחיזת עינים Sanh. 65b; 67b; Hull., p. 57a (cast a spell, bewitch, hypnotize), Levy, *Chal. Wört.*, I, p. 19; Aramaic אחד עינין, Brock., p. 11, *fascinavit;* Payn. Sm., p. 11, "one who deceives by magic arts." The explanation and translation should take the form, "A spell came over their eyes—they failed to recognize him." On the other hand, where the verse states (v. 31), "their eyes were opened and they knew him" and the verb is פקח which has the special significance "eyes that are opened with understanding," Gen. 3.7 "The eyes of both of them were opened (פקח), and they knew that they were naked."

A terminus technichus which the translator failed to reproduce is found in v. 32 of the same chapter. The passage runs, "And they said to one another, 'Did not our hearts burn within us, while he talked with us by the way, and while he opened up to us (διήνοιγεν) the Scriptures?'" In what way did Jesus "open up" the Scriptures? "Open up" represents Aramaic פתח. This word, however, has the technical meaning of "explain," often to "open a lecture with a quotation from a biblical text" but in general to "explain a scriptural passage." Compare Jast., p. 1250 for the Hebrew usage, and p. 1252 for the Aramaic. Incidentally, in v. 27 previously, "And beginning at Moses and all the prophets, he expounded ($διερμήνευσεν$) unto them in all the scriptures the things concerning himself," the verb most likely was פתר "elucidated, illustrated by." Cf. the frequent midrashic idiom פ׳ ר׳ פתר קריא "Rabbi N. N. explained the verse."

We pass to some questions of syntax. These phenomena have been handled and elucidated in a convincing fashion by Montgomery, Burney, Torrey, and Black. Torrey, for example, has shown that many declarative sentences should have been construed as interrogative sentences, and that relative particles regarded as conjunctions should have been parsed as relative pronouns. See Montgomery, p. 21; Burney, pp. 67, 79; Torrey, *Our Translated Gospels*, p. 54; *passim;* Black, pp. 70f. It is instructive that misconstructions in syntax were not exhausted by their examples. The following may be added as illustrations from Lk.

The Aramaic syntax in Lk. 12.42—43 was misconstrued by the Greek translator. The text reads, "And the Lord said, 'Who then is that faithful and wise steward ($τίς ἄρα ἐστὶν ὁ πιστὸς οἰκονομος ὁ φρόνισμος ὃν καταστήσει κτλ$.) whom his lord shall make ruler over his household to give them their portion of meat in due season?'" (v. 43) "Blessed is that servant whom his lord when he cometh shall find so doing." V. 42 asks a rather strange question, for we expect the verse to read, for example, "Who is a steward? One who is wise and prudent whom the master appoints to give food at the proper time." The answer to the question, qualifying and complementary, comes through appropriately in the next verse: "Fortunate is the steward whom the master will find doing thus," serving the food in proper time.

Patently, the translator construed all the words in v. 42 to add up *in toto* to an interrogative sentence; proleptically he understood "wise and prudent" to be immediately modifying "steward," although, as part of the predicate, we are puzzled that the steward is already described as wise and prudent, although these attributes are not discerned until the steward secures the master's approval two verses later. The translator construed the verse into too lengthy a question; he should have made a stop at "steward"; the "faithful and wise," those adjectives placed after the noun in Aramaic, he assumed to be modifying "steward." As a matter of fact they begin a new clause. The restored Aramaic brings this out clearly: מאן הוא רב ביתא? מהימנא וחכימא הוא דאקימיה מרא על בני ביתה למתן בעידנא פרסא. The translation should run, "Who is a steward of a household? He is faithful and wise, whom his master set up over the household to give their ration at the appointed time."

The reconstruction idiomatically requires a second הוא to be added (it may indeed have fallen out through haplography). The translator reproduced הוא ד by *hon.*—a normal procedure. In the next verse, "Happy" is the wrong nuance for טובוהי. The rendering should be, "*Fortunate* is the steward whom the master of the house finds doing his work conscientiously, for the master will appoint him over all his possessions." Note the wordplay in *mehaimna* meaning "faithful" and "steward."

A misconception of Aramaic syntax again appears in Lk. 18.18—19 which reads, "And a certain ruler asked him, saying, 'Good master....' And Jesus said unto him, 'Why callest thou me good? None is good, save one, that is, God'" (οὐδεὶς ἀγαθὸς εἰ μὴ εἷς [ὁ] Θεός, literally, none is good except one, God). I shall not deal with the parallel passage in Mt. 19.17 where a confusion arose in the question and answer, between "what is good" and "who is good." For the restoration there, see Torrey, *Our Translated Gospels,* pp. 16, 18, although Torrey expresses some misgiving about the thought being "a bit too philosophical." In the Lk. passage, the syntax is harsh: "None good except one—God." This sort of construction is non-Semitic, and non-Aramaic. The Greek too is awkward; note Nestle's insertion of [*ho*]. The truth seems to be that the translator failed to realize that in Aramaic the numeral may regularly precede the noun, i.e., חד אלהא and so Mk. 2.7. Accordingly the text should have been translated, "None is good save the one God," Nöldeke, *Syriac Grammar,* par. 237.

The difficult syntax in Lk. 13.8—9 is clarified too when we understand the verse in the light of the underlying Aramaic. The owner of the fig tree wished to cut it down because it yielded no fruit. His gardner sought to advise him differently: "And he answering said unto him, 'Lord, let it alone this year also, till I shall dig about it, and dung it. And if it bear fruit in the future, [well], and if not, then after that, thou shalt cut it down.'" We expect some such word as the AV inserts [well]. The Aramaic supplies the correct syntax; ואין עבדת פירין ולא לה ולא תפסיקה. When the translator saw the words ולא לה ולא, they made no sense to him. He either did not understand this combination, or thought that one ולא was a thoughtless repetition. He therefore omitted one. Actually, the first one read *wale' lah* "It will be proper, fit; it will be good!" Payn. Sm., p. 108, and the second wela'—"And if not." Note that the sense derived is explicable only in Eastern Aramaic, Peshitta Lk. 19.5; Jn. 3.7; Payn. Sm., p. 108; Brock., p. 185; Jast., pp. 372, 374. Translate, "If it bear fruit, that will be good! And if not, you will cut it down."

A difficult verse syntactically too is Lk. 16.16 (parallel Mt. 11.12) which reads, "The law and the prophets were until John; since that time the kingdom of God is being preached, and every man presseth into it" (καὶ πᾶς εἰς αὐτὴν βιάζεται) literally, and everyone into it is pressing, is forcing; biazo/פרץ, החזיק, הרס, גזל in the LXX). "Force" is probably the better meaning here. The usual interpretation is, "Everyone now can force his way to salvation,"[?] Plummer, *Luke,* p. 388, or otherwise one is compelled to take the vv. 16–18 figuratively, which is however both disjointed and far-fetched. How can one force his way into the kingdom? The verse has nothing to do with adultery either, as one commentator would claim.

The syntax was misunderstood. In Latin and Greek, the harmony of the different parts of a sentence, the concord of noun and adjective, are held within fairly confined limits. However, Hebrew, Aramaic, and Arabic allow for some wide latitude in syntax (compare Ehrlich, *Miqra ki-pheshuto* I, p. 320; II, p. 96–97; Burney, *Aramaic Origin,* p. 110). The force that is mentioned in the verse does not refer immediately to the kingdom of God, where one would enter violently, or seize violently, but to the violation of the Torah laws. V. 16 now becomes plain. The Torah, the verse asserts, was immutable and in force until John; now that the kingdom of God is in prospect, and preached about, in anticipation of the new time, everyone is violating the Torah. V. 17 in sequence vehemently protests against this: It is easier for heaven and earth to pass away, than one tittle of the Torah should fall. The regulation about adultery was probably incorporated here wrongly as if this would be a new evangelical illustration of the preceding. Note that the parallel in Mt. 11.12 is in a different setting.

The feminine *auten* refers back to the Torah (feminine), not the kingdom. The "violence" with which the Torah is "seized" would be in Hebrew חמס (compare Ez. 22.26 חמסו תורתי, Zeph. 3.4). The Aramaic word would be חטף, see presently and so Targs. to the Ez. and Zeph. passages ad loc. *The Gospel acc. to the Hebrews* as cited by Huck-Lietzmann[9] likewise has "plundered (*diarpazetai*), a good reproduction of חטף, but ultimately, though, a mistranslation as חמס תורה means "violate the Torah, pervert the Torah" not "snatch." Contrast Burkitt, I, p. 57, "snatch." חמס, Babyl. Talm. Aramaic, Yoma 24b, Levy, *Chal. Wört.,* is to be preferred. Compare further Gen. Rab. sec. 45 חומסני אתה בדברים "You use force against me with words." *eis auten = lah,* direct object of *ḥamas.*

In giving the behest that one should lend to everyone who seeks to borrow, and that one should not seek a favor in return, Lk. 6.32–33 continues, "For if ye love them which love you, what thank have ye? (ποία ὑμῖν χάρις ἐστίν) (literally, what thanks is there to you?). For sinners also love those who love them." V. 33, "And if ye do good to them which do good to you, what thank have ye" (ut supra); "For sinners also do the same." The phrase "what thanks have ye" is a little uncertain, and the dilemma of the meaning is reflected in the translations. The RSV corrects the AV to "What credit is that to you" and so Mof.[2] NEB NAB which hits upon the sense quite well. Others, "What grace do you practice" Ber.; "What merit is there in that" Gdspd.; "What recompense is yours?" Mof.[1] "What kind of thank, or favor, have you?" Plummer, *Luke*, 187. The "favor" comes from God, or the gratitude from persons loved (so Plummer, ibid); and similarly for v. 33 in the respective translations. What therefore does *charis* really mean here? The Aramaic would almost certainly be טיבו, טיבותא, and so comp. its employment for *charis* in Syriac, in Lk. p s c at 17.9; Lk. 2.40 p s, idem 6.32; Jn. 1.14.16 p c, as well as its use in the Targ. Onq. at Gen. 19.19; 20.13; 21.23 and elsewhere, although the Babylonian Aramaic חסדא (Heb. *ḥesed*), and more rarely in Eastern Aram., cannot be ruled out (Brock., p. 245; Payn. Sm., p. 150). The construction and the meaning of the word טיבותא was misunderstood by the Greek translator. The Aramaic ran מן טיבותא אית לך which should be translated "What loving kindness is there in you?" Jesus defines here *taibutha/ḥesed* much in consonance with Jewish rabbinic tradition. Thus, for example, a *ḥesed shel 'emeth,* a true act of kindness is one in which favors cannot be repaid such as actions that are performed for the dead. Compare Jast., p. 79; Gen. Rab. 96 and b. Sota 14a; Baba Meṣ. 30b. Translate alternatively: What goodness is there in you? not "thank," or "favor."

The relative particle *de,* both as a subordinate conjunction introducing a clause, and also serving as a personal pronoun are frequently confused with one another as has been exampled by the work of Montgomery, Burney, Torrey, and Black. We may add the following example, Lk. 11.8 "I say unto you, 'Though [he says] he will not rise and give him [the three loaves] because he is his friend (*dia to einai philon auton,* literally, because his being his friend) yet because of his importunity, he will rise and give him as many as he needeth.'" The logic does not quite follow. The sleeper does not give him loaves *because* he is his friend. The *de* was misunderstood. The text should read, "Though he will not rise and give him *who* is his friend, yet because of his importunity, etc."

There is one passage where the Greek translator failed to perceive a distinct nuance of the preposition *Mem.* While *m/min,* in both Hebrew and Aramaic, is generally to be translated "from," it may also bear the special significance of "without." Thus in Is. 23.1 "... is destroyed so that no one can enter in" (*mibbo'*); Jer. 10.14 *nib'ar . . . mida'at* "is stupefied so that he is without knowledge"; Ps. 109.24 " . . . is lean without fat" (*mishamen*). Comp. BDB., 583 a, b. This usage may be attested to in Aramaic as well. Compare the Peshitta and the Targums and their deployment of the *Mem* in the above verses. Now Lk. 22.41–44 describes how Jesus, the night before his arrest and after the Passover meal, withdrew from his disciples to "a place apart" and prayed. Then v. 45 continues, "And when he rose up from prayer, and was come to his disciples, he found them sleeping for sorrow (ἀπὸ τῆς λύπης lit. from sorrow) and said unto them, 'Why sleep ye?'". It would not be psychologically apt to say that all the twelve disciples were sleeping because of sorrow. In reality, people worry about the future but sorrow after the fact. Though he had returned from his private prayer and reproved the disciples three times (Mt. 26.40–45), Jesus would not have upbraided his followers if they had, in their grief, fallen asleep. The real picture is quite different. Actually they were not aware of the impending tragedy. The four cups of wine that they drank at the Passover meal overcame them (Mishna *Pesaḥim* 10.1.2). They were asleep for "heaviness" as the parallel versions give it (Mt. 26.43; Mk. 14.40), and not "sorrow" unique wth Lk. Modern versions persist in rendering "from sorrow," RSV, Mof., Knox, Arndt-Ging. 483.

lupe in the Greek means "sorrow, grief, pain." As the Peshitta suggests, however, the Aramaic word עקתא, found here in p s c phil and in Jn. 16.6.20 phil, was probably the word in the original Aramaic text. Note, for example, that in parallel texts and in the same situation, Mt. 26.37 declares that Jesus "began to be *sorrowful* (*lupeisthai*) and troubled," Mk. 14.33 states that he was "greatly *distressed* (*ekthambeisthai*) and troubled." Hence the discrepancy between Mt. and Mk. ascends to the very same Aramaic expression עקת לה having the sense of both sorrow and distress. Mk. is correctly translated. Jesus was not sorrowful but distressed. Comp. Payn. Smith, 424; Brock., p. 517. If now the alternate function and meaning of the *Mem* meaning "without" be employed for the passage in Lk. 22.45, we get a more natural description of what took place. Translate: "And when he rose up from prayer, and came to his disciples, he found them sleeping without a care!".

There are a number of instances where the reflexive was misunderstood syntactically for the passive. Thus Lk. 10.15 where we read, "And thou Capernaum, which art exalted (ὑψωθήσῃ) to heaven, shalt be thrust down to hell."

Capernaum was not exalted to heaven. It has been considered, that to get rid of the difficulty, we should assume that the clause is to be taken as a question, "Shalt thou be exalted to heaven?" and so ASV, NEB, Phi, NAB, Torrey. The rhetorical question, however, creates an absurdity. Compare the declaration and the sharp censure of the other cities, of Chorazin, of Bethsaida, and of Tyre. The Aramaic form in the text that led to the difficulty was אתתרימתי (forms may be variable, perhaps too תתרימין, cf. S c and s, Burkitt, at Lk. 10.15) which the translator opined to be a passive, whereas the correct interpretation should have been in functional terms of a reflexive. We should translate, "But thou Capernaum, who exaltest thyself to the skies ...," and then the proper sequel continues with the condemnation of her arrogance.

Similarly, the text in Lk. 10.42 was syntactically misunderstood. Martha had complained to Jesus that her sister Mary was not helping her in household duties, and that she sat idly at Jesus' feet to hear his word. Jesus said understandingly, "Martha, thou art anxious and disturbed about many things." Then, "But one thing is needful; and Mary has chosen that good part, which shall not be taken from her." The Greek text has more than its usual difficulties. I follow the text of the UBS, *henos de estin chreia,* "Just one thing is needed," which is *arguendo* partial to Mary, discriminative to Martha. The reconstituted Aramaic points to a much more pointed and relevant expression חדא מתבעיא לה "*She* is seeking one thing" i.e., the Etpe'el passive with the dative of agent. The translator took the phrase impersonally, as it was quite common, "One thing is required." Compare the Talmud Yerushalmi expression בעיא דא מילתא "This thing is needed" where the Talmud Babli would employ צריכא "it is needed." See the Glossary at the end of the Talmud Yerushalmi (Krotoschin, reprint; 1948) and the common usage in the Talmud Babli in the sense of "need, require," Kohut, II, p. 137. The sequel "Mary has chosen that good portion" forms excellent continuity. The text runs therefore, "Martha, thou art careful and troubled about many things. But one thing she wants, and Mary hath chosen that good part, which shall not be taken away from her."

There are a number of instances where misvocalizations occur. The reasonable deduction that one may make from such data is that the translator was faced with a written text which he misread. This counters the argument both of an oral transmission, and that the translator originally wrote in Greek. Thus for example Lk. 11.14, "And he was casting out a demon (שדי שידא, wordplay) and it was dumb (καὶ αὐτὸ ἦν κωφόν). And it came to pass, when the devil was gone out, the dumb (man) spake; and the people wondered" (see p. 106 for a similar example). Now the devil was not dumb, but the man was. The demon caused the dumbness. The Aramaic was read as מחרש, the 'Aph'el, and one of its characteristics aside from its service as a causative, is its stative function—it is a stative verb primarily BDB, p. 361—and the latter interpretation was used here. The translator could have vocalized *meḥaresh* "caused dumbness." But it is quite possible too that מחרש in the 'Aph'el could mean "cause dumbness"; if so, there would be but a difference in functional interpretation.

It must be allowed, however, that another construction may be placed on the clause via the Aramaic. From the Greek we see that the Aramaic ran כד שדי שידא דחרשא אית הוא (compare the Peshitta for the construction). As above, the translator regarded the syntax of "dumb" as referring to the demon as the modifying clause "because he was dumb." The translation should have followed *this* construction, "As he was casting out a demon, *because a dumb man was there . . .*" the same Aramaic דחרשא אית הוא. This interpretation may be the preferred one, as the whole passage begins quite abruptly, "Now he was casting out a demon that was dumb" but Mt. 12.22 f. more fully starts, "Then was brought unto him one possessed with a devil, blind and dumb, and he healed him, etc."

A notoriously difficult verse is in Lk. 7.8, but when the misvocalization is indicated, the passage becomes clear. A centurion had a slave at the point of death; friends interceded with Jesus to heal the slave. The centurion sent a message that he was not worthy enough for Jesus to come under his roof, and conversely he was not of worth to come to Jesus. "But say in a word, (magic word, *miltha'*. see p. 106) 'and my slave shall be healed.'" V. 8 continues, "For I also am a man set under authority (ὑπὸ ἐξουσίαν τασσόμενος) having under me soldiers, and I say unto one 'Go,' and he goeth; and to another 'Come,' and he cometh; and to my servant 'Do this,' and he doeth it." The enigmatic expression that puzzles one is that the centurion is "under authority,"[3] whereas one would expect him to say "I am a man who has authority." Moreover, what is meant by being *under* authority? Under whose authority?

By invoking the Aramaic underlying the Greek, we see how the difficulty arose through the misreading of a word. The Aramaic read אף אנא גברא אנא דמשעבד תחת שולטנא. The translator, however, read the passive דמשעבד (and this is the word employed by the Peshitta), whereas he should have pointed the word as the active participle דמשעבד, "who has authority over, subjects," Jast., pp. 1608–1609 (employed for individuals). Moreover, the ambiguous שולטנא should have been interpreted in the meaning of "governor," and not abstractly as "authority." Compare Jast., p. 1534 (partially) and שלטון

(Hebrew) meaning both "rulership" and "governor," Jast., p. 1582, and Arabic (and English) *sultan*. The translation should be, "For I also am a man having authority under the governor; and I have soldiers, etc." The meaning of this passage was unconsciously sensed and employed by that Bible reader and dramatist William Shakespeare who has Shallow say in Henry IV, Act V, Scene 3, "I am, sir, under the king, in some authority."

A charge is made against the legalists in Lk. 11.52, "Ye have taken away the keys of knowledge (ἤρατε τὴν κλεῖδα τῆς γνώσεως); ye entered not in yourselves, and them that were entering in, ye hindered." The "key of knowledge" as a locution is unusual; we expect that in the context, the thought should have conveyed the idea "You have taken away any access (or the entrance) to knowledge, and those who wished to enter were prevented." *Entrance* should have been mentioned somewhere. It is the underlying Aramaic that should have been read with a different vocalization. The consonantal text ran, ווי לכון ספריא די אחדתון מפתחין דידיעתא. The interpretation should have been "You have closed the doors (entrance) of knowledge." Then the sequel follows through in proper order. "You do not *enter*, and you prevent others from *entering*." The translator understood אחד as "take, seize"; he should have understood the meaning to be "You have closed" used frequently with "entrance, door" (Payn. Sm., p. 10, Brock., p. 12a; Levy, *Neuhebr. Chald.*, I, p. 53); and he should have read מפתחין "entrances" and not "keys." The word *pth* here has the overtone of "explain, study, expound the scriptural verse." See the explanation of *pth* in "Did he not open to us the scriptures?" p. 128; the noun likewise has the implication of the study of the Torah. Cf. Yer. Sabb. VII, 9c "It can be seen that this man has never passed through the gate of the Law" (has not studied). According to the new reading, Jesus charges the legalists for failing to liberalize and expand the Law. They do not go in this "gate," and they prevent others from coming in.

There is one interesting example wherein the passage was misheard, and which then reconstructed brings out the full meaning and flow of the verse. Unique for Lk. in this episode are some poignant sentences describing the remaining agonized emotions of Jesus just before his arrest. Lk. 22.37 reads, "... that this what is written must yet be accomplished in me 'And he was reckoned among the transgressors.' For the things concerning me have an end (καὶ γὰρ τὸ περὶ ἐμοῦ τέλος ἔχει, literally for the thing concerning me has an end)." V. 38 continues, "And they said, 'Lord, behold, here are two swords.' And he said unto them, 'It is enough' (ἱκανόν ἐστιν)."

The dialogue between Jesus and the disciples does not cohere with any meaning. If Jesus declares that his end is near, what is the sense of the declaration by the disciples that they will give him two swords? And why "two"? Then in reply Jesus says sententiously, but enigmatically, "It is enough." What is "enough"? Is it the two swords again?

Aramaic supplies the key to the problems. For "things concerning me have an end," the original Aramaic ran דעלי סיפא "For me the end is near." The disciples misheard this with their interpretation "There is a sword (סיפא, סייפא, Heb. סייף) hanging over me." The disciples reply, "Here are *two* swords!" Jesus answers shortly, "That is futile" (ספיק הוא). The latter Aramaic word usually means "enough," and this is the manner the translator rendered in its usual definition. In Eastern Aramaic-Syriac, the word bears the meaning, in the participle passive and in the Pa'el, of "futile, empty" Payn. Sm., p. 386; Brock., p. 492, and this is the only translation that makes for a cohesive thread in the dialogue. The reply is couched in the familiar rhetorical trope of the talḥin (1) Two swords will be futile (2) It is futile to talk to you. You do not understand (Jesus was vexed on a number of occasions because of the obtuseness of the disciples, Mt. 16.19.11; Mk. 8.17 and elsewhere). (3) Resistance will be of no avail as the end is near.

Chapter V

The Evidence from John

THE GOSPEL of John, no less than the Synoptists, shows full evidence of an antecedent substratal Aramaic account. The pioneering work with regard to Jn. has been J. A. Montgomery's "Aramaic Origin of St. John" and Burney's "Aramaic Origin of the Fourth Gospel" with the additional studies of Torrey and Black. As in the Synoptists, Jn. shows, with the exception of chap. 21, a goodly number of examples of all the characteristic Aramaic idioms. One proof of the underlying written text has been alluded to (p. 28). Like the other translators, Jn's translator exhibits a confusion and misapprehension of one root for another. He likewise mistranslates. He has a number of stock Aramaic and Greek equations that, in their context, make for an absurd sense. He fails to recognize obvious nuances that would be understood by one who would be at home in Aramaic, and specifically in its intimacies and depth. Particles escape him. Locutions indigenous to Aramaic are muffed. He bungles the syntax. He fails to sense the change in tempus when participles inject themselves into the text. As we would say modernly, he does not vocalize properly. The translator lapses in distinguishing the determinate and indeterminate case. Some passages have to be completely reconstructed.

An instance wherein a confusion of roots probably took place may be seen in Jn. 4.35, "Say not ye 'There are yet four months, and then cometh the harvest?' Behold, I say unto you, 'Lift up your eyes, and look on the fields; for they are white ($\lambda\epsilon\nu\kappa\alpha\iota$) already to harvest.'" Apparently the whole passage is to be taken symbolically, although there is some problem about the time element (see Bernard, *Gospel according to St. John*, I, p. 155. Hence the dialogue with the woman of Samaria (4.7f.) about the water to drink, would be in January, or early February, the rainy season, when there would have been no scarcity of water. The expression—literally, "white they are to harvest"—is puzzling. *leukos,* "white," is employed for a variety of colors ("white hair, white wine") and indeed for clouds, stones, a chair, mountains, a rock, a throne (Arndt-Gingrich, p. 473), and for fields of ripe grain as Arndt-Gingrich note for this passage, yet the explanation seems not quite appropriate and fails to convince. We should expect "is ready for harvest."

There are two possibilities. One is that the word מחוור, Pa'el passive with the fundamental root meaning "be white" (Jast., pp. 438–439), was rendered too literally by the translator, whereas he should have taken the word in a less literal sense of "clear, evident," or as Jastrow puts it, "clearly indicated." The original Aramaic undoubtedly ran ארעתא דחור לחצדא, the plural noun and the singular verb being of no moment (and so the Peshitta). The translation would be "Fields that are already for harvest" following the Greek text of UBS. One might compare the semantic development in ראה, חזי, חזא; ראוי, "ready, fit."

Less likely but to be considered is the second possibility that the translator confused two roots; (1) חר meaning in Syriac "look at, gaze" as in בחטא לא אנש חאר הוא "No one regarded the wheat" i.e., the crops were neglected in time of pestilence Payn. Sm., p. 134; also Brock., p. 222b and (2) חור "be white" as above. The first root has a number of extended meanings as "be near to, be at the point of, be soon" and compare Brock. ibid at #6 as well as the noun חורא meaning "time" at #5. Note the suggestive חור ומטי of Syriac c (Burkitt, p. 440). We will not be wrong in either case if we interpret that the verse should mean "Look upon the fields, for they are already near to harvest."

A similar confusion of roots is evident in Jn. 19.12 where the text reads, "And from thenceforth Pilate sought to release him; but the Jews cried out, saying 'If thou let this man go, thou art not Caesar's friend; whosoever maketh himself a king, speaketh ($\dot{\alpha}\nu\tau\iota\lambda\acute{e}\gamma\epsilon\iota$) against Caesar.'" The last clause is anticlimactic and a letdown. If a man makes himself a king in Caesar's empire, he does more than speak against him. He *rebels* against him. This is explicitly brought out by many translators, who obviously are dissatisfied with the AV. Thus the RSV renders, "sets himself against Caesar"; "is disloyal to Caesar" Rieu, "is defying Caesar" NEB, and most apposite is that of Mon. "is a rebel against the Emperor," which is the required sense here. The Hebrew מרה has philological association with *mri* (Syriac) "contend with," Payn. Sm., p. 298; Brock., p. 402, with *'amar*, root *mrr*, Brock., p. 401, used in the Peshitta for the Hebrew מרה Ez. 20.8, the noun *memarmerana* employed for *benei meri*, Num. 17.10.25; for *meri* "rebellion" Ez. 2.8, and similar forms for the Hebrew *meri* in Deut. 31.27; 1 Sam. 15.3. Undoubtedly, aside from the meaning of "incite, contend, provoke," the meaning "rebel" can be quite properly assigned to the Aramaic *meri,* Jast., p. 842 (see presently). Accordingly the Aramaic of our verse ran, כל מאן דעבד נפשיה מלך ממרא לקיסר "Anyone who makes himself king, rebels against Caesar." For the usage, cf. the familiar זקן ממרא "The rebellious dissident scholar." The translator, however, completely misunderstood the phrase to mean "says unto Caesar" associating the word with מימרא "saying, word." The confusion between אמר and מרי is evident elsewhere in Ps. 139.20, as well as with the ימר and מור. Compare BDB, p. 56, with additional examples of the confusions in Gesenius-Buhl[17] in 50—51; Levy, *Neuhebr. Wörtb.,* I, p. 100 cites אמר "be in opposition," although he considers some forms of the verb to be Itpe'el of *mri;* Jastr. registers the forms under *mari,* p. 842. One may add another instance of confusion of the roots in Dan. 11.11. See Zimmermann, *Biblical Books,* p. 14.

We have an appreciable number of mistranslations in Jn. Mention was made of the mistranslation of שמרי "Samaritan" and שמדי "devil" (see p. 28). At Jn. 1.18, analyzed previously by Burney, *Aramaic Origin,* chap. 1, we may note in addition the following, which likewise contains a mistranslation, "No man hath seen God at any time; the only begotten son, which is in the bosom of the Father, he hath declared (ἐξηγήσατο) him." *eksegeomai* means "explain, interpret, report, tell (so the Pesh. here in Jn.), describe," Arndt-Gingrich, p. 275 and so "tell" in Lk. 24.35, Ac. 10.8; 15.12; 21.9, and mostly for *sipper* in OT. In Jn. 1.18 the Greek verb means, "He has made known, or brought news of (the invisible God)," Arndt-Gingrich, ibid, bottom; *eksegesis* = narrative, description. Bernard I, p. 33 "Interpreted the Father," barely possible, though Rhm and Knox adopt this for want of better. RSV has hit upon the correct interpretation "He has made him known," though this cuts loose from the Greek. Since the start of the verse is "No man has seen God any time" it follows that the contrast then should be "But he in the bosom of the Father, has seen God." Or alternately, in the Johannine incarnation, "Has made God manifest."

If we adopt the reading "see," then there must have been a misreading of חזיה "seen him" which the translator saw or thought he saw as חויה "declared him." This reading would have the merit and support of Jn. 6.46 "No man hath seen the Father ... he hath seen the Father."

Alternately, the word חוי in Aramaic means "tell, declare," and this is the meaning that the translator assigned to it here, perhaps in an unclear fashion. *Ḥawwe,* however, has other meanings, in such contexts as "He showed a Sela to Rabbi L." (for examination) Y. Kil. 31a; "He showed the field" (to the officials), and also the verb's form in the Aph'el, Jast., p. 432.

Thus, the meaning is that the son "showed" the father, not only saw him in contrast to all mankind, but more appropriately made him *manifest* (Payn. Sm., p. 129), made him visible in his person to men. The whole verse seems to have a more genuine ring when either of these readings is adopted.

An extraordinary mistranslation and misconstruction is evident also in Jn. 2.4. There was a marriage to take place at Cana, but there was no wine for the feast. Jesus and his disciples were invited to the wedding. The mother of Jesus said to him, "They have no wine." V. 4 continues, "Jesus said unto her, 'Woman, what have I to do with thee? Mine hour is not yet come'" (οὔπω ἥκει ἡ ὥρα μου). The ending of the verse baffles; it seems incoherent with the preceding; it lacks pertinence to the situation at hand. The phrase is used a number of times, mostly connected with his final hours of suffering (Bernard I, p. 76) and modern translations all have their difficulties bridging the incoherence. Bernard takes the phrase to mean that the public manifestation of Jesus and his powers had not yet arrived, a reading which even Bernard himself regards as only "probable." The expression seems to be out of place and out of time, yet the Aramaic suggests a more appropriate ending and coherence. In all likelihood, the Aramaic ran זמנוני ולא אתי which may be translated "They invited me and not my miracle!" (see Dalman, *Words of Jesus*, p. 118). The rebuff is a protest. The restoration gives point to the first part of the verse "Woman, what have I to do with you?" The translator assumed that זמנוני looked something like זמני "my time," and אתי "my miracle" as if derived from אתי, participle of אתא "come." Compare *hora/zeman* Sym. Qoh. 3.1. This reconstruction would harmonize better, a familiar phrase in Jn. 7.30; 12.23; 13.1; 17.1 and elsewhere with the sequel in v. 5 "His mother saith unto the servants, 'Whatsoever he saith unto you, do it'" better than "mine hour is not yet come." זימנא with *mem* is not found in Syriac. Babylon. Talm. Aramaic has the form *zimna,* probably the more original. Cf. the Akkadian *zimanu, simanu.*

There is a section in Jn. 3.31—34 which when interpreted via the Aramaic receives a vivid clarification in a number of phrases that have hitherto perplexed commentators. The section reads;

v. 31　He that cometh from above is above all;
　　　He that is of the earth is earthly; and speaketh of the earth;
　　　He that cometh from heaven is above all.

v. 32　And what he hath seen and heard, that he testifieth;
　　　And no man receiveth his testimony.

v. 33　He that hath received his testimony hath set to his seal
　　　(ἐσφράγισεν) that God is true.

THE EVIDENCE FROM JOHN 143

v. 34   For he whom God hath sent speaketh the words of God; For God giveth not the spirit by measure (ἐκ μέτρου) unto him."

V. 31 bears the following analysis: The last clause "He that cometh from heaven is above all" is simply a variant to the first clause, "He that cometh from above is above all." The last clause came in as an explicative variant because the original Aramaic מן עילא "from on high" was ambiguous; it could mean "from on high," or "from heaven," or "from the Most High," Jast., p. 1069. It was important to the one who sponsored and inserted the last clause that it should be clearly understood that Jesus had not merely come from on high, but that he had come from God himself. Actually this is an intimation of the *talḥins* following in the verse.

The *talḥins* in the second line of verse may be illustrated by a printing schema as follows:

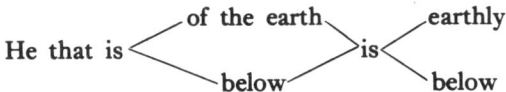

The words מן ארעא is likewise ambiguous through the talḥin "from the earth" and "from below" Levy, *Chald. Wört.* I, p. 69. Through the diagram it will be seen that the clause can be read four ways:

He that is of the earth is earthly
He that is of the earth is below
He that is below is earthly
He that is below is below.

The *talḥin* is extended to the next clause: he speaks from below and/or he speaks of the earth. I further consider that ממלל "he speaks" is an overtone and an intimation of מלי "be full" with the sense that "He is but full with but earthly images," a forecast and an intimation of the last clause in v. 34. Bernard I, 123, 125. Cf. the expression מלי מלא "speak verbosely" Payn. Sm., p. 274. In Qidd. 50a ממלי מלי עלוי "They speak against me" Jast., p. 792. Of course, there may have been a confusion of the roots ממלל/מלי as well.   In the next verse, we have a technical expression borrowed from the law courts, "seen ... heard ... testifies; no one receives his testimony." It is well known that before one could give evidence in Jewish law, he had to be investigated as to whether he qualified to give testimony—was there any suspicion about his character? That is, was he associated with lawbreakers, had he violated his oath previously, or was he deriving benefit from stolen property. The investigation was rigorous, and often prolonged. The verse stresses that John had testified what he saw and heard, and therefore was qualified beyond objection or suspicion. The Jewish Christian, who may have read this, would have been significantly impressed. The Baptist, however, knew that his testimony was not accepted in his day. The legal terminology for accepting evidence was קבל סהדותא. Compare Y. Sanh. 18b "Rabbi H. heard evidence," etc. These "testimonies" are frequent in the Tractate Eduyot; the Hebrew there is העיד. For Aramaic usage, see Jast., p. 959; Payn. Sm., p. 362.

Incidentally, the locution in Jn. 1.20 "He confessed and denied not" seems to have been borrowed from legal usage. In Hebrew the term was הודה ולא בוש which is translated incorrectly as "He confessed and was not ashamed," Jast., p. 151. The true translation is "He confessed without delay" i.e., forthrightly, *bosh* having the same sense as *boshesh* Ex. 32.1; Jud. 5.28.

The sequel in v. 33 has the peculiar expression "He that hath received his testimony (i.e., has accepted the truth of the Gospel) hath set to his seal (*esphragisen:* literally, sealed) that God is true." What is meant by "he has sealed" that God is true? It may be argued that we have here another example of legal terminology, as documents, e.g., the *giṭṭin* (documents of divorce—Akk. *gitu* document) had to be signed and sealed, and this legal requirement has seemingly the same application here to that of John's testimony that was accepted and was thereby "sealed." Similarly there may be reference here to the well-known passage "The seal of the Holy one Blessed be he is Truth" B. Shabb. 55a, cited by Lightfoot, *Hor. Heb*, ad loc. On the whole, however, the simplest explanation would be that the translator misunderstood חתם as "sealed" (Eph. 4.30, Greek and Peshitta). The better rendition of the Aramaic word should be "attest, confirm," Payn. Sm., p. 163; Brock., p. 264b. The translation should bear the thought that he who receives the Gospel attests that God is true. Or we might translate, "He who receives his testimony confirms thereby that God is true."

The next verse to be discussed in this section is v. 34 which entails both a misvocalization and a confusion of roots. The text reads, "For he whom God hath sent speaketh the words ($\tau \grave{\alpha}\ \dot{\rho}\acute{\eta}\mu\alpha\tau\alpha$) of God; for God giveth not the spirit by measure (*ek metrou*) (unto him)." The last clause in the verse is perplexing. What relation and relevance has measure to do with what God has directed his messenger to say? He has to speak the words of God, according to the verse, neither more nor less (Jn. 8.28!), and yet we are told that God does not give the words by measure. Commentators interpretively speak of "fullness" or "completeness" (Bernard I, p. 123, 125), and this would certainly be the sense required. A simple retroversion from Aramaic again supplies the solution. The Aramaic word for *rehmata* would be מליא, which the translator misvocalized, owing to the preceding "speaketh." He

THE EVIDENCE FROM JOHN 145

should have read מליא *melaya* "fullness" or מוליא *mulāyā* "plenitude, copiousness," Payn. Sm., p. 277; Brock., p. 389 which now harmonizes the different parts of the verse very well. The messenger sent by God speaks with the fullness of God's spirit because God does not give of his spirit stintingly. The passage should run,

> For he whom God hath sent
> Speaketh with the *fullness* of God;
> For God gives not the spirit by *measure*.

Note the wordplay in *memallel* and *melaya*.

Jn. 8.25 is most difficult. The text reads, "They said unto him, 'Who art thou?'" And Jesus saith unto them, 'Even the same (!) τὴν ἀρχὴν that I said unto you from the beginning.'" The Greek does not mean "*from* the beginning," expressed elsewhere by *eks arches* (16.4), or *ap' arches* (15.27; I Jn. 1.1). The LXX employs *ten archen* in the sense of "at the beginning, at the first" Gen. 43.20; Dan. 9.21 (LXX) and Dan. 8.1 (Theodotion), a usage quite classical and unexceptional. Other interpretations seek to construe the verse as a question, "Why should I talk to you at all?" Mof. 1 and Mof. 2; Gdspd.; NEB. "Even what I told you from the beginning" RSV, NAB. In this disagreement, Bernard (II, p. 301), after a balanced discussion, rejects the interrogative construction as the proposal for solving the verse's difficulties.

A clue for understanding the verse is offered by Syriac versions. Syriac s reads "The *chief* (רישא) that I should speak myself with you" (Burkitt's translation); and so some Latin texts *initium* and similarly the Vulgate *principium*. Undoubtedly then the underlying Aramaic had the Eastern Aramaic-Babylonian locution מדרישא, מן דרישא which can mean "at the beginning," and so the Greek accordingly translated. This cannot be correct however, because the verb would be required to be in the aorist, not the present indicative, i.e., not the impossible "In the beginning, I tell you." The truth seems to be that the translator missed the required sense for the verse. מדרישא means not only "from the beginning" but also "again" (Payn. Sm., p. 540; Brock., p. 728; L. Ginzberg, *Geonica*, I, p. 82). In response to the question, "Who art thou?"—people were constantly asking this question: of Jn., 1.19.22; of Jesus 8.25; 12.34–21.12—Jesus replies, "I am telling you *again* ..." i.e., he is come to the world to tell those things that he had heard from the Father (v. 26). Perhaps what "he tells again" refers to the preceding 8.14–19. However, the expression may refer also to any number of statements made previously: 7.33–34.38, 5.17.19, etc. Note now that *lalo* "I say" suits the temporal sense very well—"I tell you again," not "I told."

Jn. 8.28 has a peculiar expression, which also may be traced to a misunderstanding of the substrative Aramaic. The text reads, "Then Jesus said unto them, 'When ye have lifted up (!) (ὑψώσητε) the Son of Man, thou shalt know that I am he and that I do nothing of myself; but as my Father hath taught me, I speak these things.'" The expression "When you have lifted up the Son of Man" is incongruous—it is supposed to mean, when you have lifted me up at the time of the crucifixion, i.e., on the cross (Bernard II, p. 303). The "lifting up" however, was carried out by the Romans (Jn. 19.18.19.23). There is also some difficulty in having Jesus, even from the mystic symbolization of John, forecast his own crucifixion. The Aramaic in back of this peculiar expression was probably the root רים (compare Syriac c, the Peshitta, and the correspondent lexical equation of *hupso* and אריס Mt. 23.12; Lk. 14.11; Jn. 3.14; p and s in Lk. 1.52). In its basic meaning, אריס means, of course, "lift up"; co-equally, another meaning is "take away, remove" e.g., "Your kingdom shall be taken away," Payn. Sm., p. 535; Brock., p. 721, also #3 *dempsit* and #4 *absolevit;* Jast., p. 1460 bottom. It is also quite possible that סלק in the Pa'el could likewise have been in the text as a good synonym. The Aramaic text of the verse seems to have been כד מתרים לכון בר נשא which either is the ambiguous "When you lift up the Son of Man," and which is the path that the translator took for his rendering. Or it could also be "When I will no longer be with you, you will know who I was/am (אנא אתי, see presently for a similar ambiguity). The verse should be literally translated, "When the Son of Man will be taken away from you, you will know who I am/was." The translator perceived the construction as a passive with the Lamed of agent, and hence translated actively. The sense of the passage, however, demands that it be taken as a genuine passive, with the dative of reference. The passage certainly cannot be rendered "When you lift the Son of Man up in the air" (!) as Gdspd. does.

A mistranslation of the particle אתי *'ithai,* serving as a copulative, made for an absurdity in Jn. 8.58. The Jews had said to Jesus, "Thou art not fifty years old, and thou hast seen Abraham"? To which Jesus replied, "Verily, verily, I say unto you, 'Before Abraham was, I *am (ego eimi).*'" The translator rendered word for word according to the most literal meaning without regard for the context. The Aramaic was אנא אתי, the copulative serving most frequently in the present. Much depends however on the continuum. *'ithai* may function very well for the past tense. Comp. Nöldeke, *Syr. Gram.* p. 241, e.g. "When Adam did not yet exist," and further ibid, p. 243 bottom עד לא אתי "Before I was in existence." It follows that the translation of our verse should be naturally, "Before Abraham lived, I was in existence."[14]

An instructive misrendering occurs in Jn. 11.16. The news had come through that Lazarus was dead. For the wordplay on דמך meaning "sleep" and "die" in the whole passage in Jn. 11.11–14, see p. 158. V. 15 states finally that Jesus decided, "Let us go unto him." Then v. 16 continues, "Then said Thomas, which is called Didymus, unto his fellow disciples, 'Let us also go, that we may *die* (ἀποθάνωμεν) with him.'" This is an incredible statement. Thomas would not invite his fellow disciples to go and die with Jesus. There must be something wrong with the reading. The explanation given by Bernard, II p. 381 that "Thomas foresaw [?] only too clearly that Jesus was going to his death, and he realized, that to enter Judea as his disciple was to risk the same fate." This explanation does not fit the circumstance here which is limited to the resurrection of Lazarus. The text at the end of the discourse, manifestly should read, "Let us go that we may *accompany* him." The word that was misunderstood in the underlying Aramaic was שלם which has the meaning of (1) accompany and (2) die. Compare Payn. Sm., p. 581, Brock., p. 782. What happened is quite plain. The translator, without paying attention to the sense and drift of the passage, simply rendered word for word with the meaning of "die" in keeping with the theme running through the whole reporting of Lazarus's death. השלים = died, exists in Hebrew as well. Compare S. Lieberman, *Texts and Studies*, p. 105. Note that שלם as "die" and "accompany" is strictly Eastern Aramaic.

An error is disclosed in Jn. 11.48 which runs, "If we let him thus alone, all men will believe in him; and the Romans shall come and take away both our place and nation" (καὶ ἀροῦσιν ἡμῶν καὶ τὸν τόπον καὶ τὸ ἔθνος), literally, will take of us both the place and nation. It is assumed that "place" here refers to the Temple, as this was the special concern of the priests (Bernard II, p. 403). *topos* as "place" is used in quite a variety of senses "inhabited place, location, region, district, position, office," etc., Arndt-Gingrich, p. 830. Consequently with a wider extension of meaning, it is presumed that *topos* would have the sense "sacred place" and so RSV Mon. This is not altogether satisfactory for the natural expression would seem to be "our land and people" and so indeed the Sin. Syriac *medinatan we-amman*, translated customarily, and so Burkitt, p. 493 "Our city and our people" but which might be translated, because *medina* bears that meaning, "our land." So e.g., *medina/'ereẓ* for province, region, 2 Chron. 9.5; /*medina* Dan. 8.2; Ec. 5.17, Payn. Sm., p. 252; Brock., p. 145; Jast., p. 734. Other translations divide along the same lines "And blot out both our city and nation" Wms; "holy place and our people" Gdspd.; "*land* and nation" Mof.[1]; "our holy Place and our nation" Mof.[2]; "our temple and our nation," NEB; "Our sanctuary and our nation" NAB. However it is not usual or apt to couple "our place and our nation" as an expression, as indicated, and so following the Peshitta for the cue אתרן ועמן it is clear that the Greek translator rendered too literally with *topos* "place" whereas he should have translated אתר with "our land" meaning not only "place" but "land, country," Payn. Sm., p. 33; Brock., p. 55. Translate, "Our land and nation." Similarly, it was mistranslated in Mt. 24.7, Mk. 13.8, and Lk. 21.11 "For nation shall rise against nation, and kingdom against kingdom; and there shall be famines and pestilences and earthquakes in divers places" (*kata topous*, literally, throughout places). The Aramaic expression that the Greek represents is באתר אתר or באתרין אתרין Brock., p. 55; Payn. Sm., p. 33, which we should translate "in all countries" and so it was caught by Phi "in different parts of the world."

Jn. 5.29 is a verse in the center of a predication in which "all that are in the graves shall hear his (Jesus') voice." V. 29 continues, "And they shall come forth; they that have done good unto the resurrection of life; and they that have done evil, unto the resurrection of damnation ($\epsilon\dot{\iota}s\ \dot{\alpha}\nu\acute{\alpha}\sigma\tau\alpha\sigma\iota\nu\ \kappa\rho\acute{\iota}\sigma\epsilon\omega s$, literally, to a resurrection of judgment). The Greek *anastasis* commonly means "rising up from the grave," hence "resurrection." What, however, can the "resurrection of judgment" signify? Bernard I, p. 245 assumes that there are two resurrections, one of *life,* and one of *judgment,* but this explanation lacks support from the language, from doctrine and from content. We know that there will be a judgment, but why a resurrection? Bernard, ibid, sensed what the interpretation should be when he remarks that final "Judgment will be pronounced." The Aramaic text reads לקימא (ד)דינא. In light of the "resurrection" in the beginning of the verse, the translator took קימא to be one and the same, and so he rendered with *anastasis* "resurrection of judgment." He should have retroverted with "the fulfillment of judgment," or "to fulfill judgment" namely, execute judgment for the wicked. The retroversion for the Aramaic may take on variable forms as the noun קימא is employed for *anastasis* Lk. 2.34; 11.14 but mistranslated here, or else as a verb לקימא in the Pa'el (Jast. p. 1332) "fulfill," and Payn. Sm., p. 495 with *dina* "establish"; Brock., p. 655 *explevit*. We should translate, "And those who do evil (shall stand) for the sentence of judgment."

A section in Jn. 4.36—38 requires considerable reconstruction. The first verse reads, "And he that reapeth receiveth wages, and gathereth fruit unto life eternal; that both he that soweth and he that reapeth may rejoice together." This verse is contradicted by the next verse that runs, "And herein is the saying true, 'One soweth and another reapeth' ἄλλος ἐστὶν ὁ σπείρων καὶ ἄλλος ὁ θερίζων," literally, there is the one sowing, and another is the one reaping. V. 38 seems to confirm the statement of v. 37, "I have sent you to reap where ye have bestowed no labor; other men labored, and ye are entered into their labors."

The trouble seems to revolve around v. 37. Aside from the contradictions, there is something of a question of flying in the face of the natural order of things, where the usual round of events is that the one who sows is the one who reaps. Bernard, I, p. 159 thinks that Jesus quoted the proverb in a "cynical fashion," although Bernard feels obligated to defend it. The translator, who saw in his text the following חדא הוא דזרע וחדא הוא דחצד, misinterpreted the text on two counts: First, he misconstrued חדא . . . חדא as "the one" and "the other," whereas he should have understood and translated "the one" and "the (same) one." Second, he missed more importantly the special function of the Waw in the proverb. Frequently, the Waw joins two clauses together, especially in a proverb, with the intent that the reader should understand that both clauses are one and the same, and go together. I may quote the formulation as given by Brown, Driver and Briggs in their *Lexicon* (p. 253j):

"It is used in the formulation of proverbs (the vav adaequationis וו השתואה as Prov. 17.3; 25.3.20.25 'Cold waters to a thirsty soul *and* good news from a far country' (i.e., they are like each other) 26.3.9.14.20; 27.21; Ec. 5.2; 8.8 cf. 9.11; Ps. 19.5; 125.2; Jb. 14.11 (cf. in Arabic 'Every man and his cares' (accusative), 'Everything and its price' (accusative), i.e., they go together: 'Merchants and dogs (accus.) of Seleucia,' i.e., they are like one another.'" Thus, in its original form the text read חדא הוא דזרע וחדא הוא דחצד which may be translated, if not too literally because of the construction, "The one who sows, *and* the one who harvests *are like one another*." This comports excellently with the preceding verse *fine* "That both he that soweth, and he that reapeth may rejoice together i.e., are one and the same." However, Jesus contrastingly concludes with the message in V. 38, "I sent you to reap that whereon ye bestowed *no* labor. . . ." The "I" (*ego*) at the beginning of the verse is emphatic. Note the wordplay חדא "rejoice" and חדא "the one."

A verse that piques our curiosity contains the exclamation of Pilate in Jn. 19.5, "Then came Jesus forth wearing the crown of thorns, and the purple robe. And (Pilate) saith unto them [to the chief priests and officers, v. 6]

'Behold the man! (*idou ho anthropos*).'" The background to those events was that Pilate was playing a cat-and-mouse game. We know, from Josephus and Philo independently, that he was a bitter, barbarous, and ferocious tyrant, who disregarded both the solemn feelings of the Jews and Roman precedent, by bringing images and standards into Jerusalem. He threatened to murder those who protected others, confiscated money from the Temple treasury, and sadistically mingled the blood of the Galilean Jews with their sacrifices (Lk. 13.1). He put to death so many of the Samaritans (of a religious movement only, and non-political) that they appealed to the Syrian governor, Pilate's superior. Philo reported that Agrippa implicitly threatened to bring a bill of particulars to the Emperor's attention about Pilate's administration: his corruption, his acts of violence, his rapine, his habit of insulting people *untried and uncondemned* (italics mine), and his persistent inhumanity. (See further, E. Schürer, *Geschichte des jüdischen Volkes*, I, pp. 488 f. for sources, and discussion.)

This description provides the ominous background and the cruel irony of Pilate. Undoubtedly, as a partial justification of himself, he connived to entrap the priests and officers into a damaging statement about Jesus as a king (Jn. 19.21–22). To expose him to ridicule, Jesus was dressed in a purple robe and a crown of thorns as a mock caricature of a putative king, and the soldiers jeered at him as king of the Jews. In this context, what sense can be ascribed to "Behold the man"?

It is easily possible that the Greek translator may have failed to perceive the idiomatic deployment of the determinate case in the Aramaic. He should have rendered perhaps the emphatic case indeterminately, "Behold, *a* man!" and not the supposed king. But, there is more to this. The grotesquerie of the crown of thorns and the wearing of the purple robe, the mock insignia of royalty, points to a more pungent reading wherein the translator failed to vocalize properly. He should have read הָא גִבָּרָא "*See the mighty man! See the hero!*" for הָא גַבְרָא "Behold the man!" The remark, in irony and sardonic jest, is addressed to the assembly of the High Priest and the attendants. This interpretation is not only in character with the sadistic streak in Pilate's disposition, but significantly brings to a fitting climax the dramatic confrontation of the scene.

The characteristics of nuances have been commented upon. A nuance may hover over the boundary of a mistranslation. Nuance, by definition, is a shade of meaning that the translator may have failed to perceive but which nevertheless may produce a palpable distortion. An example is found in Jn. 2.15, "And when he had made a scourge of small cords, he drove them [the

THE EVIDENCE FROM JOHN

moneychangers] out of the temple, and the sheep and the oxen; and poured out (ἐξέχεεν) the changers' money, and overthrew the tables." The Greek word is used for pouring wine, the shedding of blood (liquids) etc., but hardly for money or coins (this but the one instance quoted by Arndt-Gingrich, p. 246). The Aramaic word in the Urtext was שדי, which, while the equivalent of the Greek, goes its own way. It is employed for hurling, casting out, throw away (solids), employed thus in the Peshitta/*hishlik* Ex. 1.22 *yarah* Ex. 15.4, as well as "pour out (water), Brock., p. 758; Jast., p. 1524. The translator missed the cue here, and should have rendered שדי by "he cast out" not "poured," the latter too literal a translation.

A nuance (mistranslation?) that escaped its proper shading is likewise to be noticed at Jn. 7.49 "But the people who knoweth not the law are cursed" (ἐπάρατοί εἰσιν, var. *epikatarasis* "cursed, vile"). It is certainly severe to say in the context that ignorant persons are to be cursed. They may be contemptible, not worthy of notice, but hardly to "be cursed," comp. Gdspd "doomed," "lost" NAB. Probably the root קלל is one of the forms which means (1) curse and (2) make light of, slight, disregard, and is probably the root in question. Note the variant forms in Jast. pp. 1375, 1378. The translation should probably run, "Those people who do not know the law are to be disregarded."

Some passages need more probing, and the solutions are larger in scope. One such section is found at Jn. 2.23–25 where the text reads, "Now when he was in Jerusalem at the Passover, in the feast (ἐν τῇ ἑορτῇ), many believed in his name, when they saw the miracles which he did. But Jesus did not commit himself ἐπίστευεν (literally "believe, trust") unto them, because he knew all [men], (v. 25) and needed not that any should testify of man (τοῦ ἀνθρώπου) for he knew what was in man (τί ἦν ἐν τῷ ἀνθρώπῳ)."

Note first, that the peculiar expression "in the feast" appears *after* "the Passover." We should expect in reverse order במועדא דפסחא "in the feast of the Passover." The locution however is elucidated most satisfactorily as the Mishnaic terminus technicus מועד "The holiday week." Compare Mishna Pesa. I. 3 בתוך המועד "during the festive week of Passover," Jast., p. 745; Levy, *Neuh. u. Chal.*, III, p. 55; Kohut, *Aruch*, V, 200. Translate: He was in Jerusalem at the Passover, during the holiday week.

Second, there is a wordplay on "many believers" (in his name) and "commit" (himself), both ascending to אמן ... הימנו, one meaning "believe," and the other understood by the translator as "commit" (transitive). According to this one interpretation, Jesus did not entrust himself to the people, because the beliefs of the throngs were formed on the basis of his miracles. Compare the previous passage and Bernard I, p. 99. It seems a little strange, however, to remark that Jesus failed to entrust himself to the Jerusalemites, even though, as Bernard assumes, this comment originates with John. The connection, moreover, between the latter part of the verse "because he knew all men" and the first part is tenuous and perplexing. What lent ambiguity to the verse finds its source in the substrative Aramaic. הוא ישוע לא אמין הוא ליה לותהון מטול דידע הוא לכלא which may be translated, "Jesus did not *continue* (remain) with them, because he knew all men." He knew, that is, that their belief based on miracles was fickle, so he did not remain with them. He knew the nature of men. The translator understood אמין as הימין as "believe, trust" instead of "remain, continue". (cf. Hebrew אמן "abide"), and Payn. Sm., p. 19—20. אמן and הימין are, of course, different in meaning, Brock., p. 25, 175, but the translator confused them.

V. 25 contains a misunderstanding of בר אנשא which the Johannine translator assumed to be "man," but which should be "the Son of Man," the term used frequently by Jesus with regard to himself. The sense of the passage is now, in Johannine emphasis and importance, that Jesus needed no one in Jerusalem to testify about the Son of Man and his miracles. The last of v. 25 admits finally of a number of interpretations. It may mean (1) He knew man's impulses, the character of men בבר אנשא (2) He דידע הוא מא דהוא בבר אנשא knew what was in the Son of Man, actually a mistranslation on the part of the Greek as simply "man"; however, בר אנשא is Jesus' denomination of himself, with the import that Jesus was aware of the divine consciousness within himself, or (3) which I prefer on the basis of the Aramaic original, "The fate that would befall the Son of Man, the destiny that was in store for him." Compare the various meanings of היה in Hebrew, BDB 224; of הוא in Brock., p. 173; Payn. Sm., p. 101b. Again, this verse may be but a comment of John who incorporated his own observation into the Fourth Gospel, as Bernard has suggestively endorsed. The passage should read, "Now when he was in Jerusalem in the Passover week, many believed in his name, when they saw the miracles which he did. But Jesus did not remain with them, because he knew everything (or all men); and he needed no one to testify about the Son of Man (himself) for he knew the fate in store for him" comp. Jn. 13.1.

A broad restoration too is required in Jn. 8.38—42. In summarizing the argument that begins at v. 33, the Jews had contended that they are Abraham's seed; Jesus countered by saying that he knows that they are Abraham's seed, but they seek to kill him. V. 38 continues, "I speak that

THE EVIDENCE FROM JOHN 153

which I have seen with my Father; and ye do what ye have seen with your father." Read perhaps with UBS (Metzger, p. 225) "Ye do what ye have heard (ekousate)." V. 39 "They answered and said unto him, 'Abraham is our father.' Jesus saith unto them, 'If ye were the children of Abraham, ye would do the works of Abraham.'" V. 40, "But now ye seek to kill me, a man that hath told you the truth, which I have heard of God; this did not Abraham; Ye do the deeds of your father (ὑμεῖς ποιεῖτε τὰ ἔργα τοῦ πατρὸς ὑμῶν). Then said they to him, 'We be not born of fornication (ἡμεῖς ἐκ πορνείας) We have one Father, even God.'" More precisely, "God is the one Father to us." The Aramaic ran: ḥad 'abba' lan 'elaha'.

It is evident that the dialogue in v. 40 *fine* and the beginning of v. 41 ensues in a perplexing fashion. Abraham, as ancestor, did not do things they want to do to Jesus in seeking to kill him. Yet v. 41 follows immediately with the statement of Jesus that "Ye do the deeds of your father." This must be Satan as commentators propose. The people's puzzling reply is that they were not born of "fornication." Moreover they have one father, God. What is the sense of this interchange between Jesus and the people? How is the retort an answer to the charge?

The answer is that the Aramaic עבר "pass over, transgress, surpass" (Payn. Sm., p. 398; Brock., pp. 507–508; Jast., pp. 1038–1039), was misread as the familiar עבד, "do." Moreover, the verb עבר, and its noun עברה, עברתא, has the additional, specific meaning of "sexual immorality, licence" (Jast., ibid). V. 41 therefore bears the following connotation: Jesus charges, "You surpass the transgressions performed by your father Satan." As in v. 44, where Satan is directly named as "father," it is Satan who now spawns these evildoers, and they exceed what Satan has practiced. "An adulterous generation" is a term employed by Jesus elsewhere, although it is employed in a metaphorical sense, most likely like the *zanah* of the Hebrew prophets. There is, however, the suggestive implication or tone that, like Satan, the people are guilty of immorality for which Satan was notoriously famed, as he had had sexual relations with Eve from way back (L. Ginzberg, *Legends of the Jews* I, p. 105; V, p. 133; also I, ch. II "Adam"; the Slavonic Book of Enoch, 29.4 ff.; II Cor. 11.3; Rev. 12.9). Satan kindles the impulse to impurity (*yezer ha-ra'*) Ex. Rab. 20. In short, Jesus charges that the people are begotten of Satan, and therefore are bastards, and Satanic in their desire to kill him. The translator confused the whole dialogue by misreading עבר עברתא as עבד עבידתא, i.e., "do the deeds" for "committed the sin."

The people in reply answer point by point. Focusing on the charge of bastardy, they deny (1) that they are the children of immorality; and as for

Satan being their father as Jesus accused them, (2) that they are the children of the one God. The use of *talḥins* throughout will be obvious. They do not follow Satan as "father" but God as "Father."

There are a number of stock translations in Jn. that the Greek translator had fixed in his mind, but which in context appear singular or incongruous (comp. the remarks on p. 43 regarding the standard equations in Mt. and Lk.). In Jn. 9.24, the man whose sight was restored was importuned by "the Jews" to state whether Jesus was a "sinner." The text then continues, "Then again called they the man who was blind, and said unto him, 'Give God the praise (δὸς δόξαν τῷ θεῷ); we know that this man is a sinner.'" After the longish episode from v. 6, "praise" in the context does not suit the sense and the point of the passage. The people are asking him in reality to *confess* before God, and this is quite the interpretation proposed by the conservative Bernard, II, p. 334, "A form of adjuration meaning 'speak the truth' as at Josh. 7.19." The latter passage, however, has been misunderstood as "praise" (תודה) as in the translations (AV RSV, Jewish Version, et al.), for "confess." (Cf. Siegfried-Stade who in their Dictionary argue for "admit, confess" but BDB, undecided, yet offer "confess," and so indeed Jerome, Kimḥi.) On the whole, it is simple to assume that אודיתא, like the later הודאה, and the liturgical use of the verb and noun in the Jewish synagogue, means both "give thanks, *praise*" (BDB, 392 Levy, *Chal. Wört.*, I, p. 207) which the translator mistakenly took here in this meaning, and secondly "give confession" the only appropriate interpretation. Similar confusions in meaning exist elsewhere, for example אנשי הודאה may signify men who confess their wrong, or men who give praise (Jast., p. 337). In Jn. the Aramaic read הב אודיתא לאלהא or אודי לאלהא "confess before God," and this should have been the translation.

There are a number of instances where *akouein* "hear" represents more than that signification, and the different shades of the Greek word, when retroverted to the pristine Aramaic, show a much more pungent meaning. In correlating *akouein* to the Aramaic equivalent, we may note שמע as meaning "understand" as in 1 Kg. 3.9, "an understanding heart." See, too, the synonymous remarks about קבל, p. 64. So for the familiar "He who has ears to hear, let him hear," Mt. 11.15; 13.9; Mk. 4.9.23; 7.16; Lk. 7.8 (with variations), the basic more pointed rendering should be, "He who has ears to hear, will understand," or "will comprehend it." The latter observation certainly applies to the verse in Jn. 6.60, "Many therefore of his disciples, when they heard [this] said, 'This is a hard saying; who can hear it?'" Obviously the translation of שמע should be, "Who can understand it?" The Greek translator however rendered too literally, keeping close to the fundamental, frequent meaning.

In Jn. 8.43, the passage which, again, contains *akouein* and is to be interpreted as "listen" should be read as a declarative, not a question, and should be rendered, "Perhaps (i.e., דלמא) you do not understand my teaching, because you cannot bear to listen to my discourse." There is a wordplay on מלתא used twice in the verse (cf. the Peshitta). The translation of AV, "Why do ye not understand my speech? Even because ye cannot hear my word" is enigmatic and awkward.

Mentioned previously was the misunderstanding, on the part of the Synoptic translators of the root פרס in the form of פריסתא meaning "morsels of bread." The translator persistently renders the word in its primitive but unsuitable meaning of "broken pieces, fragments." This fixed stock equation is likewise seen in Jn. 6.12, where instead of "fragments" we should read "morsels of bread," and similarly in v. 13 for "fragments of the five barley loaves" we clearly should read "morsels." The episode of the loaves and fishes in Jn. would seem to come from a separate Aramaic strand or tradition.

This kind of misunderstanding, of being too literal, comes through again in Jn. 12.32, where, as has been noticed before, סלק/רמי may have been mistranslated as "lifted up" (see p. 146). In the present instance, the Aramaic word that the text seems to demand would most likely be סלק. In the stock equation again of *hupsoo*, סלק is used in the Targ. for עלה "go up" in a frequent equation; note particularly in the conjugations its use for "departing from the world," Dt. 6.4, Targ., Yer. II; used of God's spirit Job 34.29; Is. 30.20 withdrawing to the heavens; in b. Ket. 106a "Elijah disappeared"; Levy, *Chal. Wört.*, II, p. 168. While *hupsoo* is usually rendered by ארים in the Peshitta, סלק "die" is particularly idiomatic in Jewish Aramaic, though with infrequent parallels in Syriac, e.g., *selqat nafsheh* "His soul ascended," he died, Payn. Sm., p. 279. Accordingly it appears that the translator bethought himself of the fundamental meaning, and rendered too literally, "be lifted up from the earth," whereas he should have rendered "disappear," i.e., die, which is the sense quite explicit here. The next verse brings this out, "This he said what death he would die;" and in the next verse, too, where the people maintain, ... "Christ abideth forever. How sayest thou, 'The Son of Man must *be lifted up*'"? i.e., erroneous for "die, disappear." The passage under discussion should therefore read, "And I, if I disappear from the world, will draw all men unto me." The latter part of the verse can but be provisionally understood, depending on whether it be regarded as a genuine prophecy or as a vaticinia ex eventu (Bernard, II, p. 442). One may observe again that for the word "draw (up)" in the verse the proper word would be סלק in the pa'el (cf. ἑλκύω/selaq Jn. 21.6 s), and it would serve with "die, disappear" as a wordplay. The sense of the passage predicates, too, that with Jesus' disappearance into heaven, he will draw up mankind to heaven, where they will live with him forever. This is in contrast to the people's belief that the Messiah will remain on earth with them.

In answer to a statement of Nicodemus, Jesus declared, "Except a man be born again, he cannot see the kingdom of God" (Jn. 3.5). Nicodemus wondered about this. He asked, can a man be born again? V. 5 carries through, "Jesus answered, 'Verily, verily, I say unto thee, except a man be born of water and of the Spirit (ἐξ ὕδατος καὶ πνεύματος), he cannot enter into the kingdom of God.'" The construction and content are a little uncertain. One might be born in and out of the spirit, but can one be born again of the water? Note also that in v. 2 Jesus says nothing about being born of water, and in v. 6 he says simply, "That which is born of the spirit is spirit," and again water is not mentioned. Bernard (I, p. 105) thinks that "born of the water" is a reflection of later Christian demand for baptism, since the matter would have been irrelevant to Nicodemus, a Jew, and hence the phrase is to be regarded as a gloss. The assumption of a gloss, however, is denied by others (Barrett in Peake,[2] p. 740a). MS. tradition supports the phrase. The Aramaic may have a contribution. Probably it ran אין לא יליד בר נשא דומיא דרוחא which may be rendered, "If a man be not born in the likeness of spirit . . ." דומיא is a noun "likeness," in apposition to בר נשא Jast., p. 286; Brock., p. 156. The translator read דמיא "of water," a misconstruing of syntax. He likewise supplied *kai* in the Greek to make it more compatible with the following phrase, "of spirit." The correct translation should have been, "If a man be not born in the likeness of the spirit, he cannot enter the kingdom of God."

An exegesis, actually based upon a misunderstanding of an Aramaic idiom is evidenced in Jn. 14.30, "Hereafter, I [Jesus] will not talk much with you; for the prince of the world [Satan] cometh, and hath nothing in me" (καὶ ἐν ἐμοὶ οὐκ ἔχει οὐδέν). This appears to be a most unusual expression, and there is much difference of opinion as to what it means, "In me indeed he can claim nothing," Mof.[1]; "He has no hold on me," Mof.[2]; "No rights over me," NEB; "No power over me," RSV; "He has no claim on me," Beck. The latter seems completely inappropriate in concept and drift. The phrase, however, is an Aramaic locution, found frequently in the Babylonian Talmud, wherein, for example, an extraneous element is introduced into a legal discussion only to be excluded with the phrase לית לן בה (לא אתי לנא בה) with the significance "We have nothing to do with this; this is not within the province of discussion; in this instance, we do not adhere to that view." The idiomatic phrase may be literally rendered, "We have nothing with this." Compare Levy, NHB, II, p. 506; Jast., p. 710. The great power of Satan as the "prince of the world" is recognized in this verse, although Satan's power is in this world only (compare L. Ginzberg, *Legends* III, p. 35). In contradistinction to the Greek *en* which usually renders the Aramaic *b*, sometimes in, sometimes with, in our passage, *en* seems a genuine mistranslation of "in/with." The present verse has the sense of "He has nothing to do with me!" or invertedly "I have no business with him!"

In Jn. 10.5, the root (אפך), meaning "turn" and "flee," was misapprehended by the translator. The previous verses describe the sheep which follow the shepherd, because they know his voice, because he calls them by name. V. 5 continues, "And as a stranger will they not follow, but will flee from him ($\phi\epsilon\acute{u}\xi o \nu \tau \alpha \iota$); for they know not the voice of strangers." The term "flee" is excessive and overdrawn; the sheep flee when the wolf comes (v. 12), but not necessarily from the voice of a stranger. Either the sheep will stand still, or else draw back, or turn aside, אפך signifying both "turn back" and "flee." For the use of the phrase in connection with sheep cf. the phrase אפך גזרא "lead, or move a flock from one place to another," Payn. Sm., p. 106 and the root נוס/אפך in Targ. Jonathan; Josh. 8.6.7; 1 Sam. 4.16.17; 1 Chron. 10.7; 19.1.15. All these examples are not only in Jewish Palestinian Aramaic, but also in Syriac, Payn. Sm., p. 106 (b). The passage should be translated, "And a stranger they will not follow, but will turn (אפך) from him."

As the reader studies the Greek of John, and is conscious of the vox memoriae of the Aramaic, wordplay so characteristic of Aramaic (and of Semitic generally) comes through. An almost classic example employed by the author of John himself, but not making sense in the Greek, is extant at John 11.11, where Jesus, now resolving to visit the "dead" Lazarus, said to his disciples, "Our friend Lazareth *sleepeth* (*kekoimetai*), but I go that I may awake him out of sleep"(*ekshupniso*). The disciples in response declare, "Lord, if he sleep, he shall do well" (*sosthesetai*, literally, he will be healed; Aram. יחי "he will recover"). V. 13 follows with, "Howbeit, Jesus spake of his (Lazarus's *death* (*thanatou*); but they thought he had spoken of taking of rest in *sleep*" (*hupnou*). V. 14 continues "Then said Jesus unto them plainly,

'Lazarus is *dead*" (*apethanen*). The passages contain a play on the root דמך meaning "sleep" and "die," semantically the same as the Hebrew and Aramaic שכב. When Jesus spoke at first about Lazarus's sleeping, to awaken him from his sleep, he apparently used the term שכב/דמך, and the disciples thought—as they were thinking of the meaning "sleep" and not "die"—that Lazarus would get well. But then Jesus employed another word ("plainly"), and fixed the meaning with "Lazarus is dead" (מית). This kind of *jeu de mots* is reflected elsewhere where Jesus made use of this device. Thus in Mt. 21.3 in the requisition of the ass and colt, ("the Lord hath need of them") there is the wordplay of מרא (1) Lord and (2) owner(!)

Moreover, there is a whole section in Jn. 8.30—35 in which there are a number of wordplays, plays in sounds and consonants, plays on meanings, and overtones (*talḥin*). The passages run, with the wordplays emphasized:

V. 30 "As he spake these words, many *believed* (*episteusan*) on him."

V. 31 "Then said Jesus to those Jews which *believed* on him, 'If ye *continue* (*meinete*) in my word, then ye are my disciples *indeed* (*alethos*).'"

V. 32 "And ye shall know the *truth* (*aletheian*), and the *truth* shall make you free."

V. 33 "They answered him, We be Abraham's seed, and we were never in *bondage* (*dedouleukamen*) to any man. How sayest thou, 'Ye shall be made free'"?

V. 34. "Jesus answered them, '*Verily, verily* (*amen*), I say unto you, Whosoever *committeth* (*poion ten amartian*) sin is the *servant* (*doulos*) of sin.'"

V. 35 "And the servant abideth (*meno*) not in the house forever (literally, unto the age); but the Son abideth forever."

The root אמן "believe, be continued," and its pe'al formation and idem in the pai'el הימן, as well as in the Ethpe. "persist in, continue in" Payn. Sm., pp. 19—20; Brock., p. 25 carries through the whole of the section. Again,

V. 30 "believed" הימנו.

V. 31 contains three wordplays: "believed," "continue" as אמן supra. "Indeed" (*alethos* "truly") is אימנאית (and so in the Peshitta).

V. 32 "truth," הימנותא (bis).

V. 34 "verily, verily" is undoubtedly אמן, אמין in Syr., אמן in Heb. Moreover the phrase "committed sin" is עבר עברה (Aramaic!) Jast. 1038—1039 and is a play upon עבדא "servant."[15]

V. 35 "servant" is עבדא again; "abideth" may have a number of retroversions, but it probably is מתאמן "continue in" carrying through the wordplay.

There is one mistranslation. "Forever," (εἰς τὸν αἰῶνα) or literally, unto the age, is Hebrew-Aramaic לעלם and prefaced by לא means "not at all, never"; in talmudic usage the same meaning obtains. We should translate, "The servant never stays in the house; but the Son abides always."

There are, in summary, some six occasions in which אמן with its meanings and nuances are played upon, and some four times in which עבד is punned upon.

From the point of view of exegesis in v. 32 the expression "And ye shall know the truth, and the truth shall make you free" the talḥin meaning "faith" *and* "truth" could, to the more sophisticated listeners, imply "Faith shall make you free" i.e., free from sin, *men ḥatitha* as Nestorius has it metaphorically (Brock., p. 89; Bernard, II, p. 305).

In v. 35 the argument is difficult to follow (Bernard, II, p. 308). The overtones in the verse however, "And the servant (sin) stays not with the family (*baitha* may mean "household, family") at all, but the Son (*bar*, with a play too on *bar* "innocent, clear of sin") abides," a *talḥin* of sin and innocence is contrasted. Simply, however, though pregnant with meaning, the verse signifies, "A slave can never stay on in the ancestral house, but the Son continues always."[16]

A further wordplay is understood through the Aramaic retroversion in Jn. 7.6.8. Jesus had performed miracles, and had been told by his brothers to go to Judea and "show thyself in the world. Then Jesus said unto them, 'My time (*kairos*) is not yet come; but your time (*kairos*) is always ready'" (*etoimos*). V. 8 continues, "Go ye up unto this feast (*eorten*); I go not up yet unto this feast; for my time (*kairos*) is not yet full come."

V. 6 contains the wordplay *zimna* "time" (Peshitta *zabna*) and *zemin*, *mezamman* "ready, prepared" (Jast., p. 404). While זבן is usual in Syriac, זמן is to be preferred as previously mentioned, as the forms alternate in Aramaic Inscriptions (compare Cowley, *Glossary of Aramaic Inscriptions*, p. 48), and the form is good Jewish Aramaic as in Biblical Aramaic, the Targs., Babylonian Talm. Aramaic, as well as Akk. *simanu* (Brock., p. 187). The exegesis of the verses in the light of the literary rhetorical device presented changes the sense of the passage. In effect, Jesus declares "Your time is fixed by the calendar to go regularly to the feasts. My time is not ordered that way."[17]

A most perplexing dialogue begins at Jn. 4.31. The disciples are concerned that their teacher and master did not eat, "And they prayed to him, 'master, eat.'" V. 34 continues, "But he said unto them, 'I have meat (βρῶσιν = food) to eat that ye know not of.'" V. 34 then elucidates, "My meat (βρῶμα food) is to do the will of him that sent me, and to finish his work." This is a type of discourse, in Jn. mainly in ch. 3.4.6, that has been denominated by some critics as "schematism," in which Jesus first propounds an enigmatically phrased statement; the disciples do not understand this; then Jesus elucidates, either wholly or partially, with some appropriate explanation. Such tropes are found elsewhere. Thus, Jesus tells the woman of Samaria that he would have given her "living water" (4.10). The woman does not understand. The מיין חיין ordinarily means "fresh water, water from a spring," but Jesus had indulged in a wordplay where the phrase also means essentially "water of life, eternal water," similar to the rabbinic explanation of the verse of Is. 55.1, "All ye who are thirsty, betake yourselves to the water" which the Rabbis interpret as meaning not water, but the eternal Torah. This type of discourse is seen and has been discussed in Mt. 16.6.12; Mk. 8.15—21 (see p. 41f.). In our passage under discussion, what does "my food" signify, and in what sense is it God's work to be accomplished?

It is apparent that the Aramaic סיברתא has been utilized with a double meaning; (1) My *burden* (cf. Hebrew *massa'* = burden, oracle, message, Jer. 23.33) is to do the will of the one who sent me"; (2) referring to the disciples' remark about "my food," סיברתא is employed for *broma* in Mt. 14.15 p s c; Lk. 9.13 and is derived from סבר, (so Payn. Sm. 359, but according to Brock., p. 457 there are two roots) a noun which means "food," but may also carry the meaning of "that which is borne, endured" from the Aramaic *saibar* "bear, carry." Cf. the Ethpai'al in that sense (Payn. Sm., p. 359). In Jewish Aramaic the form appears in the Po'el *sobar,* used as a verb "support, supply, provisions," Jast., p. 952, whence we have denominatively the derived sense of "support, food, provision" (Payn. Sm., p. 359 reverses this). In the Greek, "food" by itself conveys little sense. Here in the Aramaic, the double meaning, repeated in "food" and "burden" would be understood in a palpable fashion by the Aramaic reader.

Undoubtedly, the same wordplay is extant in Jn. 6.27 where Jesus speaks to the multitude that had been fed, "Look not for the meat (*brosin,* food) which perisheth, but for that meat which endureth unto everlasting life, which the Son of Man shall give to you; for him hath God, the Father, sealed" (*esphragisen*).

Taking the last clause first for elucidation, "sealed" is a mistranslation of

חתם meaning not "sealed" in this instance but "affirmed, confirmed, attested to" (see p. 144 for a similar confusion).

The "meat that perisheth" is the food that is consumed and "lost"; (τὴν βρῶσιν τὴν μένουσαν) סיברתא דהימנותא is translated, on the surface, "the food that endures." Nevertheless, what is this "food that endures" and what are its implications that Jesus seeks to convey to his listeners? This is a wordplay, a *talḥin*, perhaps even a mistranslation with the message that it is the nourishment of faith, "support of *faith*" (*haimanutha*) "to eternal life which the Son of Man shall give to you." And what furthermore is this "support of faith"? V. 29 gives the answer, "That ye believe (*haiman* again and punning on *haimanutha* supra) on him whom he hath sent." Note as well that סיברתא can be a *talḥin* for סברתא "the Gospel" literally, "tidings" (Payn. Sm., p. 329), used for the Evangel in Mk. 1.44; 8.35 p s; Mt. 4.23 p s c., and can be associated readily in a reader or listener's mind with "my food" and "burden."

In this category of wordplays we may notice Jn. 4.36, "They shall rejoice together" יחדון כחדא. For the full discussion of Jn. 4.36—38, see p. 149.

Notice too, the following wordplays, tacitly confirming again his Aramaic origin. Thus, Jn. 12.24 "Except a corn of wheat ... die, it remains as one" (see p. 149) "But if it die, it bringeth forth much fruit." A play is on the words מיתא "die" (bis), and מתיא "bringeth forth." Similarly, words are played upon in the famous text, Jn. 11.25, "I am the resurrection and the life," אנא חית מיתא וחיתא, 'ena hăyāth mīthē we-ḥayātha, cf. Payn. Sm., p. 141; Brock., p. 229; Jewish Aramaic is אחיותא, Jast., p. 40; *hayath mitha/anastasis* p s Mt. 22.23; s Mt. 22.28. Jn. 19.42 "For the sepulchre was nigh at hand" (*eggus*) i.e., קריב לה קוברא.

We pass on to considerations of syntax, misconstrued by the Greek translator. Quite a puzzling text is Jn. 8.15 which enigmatically reads, "Ye judge after (according to) the flesh; I judge no man" (ἐγὼ οὐ κρίνω οὐδένα). A distinctive doctrine in Jn. predicates that Jesus does not judge any man (3.17); although on the last day, the spoken word might judge him (12.48); but as an ethical principle "I judge him not, for I came not to judge the world" (12.47). The present verse, however, seems weakened by a retraction in the sequel, "But if I do judge ..." and the reader remains uncertain. The construction in Aramaic seemingly for "I judge no man" would be אנא לאנש לא דן אנא "I do not judge any one," and so on the surface. This would be the natural interpretation, which the translator adopted. It does not, however, provide the correct antithesis to the first part of the verse

"You judge after the flesh," i.e., in a human fashion. The latter part of the verse should have construed לאנש by "*as* a man," the Lamed being mistaken for the sign of the accusative instead of "as, like." This function of the Lamed meaning "as" is found frequently in Hebrew (BDB, p. 512.4). The same usage is found in Aramaic (Jn. 8.15 s). Cf. moreover Dan. 4.27 "as a royal residence ... and as an hour for any majesty," and for almost an exact parallel e.g. Nöld. *Syr. Gram.*, par. 247 "If one buys a slave as a good slave." *l'abda' taba* to the verse under discussion. We should now translate, "You judge in a human fashion; I do not judge as a man."

An obscure meaning and problematic syntax are present in the verse at Jn. 9.27. In the preceding section Jesus had cured a man of his blindness. The Pharisees made inquiry as to how the man was cured and of what character was Jesus who had healed him. V. 26 runs, "Then said they to him again, 'What did he to thee? How opened he thine eyes?'" V. 27 gives the reply, "I have told you already, and ye did not hear; Wherefore would ye hear it again? Will ye also be his disciples?" (μὴ καὶ ὑμεῖς θέλετε αὐτοῦ μαθηταὶ γενέσθαι). In the context, the latter question is obscure. Bernard (II, p. 335) assumes that this must be "an ironical jibe," as the man wanted to irritate the Pharisees, and renders "Surely you do not wish to become disciples of his?" Irony, however, in this passage is misplaced—the coherence is weak, and the syntax remains difficult. The same may be said with regard to the modern translations "Do you want to be disciples of his?" Mof.[2]; similarly Gdspd.; NEB, and more smoothly, NAB. The Aramaic tells us what the original sense was because the Greek misunderstood the syntax. The original probably ran דלמא אנתון בעין דתהוון יליפין לה. The translator interpreted or thought he read ילופין "students," Payn. Sm., p. 192, whereas he should have read יליפין the pe'il form with the Dative of Agent "by him," not "pupils to him" as a preposition. The rendition now takes the shape of "Perhaps you should be taught by Jesus himself?" We now have a logical sequence: "I told you already; you did not listen; do you want to hear it again? Perhaps you should be taught by *him*?"

The Aramaic origins of Jn. show up again in a passage at 12.24 which reads, "Verily, verily, I say unto you, 'Except a corn of wheat fall into the ground, and die, it abideth alone (αὐτὸς μόνος μένει, literally, it remains alone); but if it dies, it bringeth forth much fruit.'" The verse obviously purports to teach both a contrast and a paradox: if the kernel is not buried in the ground ("dies"), it remains by itself alone, i.e., solitarily sterile; if however it "dies," it produces a good yield. The contrast is not brought out starkly enough in the verse; "yielding much fruit" is not the correct antithesis to "abiding alone." The varied translations give a more adequate rendering by "It remains a single grain," Mof.², Wms.; "a single kernel" Mon.; not "it remains solitary," TCNT, nor "it remains alone," RSV, Torrey. Wey gives the sense acutely, "It remains what it was—a single grain," and similarly NEB, Gdspd.; NAB "It remains just a grain of wheat"; Mof.¹ "It remains by itself alone." Apparently the Greek translator did not quite catch the shade of meaning in the verse. The Aramaic probably ran קם לחדא (variantly לחודיה), which the translator, without looking at the drift of the verse ahead, took to mean "alone." The proper rendition should have conveyed the sense, "It remains as *one*" Nöldeke, *Syriac Grammar*, par. 247. Comp. *monos*/בלחוד Mt. 14.36 Syriac p s c; Mt. 8.8 p c as well as Mt. 12.4; 21.19; *meno*/קים Dan. 4.23; 6.26; and *meno*/עמד in the LXX frequently. For the latter, שאר and יתר would likewise be good synonyms.

If the translator had rendered לחדא as "one," the contrasting *stichoi* would have shown the proper antithesis and sharper point, "Unless a grain of wheat falling to the ground dies, it remains as *one;* but if it dies, it bears much fruit." For the construction, cf. Ez. 37.17.

A syntactical construction of a different sort appears in Jn. 12.16, "These things understood not his disciples at the first; but when Jesus was glorified, then remembered they those things were written of him, and that they had done (ἐποίησαν) these *things unto him.*" As Bernard (II, p. 427) queries, what things did they do to him? The explanation offered attempts to refer the text to the search for the ass Mt. 21.2; Mk. 11.2; Lk. 19.30 which indeed the Synoptists report, but which is not however found in Jn. The Aramaic locution and syntax in the verse were misunderstood. The root עבד "make, do" has the idiomatic definition of "occur, happen," Levy, *Chal. Wört.*, II, p. 196, and compare עובדא = מעשה "story, event, happening." The Aramaic of our text ran הלין עבדו לה or והלין דעבידין לה, as the Peshitta has it, which should have been rendered by the Greek translator as "and those things that *happened* to him." This clears away the enigmatic inexplicable statement of "what they did to him," and per contra, puts the thought in a natural sequence as per the translation, "Then remembered they that these things were written of him, and those things that happened to him."

In this classification of syntactical misconstruction, we may mention the particle *de* which may mean "who, that which, so that, (with the imperfect), because," and reference may be made to the treatises of Burney, Torrey, and Black. One more case may be noted. Jn. 9.17 runs, "They say unto the blind man again 'What sayest thou of him, that (*hoti*) he hath opened thine eyes?' He said, 'He is a prophet.'" The sentence structure is awkward. While *hoti* might govern the direct discourse in Greek, the construction is different here. It is evident that the verse should run in a much more smooth fashion, "What sayest thou of him *who* opened your eyes," where it is clear that *de* is the relative, not the conjunction. The Greek translator made the same mistake in a nearby verse 9.8.

An Aramaic locution likewise misunderstood appears in Jn. 5.6. The previous verses describe how a large number of sick gathered at the Bethesda pool (this is the only reading incidentally that makes sense; בית חסדא aetiologically means "place of grace") to be cured of their ills. They awaited the stirring of the water, and then would go, and immerse themselves to be cured. V. 5 follows with, "And a certain man was there who had an infirmity thirty and eight years." V. 6, "When Jesus saw him lie, and knew that he had been a long time (in that case, AV, literally, that much time he has already, (ὅτι πολὺν ἤδη χρόνον ἔχει), he saith unto him, 'Wilt thou be made whole?'" The Greek is difficult and abrupt; the AV has to supply words for intelligibility. What is meant by saying, "He has a long time?" The Aramaic reproduction of this phrase would be זימנא סגיא אית לה which in turn bachylogically means that he had this illness for a long time, literally, it was to him a long time. Compare Nöl. *Syr. Gram.* p. 241, middle of the page, *zabna sagiaya ith ad* . . ., "It is long, till . . ." Cf. also Burkitt, p. 493 on Jn. 11.40 ארבעא לה יומין as well as the Peshitta, ibid, with the same reading as well as Jn. 11.17.

In the area of misvocalization, a number of verses have remained incomprehensible because the translator did not point his text correctly, a clear indication as the examples will show that the translator had a scroll or codex before him, a written text. Thus Jn. 8.44, "Ye are of your father the devil, and the lusts of your father ye will do. He was a murderer from the beginning, and abode not in the truth, because there is no truth in him. When he speaketh a lie, he speaketh of his own; for he is a liar, and the father of it" (καὶ ὁ πατὴρ αὐτοῦ). Among the questions that puzzle one are:

(1) How was the devil a "murderer"? Whom specifically did he murder? And from what "beginning"?

(2) What is meant by his being a "liar"? How is he the "father of *it*"?

(3) What is meant by the phrase "and abode not in the truth"? literally, he does not stand (ἔστηκεν) in the truth.

We answer these questions—and we start with (2)—by noting that שִׁקְרָא, "falsehood" was misread as שַׁקָּרָא "liar," Jast., p. 1626; Payn. Sm., p. 595; Brock., p. 801. Torrey's *beʻel sheqar* is correct pro forma but is unsupported, and does not reflect the Greek accurately enough. Montgomery *Aramaic Origin*, 21 knew that "liar" must be wrong and argued for "the son of the lie" but did not spell out the Aramaic. The misreading of שְׁקָרָא/שִׁקְרָא threw the whole sentence out of kilter. The translation should have been "For he is a deception (or fraud) and the father of *it*." "Father" of course, simply means, as common in Hebrew and Aramaic, "producer, generator," BDB, p. 3.

With reference to (1), "murderer" is the Greek translation, based on the Aramaic root חבל, fundamentally meaning "to wound," but more frequently "kill, murder," Brock., p. 211 (*necavit*); Palm. חבל "*mortuus*," cited by BDB, p. 287; *ḥabel nafsheh* (Payn. Sm., p. 124) "he destroyed himself," he killed himself, and in other expressions with the same verb: He was killed by lightning, by fire, etc. Still Satan is no "murderer." I consider that Satan may be the earlier מלאך המשחית, 2 Sam. 24.16.17 and 1 Chron. 21.12–30. Targ. is מלאכא דמחבל) and hence as in the later phrase one of the מלאכי חבלה "the destroying angels." In our text, the Aramaic was (חבלנא) which the Greek translator misunderstood as "killer" instead of "destroyer." In this connection, "from the beginning" is almost a terminus technicus, i.e., מבראשית meaning "from the start of all things, from Creation"; because the word begins the Pentateuch, it has served as shorthand for "beginning." Compare in this usage Is. 41.4; 28.29 and the familiar *ma'aseh bereshit*, the secret study of how God created the world, Mishna Ḥag. 2.1 as well as its technical use by the Peshitta in our NT passage. Satan, as the accuser of man, is regarded thus as "a destroyer from the beginning" in that he was the primal cause for the exile of Adam and Eve from Paradise. In a (late) passage in Baba Batra, Satan and the Evil Inclination and the Angel of Death are regarded as one and the same. The phrase "he speaketh of his own" (ἐκ τῶν ἰδίων) Aramaic מן דילה means he tells a lie "of his own invention."

Finally, for the explanation of "and abode (*esteken* = stood) not in the truth," the root *qum*, in Aramaic as in Hebrew, bears a number of significations. In Aramaic, the root has as one of its meanings the sense of "profess, stick to, be occupied in," construed with *b*, Payn. Sm., p. 494; Brock., pp. 652, 657; for example with *miltha'* "stand by one's word," Hebrew עמד בדברו, also as in קם ליה בהימנותא "remain trustworthy," b. Git. 45a; Abod. Zara 8b, 9a; or with *maumatha* "stand by an oath, keep one's oath." Hence the thought of our passage should be, "He is not concerned with, or does not persevere in, or does not stand by the truth, for the truth is not in him." The translator rendered too literally "And stands not in the truth." He apparently did not recognize the idiom.

Chapter VI

Texts and Doctrines

A FEW selected texts have been allocated to this chapter because of their more than ordinary philological interest. They involve a certain historical importance and, indeed, are significant for their theological implications. A number of ideas and doctrines have been founded upon these passages. These texts, however, have been based upon Aramaic, as the preceding pages have sought to affirm. Had these texts been translated correctly, movements and ideas in religion, philosophy, and art, might have taken a different turn, and would have headed in a different direction.

One such example is found in the opening verses of the Gospel of John. "In the beginning was the word (*logos*), and the word was with God, and the word was God." (Perhaps we should translate with Alfred Marshall "And God was the word" as *theos,* the subject, lacks the article, and so interestingly the Peshitta and the Vulgate.) V. 2 continues, "The same was in the beginning with God," and v. 14 states remarkably "And the word was made flesh, and dwelt among us." One must ask in all innocence who is, what is, this word, and how did it become flesh? Moreover, how is it that this doctrine does not appear at all in the body of the Gospel itself? Most perplexing is that Jesus does not use the title *logos* for himself, nor does Jn. apply it to him.

The thesis is advanced that the Logos is the philosophical exposition of the Christian Gospel; that Jesus was the divine Logos (Thomas Aquinas: an intellectual emanation of God); that some parallel may be adduced from the doctrine set forth in Prov. 3.13f.; 4.5f. and especially 8.22 where Wisdom declares "I was set up from everlasting; from the beginning, or ever the earth was." The question of the influence of Greek wisdom (and its personification) upon Hebrew thought seems inextricably complicated. Affirmations of Greek penetration are argued for by C. Siegfried, HDB, IV, p. 925 and S. Holmes, in Charles, II, p. 525 and denied by E. Meyer, *Origin and Beginnings of Christianity,* II, p. 105 f. and Heinisch, *The Personal*

Wisdom of the Old Testament, cited by O. S. Manson, *Israel's Wisdom Literature,* p. 227f. Siegfried's argument that the "sudden" appearance of Wisdom can only be accounted for as coming from outside Judaism, because it would otherwise conflict with the monotheism of the Jews, is erroneous. A religion is not a system of philosophy. The personification of Wisdom is no more in conflict with Jewish tenets than the function of angels, Satan, the Messiah, however he be conceived, and the Torah itself as an emanation of God (it is in "the lap of God"; the passage is quite late; L. Ginzberg, *Legends,* I, 3). Secondly, I would share the view with E. Meyer in his claim that Wisdom is intrinsically, natively, and inherently Jewish although for different reasons. The word *ḥakam,* both in noun and verb, is found more than 450 times in Hebrew Scriptures, with some passages quite early as in 1 Kgs. 5.11f. (Solomon's wisdom), Prov. 1.5; 24.23; 3.19 (God created the world with *ḥokma*), as well as in the tripartite avenue of revelation that the people knew about and could resort to (Jer. 18.18, "For the law shall not perish from the priest, nor counsel from the wise, nor the word from the prophet." See M. L. Margolis, *The Hebrew Scriptures in the Making,* p. 54). To be sure, *ḥakam* and *ḥokma* are used in wide senses from simple cleverness to Divine Wisdom. The personification of Sophia in *Greek,* in concomitance with other personifications of Truth, Justice, Harmony, Virtue etc. is not especially distinctive, like Wisdom or Torah as children of God. As Liddell and Scott observe in their dictionary, Sophia as an hypostasis among the Jews had been "recognized first as an attribute of God and later identified with the Spirit of God," Prov. 8, and Ben Sira ch. 14 et seq.

Reference by scholars to Wisd. 9.1, for the Logos "You made everything with your word" is not happy, as 9.1 is undoubtedly based on Ps. 107.20; 119.50. Nor does the *memra* of God have anything to do with the Logos. *Memra* is an anthropological locution to avoid speaking in human terms about God. Rev. 19.13, based upon a Semitic document, will be fully discussed infra, p. 209.

Loisy, with good instinct and fine scholarship, wrote that the "theology of the Incarnation is the key to the entire book, and which dominates from the first line to the last" (from *La Quatrième Évangile,* p. 98). Bernard's counter to this is not justified. If the purpose of this Gospel is to show "How can God reveal himself to man?" (Bernard, I, *Introduction*) the simplest answer, as in the other Gospels, would be that Jesus in his own person would have been the better manifestation of that revelation. Logos is an attribute ascribed to Jesus by later theologians as were other qualities, tenden-

TEXTS AND DOCTRINES   169

tiously supplied to him. He had to be a firstborn, born of a virgin, a son of
God, a Messiah, and he had to be born in Bethlehem according to prophecy,
of royal blood, a king, a High Priest, a redeemer of Israel, a redeemer of
mankind, and so, he was also designated a Logos to satisfy philosophers.

The whole matter of Logos, however, is founded upon a mistranslation.
Burney attempts to solve the text in 1.1 by assuming that טליא, meaning
both "lamb" and "child, child of God" was played upon. This solution
however has raised the problem, where did Logos, "word," come from?

One of the main differences between the Synoptists and the Fourth
Gospel is that, in the former, Jesus sought to save the Jewish people by
ushering in the Kingdom of God at the most apposite season of the Passover. This was the great feast of liberation from Egyptian slavery. It was felt
somehow that as a typological replica of what had taken place a millennium
before with the great miracle of redemption, "with the strong hand and the
outstretched arm," a similar miraculous event must take place again "like
lightning that shines from the east to the west" (Lk. 19.11). Jesus came to
Jerusalem to eat the Qorban Pesah, the Paschal Lamb, with his disciples,
and with the conscious anticipation of ushering in the Kingdom.

In the Fourth Gospel, there is an entirely different conception. Jesus did
not come to eat the Paschal Lamb: he *is* the Paschal Lamb. He did not come
to save the Jewish people. He came to save mankind. He is the Lamb who
will be sacrificed, and whose blood will be shed to redeem humanity. So important did the author of the Fourth Gospel consider Jesus in this role of the
lamb and its sacrifice, that he focuses on this motif at the crucifixion itself,
where Jesus did not have his bones broken Jn. 19.36 (as he was a political of-
fender). In contrast, the thieves had their legs broken. This was of prime
significance to the Johannine narrator. Jesus as the Paschal Lamb was intact, not disqualified by a broken bone. He was symbolically the true Paschal
sacrifice, as the Scripture has it, "A bone ye shall not break in it" Ex. 12.46;
Num. 9.12. It is this motif that unites the beginning and the end of this
Gospel. Such an unblemished sacrifice now becomes acceptable to God.

In the very first verse of the Gospel, the Greek translator saw the word
אמרא. Whether deliberately or out of simple carelessness or ignorance, or
whether he was influenced by Alexandrinian hermeneutics, he translated the
Aramaic as "word." This, however, was not the intention of the Aramaic
author. It was his conviction that אמרא was to be considered as אמרא "lamb"
not אמרא "word."

The proof that the writer of this Gospel wished to impress his readers
with this concept of Jesus as a lamb, is brought home to us immediately

after the Prologue, and his emphasis on the lamb in Jn. 2.29. John sees Jesus on the street coming to him, and proclaims in sudden designation, "Behold the Lamb of God." Note that he did not say "Behold the Messiah," important as this was and note its emphasis in the same chapter, v. 41; nor did he say, "Behold the Son of God," or "the son of David." He said what the Aramaic author had uppermost in his mind—Jesus was the Lamb of God.

As if to drive home this point, he repeats the salutation once more in v. 35f. "Again the next day, John stood with two of his disciples, and looking upon Jesus as he walked, he saith, 'Behold the Lamb of God!'" The interpretation advanced here has the additional merit of showing the inherent connection and concourse between the Prologue (1–18) and the narrative that follows (19–51), the key word being the Aramaic "lamb," which connection indeed had eluded commentators. As mentioned, this connection persists to the end when at the crucifixion, the Lamb's legs were not broken and the Aramaic author carefully inserted, "For these things were done, that the scripture should be fulfilled, 'A bone of him shall not be broken.'" In short, one may with some certainty conclude that the Aramaic writer had no conception of Logos. The Prologue conveys what he thought:

    V. 1 In the beginning was the Lamb, and the Lamb was with God, and the Lamb was God.

    V. 2 He had been in the beginning with God.

    V. 3 And the Lamb became a man הוא לבסרא (cf. Jn. 8.15 s) and dwelt among us.

Note that v. 2 would be replicative of both language and thought of v. 1, and there would be no point of repeating. It is quite likely that a syntactical misinterpretation took place. The passage appeared to the translator as הוא בברישית לות אלהא which he should have interpreted as a pluperfect in point of time which bears the sense that he had always been with God, this in continuation of the first statement. For such pluperfects, see היה/הוה pluperfect, in MT Gen. 26.1; 30.29; Ex. 1.5 and Onqelos; Nöldeke, *Syriac Grammar*, par. 251.[18]

With significant implications, another interesting example is found at Mt. 3.16 (parallels Mk. 1.10; Lk. 3.22), "And Jesus when he was baptized, went up straightway out of the water; and lo the heavens were opened unto him, and he saw the Spirit of God descending like a dove (ὡσεὶ περιστεράν), and lighting upon him."

The explanation that the Spirit fluttered down upon him somehow like a dove because, as some interpret, the dove being a frequent symbol of Israel

TEXTS AND DOCTRINES 171

and consequently might have an association here, does not hold up as good exegesis. Why the spirit should be like a dove is a mystery.

The truth is that, once again, the Aramaic was misread by the Greek translator. He saw the word כיונא which he imagined to be "like a dove" (the form is with Aleph in Aramaic). He should have read the word with the same consonants כיונא "immediately, directly, straightway," employed frequently in the Targs. for נכון Deut. 13.15; 17.4; Gen. 42.11.31; 42.19.33.34 with the sense of "right, straightway, true," and more to the purpose here, in the sense of the Hebrew כיון which means "directly," Jast., p. 631, as in phrases like Pes. 37a "He may form the dough in a mould, and attach it to the cake *directly*" (*keiwan*); Tamid 3.6 "A priest puts his hand in an opening of the door, and another priest opens with the other key *directly*," and Baba Meṣ. 33a (Levy, *Chal. Wört.*, I, 356 *alsbald*). The sense of our passage becomes simple and clear; the moment Jesus was baptized and "went straightway out of the water, the Spirit of God came down upon him directly."

The original Aramaic restores the rite of the Eucharist to its basic and understandable significance. The worshipper, in eating the bread and drinking the wine, enters into communion with Christ. The fundamental passage that portrays this activity is found in Mk. 14.22 (parallels Mt. 26.26f.; Lk. 22.15f.) and reads as follows:

V. 22 And as they did eat, Jesus took bread ($ἄρτον$), and blessed and brake it, and gave it to them, and said, "take, eat; this is my body."

V. 23 And he took the cup, and when he had given thanks, he gave it to them, and they all drank of it.

V. 24 And he said to them, "This is my blood of the new testament which is shed for many."

There are but slight differences in the parallel accounts. The Fourth Gospel does not mention the Eucharist; Paul's explanation contains matter and interpretation advanced by himself, i.e., that the body of Christ is one, and "we are members of his body" (Eph. 5.30), and that the body is the church. All this is a later development and interpretation. The earlier writers, Clement, the Didache, and Ignatius had different but less significant conceptions of the Eucharist (cf. J. Armitage Robinson, art. "Eucharist," EB cols. 1418 et seq).

There is one fundamental question, seldom noticed, that bears on the elucidation of this scene of Jesus and the disciples, as they sat round the "table" for the Passover meal. We know that a covenant had now been made between Jesus and the disciples, and that covenants, as in the Hebrew Bible, were sealed with blood, Ex. 24.8 and elsewhere, and by a meal eaten together, ibid., v. 11. We further understand how wine, through its reddish color, may symbolically represent blood, and the drinking of the wine may serve symbolically for the drinking of the blood of the covenant. But how does the bread signify the body of Jesus?

The answer to the question is found in the description of the primitive Eucharist as given by Paul (1 Cor. 11.24), which reads, "For I have received of the Lord that which I delivered unto you: that the Lord Jesus the [same] night, in which he was betrayed, took bread. And when he had given thanks, he brake it, and said, 'Take, eat; this is my body, *which is broken for you;*[19] *this do in remembrance of me.*'"

This passage has been much disputed (J. Jeremias, *Das Abendmahlsworte Jesu*[4] (1967); H. Conzelmann's article on the Eucharist in Kittel-Friedrich-Bromiley, vol. IX, p. 411 f.), but I adhere to the view that the Pauline pristine characterization has been neglected. First, commentators frequently use the term "loaf" which beclouds the original meaning of the rite (so Robinson, ibid., throughout his article; similarly "bread" by G. H. Clay in his article in Hastings, *Dictionary of the Apostolic Church*). It was *maṣah* at the Passover, the unleavened flat cakes that are eaten at the Passover time. Jesus did not eat bread. Probably the Greek *arton* in the text was misleading; commentators should have realized however that *artos* is employed by the LXX for *maṣah*.

Second, the central idea that should be stressed is not that the disciples ate the *maṣah* as a sign of the new covenant, though unquestionably this was part of the rite, but that the *maṣah* was *broken*. Compare "This is my body broken for you" Mof.[2]. It is this *act of breaking* that Jesus enjoins his disciples to perform, the main action in the ritual, as a reminder of his broken body. And this they should continue to do "in remembrance of me." At this last night, Jesus was aware that he would be arrested, Lk. 22.37 and elsewhere.

The Aramaic in Mk. 14.22 was curtailed. It contained the words פגרי דין מפגר meaning "this is my broken body." First, פגרא in Eastern Aramaic, and in contradiction to Hebrew, may mean a live person, a live body, as well as a "corpse," Payn. Sm., p. 434; Jennings, Levy, *Chal. Wört.*, II, p. 254. The Greek translator, in looking at the similar letters may have left one word out, either thinking that מפגר was a thoughtless repetition, or through haplography. As "broken, crushed, wounded," the word is found in Babylonian Talmudic Aramaic as well (Jast., p. 1135 and note Niddah 66a where פגר is used specifically for "wound to the body," and cf. Levy, *Chal. Wört.*, II, p. 254 a, b). Note, in passing, the wordplay, as well as the overtone of פגרותא "bread" (dried), Brock., p. 557. Second it may be surmised, too, that the breaking of the *maṣah* was not performed in a haphazard fashion, but accomplished in a certain kind of way. Compare Lk. 24.35 "How he was known to them in the breaking of the bread" and Acts 2.42.46; 20.7 (probably). Inasmuch as the breaking of bread—the flat waferlike cakes—was an everyday procedure all the year, it must have been the ritual handling of the bread, and the ritual way it had to be broken, that was an essential part of the Eucharist.

An analogy, perhaps only a suggestion of this original idea of the Eucharist, is found in the בוכרא "very often used of Christ; hence in the Nestorian Liturgies, the holy bread is called 'The First born of all creatures.'" In the service, the description is כהנא קצא לבוכרא לתרין מנון "The priest shall break the Bukhra into two portions," Payn. Sm., p. 38. The Eucharist therefore had these three parts (1) the drinking of the wine (2) the breaking of the *maṣah* in memory of Jesus' crucifixion (3) the eating of it as consuming the body of Christ.

The word *dunamis* in the NT has a number of varied meanings. The article by W. Grundmann in the *Theological Dictionary of the New Testament*, II, pp. 284f. leaves little to be desired. What I have to propose, is by way of supplement, and the particular contribution that Aramaic may offer. The word *dunamis*, "power," is employed in connection with the cosmic powers of the sun, moon, and stars, but it is not completely clear to scholars how this term came to be applied to these heavenly bodies (Grundmann, ibid, p. 295). "Its origin is to be sought in the title *kurios ton dunamon* ... the *dunameis* ... are the heavenly hosts, *dunameis* being used for צבאות ה'." The word *ḥaila* in Aramaic, the equivalent of *dunameis*, may provide an interesting suggestion. *ḥaila* meaning "strength" evolved to the function and meaning of "heavenly powers."

A standard equation that the translator may have had fixed in his mind becomes, in turn, the basis for further proliferation and (mis)interpretation. Compare for example, the evolution of the term *mashiaḥ*, from "the anointed" to the "redeemer" in Israel and Christianity, of *ṭebilah* from "immersion" to the sacramental baptism, of *satan* from "adversary" to the Antichrist, from Gehenna, the burial place outside of Jerusalem, to Hell itself.

Something of the same developmental process we see in the employment of *haila*, "strength" and "host."

hailin, meaning "powers," and concomitant with *dunameis*, the latter a rendition of the former, came to be associated with "angelic or cosmic powers," and so used in En. 61.10 "powers which are on the dry land, and above the water"; for "powers that go round in circles" En. 82.8; of the "powers of motion" (Grundmann, ibid, p. 296). Undoubtedly, the idea of "powers" and "principalities" (Rom. 8.38), and "all principality, and might" Eph. 1.21, became widespread in NT times. There are, however, a number of NT passages that with difficulty can bear that interpretation.

(1) In the Hebrew Scriptures, צבא is used metaphorically and as a description of the sun, moon, and stars as they were constellated to rise and set in military formation at the command of God. Compare Gen. 2.1; Ps. 107.4, and hence the translation "host (s)." (2) In Aramaic צבא is almost uniformly rendered by Onqelos and the Peshitta as *haila*. And so, for example, "And the heavens and the earth were finished, and all their host of them," Onqelos חיליהון, and so Targ. Jonathan and the Peshitta. However, in a number of NT passages, the term needs a new interpretation. Briefly, *hailayya* was mistranslated. It should have been rendered as "hosts"; it was mistranslated in its other meaning as "powers."

Thus, Mt. 24.29 reads, "Immediately after the tribulation of those days shall the sun be darkened, and the moon shall not give her light, and the stars shall fall from heaven, and the powers (*dunameis*) of the heavens shall be shaken." It is assumed that this verse is a borrowing and reflection of Is. 13.10 (so Allen; LXX, however, has *kosmos*, not *dunameis*; Is. 34.4 is apparently an addition by Origen *sub asterisko;* Rhalfs does not print it in his edition). The immediate phrases before, about the sun, the moon and the stars that shall "fall from heaven" give rise to the judgment that "powers" in the sequel must be synonymous with the constellations mentioned, and furthermore Is. 34.4 contains the telltale צבא השמים. There is no genuine allusion to "powers." We must conclude that *dunameis* mistranslates חיליא as "powers" instead of "hosts, constellations." We should accordingly render Mt. 24.29; Mk. 13.25; Lk. 21.26 "The constellations of heaven shall be shaken."

In the Transfiguration account, Mt. 17.5; Mk. 9.7, Lk. 9.34, a bright cloud "overshadowed" ($\epsilon\pi\epsilon\sigma\kappa\iota\alpha\sigma\epsilon\nu$) Jesus. James, John, and Peter, the three disciples, who were with him, were likewise enveloped by the cloud. Peter had prepared three "tabernacles," one for Jesus, "and one for Moses and one for Elias." In what manner the bright cloud "overshadowed" them

TEXTS AND DOCTRINES 175

is not clear, as Plummer, Luke, p. 252, remarks, "Strictly speaking, a luminous cloud cannot overshadow." It is without parallel in any revelation account. Ex. 40.34—35, to which this passage is generally compared, reads, "Then the cloud covered the tent of meeting, and the glory of the Lord filled the tabernacle. And Moses was not able to enter the tent of meeting because the cloud abode (שכן) thereon, and the glory of the Lord filled the tabernacle." It is to be noticed, however, that the verb is *shakan* "rested," the apposite required sense in the NT passage. The remarks made on p. 100 with regard to the spirit "overshadowing" Elisabeth, where it was indicated that *gnn* was mistranslated there, i.e., "rest upon" for "overshadow," apply here as well. Our conclusion is irresistible. In the light of the Exodus account where the cloud "rested," it can hardly be gainsaid that here, too, the cloud rested upon Jesus and the disciples. The Eastern Aramaic word, again, was *gnn* meaning mostly "protect, overshadow," but also "rest upon," used expressly for "resting upon" of the spirit, Brock., p. 123 *incibuit* (*spiritus*) and the noun *incubatio* (*spiritus*), and this certainly should be the sense here, not "overshadowed."

In passing, we may suggest the reason why Peter made three tabernacles "one for Moses, one for Elijah, and one for Jesus," which is as Plummer puts it (ibid, p. 252) "a strange proposal." The Greek word in question is *skenai*, usually translated as "booths, tabernacles" but means actually "tents," corresponding to the Hebrew אהל, and so the LXX translates it that way some 150 times in the Hebrew Bible. It is also employed in the phrase אהל מועד "tent of meeting," the sacred place where God revealed himself previously to Moses. Just as God made use of this tent for revelation, and furthermore revealed himself to Elijah the prototype of the prophets who was to be the harbinger of the great day of the Lord, so now a new tent, the abode of God, where a new revelation was to take place, was constructed by Peter, though surprisingly he himself did not know what the purpose was (so Lk. 9.33). Moses and Elijah furthermore had come upon the scene conversing (Lk. 9.30), not only to show parity with Jesus, but because the one was transmitting to the other the divine tradition. Now a new tent was made, and the voice in the cloud gave Jesus equal and new authority, "This is my son; hear him." The purpose of the Transfiguration becomes clear. Jesus had gone up on the mountain, as Moses previously did at Sinai (typology), to receive the divine commission, the new and further revelation. The presence of Moses and Elijah was to confirm the chain of tradition—the arrival of Jesus on the scene was a continuation of the tradition, while, at the same time, the voice proclaimed a new revelation. Elijah, of course, was a much more important figure to the apocalyptists, and indeed to the mass of the people of the time rather than Isaiah or Amos, because he was the harbinger of the Messiah, and herald of the kingdom of God. Note the emphasis even in Ben Sira 48.1—14 on Elijah, and the scant line or two to the other prophets.

The ruling of Jesus on divorce confusedly originates from the discrepant texts in the Gospels. Mt. 5.32 prohibits divorce except on the ground of unchastity, while the other Gospels make no such exception. It had been noticed by Torrey that in Mk. 10.12 "And if she divorces her husband and marries another, commits adultery against her," the true rendering must be "She who is divorced by her husband" פְּטְרָא לְבַעֲלַהּ, was misread as פְּטְרָא לְבַעֲלַהּ, "divorced her husband"; under Jewish law at the time of Jesus no woman was permitted to divorce her husband (Jos. Ant. 15.7.10). However, the passage in Mt. 5.32 has the peculiar statement "But I say unto you, 'That whosoever shall put away his wife, saving for the cause of fornication, causeth her to commit adultery ($\pi o \iota \epsilon \hat{\iota}$ $\alpha \dot{\upsilon} \tau \dot{\eta} \nu$ $\mu o \iota \chi \epsilon \upsilon \theta \hat{\eta} \nu \alpha \iota$); and whosoever shall marry her that is divorced committeth adultery.'" The question is, if a man divorces his wife, and thereby she becomes free and unmarried—how does he make *her* an adulteress? The most obvious explanation would be that she would marry again. Mont. *Synoptic Gospels*, II, p. 66, and others say it is as *if* she married again and thereby became an adulterous woman. This begs rational understanding. She may not want to remarry after the divorce, but if she did, why should she be prevented from remarrying by having the stigma of "adulteress"? The statement of Jesus that the husband makes *her* an adulteress could not be true, but if we resort to the Aramaic, the solution becomes simple. The Aramaic ran מגיר לה which the translator misread as the preposition *lah* instead of *leh;* the translation should not read, "he makes her an adulteress" but "makes *himself* an adulterer."

Chapter VII

Logia of Jesus and Their Aramaic Source

IT IS well known that there are sayings of Jesus that are not in the canonical Gospels. The book of Acts, for example, records a statement of Paul (20.35) wherein he quotes such a saying, "I have showed you all things, how that so laboring ye ought to support the weak, and to remember the words of the Lord Jesus how he said, 'It is more blessed to give than to receive.'" Many other sayings of Jesus are quoted, or alluded to, by the early church fathers. A problem now arises, is the statement attributed to Jesus, not infrequently varying from the canonical Gospels, a direct quotation from a written text, or did the saying come to the church father through an oral channel? Moreover, the fact that many of these "quotations" are prefaced by *hos gegraptai,* or *phesin* "as it is written, as it (he) says" which may or may not be authentic, complicates the investigation even more. (Compare Koster, *Synoptische Uberlieferung bei den apostolischen Vätern* [1957] for analysis and discussion; and J. Finegan, *Hidden Records of the Life of Jesus,* p. 123f.) In addition, frequently a passage is cited as being a genuine logion of Jesus, but there is no parallel for it in the Gospels. Some texts may have been wrongly attributed to Jesus, still others are imagined to be statements by him. The question is a complicated one, but I have concluded that the earlier the church father the more likely that he was quoting an authentic saying, whether written or oral. Much of the Nag Hammadi material, though most interesting from the historical and religio-cultural development, and most important for Gnostic research, did not serve the purpose for the recovery of text, or for interpretation and philology. In my studies, I have been strongly sensible of the guidance of scholars with their pronouncements of what is, and what is not, seemingly genuine. See Alfred Resch, *Agrapha* (1906); Leon E. Wright, *Alterations of the words of Jesus as quoted in the Literature of the Second Century* (1952).

I would take the view therefore that the majority of quotations, prefaced by "it is written," "as it is said," "as he says"—corresponding to the frequent דכתיב, שנאמר, הכתוב שאמר זה, in the tannaitic writings—are probably genuine. Perhaps now the original Aramaic may offer its contribution for the solution of some puzzling texts, and, if so, would provide further confirmation of the genuineness of the statement, and would come through again as evidence for the original Aramaic wellhead of both the logia and their ultimate source in the Aramaic Gospels.

There are some inhibitions and handicaps. Judgment on whether a text is difficult or not is internal within the context itself. The difficulties in the text provide the analysis. Rarely are there comparative texts to aid one; no multifarious readings in the Mss. to provide a point of reference, even to know what is a wrong reading. No comparative translations from the Syriac, or Latin provide a surer footing. As Lagarde formulated in his first canon of criticism for the guidance of the critic, "His chief aid [in restoring readings based upon the LXX] will be the faculty possessed by him of referring the readings that come before him to their Semitic origin...." With these caveats, I hope the following discussions will prove to be of some interest.

The Letter of Barnabas is considered usually as a part of the "Apostolic Fathers," extant in the Old Latin translations, though not in the Vulgate, and excluded from the King James Version. The "Apostolic Fathers" consist of some dozen works, written by authors who are reputed to have known the Apostles, or those immediately following them. Among others listed with the Letter of Barnabas are 1 Clement, or the First Letter of Clement to the Corinthians, 2 Clement, or the Second Letter of Clement to the Corinthians, and the Shepherd, or the Shepherd of Hermas (compare Finegan, op. cit., p. 43, and for the literature, n. 2).

An interesting quotation is found in Barnabas 7.11 which runs: "Thus, he says, 'Those who wish to see me, and to take hold of my kingdom ἅψασθαί μου τῆς βασιλείας) must through tribulation and suffering obtain (*lambanein*) me.'"

Commentators assume that the saying is reminiscent of Acts 14.22 which reads, "And that we must through much tribulation (*dia pollon thlipseon*) enter the Kingdom of God." Actually, as the reader will readily perceive, the connection between Bar. 7.11 and Acts seems slight, though "tribulations" is the expected common condition forecast by Jesus for the disciples and for the world generally (Mt. 13.21; Mk. 13.19; Jn. 16.21 and elsewhere), as well as for the suffering that he and the disciples must undergo. The difficulties in the Bar. citation are the unusual "take hold of my kingdom" and the strange "obtain me." The Greek verb *hapto* in Mid. means "fasten, or bind to, join," metaphorically "take hold, cleave to," and is

LOGIA OF JESUS

peculiar to Bar. 7.11 (Arndt-Gingrich, 102; Finegan, p. 128). The Semitic scholar, however, will recognize the Aramaic locution קבל מלכותא Dan. 6.1, not "receive the kingdom," but "took" (NEB), or "succeeded to the kingdom" (NAB). At any rate, the Aramaic root was קבל, Brock. 642 #9. *Lambanein* as a synonym in "receive a kingdom" Lk. 19.12 might be admissible as evidence but is problematic and perhaps based upon a misunderstanding of the underlying document in Aramaic. קבל מלכותא should be rendered in that Lucan passage that the nobleman went "to welcome the royal presence." The root קבל was misunderstood in this present citation, as the word has quite a number of meanings (see p. 64, 104) and in the transmission wrong meanings were selected. *qabbel* has the meaning of (1) take, used frequently for לקח in Onqelos, Gen. 4.11, 14.24; 21.30; 27.35.36; 33.10.11 and often, and (2) welcome. The saying should have borne the following sense, "Those who wish to see me and *acquire* the kingdom (or *succeed* to the kingdom), must *welcome* me through trial and suffering." There is a wordplay on *qabbel* "acquire" and "welcome," but the translator in both cases of *qabbel* misinterpreted the word.

The root *qabbel* is the source of confusion in another passage in the Dialogue with Trypho, 47, where Justin Martyr quotes a saying of Jesus, "Wherefore also our Lord Jesus Christ said, 'In whatever things I shall take you ($καταλάβω$), in these I shall judge you.'" The usual parallels adduced, Ez. 33.20, "I shall judge you each according to his ways" (Mt. 24.40—42 parallels Lk. 17.34f.39 for the thought), are only slight and fortuitous. The puzzling phrase in the quotation is "I shall take you," contextually inappropriate and incongruous. It would make for much better sense to frame the quotation with the meaning,

In whatever things I shall *charge* you
In these I shall judge you.

"Charge" means "complain against," a quasilegal term, in English "complaint, charge" (compare Jast., p. 1309b). Jesus would then say, "Whatever legal charges that I would level against you (as if in a court action), those very charges will be used against you." The translator confused the separate meanings of *qabbel*, of (1) take and (2) complain. (Compare further, M. L. Margolis, "Lambanein and its Hebrew-Aramaic Equivalents in Old Testament Greek," AJSL, XXII, pp. 110f.)

A misconstruction of syntax, which leads to a miscomprehension of the Aramaic, appears in another saying. Epiphanius in *Pan. haer.* 76.42.8 (see *Die griechischen christlichen Schriftsteller der ersten Jahrhunderte*, Deutsche Akademie für Wissenschaften zu Berlin; Finegan, XXV), following a quotation of Jn. 1.12 and immediately before a question of Jn. 5.46, gives the following citation from Jesus: "And therefore he says, 'He who speaks in the prophets, behold I am here'" (καὶ διὰ τοῦτο λέγει ὁ λαλῶν ἐν τοῖς προφήταις ἰδοὺ πάρειμι). The passage implies that the one who speaks in the prophets is the same one who is before you now. If that be the sense, it is awkwardly expressed. Jesus is not the one who "speaks in the prophets." An easy retroversion to Aramaic yields a much more intelligent thought. The Aramaic probably ran הוא דאמר בנביאיא הא אנא הוא which may be translated, "He that is spoken of in the Prophets, behold it is I." The transmitter or translator had difficulty with דאמר, not realizing that the construction is impersonal "He that one speaks of." There are other alternatives that add up to the same thing. It is possible that the form was אמיר, passive pe'il, found occasionally in Jewish Aram. Levy, NHB I, p. 37b, but frequently in Syriac. דאמר also may be a shorthand locution for "As the text says," compare the talmudic expression ואומר in the sense of "as another text has it." The term בנביאיא is a terminus technicus for the second section of the Hebrew Bible, cf. Tosef. Megill. IV (III) 18 (ed. M. S. Zuckermandel, 226); Mish. Meg. 4.1, Jast., pp. 868–869. Ha' 'ana' hu' is idiomatic for "Behold I am the one." The Aramaic conveys the thought paralleled elsewhere. Compare Jn. 1.45, "We have found him, of whom Moses in the law, and the prophets did write."

There is an extraordinary quotation reported by Clement, quoting a teacher in Egypt, Julius Cassianus, who came from the school of Valentinus, and was the founder of Docetism (see Finegan, p. 144). Cassianus had written a treatise "On Continence," from which Clement quotes two quotations which reject sexual intercourse. A third quotation is introduced as follows,

> Accordingly Cassianus says, "When Salome had inquired about the things she had inquired about would be known, the Lord said,
> 'When you have trampled upon the garment of shame
> (τὸ τῆς αἰσχύνης ἔνδυμα)
> And when the two become one,
> And the male with the female,
> Neither male nor female.'"

this teaching is supposed to be a reflection of, or dependent on Gal. 3.28, "There is neither Jew nor Greek, there is neither bond nor free, there is neither male nor female, for ye are all one in Christ Jesus."

It is thought that the Gospel from which this quotation was cited, *the Gospel according to the Egyptians,* existed in the early part of the second century (cf. Finegan, p. 145). If so, the possibility of an Aramaic source then should be admitted. The question that now comes to the fore is, what is meant by the "garments of shame"? It cannot mean that humankind is expected to walk around naked, nor "nakedness of soul." Although there are traces of this in classical literature, Deissmann, *Light from the Ancient East,* p. 292 (address of Hadrian to his soul; queried by Diessmann) and in NT II Cor. 5.3 (the text somewhat problematic), it can hardly be implied that, between the pre-Parousian period and the ultimate judgment for the non-believers, bodies are to be in a state of nakedness, Phil. 1.23 "to be with Christ" (in death). There are strains wherein the souls of the damned were considered as naked as in the Samaritan liturgy for the Day of Atonement where the non-Samaritans will be resurrected naked but the righteous will rise with the clothes in which they were inhumed (דבון היו) (?) בסבלותם יקומו מקברין). The passage must be very late; note the language. (See A. Merx, *Der Messias,* 1909, pp. 15, 13 cited by Oepke, *Thelog. Dict.* of the *NT,* I, p. 774). Ishtar's descent to Hell in which she divests a portion of her clothing before the different gates so that she appears naked before Hell's queen has nothing to do with the question. No, souls are not naked. (In the above passage סרבלותם "their clothes"/סבלותם should be read.) The heavenly Adam and the angels all wore clothes. Compare L. Ginzberg, *Legends,* III, p. 17; I, pp. 79, 80, 177; idem, pp. 135, 139 (clothes of the heavenly Enoch), as well as the express statement "The righteous will rise in the future with their clothes on, argued *a fortiori* from a wheat kernel" Ket. 101b, Sanh. 90b and compare F. Cumont, *Oriental Religions*[3] (1931), p. 290.

If as the text has it, the male is to be female, and the female male, and then they become neither male nor female, this can only be conceived as bodies which have no sexual organs, i.e., the male having no genitals, the female having no breasts. Then only a quasi-equality and similarity may be achieved. Women will not give birth; men will not procreate; they will be spiritualized human beings.

The tenor of this interpretation is borne out by other passages in a question and answer dialogue, in which Salome figured as the questioner. Thus one passage runs, "When the two shall be one, and the outside as the inside, and the male with the female, neither male nor female" (Finegan, p. 143). Compare also these texts:

Salome: How long will death have power?
The Lord: As long as you women bear children.

* * *

The Savior said: I came to destroy the works (*ergai*) of the female. Salome: I have done well then in not bearing children as if "it were not fitting to participate in procreation" (on the above texts, see Finegan, pp. 143–147).

Referring back to the passage under discussion, for "garments of shame," the Aramaic phrase was probably מאניא דבהחתא. The Greek in the transmission misconceived מאניא as "garments, clothes." The word should have been understood by its other meaning "The instruments, or the tools (of shame)" (Jast., p. 723; Payn. Sm., p. 247: Brock., p. 373). The instruments of shame would naturally be the characteristic sexual members of men and women. For the locution, cf. מאני דזרעא "organs of reproduction" Payn. Sm., p. 247. The context with the other passages form a consentaneous whole in all parts of the statement, Translate, "When you have trampled upon the organs of shame."

Another example of evidence of an Aramaic transmission appears in Hegesippus, cited by Eusebius in his *Ecclesiastical History*. Eusebius states (4.22.8) that Hegesippus made extracts, i.e., quotations "From the Gospel according to the Hebrews, and from the Syriac, and particularly from the Hebrew language he makes some extracts" (Finegan, p. 147 whom I follow). Apparently Hegesippus made use of two works, (1) the Gospel according to the Hebrews, and (2) another Gospel written in Syriac. Eusebius remarks that Hegesippus was a convert from the Jews as he had an interest to quote "from the Hebrew language," by which Eusebius means Aramaic as a rule. "Therefore the quotations from the Aramaic ('Hebrew dialect') were from the Aramaic ('Syriac') Gospel" (Finegan, p. 148). The other work was written not in Aramaic, but in Greek, and the *Gospel according to the Hebrews* was probably in use with Jewish Christians. Was this Gospel written originally in Greek, or is there a possibility that it may have had an Aramaic origin? The following example may indicate a tentative solution.

Clement in his *Stromata*, II, 9.45,5 gives the following as having been written (*gegraptai* i.e., as if a scriptural quotation) in the *Gospel according to the Hebrews:*

He who wonders shall reign,
And he who reigns shall rest.

An apparently fuller text is cited in *Stromata* V, 14.96,3, without the indication whether it is scriptural:

He who seeks will not cease until he finds;
And having found he will be astounded;
And being astounded, he will reign ($\beta\alpha\sigma\iota\lambda\epsilon\acute{\upsilon}\sigma\epsilon\iota$)
And reigning he will rest.

This saying had some currency, found fragmentarily in Oxyrhynchus Papyrus 654, and in the Coptic Gospel according to Thomas, and hence we need not in this *sorites* assume that "rest" was the apex and the objective of Gnostic thought (Finegan, p. 149, differently). The exegesis of the passage remains, however, problematic. Critical in the interpretation is the sequence, where the searcher, after being astounded, "reigns," and in reigning (?) he will find rest. Presumably the text deals with the seeker of the true religion, the true light, who when he finds it, will wonder and then ponder on what he has seen, and thereby will find rest, a surcease from internal restlessness and turmoil. "Reign," however, seems to be awry, and our problem in the passage.

Apparently the logion was misinterpreted in one particular. The translator or transmitter from Aramaic to Greek misunderstood the word מלך which bears the signification of "rule," the more common meaning which the translator followed, and II מלך "think, consider, take counsel, reflect." It is the latter מלך that should have been translated, and this makes for the required sense. Patently "being astounded" and "reflect" are naturally associated with one another, and not only follow well in the context, but quite apposite in the *sorites* here. The passage should now read, "He who seeks will not cease till he finds; and having found he will be astounded; and being astounded, he will reflect, and reflecting, he will find rest." This means that the one who reads the Gospels will be impressed with its message; at first will be astounded with its story, but then on reflecting, will find rest.

Origen quotes from the *Gospel according to the Hebrews* in his *Commentary on John* (supposedly written in 226–227 C.E.). He declares that Jesus had said (Finegan, p. 149): "Then my mother, the Holy Spirit (*he meter mou, to hagion pneuma*) took me by one of my hairs, and carried me off to the great Mount Tabor." The idea that the Holy Spirit is the mother of Jesus undoubtedly stems from the fact that the Aramaic *ruḥa dequdsha* is feminine, although the Greek *to hagion pneuma* is neuter. The source then would be Aramaic.

Jerome remarks in his Commentary on Isaiah 4,11.2 that in the Gospel which the Nazaraeans (*Nazaraei*) read there occurs the following passage (*scripta*): "And it came to pass, when the Lord came up out of the water, the whole fount of the Holy Spirit descended, and rested upon him, and said to him, 'My Son, in all the prophets I was waiting for you, that you might come, and that I might rest in you (*et requiescerem in te*); for you are my rest (*tu es enim requies mea*); you are my firstborn Son, who reigns forever.'"

One problem cannot easily be dismissed. However early Christianity had magnified the character and function of Jesus as savior, Messiah, king, for whom God waited to appear in the prophets, and now seeking "rest" in him, it is improbable that Jesus should be God's "rest,"; this would not be, among other things in character with the Deity who always retains his omnipotent function in the NT, Mt. 4.10; 6.30; Mk. 13.19. "Rest" cannot signify the Incarnation either; Jesus among the Nasoreans (=Mandeans) and so many scholars, is simply *manda' deḥayye* (see ERE, VIII, p. 380f.). Then again, the passage quoted in connection with Mt. 3.17; Mk. 1.11 speaks not of "rest" but "Thou art my beloved son." I have shown elsewhere (p. 56) that the original meaning was "whom I have chosen," though the meaning "well pleased," certainly by the time of Jerome, had become traditional and well entrenched. I would suggest that the verb נח, noun ניחא (Payn. Sm., p. 338; Jast., p. 886, 904), "be pleasing, agreeable, content," as, for example, *damniḥ beh 'Aloho'*, "with whom God is well pleased" (and see other examples in Payn. Sm., p. 331b.), had been understood by the Greek transmitter-translator in the sense of "rest," which is not appropriate. The translation should now read, "In all the prophets I was waiting for you, so that you might come that I might *delight* in you. For you are my *delight;* you are my firstborn son, who reigns forever."

Jerome also mentions that the *Gospel According to the Hebrews,* used by the Nazaraeans, is also *the Gospel According to the Apostles,* or the *Gospel According to Matthew,* and exists according to him in a single copy in the library in Caesarea. He quotes from it the following passage: "Behold the mother of the Lord and his brothers said to him, 'John the Baptist baptizes for the forgiveness of sins; let us go and be baptized by him.' But he said to them, 'In what have I sinned that I should go and be baptized by him? Unless perhaps what I have said is ignorance'" (*nisi forte hoc ipsum quod dixi ignorantia*).

Commentators (Huck, Lietzmann, Finegan) translate by the insertion of parenthesis the words "sin of" so that *ignorantia* should contain the meaning of "sin" in some fashion. There is no point to the passage otherwise, because it tries to give a reason why Jesus should not be baptized by John; the text should have something of the meaning and significance conveying "sin."

It is quite likely that the word for *ignorantia* was originally the Aramaic *shalutha*. The word is employed, for example, in the Targs. for "forgetfullness, mistake" but also for "unwitting sin," Hebrew שגגה.[20] It seems probable that שלותא was misunderstood as "ignorance" rather than "sin."

The translation should have read, "Unless what I said is sin," the required sense.

Jerome, again, in his *Commentary on Matthew,* on the verse in 6.11 observes that in the Gospel called "According to the Hebrews" for the phrase "bread necessary to support life" (*supersubstantiali pane;* AV "our daily bread") he found *mahar* which signifies as he interprets it by *crastinum* "of tomorrow." The sense of the passage now becomes, as his Latin has it, *panem nostrum crastinium, id est futurum, da nobis hodie,* "Our bread of tomorrow, that is of the future, give us this day." The Greek of the passage contains the puzzling word *epiousios,* interpreted variously as (1) necessary for our existence (2) for the current day (3) for the following day (4) the future (Arndt-Gingrich, p. 296f.), all of which, however, we cannot discuss at this point, except to observe that (1) is the best interpretation founded on the biblical and rabbinic tradition (Strack-Billerbeck, I, p. 420). The third, while given support by authorities, would go somewhat against Jewish tradition. Thus, for example, Hillel's exhortation to be concerned for one's daily food and its preparation on the principle of "Blessed be God day by day" (Ps. 68.20), is in contrast to Shammai who ruled that whatever food one buys one should always have the Sabbath in mind (Beṣa. 16a). Compare also Soṭ. 48b, "Rabbi Elazar the Great declared 'He who has bread in his basket, and says "What shall I eat tomorrow," he is but one of those who have little faith.'" Anyway, as Allen declares *Matthew* a.l. in effect, that to pray "Give us bread the following day" is out of focus; AV is the best "Give us this day our daily bread." If Jerome, as he himself says, found *mahar* (this would be Aramaic, cf. the Elephantine Papyri, passim, and *maḥra demaḥar* "the day after tomorrow," Jast., p. 764) *in the Gospel According to the Hebrews,* this would agree with (3), though (4) is quite within the range of possibility as *mahar* can mean "future time." Compare again the Elephantine Papyri, passim. Still, Jerome quotes *mahar* deliberately in contrast to his own version *superstantiali pane* "bread necessary to support life." Allen significantly asserts (*Commentary on St. Matthew,* p. 59) that "It is difficult not to think that *ton epiousion* rests upon misunderstanding (false transliteration?) of an original Aramaic phrase or upon a Greek corruption." Allen properly sensed that there was something wrong in the translation of transmission of our Mt. text. I would venture to suggest that the Aramaic לחמא דמחרא is an early corruption of לחמא דמחסרא, literally, bread of our necessity (Jast., p. 437), and the liturgical use of בורא נפשות רבות וחסרונן b. Bera. 37a; 44a, 45a; Kohut, Aruch, V, 369; "(God) who creates the many souls and their needs."

There is also an observation by Jerome of the fact that Barabbas, surrendered to the people by Pilate, was interpreted in the *Gospel According to the Hebrews* to mean "son of their teacher" (*filius magistri eorum*). Bar Abbas (בר אבא) would mean literally "son of the father," although Abba acquired the character of a personal name and an attribute of honor and distinction. Compare Ginzberg, *Supplement to the Aruch Completum*, p. 417 s.v. אבא; שם תאר כבוד לחסידים ואנשי מעשה. The interpretation cited by Jerome implies really בר ראבא with Aleph (so spelled) "son of the teacher" and is frequent in older rabbinic texts. So Ginzberg, *Geonica* II, p. 417, it being clearly understood that Rabba as a formal title for "teacher" is not found before the Destruction.

At Ps. 22.1 (v. 2 in MT), Aquila translates and so Eusebius, *Demonstratio evangelica* 10.8 (Finegan, 233), Eli, Eli "My God, my God" by the extraordinary "My Power, my Power," to be explained no doubt by tannaitic exegesis that אל might mean, as an appellation of the Deity, "power." Compare their use of גבורה as a name for God, Jast., p. 205; *ischuros/'el* in Aquila is found elsewhere Is. 9.6; Ps. 80.10; Mi. 2.1. In a parchment codex of Akhmin, written in Greek, there is a statement that on the cross the last words of Jesus were "My power, my power" (*he dunamis mou*). The tradition of Peter that is extant in his Gospel (5.19) records the same "My Power, my Power." The readings of Aquila and Peter, however, are to be differentiated. That of Aquila is based upon the root meaning *'el*, assumed to mean power as mentioned supra. According to Mt. 27.47, however, some persons attendant at the crucifixion thought that Jesus was calling upon Elijah (אליה). Peter, a Galilean, did not distinguish the gutturals Aleph and Ḥet, and, as he understood the cry, it was heard as if *ḥaili*, Aramaic, "my Power." See the writer's article "The Last Words of Jesus," JBL, 66, pp. 465 f. (1947).

In the finds of Grenfell and Hunt, "Sayings of our Lord" (1897), Oxyrhnchus Papyrus, I, 11.4–11 (Finegan, p. 195), there is a puzzling passage that reads, "Jesus says, 'If you do not fast ($\mu\dot{\eta}$ $\nu\eta\sigma\tau\epsilon\dot{\upsilon}\sigma\epsilon\tau\alpha\iota$) to the world ($\tau\grave{o}\nu$ $\kappa\acute{o}\sigma\mu o\nu$), you will not find the kingdom of God; and if you do not keep the Sabbath as Sabbath ($\tau\grave{o}$ $\sigma\acute{\alpha}\beta\beta\alpha\tau o\nu$), you will not see the Father.'"

The attitude of Jesus toward fasting is a knotty one, and some conclude that "There is no more any clear awareness of the way in which Jesus viewed fasting" (J. Behm, *Theolog. Dict. of NT*, IV, p. 935). Others claim that Jesus (despite his statement about John's followers, Mt. 9.14) did not oppose fasting (Mt. 6.17), but put it on a different level, as with his fasting forty days in the wilderness. Our present passage would indicate that Jesus held that fasting was of some importance, as well as the observance of the Sabbath, without which one would not be able to see the Father. The expression "fasting to the world" is peculiar, however. How does one fast *to* the world? While Arndt-Gingrich, p. 540 pose the difficulty, they say that it "has not yet been satisfactorily explained" and query whether it may not mean "abstain from the world." If abstinence is implied, the sense and the syntax remain puzzling. The admonition for the keeping of the Sabbath prompts the inference that the logion must belong to the Mt. tradition. This is based, first, on Mt. concern with the observance and recording of Jewish practices (Mt. 5.18; 10.5; 23.2.3 and 23); and second, on the fact that Jesus and his followers certainly did not abjure fasting entirely, as much fasting was part of the Jewish calendar. These fast days included the day of Atonement, the four fasts mentioned by Zechariah (8.19), as well as the many individual fasts presupposed by the *Megillat Ta'anit*. See further Ps. 35.13; 69.11; Ezr. 8.21.

It would seem that in the transmission of the logion a misunderstanding of an Aramaic locution took place. Hebrew gives more examples of this construction than Aramaic. לעולם, which has served as illustration before (see p. 159), has a variety of meanings (1) universally, generally, and with the negative לא signifies "never, never at all" (Payn. Sm., p. 415). It is this expression לעולם that the translator missed by rendering literally "to the world." The Aramaic ran

אין לא תצומן לעלם, לא תשכחן מלכות שמיא
ואין לא תשבתון שבתכון, לא חזין אנתון לאלהא

which we should translate, "If you do not fast at all, you will not find the Kingdom of God; and if you do not observe your Sabbath, you will not be seen of your Father." For this misvocalization, see p. 69. Note also the clinching locution found in the strange Greek *sabbatisete sabbaton*, literally, "sabbath your sabbaths," apparently unique, see Arndt-Gingrich, p. 746 for this single example, but, by contrast, a normal Hebrew-Aramaic idiom Lev. 23.32; 25.2; 26.34. where the Aramaic is שבת שבתא Lev. 25.2 Peshitta; the Targs. are halakhic. This passage of "fasting to the world," found also in the *Coptic Gospel According to Thomas*, and similarly in the *Stromata* of Clement of Alexandria, seems later (Finegan, p. 248).

Chapter VIII

The World is a Bridge...
Another Logion of Jesus

IN HIS excellent and thorough book on the unknown sayings of Jesus,[21] J. Jeremias discusses one of the apagrapha beginning with the words "The World is a Bridge" listed as #20 in his collection. The present analysis purports to follow through as a continuation and supplement of the discussion which he initiated in his exposition of this logion. A short summary of the history and background of this saying may be in order.

An Arabic inscription was found in the ruined city of Fathpur-Sikri which is situated about 100 miles south of Delhi. Akbar the Great (1542–1605) made a memorial on the occasions of his great victories and set up an inscription on the main portal of the great mosque at Fathpur-Sikri. The inscription runs as follows: "Jesus, on whom be peace, has said: This world is a bridge. Pass over it. But build not your dwelling there."[22] There is a similar inscription on a nearby archway of the same mosque which takes a different form and wording: "Said Jesus Christ, blessings upon him, The world is a lofty mansion; So take a warning and do not build on it."[23] Unfortunately, the Arabic text was not made available.

"The world is a bridge" motif occurs also in the *Disciplina clericalis* of Petrus Alfonsi, a baptized Spanish Jew who served as physician to King Alphonso I of Aragon (1105–1134). This *Disciplina clericalis* is a collection of oriental proverbs containing a number of sayings including the logion under discussion. "The world is a bridge" is attributed to "a philosopher." The passage reads: "The world is a bridge; so pass over it; and do not stay on it" (*Saeculum est quasi pons: transi ergo ne hospitaris*). Jeremias traces this saying through Mohammedan authors up to pre-Mohammedan times (p. 114). Very notable, in addition, is the saying in Petrus Alfonsi's collection immediately before "The world is a bridge." The passage reads: "The world is like a transition" (*saeculum est quasi transitus*), quite evidently a variant.

The statement concludes with: "because short is the course of life" (*quia brevis est cursus vitae*). The obvious conclusion to be reached here in the interpretation of "world," as we may infer from the verse, is that "world" means not the world proper, but human life in the world. At any rate, the second statement is clearly related to the first. The second declaration seems to take on a more abstract philosophical form.

The question that now confronts us is, as sayings outside the canonical literature, are these genuine traditions or logia of Jesus? In what way are these logia specifically related to one another?

I will bypass for the nonce the discussion of Jeremias (p. 114) and the comprehensive study of the appearance of this saying "The world is a bridge. Pass over it" in such Arabic authors as Al-Ghazali (1059—1111), Abu Talib al-Makki (tenth century). and even ascending to a "companion" of Mohammed, Ibn Omar (seventh century). This seems to be an impressive tradition, (Jeremias), although the metaphor of the bridge does not exist in the 77 Mohammedan agrapha offered by D. S. Margoliouth.[24] The logion in the Gospel of Thomas #42 "Become passersby," the Greek of which is restored by Jeremias γίνεσθε παράγοντες,[25] seems to him to be the first link in the chain. It is also hypothesized that the original intent of the saying was that life was a pilgrimage; the figure of the bridge in the statement, however, is a secondary accretion. Such an addition, it is further contended, could only have originated in Egypt.[26] It is at this point that I cannot follow Professor Jeremias's line of reasoning and must part company with his conclusions.

I would like to offer the following suggestions:
1. The source of the saying appears to have been originally phrased in Aramaic.
2. The native habitat of the saying seems to be Palestine.
3. The saying and its figure of the bridge, framed in the various forms indicated below, found expression in the talmudic and midrashic literature, and in the literature of Jewish poets and philosophers. The relevancy of this will be indicated.

First of all, it is quite clear that the mode of expression, the syntax, and the figures employed in the simile are not only Palestinian but when retroverted, the language in which the phrasing is pitched manifests the underlying Aramaic. This can be shown by the circumstance that the wording for "bridge" and for "transition" ascend to the Aramaic מעברא. The primary meaning of the word is "a passing through," but also has the meaning "bridge."[27] It is now clear what took place. The original cast of the saying read: "This world is like a bridge. Pass through by means of it." Another version had it: "This world is a passing through."²⁸ Both ascend to the same Aramaic word מעברא. Note also the idiomatic retroversion עבר בה not "Pass through it" but "Pass through by means of it," the Beth instrumenti.

It seems also clear that the origin of the saying had its currency, even its birth, on Palestinian soil. R. Ya'aqob stated: "This world is like an antechamber to the world to come; prepare yourself in the vestibule before you come into the dining hall" (cited by Jeremias, p. 115).

This formula "The world is like" is repeated elsewhere. Thus, for example, we read in Baba Batra 25a: "Rabbi Eliezer says, 'The world is like an exedra'" (Greek: a covered place in front of a house, the northernmost side of which is not covered); "R. Joshua says, 'The world is like an enclosed tent'" (so the commentators); others opine an "arch."²⁹ Note that these statements are of the second century C.E. Similarly, another statement runs: "And why is this world created with the letter He (referring homiletically to the small He in the text of Gen. 2.4a)? Because it is like an exedra, and anyone who wishes to go forth may do so."³⁰ Then with changes in the figure, the world is compared to a night,³¹ and in the famous statement of Samuel to a wedding feast, "Snatch at the food, and snatch at drink; for this world that we depart from is like a wedding banquet."³² Noteworthy is a passage wherein the son of R. Simon b. Yoḥai came to his father for an explanation of a very peculiar blessing given to him by some contemporary scholars. It was paradoxical by nature, full of turns and odd expressions, supposedly containing prayers and blessings for a rich bountiful life, but in fact enigmatic and obscure, and ending with a declaration to the effect: "May your temporary abode be established, may your permanent home be destroyed." It took the acuity and insight of the rabbinical scholar to clear up matters. "Your permanent house shall be destroyed, and your temporary dwelling shall be inhabited—for this world is only a temporary dwelling, and the world to come is the real house."³³

This reflection on what the world may be like is continued, with the same similes of our passage under discussion, in the mediaeval Hebrew poets and philosophers. Thus the Hebrew poet Moses ben Ezra employs the figure in his poem "My Soul Desireth Thee":³⁴

See the world is a ferry, (or bridge)....
Rise, rise, my soul,
At the beginning of the night-watch.

The poet Ibn Gabirol likewise makes use of a similar metaphor, wherein the world is compared to a bridge, and all those who pass back and forth are but as sojourners.[35] Again, the idea is used also by the author of *Beḥinat Olam:* "The world is like a turbulent sea, with great depths, wide in expanse, and time but a shaky bridge built upon it."[36] In v. 8 in the same chapter and in a resumption of the figure, the author speaks of "your habitation" and the possibility of it being destroyed, which is quite akin to the admonition of "not building your habitation on it" in one version of the saying considered at the beginning of this discussion.[37]

It may be confidently hypothesized therefore that these similes and figures of what the world is like ultimately ascend to a Palestinian origin. While it could be argued that the later writers, the Hebrew poets and philosophers, may have been influenced by Arabic writers, it would seem much more probable and logical to counter that here the Hebrew writers were simply making use of their familiar Jewish tradition. If our agraphon were to be attributed to Jesus at all, it would have certainly been native to the surroundings in which he grew up rather than to Egypt. The Gospel of Thomas would not be the primary source for the saying. Moreover, the Bible itself constantly makes use of the term *maʿabarot*,[38] meaning bridges over streams and rivers so that the argument that the figure of the bridge over water seems to fit the conditions of Egypt rather than Palestine is not decisive.

Although there seem to be two possibilities for the interpretation of *maʿabara*—the world is either a bridge or a thoroughfare, I do not believe that we have plumbed the ultimate version of the saying. If the reading of the world as a bridge be selected, then it seems to be quite an odd behest not to build a habitation on it.[39] A more acceptable possibility is that one does not build a habitation in a *transitus*, a thoroughfare where people are travelling back and forth, presumably because it may be subject to abuse and lack of privacy. Per contra, one might still argue that the building of such a habitation is perfectly within the bounds of good reason, and therefore the erection of such a house, while perhaps unusual, could be quite possible.

I am inclined to think, however, that there is another interpretation of *maʿabara*, a nuance which would fit the intent of our saying in a much more related and coherent fashion. *Maʿabara* also has the meaning of "ferry, ferry-boat" (Jast., p. 813a). The gist of the saying would now be: The world is like a ferry-boat, pass through by means of it: and don't build a permanent habitation on it; i.e., ביתא as opposed to אושפיזא *ut supra,* n. 33. The whole verse now hangs together in a harmonious frame with all the components in concord. If one travels on a ferry, one's preoccupation and anxiety is to arrive, and one never contemplates building a permanent dwelling upon it. The Aramaic may be presumed to have run:

עלמא הדין דמי למעברא
עבר ביה לא תבנא לך ביתא עלוהי

Actually if the saying be cast with feminine terminations, we obtain a parallelismus membrorum of four beats each:

'Alma' hadên damé lemá'abarta
'Abar báh la tibneh lák baitha 'alah

If not completely parallel, it is striking that the author of the *Eben Bohan* seems to give an echo of the earlier Aramaic proverb: The world is a great ocean, and great in expanse, and man is like a boat, coursing (helplessly) through it.[40] The figure was changed in the course of transmission.

The logion in Arabic sources quoted at the head of this section remains quite a puzzle. Certainly it must have been quite an enigma to the inscriber that the world should be a lofty mansion; so take warning and don't build on it (!)—a simple contradiction in terms. I would venture to say on pure speculation, without an Arabic text to go by, that this version is a corrupted transmission of "The world is a bridge. Pass through...." The Arabic *qantara*, (*Arabic-English Dictionary*, Hava, p. 630) means "to arch, to vault": the noun *qantarat* means "a vaulted bridge"; in the dialect of Syria, it signifies "a vaulted passage" but side by side with these meanings it has the signification of "large building." The Arabic word has its associations in Aramaic קנטינר with various spellings (Jast., p. 1389, see further Krauss, *Lehnwörter*, p. 553), the word being connected with *centenarium* and explained by the Gemara (Baba Batra 98b) as being a courtyard adjoining a villa תרבץ אפדני. Although apparently derived from the Latin/Greek, the usage in Aramaic seems to point to a larger court and indeed derivatively an additional comment to the Mishna in Baba Batra, supposedly, ibid, as of 12 x 12 cubits. The area of the courtyard could very well be transferred to the building proper. Compare the English "court" which means (1) "a clear space inclosed by walls or surrounded by buildings; a yard, a courtyard" and (2) "a large building or set of buildings standing in a courtyard; a large house or castle" (*Oxford English Dictionary*, s.v. court).

The root in Arabic, moreover, "take warning" is *'abara* (Hava, p. 450) found thus in the VIII, as a noun *'ibrat* "warning," as well as the usual meaning "pass, pass through."

It would follow now that in the transmission of the Arabic saying, by word of mouth, someone misunderstood the whole meaning and context of the phrase, confusing *qantarat* as "large building" instead of vaulted bridge, and then misunderstood *'abara* in the sense of "warning" instead of the more frequent "pass through." As advanced before, it would appear that the saying is a corrupted version of "The world is a bridge" and is to be discounted as a secondary reading.

Appendix I

Aramaisms in Acts

THE PROOF that the first part of Ac. corresponding mostly to chs. 1—15, had originally an underlying Aramaic was offered by the significant monograph of C. C. Torrey in *The Composition and Date of Acts* (Cambridge, Mass., 1916). The evidence has been subjected to searching criticism by a number of authoritative scholars, among them F. C. Burkitt in "Professor C. C. Torrey on Acts," JTS, xx (1919), pp. 321f.; H. J. Cadbury, "Luke—Translator or Author?" Am. J. Theol., xxiv (1920), pp. 436—55; E. J. Goodspeed, "The Origin of Acts" JBL, xxxix (1920), pp. 83—101; and some of Torrey's replies in "Facts and Fancies in Theories concerning Acts," Am. J. Th., xxiii (1919), pp. 61—86 and 189—212. To offset the claimed Aramaic substratum for Ac. opposing scholars made use of the familiar procedure of citing Greek usages from the literature and the papyri, far and wide, and the usages of Greek locutions within the Gospels, and Christian writings generally, to explain a peculiar idiom and construction in the passage under investigation. After all is said and done, however, students are perforce admitting that there is an Aramaic background to the first half of Ac. (just as they now recognize the Gospels). The Aramaic element is firmly recognized despite the reservations scholars may cling to either to minimize or even disqualify the Aramaic hypothesized presence. Compare Max Wilcox, *The Semitisms of Acts*.

Torrey's argument about the Aramaic origin of Ac. I still stands, a little battered perhaps, but holding up well. While one may take exception to some examples, as a pioneering work, the main contention is brilliantly conceived, and the thesis well substantiated. The following examples may serve additionally to explain a number of puzzling texts via the Aramaic that have hitherto escaped notice.

1:14: "These all continued with one accord in prayer ($τῇ\ προσευχῇ$, literally, in the prayer) and supplication, with the women, and Mary the mother of Jesus, and with his brethren." While the English text is copied from the current AV, the words "with supplication" should be omitted, because, as is well known, the textus receptus is based upon late Mss. Compare Nestle, *Introduction to Novum Testamentum Graece,* subheading "The Greek Manuscripts," 69*, who does not print the words, nor UBS, and compare further, Metzger, *Textual Comm.,* p. 284. Note, however, the definite article in *te proseche,* and similarly 16.16. "Certainly, the use of the article here implies something more definite than merely 'prayer'" A. W. F. Blunt, *The Acts of the Apostles,* p. 134, and similarly, Foakes-Jackson-Lake, I, p. 10 who translate "Place of Prayer" and who argue that *proseuche* must mean "Place of Prayer, or Synagogue." Objections are raised by Arndt-Gingrich, p. 720, that *proseuche* in Ac. 16.13.16 was not a regular synagogue as it was attended only by women (v. 13), and the word *sunagoge* is the usual one, elsewhere *oikos proseuches* Mt. 21.13; Mk. 11.17; Lk. 19.46. The trouble is resolved when we become aware of the mistranslation. The Aramaic read בית צלותא which means *aedes sacra* (Brock., p. 70; Payn. Sm., p. 479) and which varies with "oratory" meaning "private prayer place." Most likely, the phrase *bet ṣelotha* means "synagogue," (cf. בית תפלה), as its provenance was Eastern Aramaic instead of the usual *bet kenishta.* The Greek translator did not understand; and, taking *bet* as the preposition "in" instead of the noun "house of," he rendered *bet ṣelotha* as "in the prayer." The determinate ending in the Aramaic accounts for the definite article in the Greek. The same mistranslation took place in Ac. 16.13.16 where again the translator rendered "in the prayer" instead of, simply, "the synagogue." *Bet ṣelotha* "house of prayer" idiomatically means "the synagogue"; cf. the familiar בי מדרשא, בי כנישתא, בי רבנן "college" Ber. 17a. Two incidental corrections are to be made with regard to Ac. 16.13.16. From Temple days, women did not have, as is alleged, a special synagogue for themselves, but joined with the men in prayer, although in a segregated part of the synagogue Midd. 2.5. A synagogue, moreover, if at the river (Ant. 14.10.23), was not so legally required, but was for the convenience of those who wished to wash their hands before prayer (Foakes Jackson Lake, p. 191), or for those priests who became unclean and had to bathe in order to eat of their priestly share (Ber. 2b). It was also covenient for the *ṭoble shaḥrit* (ibid, 22a) "the morning bathers," who wished to be cleansed, for example, after *pollutio noctis,* and for the *ṭebul yom,* the one who has bathed early in the day (though he had to wait for the sunset to be clean), as well as for immersion for the postmenstrual woman, instead of the *miqva* bath.

The Aramaic substratum shows up again in the peculiar phrase, designating Jesus, in the passage of Ac. 3.15 which runs, "And [you] killed the Prince of life (ἀρχηγὸν τῆς ζωῆς) whom God hath raised from the

APPENDIX I 197

dead; whereof we are witnesses." The word *archegon*, "leader, ruler, prince," and possibly "originator, founder," is used in the LXX for *rosh, sar, nasi', qaṣin;* these meanings limit what *archegos* should mean; however "Prince of life," is an incongruous phrase, without parallel. Other translations only certify to the perplexities and confusion that persist, as for instance, "Princely Leader of Life," Rhm; "Guide to Life," TCNT; "The leader of Life," Mof.;[1] "The pioneer of Life," Mof.[2]; "The source of life," Gdspd.; "author of life," Knox; "Author of life," Rieu; "Who has led the way to life," NEB; "Author of life," RSV, NAB. All the translations, however, with the best of intentions, seem to cut themselves adrift from the special sense of *archegos,* from the oddity of the phrase, and from the elusive meaning (Foakes Jackson-Lake: the Captain of life [!]). The Aramaic behind the Greek seems to offer the proper understanding of the phrase. Undoubtedly, the Aramaic term for *archegos* was רב, רבא, "master, chief, teacher," and the choice of this word is based on its usage as a comprehensive blanket term for *'luf, bekor, ba'al, gebir, gadol, nasi', saris, sar,* even *'ab, 'elohim, mashiaḥ* (*ha-kohen hamashiaḥ*), used in the Targums for the non-Hebrew priests Potifera and Jethro, Gen. 41.45.50; 46.20; Ex. 2.16; 18.1, and this quite matches up with *archegos* in the LXX as used for *'aluf, nasi', qaṣin, sar, rosh* (Hatch-Redpath, *Concordance to the LXX,* p. 165). The second word in the phrase gave the confusion and trouble: חייא. The Greek translator assumed that he had in front of him the word for "life." He should have rendered by *soteria* "salvation." For *ḥayye* as "salvation" compare Payn. Sm., p. 139; Brock. p. 229; it is a frequent equivalent in noun and verb for *sosai, soteria* "save, salvation," Mt. 1.21; Lk. 17.19 (vb.); Lk. 19.9; Jn. 4.22; Lk. 1.77 (noun). Note, however, that חיא is employed for *zao* "live," and the noun חיא/חייא (the latter with one yud as in Syriac) is used equationally for *zoe,* "life." These two meanings of "life" and "saving" were mistaken for one another. The Aramaic phase רבא לחייא or רב לחייא, is probably a reminiscence of the familiar רב להושיע, compare Is. 63.1, and its liturgical use in the *Shemoneh Esreh,* as well as Is. 19.20 and Zeph. 3.17. The translation should have borne the thought that Jesus was mighty in his saving power. Note the same thought in Ac. 5.31. Translate "master (or "great") in salvation."

This same mistake of "life" for "salvation, *rescue*" is found in Ac. 5.20. The preceding verses tell of the apostles' rescue from prison and the part that the angel played in this rescue. He then enjoins them "Go, stand, and speak in the temple to the people all the words of this life" ($\tau\grave{\alpha}$ $\dot{\rho}\acute{\eta}\mu\alpha\tau\alpha$ $\tau\tilde{\eta}s$ $\zeta\omega\tilde{\eta}s$ $\tau\alpha\acute{v}\tau\eta s$). The observation of Foakes-Jackson-Lake in their commentary refuses to draw a precise conclusion, "Whether this phrase translates an Aramaic original or not, it doubtless represents a word [?] which could be rendered both by *zoe* and *soteria,* just as conversely חיי 'life' is used in Syriac to render *soteria.*" Why not say, "The Aramaic had חיי; the Greek translated with 'life' whereas he should have rendered with *soteria,* 'salvation,' or better in this instance, preferably, 'rescue' from jail"? This is exactly what took place. The angel simply said to the apostles, "Tell the people how you got rescued." Or rendered verbatim, "Tell in the temple to the people all the details of this rescue," Aramaic מליא דחיי. The Greek translator again mistook *millayya* as "words" and *ḥayye* as "life." The word "this," which was enigmatic to the above commentators now takes its rightful place, "the events of *this* rescue" not "this life."

Ten verses later, in reply to the High Priest's charges, Peter and the apostles said, "The God of our fathers raised up Jesus whom ye slew and hanged on a tree (κρεμάσαντες ἐπὶ ξύλου)." It is idle to explain that the author had Deut. 21.22 in mind "You shall hang him on a tree," or to employ the Latin inscription *infelici arbor reste suspendito* where the accursed tree is euphemistic for the gallows or gibbet; and furthermore, to advance Mommsen's assertion that *suspendere* remained from the old Roman custom of crucifying slaves, and that the wooden yoke (*furca*) eventually evolved to the *crux*. It is assumed that ξύλον, meaning both tree and pole, found its way into the *koine* from the LXX (See Foakes Jackson-Lake in n., p. 59). Some difficulties remain: It is extraordinary that *xulon* goes flatly against the tradition of the Four Gospels which use *stauros* and *stauroō*, "cross" and "crucify" over fifty times and do not once mention hanging on a tree. Although *stauroō* as the verb is found twice, Ac. 2.36; 4.10, *xulon* is limited to Ac. 5.30; 10.39; 13.29. Gal. 3.13, of course, is a quotation from Deut. 1 Pet. 2.24; if it were written by Peter, this would have been at least twenty years after the death of Paul (Moffatt, the *Historical New Testament,* pp. 242–243), and therefore the passage is simply derivative from Ac. Moreover, *xulon* remains in the text, and the modern translations are divided in their interpretation. Thus, "on a gibbet" is the translation offered by Mof. 1 and 2; NEB, Gdspd. "on a cross," TCNT; "on a cross of wood," Phi; but "on a tree" is the rendering of ASV, RSV, NAB, Mon. Even Foakes Jackson-Lake, after their stimulating and learned discussion translate "hanging on a tree." In the midst of these disagreements, the Aramaic may offer a helpful suggestion. The expression used for hanging is צליב בקיסא "hanged upon a tree" (cf. Levy, *Chal. Wört.* II, p. 326; and also צליבת קיסא, a death sentence by impaling on a beam; Heb. צלוב על הצלוב "hanged on a gibbet"); Abraham carried the wood for the sacrifice of Isaac כזה שהוא טוען צלובו על כתפו "Like one who carries his cross upon his shoulder" because Isaac's sacrifice and death was imminent, Levy, ibid, p. 326. אע, like קיסא, and like עץ, has the meaning of "wood" and "tree" and it can readily be seen how the meanings could be confused. Payn. Sm., p. 504; Brock., p. 665. Note for the translation the following example in Gen. 40.19 ותלה אותך על עץ, Trg. O. ויצלובן יתך על קיסא Trg. Yer. I ויצלוב יתך על צליבא. On the basis of the examples presented we should translate our Ac. passages consistently "impaled upon a cross" or "crucified upon the cross," Ac. 13.29 "took him down from the cross," not "tree."

Ac. 8.23 reads, "For I perceive that thou art in the gall of bitterness (χολὴν πικρίας), and in the bond of iniquity." This passage is within the general charge of Peter against Simon Magus, who was accused of trying to buy power to confer the Holy Ghost on people. Peter says that Simon will have no part in this power; he is "not right with God," and is simply full of "wickedness." To say, however, that Simon is "in the gall of bitterness" is peculiar. The meaning is obscure, and the expected parallel is lacking. The passage in Deut. 29.17 "a root that beareth gall and wormwood (ראש ולענה)," cited in this connection does not apply. The Aramaic phrase in back of the Greek was most probably מרתא מרירא. The translator understood both words as being associated with מרר, "be bitter," and מרירא or מררא as "gall." It seems evident that the translator misread his text מרירא for מרידא, Resh for Daleth, "bitter rebellion." מרד and מרר are frequently mistaken for one another (Jast., p. 843b). We should translate "In bitter contention" (or "rebellion"). Note that the following "iniquity" offers a good parallel to "contention."

Ac. 9.1 runs, "And Saul, yet breathing out (ἐμπνέων) threatenings and slaughter against the disciples of the Lord, went unto the High Priest." The next verse describes how Saul-Paul sought out warrants for the arrest of men and women to bring them bound to Jerusalem. The term "breathing out" is an old difficulty. A parallel is sought in Theocritus 22.82 (Arndt-Gingrich, Introd., XXV) (Bauer). The modern translations follow in the main the term "breathing" and only one seems to have caught the natural sense "uttering murderous threats" TCNT. The Greek translator saw the Hebrew-Aramaic word יפיח (compare the compound διαπνέω/פוח in Cant. 2.17; 4.6) which he translated too literally, though indeed, "breathing" is the fundamental meaning of the word. It has, however, the secondary, derived meaning of "utter," compare BDB, p. 806 and Prov. 6.19; 14.5.29; 12.17. We should translate therefore, "And Saul uttering murderous threats against the disciples of the Lord...." "Threats and murder" is hendiadys for "murderous threats."

Ac. 17.3 is a description of Paul's activity in the synagogue at Thessalonica "where he reasoned with them out of the scriptures" and v. 3 "Opening up ($\delta\iota\alpha\nu o\iota\gamma\omega\nu$) and alleging," etc. This action of "opening up" is the Aramaic פתח meaning "explain" (discussed above, p. 128), but which the Greek mistranslated. Hence, the Aramaic document did not end at ch. 15, though the point at which it ended cannot for the moment be determined.

Ac. 13.11 sets forth Paul's imprecation on Bar-Jesus, the sorcerer (Elymas), "And now behold, the hand of the Lord is upon thee, and thou shalt be blind, not seeing the sun for a season ($\mathring{\alpha}\chi\rho\iota\ \kappa\alpha\iota\rho o\hat{\upsilon}$, literally, until a time). This expression was discussed in Lk. 4.13 where it was shown that it was an Aramaic locution עד זימנא or alternately עד עידנא, too, which the translator rendered too literally instead of "for a while" (see p. 128).

Some phrases are problematic in exegesis. The text in Ac. 5.12—13 reads, "And by the hands of the apostles were many signs and wonders wrought among the people. And they were *all* of one accord in Solomon's porch. And the rest durst no man *join* himself to them ($\tau\hat{\omega}\nu\ \delta\grave{\epsilon}\ \lambda o\iota\pi\hat{\omega}\nu\ o\mathring{\upsilon}\delta\epsilon\grave{\iota}s\ \mathring{\epsilon}\tau\acute{o}\lambda\mu\alpha\ \kappa o\lambda\lambda\hat{\alpha}\sigma\theta\alpha\iota\ \alpha\mathring{\upsilon}\tau o\hat{\iota}s$), but the people magnified them." Most likely "all" in the verse alludes to the apostles who used Solomon's portico to instruct the people. What the "rest" means is difficult to explain. It is hypothesized that it signifies (1) the non-Christians, and the "people" in the text adversatively refers to the lower classes; (2) "rest" refers to the Christians, who dared not join, presumably not to infringe on the prerogatives of the apostles, whom the "people" collectively extolled; (3) "The Greek expression is strange," and it is argued the "rest" may be an early correction of the text. The suggestion is made that "rulers" be read for "rest" to make sense, Peake² (*Acts*, p. 892).

The Aramaic would suggest a simple clear-cut solution ודי מיתרין לא אמרחו למדבק להון with the meaning, "And the nobles (or "affluent," "honored ones") dared not persecute them." The Greek translator thought of the root יתר meaning "rest, remaining" and so rendered accordingly. דבק means not only *kollosthai* "adhere, join," but is a good synonym of רדף, signifying "persecute, hound." Compare Levy, *Chal. Wört.*, I, p. 160, and the equation of דבק/*kollamai*, and Lk. 10.11 Syriac p s c which דבק otherwise would be rendered by *akoloutheo*, Mt. 9.27 and elsewhere; as well as השג "overtake" in Onqelos, Gen. 31.25; 44.4.6 often after רדף "run after," BDB, p. 673. מיתר in the sense of "honored" is found in Mt. 20.28 Syriac c (Burkitt, p. 119)

APPENDIX I

where interestingly the D version adds, "It will be of greater profit (*chresimon* = יותרנא!) to thee," another interpretation of יתר, and compare further מיתר "honored" as in או מיתרא "O excellent man!", *The Chronicle of Joshua, the Stylite,* Proem, ed. W. Wright; Payn. Sm., p. 200; Brock., p. 313. Our passage now should bear the sense, "And the rich class did not persecute the apostles; however, the common people honored them."

In Ac. 8.26 we read, "And the angel of the Lord spoke unto Philip saying, 'Arise, and go toward the south, unto the way that goeth down from Jerusalem unto Gaza, which is desert (αὕτη ἐστίν ἔρημος).'" The tag at the end "which is desert" has elicited suspicion on the part of critics, and rightly so. There are a number of questions (cf. Foakes Jackson-Lake, p. 95): is it the city that is deserted, or the road? (1) if the road, it was not deserted; Josephus says that it was not deserted until after 66 C.E.; (2) perhaps this is a gloss; (3) there were two cities called Gaza, the old Gaza destroyed in 96 B.C.E. by Alexander Janneus; the new Gaza, built under the Romans and demolished in 66 C.E. as mentioned. It is maintained that the name "desert" stuck to the old Gaza; the new Gaza on the sea was qualified as "maritime."

It is difficult to fathom and settle on the alternatives we have in "deserted" Gaza, or the "deserted" road (the latter "a curious note" in the text according to G. W. H. Lampe, *Acts,* p. 897 in Peake[2]). George Adam Smith decidedly concludes (*Historical Geography of the Holy Land,*[4] p. 186), "No possible route from Jerusalem to Gaza could be called desert." And in n.3, ibid, "But it seems to me so impossible to describe any route from Jerusalem to Gaza as desert. . . ." He argues for a new and old Gaza. Pertinently, the Peshitta has a different order, "Go south on the desert road that goes down from Jerusalem to Gaza." The modern translators, as editors making a judgment on deserted Gaza or deserted road, are completely at odds with one another, and translate as follows: "The same is desert" ASV; "(it is now deserted)" TCNT; "crossing the desert" Wey; "The road is desert" Mof.[1]; "(the desert route)" Mof.[2]; "(The town is now deserted)" Gdspd.; "This is the desert road" Wms., NEB; "a lonely road" Ber.; "out in the desert" Phi; "it is a deserted road" Beck. The parentheses indicate a gloss in the opinion of the editors.

The origin of the confusion may have been in the Aramaic antecedent document. Taking a cue from the Peshitta, I would restore the text to read אורחא דמדברא נחתא מן ירושלים לעזה which should be translated, "The road leading and going down from Jerusalem to Gaza." The root דבר in Aramaic means generally "drive, lead," and relative to the verse are such nouns as דברא "drive, way of moving," Targ. 2 Kings 9.20, and especially Targ. Jud.

5.21 כוכביא מכבשי דבריהון "stars from the roads of their "leading," i.e., where they are being led in their course; then in a different form as in דברונא דנהרא (Ms. Munich, Rashi דברונא דמיא) "course of the river," Jast., p. 279; Levy, *Chal. Wört.*, I, p. 161, and Ex. 13.2 לדברותהון בארחא "to lead them on the road." The translator, however, saw and interpreted אורחא דמדברא (note that אורחא is feminine, Dalman, *Wört.*, p. 38) "the desert road," which made for confusion in the Greek translation. Subsequently, "desert" for stylistic glossing was transferred to the end of the verse, as copyists were accustomed to do. See the writer's article "The Perpetuation of Variants in the Masoretic Text," JQR, 1944, 459ff. The asyndeton in the two verbs would be idiomatic Aramaic. We should translate, "the road leading and descending from Jerusalem to Gaza."

An extraordinary action in the freeing of Peter from prison occurs in Ac. 12.7. When the angel appears to liberate Peter, he *strikes* Peter on the *side*. The Greek reads πατάξας δὲ τὴν πλευρὰν τοῦ Πέτρου, "He smote Peter on the side" AV. This is a very unusual act on the part of a divine messenger. Generally, God or the messenger of God, has but to appear and a man becomes conscious of the divine presence. The *yad 'adonai* that comes upon Ezekiel, for example, is a divine trance (Ez. 8.1 and elsewhere), although a hand for a specific purpose does play a part for picking up Ezekiel by the hair of his head (ibid, 8.3), or extending a scroll to him (ibid, 2.9). At most, the angel touches a man (Dan. 10.10). The Greek word *patasso* means "strike, beat, wound," corresponding to מחא in the Aramaic, equated similarly in Lk. 22.49; Mt. 26.31; Mk. 14.27. The modern translations show their dissatisfaction with the conventional rendering, although Rhm, Wey, Wms, Mof.¹ Mof.², Gdspd. adhere to "striking." Ber. however, translates "touching Peter in the side"; Phi, "He tapped Peter on the side and woke him up"; Rieu, "The angel woke Peter with a touch on the side"; NEB, "He tapped Peter on the shoulder and woke him," similarly NAB. We must surmise that the Greek mistranslated. מחא has the fundamental meaning of "strike, beat," but in Syriac the verb goes its own way to signify "to slap," "to clothe or gird oneself," to "bend (the head, knees)" and most pertinent for the interpretation in our verse "to put, lay one's hand to," Brock., p. 380, #9. That is what the angel did: he touched Peter; this corresponds to the Hebrew biblical usage נגע.

The translator however misunderstood another word. He thought that לצד, also לציד, means "the side of." It also has the function, however, of a preposition, found likewise in Palestinian Aramaic and Syriac, having the signification of "by, at, to, with." Compare Brock., p. 626; Jast., p. 1274; Levy, *Chal. Wört.*, II, p. 320; Payn. Sm., p. 477. The Aramaic probably ran: ומחא לציד פטרוס which we may translate simply, "And he touched Peter."

Appendix II

The Book of Revelations and Its Underlying Document

THE BOOK of Revelations is filled with bristling, complicated questions, among which the question of the original language of the book is important. R. H. Charles in his valuable and suggestive commentary (*The Revelation of St. John*, 2 vols., 1920) spoke out boldly for his thesis that this is a translation from the Hebrew, endeavoring to prove that the seer was translating from that language. C. C. Torrey, *Documents of the Primitive Church*, pp. 149f. was equally convinced that the Greek, with its extraordinary peculiarities, originated from the Aramaic. His investigations and his conclusions are formulated with a depth and thoroughness that are impressive.

In going over the ground carefully with regard to the linguistic character of Revelations, it seems to me that Torrey's position is stronger and more convincing. Charles's examples appear in a number of major points to be doubtful, if not erroneous. More importantly, Charles failed to reckon with the possibility that the Greek may have been translated from the Aramaic, and not only from the Hebrew. It should be noted incidentally that, on the one hand, he assumes that *"While he [John] writes in Greek, he thinks in Hebrew"* (Charles, I, p. xcliii; italics his); on the other hand, he argues that "Our author makes use of sources some of which were Greek, though originally written in Hebrew; others which he found in Hebrew, and rendered into Greek" (ibid, cl; and II, p. 207). In the main, the objections to his hypothesis consist of the old counterclaim, sometimes quite real, that the Greek can be paralleled and exemplified elsewhere (so Moulton, Swete, *Apocalypse of John*,[2] cxxiv, note, Grenfell, Hunt, Thumb, et al.). Mistranslations from the Hebrew would be a powerful argument, but it must be confessed that his examples left something to be desired. Thus, his citation and reconstruction of 13.3 c ותתמה כל הארץ מאחרי החיה which he details in his Introduction p. cii; he restores מאחרי/בראות, bringing the reading in line with

17.8 "shall wonder when they see the beast." I have no convincing suggestion on these discrepant texts, although as a counter proposal, I suspect a misunderstanding of לאחורי (Aramaic, cf. Ex. 26.12; Num. 3.23; Ez. 2.9) as if from חר "to see, gaze at," (see p.55 for another example). At any rate, the Aramaic is equally a possibility. Or, in 13.11 "He spoke like a dragon," Charles emends to ותאבד from ותדבר which he translates "He was a destroyer like a dragon" without realizing that for the dragon he has a feminine form, to say nothing about the change from the unseen ותדבר to ותאבד, though as an illustration, he compares aptly 2 Chron. 22.10 with 2 Kings 11.1 (see, however, p. 210 for the Aramaic explanation).

More fundamentally, the idea that much of the bizarre Greek is based on the presumed source of the Hebrew, (as is presented in his second lecture in *Lectures on the Apocalypse,* p. 30) is beside the mark. The classical Hebrew constructions, wherein the participle before the finite verb then introduced by *kai,* as well as constructions with the Waw Conversive *ut supra,* and referred retrojectively to "classical Hebrew" had but sparsely flourished in the first century C.E. Compare M. Segal's remarks in *Mishnaic Hebrew Grammar,* par. 104 "In the field of syntax, Mishnaic Hebrew lost many constructions which imparted such beauty and distinction to Biblical Hebrew, such as the use of the cohortative and the jussive, *and of the consecutive tenses*" (italics mine); and beginning par. 308 notes ". . . the absence of the imperfect consecutive in Mishnaic Hebrew. . . ." On a number of counts, therefore, Charles' hypothesis of a *Hebrew* translation could be questioned: on the score of the restorations; on the questionable chronological period for Hebrew in Revelations; on his doubtful restorations based on Greek syntax, which could be exampled—as he himself admits—from the LXX (see further p. cxliii of his Introduction). As mentioned, he did not reckon with Aramaic, the *koine* of the Jewish people; his employment of Hebrew is anachronistic.

The following material, presented as an addition to Torrey's article on Revelations, should prove enough continued justification to argue for an Aramaic original.

The evidence for Aramaic, underlying the Greek, is recognizable in Rev. 2.24, a section of the letters that the seer had written to the several churches. The passage reads, "But unto you I say, and unto the rest in Thyatira, as many as have not this doctrine, and which have not known the *depths of Satan* ($\tau\grave{\alpha}\ \beta\alpha\theta\acute{\epsilon}\alpha\ \tau o\hat{\upsilon}\ \sigma\alpha\tau\alpha\nu\hat{\alpha}$) as they speak; I will put upon you no other burden." John, after denouncing the evil inhabitants of Thyatira, and their "Jezebel" female leader, shunts off his searing condemnation of the remaining loyal religionists who have not espoused false teachings, and who have not known the *depths* of Satan, *as they speak*. Commentators cite 1 Cor. 2.10 "the depths of God," "the depths of divine knowledge," 1 Cl. 40.1 (Arndt-Gingrich, p. 129), and therefore this divine "depth" is regarded as a parallel in thought and usage to the "depths" of Satan. (For the depths of God, however, we could go back to the Bible, Ps. 92.5 "Thy thoughts are very deep.") The depths of Satan, however, are quite different. What can these "depths" consist of? Charles, I, p. 73 offers two interpretations: (1) The libertine section, or party in the Church of Thyatira; (2) The Gnostic element which claimed that to know the deep elements of Satan, one must first experience the pagan sacrificial feasts, and the heathen immoralities (so Spitta, Zahn, Bousset, and others, Charles, ibid). Still, the use of "depths" of Satan is peculiar, and seemingly unprecedented. The difficulty is felt by the modern translations, "The 'secrets' of Satan, as men call them," TCNT; "The deep mysteries (as they are called) which Satan offers," Knox. The problem, however, is not too complicated when we refer to the underlying Aramaic. Thus the Aramaic עומקא would give the proper solution to the enigma. The word means "wiles, perversity," and indeed, may simply be a variant for עקם "be perverse, deceitful." We have some six examples of עמק in the sense of "wiles, perversity." See Levy, *Chal. Wört.*, II, p. 24. We should translate, "[those] as have not this doctrine, and who have not known the wiles of Satan." Note the correct complement now "wiles of Satan"— deceitful words—"as they speak."

A phrase that the translator misconceived is evident in Rev. 5.2. The text reads, "And I saw a strong angel (ἄγγελον ἰσχυρὸν) proclaiming with a loud voice, 'Who is worthy to open the book...?'" A "strong angel" is mentioned again in 10.1; 18.21. It is perplexing that the angel is portrayed as "strong," and it is without parallel. The text that the Greek translator had before him was מלאך גבורתא "angel of the *Almighty*." Compare Jast., p. 205. The Greek is a mistranslation. The Rev. passage should bear the translation, "And I saw an angel of God," the earlier OT מלאך יי.

In Rev. 6.6, the text states that with the opening of the third seal, a famine will spread in which there will be a dearth of wheat and barley, oil and wine, the staples of workers and slaves. The average daily wage for the worker was a denarius (see Charles, I, p. 166, and the sources there cited), consequently the Rev. writer forecasts a disastrous future. The verse that describes this famine reads, "And I heard a voice in the midst of the four beasts say, 'A measure of wheat for a penny (so AV; actually a denarius), and three measures of barley for a penny, and see thou hurt not (μὴ ἀδικήσῃς: literally, do not wrong) the oil and the wine.'" Scholars deduce that, while there will be a famine in wheat and barley, wine and oil will be abundant. No positive conclusion, however, can be reached about the genuineness and validity of this hypothesis. Bousset and Swete accept the idea of the dearth of bread, but also the abundance of oil and wine; Holtzmann doubts it; Wellhausen rejects it, and his view is shared by Charles. The quoted talmudic sources by Charles, Sotah 49b "In the times when the Messiah is at hand, shamelessness will increase ...," and other citations from San. 97a, are chronologically out of joint with Rev. and are of no pertinence (Charles, ibid, I, p. 168). The Greek translator again did not understand his Aramaic text. The Greek *adikeo* meaning "act unjustly, wrong, injure" is supposed to signify here "damage, spoil"; this would still leave the previous question of the scarcity of bread and, contrarily, the abundance of oil and wine puzzling and unresolved. The translator saw the word תחסר "hurt, injure" *nocuit* (Aph'el) (Brock., p. 248; Payn. Sm., p. 152), and this is the way he translated. Instead, he should have taken חסר in the Pe'al, or Pa'el in the sense of "lack, want." Note the same semantic development in נכי "injure" and "subtract," Jast., 910. In this instance, the translator failed to recognize the brachylogy in the sense of "Let there not be lacking, missing, omitted in your account" Ct. 7.3. Or as we would say, "There will be a scarcity of bread and barley, to say nothing of oil and wine." For "lack, omit,"cf. Ker. 6a "If he left out (חיסר) one of the ingredients." Erub. 13a "If you omit (מחסר) one letter ...," Jast., p. 489; Levy, NHB, II, p. 91. Other passages of a still different character in Rev. 2.11; 7.2f. are not in the same category of the present verse.

In the description of the opening of the sixth seal, part of this apocalyptic vision reads (6.14), "And the heavens departed" (ἀπεχωρίσθη) meaning "separated," so the Peshitta פרש, Vulgate *recessit* "pass away," is usually explained (perhaps following the latter, or ad hoc to mean "will vanish" or something similar) "as a scroll that is rolled together (ὡς βιβλίον ἑλισσόμενον); and every mountain and island were moved out of their places." There is an illogicality here: if the heavens are parted or separated, then they cannot be compared to a rolled up scroll. This passage is based upon Is. 34.4 ונגלו כספר שמים "And the heavens shall be rolled together as a scroll," and similarly the LXX which read the same as MT; the Greek verb in the Rev. passage was taken from the isainic Greek. It is clear that the meaning of the Mt. passage follows the sense as was translated above: the heavens like a scroll will be rolled *up*. Whereas the Isaiah writer thought in terms of how the scroll would be rolled up, the Rev. conception is that the

APPENDIX II

scroll, already rolled, will be unrolled, or spread apart. Actually there was a misunderstanding of the Hebrew-Aramaic root פרש/פרס, Levy, *Chal. Wört.* II, p. 301, which the Rev. writer assumed to mean "separate," and which he should have interpreted as "spread apart," Jast., p. 1232. The translation should be, "And the heavens were spread apart like a scroll that is rolled out."

The "Word of God" (*logos*) appears in Rev. but once. It is assumed that this "Word" is an appelative attribute of Jesus in common with Jn. 1.1.2.14. In an abrupt fashion, with the portrayal of his marriage to his wife, the Lamb is introduced in 19.7. In v. 11, the heavens are opened disclosing a rider "Faithful and True," on a white horse, ready to make war. V. 12 then describes that the rider had "many crowns," and he had a name no man knew, but he himself. V. 13 continues, "And he was clothed in a vesture dipped in blood, and his name is called the 'Word of God.'" V. 16, all part of this description asserts that he has another name—"King of Kings and Lord of Lords." Restating, there are a number of problems that require solution:

V. 12 says that he had a name written that no man knew (*oiden*) but he himself.

V. 13, per contra, alleges that his name was "Word of God."

V. 16 asserts, however, that his name was "King of Kings and Lord of Lords."

Hence, v. 12 contradicts vv. 13 and 16; vv. 13 and 16 contradict each other. Through the instrumentality of the Aramaic, a satisfying reconstruction is possible.

To reconcile these discrepancies, scholars such as Charles (II, p. 132) regard 12c as an interpolation because of the interruption in thought, and because of the contradiction that exists in 13b. On the other hand, the latter clause is regarded as a scribal addition by Spitta, Hilgenfeld, Bousset, though not by Charles, II, p. 134. The inconsistencies, if formidable, may be resolved, and a reasonable coherence may be construed. It is easy to retrovert from the Greek; the relevant restored Aramaic ran, with translation and notes:

12. ועל רישיה תגא סגיא, ולה שמא כתיבא דלא ידע אנש אלא הוא.
13. ומעטף הוא מאנא כד מטמע בדמא ומתקרא שמיה אמרא דאלהא.
16. ואית ליה על מאניה ועל דגלה שמא כתיבא מלכא דמלכיא ומרא דמרותא.

Translation:

V. 12 "And on his head, there was a *great crown;* and there was a name written which no one knew except himself."

V. 13 "And he was clothed with a vesture immersed in blood, and his name was called *'Lamb of God.'*"

V. 16 "And there was on his *weapon* (sword), and on his *banner* a name written 'King of Kings and Lord of Lords.'"

It is possible to maintain the text by advocating reasonably that the names, which Christ as a warrior would bear, would reflect the different attributes of his nature and action; one attribute on his crown, one attribute on his bloodied vesture, and one attribute spread on his martial equipment, on his sword, and on his banner.

V. 12. "many crowns," seems bizarre in the Greek. The plural, mistakenly assumed, rose from the translator's thought that the crowns were the separate crowns of kings that Christ would appropriate after he had conquered the world's armies and kingdoms (19.18). Wearing so many crowns upon his head (one on top of another?) would be a grotesquerie; and was there a single name written on all of them? There was actually *one* crown of supreme lordship. The translator mispointed תגא סֹגִיאא (I give the Syriac spelling) for תגא סגיאא. The name on this crown was to be secret and ineffable, lest someone, by learning it, would gain magical power over it, as would one who learned the secret name of God (Yahweh). Such an individual would acquire supreme lordship, and be the conqueror of the world as well.

V. 13. Since the Lamb of God is mentioned in vv. 7, 9, it follows that the "Word of God" introduced but once in Rev. is unrelated to the scene at hand and is a misnomer. Commentators are constrained to admit that "The phrase is used in an entirely different context in the two books" [John and Revelations] (N. Turner, *Revelations,* in Peake,[2] p. 1057). Again, the translator misread אמרא as "word" instead of אמרא "lamb," the only appropriate reading in the passage introduced as he was in v. 7.

Parenthetically, one should add here the difficult phrase in Rev. 13.11, "And I beheld another beast coming out of the earth; and he had two horns like a lamb, and he spake as a dragon" (ἐλάλει ὡς δράκων). Now a dragon does not speak. From the antecedent verses, which dealt likewise with a beast ("seven heads, ten horns, ten crowns"), and the dragon which had given the beast power, all worshipped this beast. Then v. 11 describes another beast coming out of the earth, which our verse seems to delineate as Nero (so commentators). This lamb in the verse has to be differentiated from the Lamb in the author's thoughts. His Aramaic read ואמרא הוא היך תנינא which the translator imagined to mean "He spoke as a dragon," making for an absurdity (as if ואמר הוא). He should have rendered ואמר in the phrase

APPENDIX II   211

as "And the lamb was like a dragon." This phrase had the intention of signaling the unsophisticated reader that this was not the Lamb of God, but another lamb, "his antitype" i.e., Antichrist as J. Jeremias, (*Theological Dictionary of the NT,* I, p. 341) identifies it.

Returning to v. 16, "vesture" in v. 13 already had the Lamb of God inscribed on it as a name, and therefore "vesture" in v. 16 has no place here. מאנה (מאנוהי in the plural could equally be idiomatic) means not only his "vesture," but his "armor," Payn. Sm. p. 247. The translator confused the two. For his "thigh" on which was written the third name as the verse has it, the proposal of Torrey, *Documents of the Primitive Church,* to emend רגליה "his thigh" to דגליה "his banner" is a sterling suggestion which I follow. The sense of the passage that there was a name written on his armor and his banner is quite fitting. The translation with the concordance of all the members in the verses, should be followed as given above.

The passage in Rev. 22.1f. is somewhat intricate, and contains a number of elements requiring a preliminary background and exposition. V. 1 in the AV tells of the revelation to the seer of a "pure river of water of life, clear as crystal, proceeding out of the throne of God and of the Lamb." V. 2 continues, "In the midst of the *street* of it ($\dot{\epsilon}\nu\ \mu\dot{\epsilon}\sigma\omega\ \tau\hat{\eta}s\ \pi\lambda\alpha\tau\epsilon\dot{\iota}\alpha s\ \alpha\dot{\upsilon}\tau\hat{\eta}s$) and on either side of the river was there the tree of life, which bare twelve manner of fruits, and yielding her fruit every month: and the leaves of the tree were for the *healing* ($\epsilon\dot{\iota}s\ \theta\epsilon\rho\alpha\pi\epsilon\dot{\iota}\alpha\nu$) of the nations."

The verse, when analyzed, presents a confused picture, difficult to conceive. If there is a river emanating from God's throne, what is meant by its course as bounding through the street thereof? Perhaps one must explain that the phrase in v. 2 is a continuation of v. 1 and that the imagery of the river, coursing through the street ("of the city," so the addition of RSV), is borrowed implicitly from the previous chapter, although not mentioned in this chapter. Since the syntax is at any rate difficult, some take the view (Charles, II, p. 176) that the phrase "in the midst of the street thereof" is to be taken with the sequel, although there is the difficulty that there is a "space" (Charles, ibid) between the street and the river, which were parallel to each other, side by side, with the trees of life on both sides of the river.

As scholars have noticed, the seer is modelling his description on the passage in Ez. 47 where the guide, divinely sent, pilots Ezekiel from the temple in Jerusalem, as water issued from the altar south and west. The water first was ankle deep (47.3), then knee-deep, then up to the loins (v. 4). However, in v. 5 the water becomes so deep, "And it was a river that I could not pass through: it was deep enough to swim in; a river that could not be passed through." V. 7 continues, "As I went back, I saw on the bank of the river very many trees (עץ רב מאד, a collective) on the one side and on the other. The trees will bear fresh fruit every month for food . . . their leaves for healing (עלהו לתרופה)." A number of questions now arise: what is meant by 'in the street thereof," and what are the *trees* of life?

The Aramaic provides a clarifying solution. "In the midst of the street thereof" was most probably בי פתאה where, first, the translator misjudged by thinking that בי means "in the midst, in the center" as if בי < בית < בינת and פתאה as if meaning "a street." However, בי פתאה means "at its widest extent," i.e., בי has the sense of "with, at," French *chez* (see Dan. 8.16 בין אולי, where too the Danielic translator from the Aramaic into Hebrew thought that בית אולי was "*between* the River Ulai" instead of "at the River Ulai." Cf. the writer's *Biblical Books Translated from the Aramaic*, p. 18 for other examples). Specifically "in the midst of the street thereof" is a mistranslation for "at its widest extent"; that is פתאה "street," see Levy, *Chal. Wört.*, II, p. 307 equationally for Hebrew רחוב, the form variable as פְּתָאָה Onq. Deut. 13.17 (compare Dalman, *Wörterbuch*, p. 340; Sperber, p. 315). The widest extent of the river would be a summary of Ez. 47.5 where the prophet had described the depth of the water, where it was at first ankle deep, then knee deep, then up to the loins, and then at last, where he could not pass through as it was the deepest and widest part. The description in Ez. 47.1—5 was encapsulated in the Rev. text as, per the restoration, "the widest part." In addition, the "trees of life," in Aramaic אע דחיי—a collective based upon Ez. 47.5—seems incorrect. First, in Paradise, the prototype found both in Ezekiel and Genesis, there was but one tree of life. Moreover, if the function of the trees is to provide leaves for healing, as the Rev. verse has it, then אע דחיי must mean "trees for healing," i.e. it was mistranslated as "trees of life" instead of "trees for healing." The verb in חיי in the 'Aph'el (Payn. Sm., p. 139; Jast., p. 454; Brock., p. 229 #3) bears that meaning. "Trees for healing" then forms a wordplay on the "healing of peoples" in our Rev. passage, perhaps אע דחיי . . . לחיי עממיא. Recourse to the Aramaic, then, solves our problems. Translate, "At its widest extent, on either side of the river, were trees of healing . . . and the leaves of the trees were for the healing of nations."

A clear-cut mistranslation appears in Rev. 22.15 where the text reads, "For without [the city] are dogs, and sorcerers, and whoremongers, and idolators, and whosoever loveth and maketh a lie" (καὶ πᾶς φιλῶν καὶ ποιῶν ψεῦδος). There are two perplexing readings: First, in the midst of all the evil-doers, the sorcerers, whoremongers and murderers, it is surprising

APPENDIX II

that the verse ends with "those who love and make lies." Second, it is a peculiar expression to say that one "makes lies." Beyond the linguistic singularity, as a moral evaluation "loving lies" is hardly on the same footing with the preceding murderers and idolators. Some Mss., in a reverse fashion, vary with, "Those who do and love lies," perhaps an unconscious correction. It seems likely that *pas philon* is a phrase to be taken by itself, and it represents the Aramaic והלין דמחבין which the translator confused with the root חבב "love" instead of חבין "those who sin," the proper reading (Payn. Sm., p. 122; Brock., pp. 208, 218). In addition, the translator did not quite perceive the nuance in שקרא, meaning "lie"; with the "doing," however, the sense should be "wickedness, deception, perjury," Payn. Sm., p. 595. For the "doing" of wickedness, cf. עשה שקר as in 2 Sam. 18.13; Jer. 6.13; 8.8. We should render the phrase "all those who sin, and do iniquity." This interpretation, accordingly, would be quite the correct summing up and climax of the previous "evildoers."

Notes

[1] For the literature, see the full bibliography in Blass-Debrunner-Funk, pp. xxvf. where the most up-to-date material is listed.

[2] See J. Moffat, *Introduction to the Literature of the New Testament*,[3] pp. 185—191 where the tradition given by Papias is presented with an evaluation. Most scholars are skeptical of the traditions Papias reports about the gospels of Mk. and Mt.

[3] Jn. 21 has a distinctive Greek style, not translation Greek, different from the recognizable renderings of the Aramaic idiom in the other chapters of the Synoptists, and contrastingly to the other chapters in Jn. Lightfoot, Harnack, Sanday, W. Bauer defend its genuineness; Pfleiderer, Moffat, Stanton consider that Ch. 21 was a later addition. Compare Bernard, *Gospel according to St. John*, II, pp. 683f. The lack of translation Greek in Jn. 21 is the first marked characteristic that its source may not be Aramaic, very much as Ac. I is translation Greek, while Acts II is written in a free-flowing, lively Greek style. Jn. 21, anyway, is a complicated question as to its proper place in the Fourth Gospel, Mof. ILNT, pp. 570—579.

[4] As will be shown in the chapter on Lk. (p. 97f.) the narrative portions in Lk. 1—2 were written in Aramaic, but the prayers therein were composed in Hebrew.

[5] Compare Deissmann's *Light from the Ancient East,* trans. from the 4th German ed. by L. R. M. Strachan, p. 64 "Moreover, the oldest record of the words that Jesus spake, the record of his apostle Matthew, was no doubt written in Aramaic for the Palestinian Christians who spoke that language ... The earlier Aramaic copies vanished before the multitude of Greek Mss." etc.

[6] Compare the remark also in Moulton, II, p. 419 "Inasmuch as the teaching of Jesus, and the original record of it, is assumed throughout this grammar to have been in Aramaic, and the Semitic coloring of our Greek documents in these parts is not in dispute, no more need be said."

[7] Transmitting the tradition in the language of one's teacher in this passage in Eduyot has been questioned as a gloss. (See Ben Yehudah, Introduction, p. 46 for the discussion; for another view, see J. Z. Lauterbach, *Rabbinic Essays*, 1951, p. 219f.) We know that Hillel lay great store on the Qabbala (tradition) as, for instance, in his countervailing argument against his predecessors the Benei Bethira. Compare Bacher, *Aggadot Ha-Tannaim,* trans. A. Z. Rabbinowitz, from the German into Hebrew, 2nd ed. I, p. 2 n. 4; Z. Frankel, *Darkei Ha-Mishna,* p. 40. Bacher, ibid, p. 8 gives the references where Hillel sometimes transmits traditions in Hebrew, other times in Aramaic, and yet other times in a mixture of both (cf. further, Ch. Albeck, *Mabo' La-Mishna,* p. 70).

[8] Comp. Strack, *Introduction to the Talmud and Midrash* (English), p. 12 f., 19. Add now: Y. N. Epstein, *Mabo' Le-Nosaḥ Ha-Mishna*, II, 609f.; Ch. Albeck, *Mabo' La-Mishna,* 114—115; Ch. Tchernowitz, *Toledot Ha-Halaka*, I, 6—7.

[9] In the *Antiquities,* 20.11.2, Josephus says,

> I have also taken a great deal of pains to obtain the learning of the Greeks, and understand the elements of the Greek language, although I have so long accustomed myself to speak our own tongue [Aramaic], that I cannot pronounce Greek with sufficient exactness; for our nation does not encourage those who learn the languages of many na-

tions ... because they look upon this sort of accomplishment as common, not only to all sorts of free-men, but to as many of the servants as please to learn them. But they give him the testimony of being the wise man who is fully acquainted with our laws, and is able to interpret their meaning ...

The deduction is obvious—he spoke Aramaic as his mother tongue; Greek he learned with some competence, and knew enough of it to compose, with the help of assistants, his histories. Parenthetically, as is well known, Paul spoke Aramaic to the crowd (Ac. 21.40; 22.2), from which Schürer implies that the people did not understand Greek (*History of the Jewish People in the Time of Jesus Christ*, Eng. ed., II, pp. 1, 48).

[10] One Galilean is referred to as a "gabbling Galilean," גלילאה שוטה. Compare Margolis, *34; Levy, *NH Wört.*, I, p. 336.

[11] Jast., p. 129; Levy, *Chal. Wört.*, I, p. 72. The Aleph is simply prosthetic Aleph, not *aeshma daeva*. The treatment of Asmodeus with but one line in Kittel's article "Daimon" in the *Theological Dictionary of the New Testament*, II, p. 15 is a shortfall, as Asmodeus was "king of the demons," Trg. to Qohelet 1.12, and compare L. Ginzberg, *Legends*, IV, pp. 100, 132, 166 (he ascended to heaven daily), 169 (he supplanted Solomon as king).

[12] English would be "Ethics and Law in Israel." See further on this principle of acting more stringently with oneself than that which the Torah requires: b. Bab. Qam. 99a; Bab. Meṣ. 84a (two examples); Ket. 97a and compare the Tosafot Bab. Meṣ. 24, lemma "Lifnim." Aside from the principles of *peshara* and *lifnim meshurat ha-din*, there are scores of others which permeate the whole system of Jewish jurisprudence, as in the practical abolition of capital punishment (see Federbusch); the "law (*nomos*)," as Paul describes it, is a false interpretation of the word Torah, as Federbusch declares. While it may be objected that some of the principles mentioned above may be late tannaitic, or amoraic, the fact is that the Holiness code and Deuteronomy presuppose these ethical maxims, compare, for example, Deut. 24.10f., 15, 16, 17, 19, 20 and the ethical elements involved.

[13] As if indirect proof were further needed that a mistake could be made between *beʻel debaba* and *beʻel debuba*, the vocalization appears incorrectly in that article.

[14] Equally possible would be the idiom אנא אנא, cf. Montgomery, p. 19, or אנא הוית (sic), Nöldeke, *Syr. Gramm.*, par. 256.

[15] Agnes Smith Lewis in *Light on the Four Gospels from the Sinai Palimpsest* (cited by Black, p. 128) pointed out that there may be a wordplay on "two Aramaic words" *ʻabed* 'to do' and *ʻabd* 'a slave.'" עבר עברה seems more idiomatic.

[16] There may be a further allusion, or perhaps a *talḥin* by extension implying the phrase בר ביתא having the sense of "prince," so defined by G. R. Driver as found in the Aramaic documents of the fifth century B.C.E. Cf. his edition (abridged and revised) *Aramaic Documents of the Fifth Century*, Oxford, 1957 pp. 4, 21, 22, 25, 33. The readings on pp. 21 and 33 are certain. The others are supplied on the basis of similar contexts. "Prince," contrasted with "servant, slave," would provide the correct antithesis.

[17] There is the further possibility that עידנא "time," מועדא 'feast," אייעד "make ready" are played upon, with the reservation that *yaʻad* is found only in Babylonian Aramaic, Jast. p. 584, but not in Syriac.

[18] In passing, we may notice Jn. 5.2 "Now there is (*estin*) at Jerusalem by the sheep market, a pool," where it is argued by Torrey, HTR, 1923, p. 334, in prosecution of his theory that all the Gospels are early, that this chapter would presuppose an early date. הוא, however, can easily mean "there is" or "there was," so variable is the temporal fluctuation.

NOTES

[19] The Greek reads *touto mou estin to soma to huper humon klomenon*. The last word "broken" is considered spurious, is not printed by Nestle, followed by UBS, and bracketed by Von Soden. A respectable number of Mss., however, carry *klomenon* "broken," with the synonymous *thruptomenon* "broken in pieces" in D. Metzger, p. 562, states that the participles are attempts to explicate the abrupt *to huper humon*, which, it is alleged, is characteristic of Paul's style. Nevertheless, I do not share this view. By itself, "This is my body on behalf of you" does not convey the message directly enough, nor does it have enough pointed significant meaning. It is the *breaking* that gives significance to the bread, and "This do in remembrance of me." The breaking of the *maṣah* reminds one of the broken body, i.e., the crucifixion. See further in the text.

[20] Compare *shalutha'* for *shegagah* in Targ. Onqelos Lev. 4.2 and often; as well as *shela* for *shagag*, Lev. 5.18; Num. 15.28; *shalu* for *mishgah*, Gen. 43.12.

[21] J. Jeremias, *Sayings of Jesus*, trans. by R. H. Fuller, 2nd English edition, London, 1964.

[22] B. Pick, *Paralipomena. Remains of Gospels and Sayings of Christ*, Chicago, 1908, p. 100, #107 cited by Jeremias, op. cit., p. 112.

[23] V. A. Soith, *Akbar, the Great Mogul*, Oxford, 1917; Jeremias, p. 111.

[24] *Dictionary of Christ and the Gospels,* II, Edinburgh, 1924, pp. 882–886; there does seem to be a trace of the saying in Jaqut's *Geographical Lexicon:* Jesus said: "The world is a place of transition, full of examples (מתלין error for מתקלין "pitfalls"); be pilgrims therein, and take warning by the traces of those who have gone before." Compare Ropes, art. Agrapha, *Dictionary of the Bible* (J. Hastings), Extra Volume, p. 350.

[25] Jeremias, op. cit., p. 114, n.7.

[26] Ibid, p. 115.

[27] Compare Levy and Jastrow in their Talmudic dictionaries.

[28] It is interesting that this interpretation caught the attention of Chaucer in the Knight's Tale 1.1989:

This world nis but a thurghfare ful of wo
And we ben pilgrims, passing to and fro
Death is an ende of every worldly sore.

[29] תניא ר׳ אליעזר אומר עולם לאכסדרה הוא דומה ורוח צפונית אינה מסובבת וכיון שהגיע חמה אצל קרן מערבית צפונית נכפפת ועולה למעלה מן הרקיע. ור׳ יהושע אומר עולם לקובה הוא דומה . . . קובה =אוהל שכולו מוקף. (Rashi)

[30] *Menaḥot 29b:* ומפני מה נברא העולם הזה בה׳ מפני שדומה לאכסדרה שכל הרוצה לצאת יצא.

[31] *Baba Batra 83b:* . . . . תשת חשך ויהי לילה. זה העולם שדומה ללילה.

[32] *Erubin 54a:* חטוף ואכול חטוף ואשתי דעלמא דאזלינן מניה כהלולא דמי.

[33] *Mo'ed Qatan 9b:* ליחרוב ביתך וליתוב אושפיזך דהאי עלמא אושפיזא וההוא עלמא ביתא.

[34] In the poem התבוננו כי העולם מעברות (מעבורת ?); עורי עורי beginning: נפשי אויתיך לראש אשמורת.

[35] *Carmina Sancta,* וכאשר נחשב (העולם הזה .sc) לבל יהי נושב וכל עובד ושב כגרים נמשלים *Salomonis Ibn Gabirol* by Senior Sachs, Lutetitia-Paris, 1868, p. 15. Hebrew Title: שיר השירים אשר לשלמה בן גבירול; שניאור זק״ש.

[36] *Beḥinat Olam,* VIII, 1–2: העולם ים זועף רב מצולה רחב ידים והזמן גשר רעוע בנוי עליו.

[37] *Ibid,* מה תעשה לזעף הים והמונו כי יתגעש ושטף ועבר ובית מלונו אף הוא יחשב להשבר. A number of other parallels may be found in I. Davidson, *Thesaurus of Proverbs and Parables from Mediaeval Jewish Literature,* Jerusalem, 1957, of which #2901, p. 176 is most apposite

ed. בן המלך והנזיר לר' לוי בר אברהם בן חסדי ,further .Cf. העולם הזה כגשר עברו עליו אל תשבו בו
A. M. Haberman, p. 102, and p. 70: Immanuel of Rome (מחברות). התבל דומה לגשר רעוע, and
Davidson #2898 העולם הזה דרך ומעבר לעולם הבא.

[38] Compare Gen. 32.23; Jos. 2.7; Jud. 3.28 12.5.6.

[39] It is quite possible to explain, however, and this may be considered with some seriousness that "don't build a habitation on *it*" refers to world and not to bridge. While in Greek, Latin, and English especially the antecedent has to be clearly indicated by its position, this is not the case in Hebrew where the antecedent may be set farther off in the sentence. Compare Ehrlich, *Miqra Ki-pheschuto,* II, pp. 407, 413, 417. Follow, however, the interpretation in the text.

[40] העולם ים גדול ורחב ידים והאדם ספינה משוטטת בתוכו, *Eben Boḥan,* by Menahem ben Shelomoh, ed. L. Dukes, Esslingen am Necker, 1846, p. 78.

Select Bibliography

Versions and Texts

NT	*Novum Testamentum Graece,* cum apparato critico 25th edition by E. Nestle and Kurt Aland, 1964.
UBS	*The New Testament in Greek and English:* the Greek Text of the United Bible Societies: ed. Kurt Aland, Matthew Black, Bruce M. Metzger and Allen Wikgren. For the sigla in the Greek MSS. the reader is referred to the ones listed in this third edition (1968).
Von Soden	Hermann von Soden, *Die Schriften des Neuen Testaments,* Text und Apparat, Teil 2.
itala	Old Latin witnesses to the NT.
vulg. vg.	*Biblia Vulgata,* Madrid, 1953.
Burkitt c	*Evangelion da Mepharreshe:* The Curetonian Version of the Four Gospels, with the readings of the Sinai palimpsest and the early Syriac Patristic evidence; edited, collected and arranged by F. Crawford Burkitt, 2 vols. 1904.
s	Sinaitic version of the Syriac.
p	Peshitta. The New Testament in Syriac, London, 1962 ed. by G. H. Gwilliam.
Phil	*Versio Philoxeniana,* ed. Joseph White, 1778.
MT	Masoretic Text: *Biblia Hebraica:* textum masoreticum curavit P. Kahle: 3–4 ed. A. Alt et O. Eissfeldt 1949. There are later editions of single books.
Trg.	Targums, Onq(elos), Targ. Yerushalmi, and Jon(athan) as found in the standard Rabbinic Bibles;

Sperber	A. Sperber, *The Bible in Aramaic*, 5 vols. 1959 f.
b.	*Talmud Babli*, Vilna edition, 1928.
y.	*Talmud Yerushalmi*, Krotoschin, repr. 1948. idem, 6 vols. with commentaries, Jerusalem, 1969.
midrash	midrash, midrashim: *Bereshit Rabba*, ed. J. Theodor-Ch. Albeck, 2nd ed. Jerusalem, 1965.
Num. R.	Numbers Rabbah
Qoh. R.	Qohelet Rabbah
Jos.	Josephus, *Jewish War; Jewish Antiquities*. Greek text ed. B. Niese; latest ed. in the Loeb Classics by Thackeray-Marcus-Wikgren-Feldman.
LXX	Greek version of the Hebrew Bible
A	The Alexandrine version of the LXX
B	The Vatican version of the LXX
sa	Sahidic version of the NT
bo	Bohairic version of the NT

Standard Works, Commentaries and Special Studies

W. F. Albright	*From the Stone Age to Christianity*, 2nd ed. 1957. *Archaeology of Palestine*, 1961. *Commentary on Matthew*, with C. S. Mann 1971.
W. C. Allen	*A Critical and Exegetical Commentary on the Gospel of S. Matthew*, repr. 1957.
M. Black	*An Aramaic Approach to the Gospels and Acts*, 2nd ed. 1954; 3rd ed. 1967.
J. H. Bernard	*Gospel according to St. John*, 2 vols. 1958 (repr.)
A. Büchler	*Die Priester und der Cultus*, 1895.
C. F. Burney	*Aramaic Origin of the Fourth Gospel*, 1922.
R. H. Charles	*The Apocrypha and Pseudepigrapha of the Old Testament*, 2 vols. 1913.
idem	*A Critical and Exegetical Commentary on the Revelations of S. John*, 2 vols. 1920.
G. Dalman	*Words of Jesus*, trans. from the German *Die Worte Jesu*, 1902; 2nd ed. 1930.
A. B. Ehrlich	*Miqra ki-Pheschuto*, 3 vols. 1899 f.; *Randglossen zur hebräischen Bibel*, 7 vols.
Y. N. Epstein	*Mevo'ot lesifrut ha-Tannaim* (Introduction to Tannaitic Literature) 1957.

J. Finegan	*Hidden Records of the Life of Jesus*, 1969.
L. Ginzberg	*Legends of the Jews*, 7 vols. 1913—1938.
idem	*Geonica*, 2 vols. 1909.
E. Z. Gould	*A Critical and Exegetical Commentary on St. Mark*, 1955.
F. J. Foakes Jackson-Kirsopp Lake	*The Beginnings of Christianity*, vol. IV, 1933.
A. Meyer	*Jesu Muttersprache*, 1896.
G. Kittel-G. Friedrich-G. W. Bromiley	*Theological Dictionary of the New Testament*, 10 vols.
E. Nestle	*Philologica Sacra*, 1896.
Arthur S. Peake[1]	*A Commentary on the Bible*, 1919; A. J. Grieve (NT).
Peake,[2] M. Black-H. H. Rowley	*Peake's*[2] *Commentary on the Bible*, 1962.
J. Moffatt	*Introduction to the Literature of the NT*, 3rd ed. 1961 (rep.).
J. A. Montgomery	*Origin of the Gospel according to St. John*, 1923.
A. Plummer	*Commentary on St. Luke*, 1960 (rep.).
E. Schürer	*Geschichte des jüdischen Volkes in Zeitalter Jesu Christi*, 3—4 ed. 1901—11; Eng. trans. *History of the Jewish People in the Time of Jesus Christ*, 5 vols. 1885.
H. L. Strack-P. Billerbeck	*Kommentar zum Neuen Testament*,[3] 6 vols. 1926.
H. B. Swete	*The Gospel according to St. Mark*, 1927.
C. C. Torrey	*Composition and Date of the Acts*, 1916. *The Four Gospels*, a new translation, 1933. *Our Translated Gospels*, 1936.
J. Wellhausen	*Einleitung in die drei ersten Evangelium*, 1905; 2nd ed. 1911.
Y. Yadin	*Bar Kokhba*, Eng. ed. 1972; Heb. ed. 1971. *Ha-ḥippusim aḥar Bar Kokhba*.

Grammars

Dalman	G. Dalman, *Grammatik des jüdisch-palästinischen Aramäisch*, 2nd ed., 1905; *Aramäische Dialektproben*, 2nd ed. repr. 1960.

Margolis	M. L. Margolis, *A Manual of the Aramaic Language of the Babylonian Talmud*, 1910.
diq.	Y. N. Epstein, *Diqduq Aramait Bablit*, 1930.
Nöld.	T. Nöldeke, *Compendious Syriac Grammar*, trans. by J. A. Crichton, 1904; idem, *Mandäische Grammatik*, 1875.
M. H. Segal	*Mishnaic Hebrew Grammar*, 1927.
Arndt-Ging.	William F. Arndt and F. Wilbur Gingrich, *A Greek and English Lexicon of the New Testament and other early Christian Literature*, 1957.
Liddell and Scott	Henry George Liddell and Robert Scott, *A Greek and English Lexicon*, revised by Henry Stuart Jones and Robert Mackenzie, 9th ed.
Lewis and Short	Chalton T. Lewis and Charles Short, *A Latin Dictionary*, 1958.
J. H. Moulton	*A Grammar of New Testament Greek*, 3 vols., I by J. H. Moulton, II, with W. F. Howard, III by Nigel Turner. 3rd edition, 1949 f.
Blass F.-Debrunner A.-Funk R. W.	*A Greek Grammar of the New Testament*, 1961.

DICTIONARIES

Levy, NH Wört., Chaldä. Wort.	J. Levy, *Neuhebräisches und Chaldäisches Wörterbuch über die Talmudim und Midraschim*, 4 vol., 1876—1889; idem, *Chaldäisches Wörterbuch über die Targumim*, 1881.
Kohut.	A. Kohut, *Aruch Completum*, 1878—1892, repr. with supplementary vol. 1955.
Jast.	M. Jastrow, *Dictionary of the Targumim, the Talmud Babli and Yerushalmi, and the Midrashic Literature*, 1886—1903.
Dalman	G. Dalman, *Aramäisch-neuhebräisches Handwörterbuch zu Targum, Talmud und Midrasch*, 1901.
BDB	F. Brown, S. R. Driver, C. A. Briggs, *Hebrew and English Lexicon of the Old Testament*, 1907.

Ges.-Buhl	William Gesenius, *Hebräisches und Aramäisches Handwörterbuch des A.T.* 17 ed., repr. 1949.
Ben Yehudah	E. Ben Yehudah, *Millon Ha-Lashon Ha-Ibrit* with supplementary notes by N. H. Tur Sinai, 1948.
Payn. Sm.	J. Payne Smith, *Compendious Syriac Dictionary*, 1903, founded on the Thesaurus Syriacus of R. Payne Smith, 1876.
Brock.	C. Brockelmann, *Lexicon Syriacum*, 2nd ed. 1928.
Schultess	F. Schultess, *Lexicon Syropalaestinum*, 1903.
Jennings	*Lexicon to the Syriac New Testament* by W. Jennings revised by Ulric Gantillon, 1926.
Oppenheim	A. L. Oppenheim et alii, *The Assyrian Dictionary*.
Lane	E. E. Lane, *Arabic English Lexicon*, 8 vols.
Hava	J. G. Hava, *Arabic-English Dictionary*, 1926 repr.
Krauss, S.	S. Krauss, *Griechische und Lateinische Lehnwörter in Talmud, Midrasch und Targum*, 1898.

General Index

I

Abode (temporary) vs. permanent home, 191
Acts, Book of, Chs. 1—15, composed in Aramaic 195; Aramaic did not end at Ch. 15, 200
Adam, not "Son of God," 110
aeshma daeva, 216
Albright, W. F., Aramaic and Greek Gospels, his views, 6f; refutation of these, 8f.
Angels, destroying, 165
Anthropomorphism, avoidance of, 68
Apagrapha, Ch. 7—8, 189
Arabic authors, Jesus' logia in, 190
Arabic *fa*, 75
Aramaic dialects, 6
Aramaic, Eastern, 21, 23, 96; complex of 21
Aramaic, Hebrew and, 17; on a special footing in the Second Commonwealth in Maccabean times, 11; Aramaic, Hebrew and Greek 15; dialogue in Aramaic, narrative in Hebrew; dialogue in Hebrew, narrative in Aramaic 14; Paul and A. 15
Aramaic, Western, 13
asartha, 10
Asmodeus, 28, 216
Astrology, 72

Babata, 15
Baptism, 15, 123; two meanings of, 91f.
Bar Abba, 186
Bar Kokhba, finds of, 14

Barnabas, Letter of, 178
Beel Zebub, 109
Bet Hillel, 80
Bet Shammai, 80
Bethsaida, 46
Boarneges, as Bene Re'esh, 10
Burial of the dead, 51

Caesar, J., 61
Cana, 142
Capernaum, 133
chiliarchi, 88
Citation, method of, in rabbinic literature, 180
Clothes, worn by heavenly Adam, angels, and Enoch, 181

D Version, 201
Demons, 46
Devil (Satan), 164
didache, 42
Divorce, 80; Jesus' ruling on, 176
Docetism, 180

Elephantine Papyri, 185
Elijah, 186
Elisabeth, barreness of; her pregnancy, 99.
Endurance, 118
Enoch, Book of, 9
Episodes, interrelation of three episodes: Mt., 24, 45; Mt. 25.1 and 14, 67

Eucharist, interpretation of, 172; Paul's description, 171
Ezekiel, 211
Ezra, Book of, 10

Fasting, 186—87
ficus carica, 82
ficus sycomorus, 82
Fig tree, 82
First born of all creatures, 173
Fist, 94, 95

Gadara, 88
Gamaliel I, 12, 13; Epistles of, 13
Gamaliel II, 12
Galilee, 88, upper and lower, 13
Galileans, did not enunciate gutturals clearly, 216
Gaza, two cities, 201
Gifts, by pagan rulers to the Temple, 117
Gospels, question of original language, 3; written in Aramaic, 23, 25f. 124 and *passim;* Chs. not written in Aramaic originally, 4
Gospel, Fourth, differences from the Synoptists, 169; Jesus as lamb in, 169
Gospel acc. to the Hebrews, 52, 131
Gospel, Coptic acc. to Thomas, 183
Greek, fallacy of thinking in Grk. and writing Hebrew 205f; "Palestinian Jewish Christian" Gk., 97

hetiyat, not necessarily Samaritan, 21
Herod, 84
Hesychius, 56
Holiness Code, 216
Hope, 35, 118

Immersion, 52; not the same as baptism, 123
Immorality, 153

Jerome, 52
Jesus, his Galilean Aramaic understood by Judeans, 22; carpenter, 26; acts on his own authority, 120; "Son of the Highest, 126,; vexation with his disciples, 137; his different attributes in Rev., 209; political revolutionary, 62; as spoken of in the Prophets, 180; non-canonical sayings of, ch.8, 177 f. understood and spoke some Greek, 17; as the Paschal Lamb in Jn., 169; as Logos to satisfy Hellenistic philosophers, 169; misunderstood by disciples 42; his sensitivity, 59.
John, the Baptist, 79
John, comment of, in the Fourth Gospel, 152
John, translator of, confuses Aram. roots 139 f; characteristics of his Greek translator, 139
Josephus, 150; knew Aramaic and Greek 216; his transliteration of Aramaic, 10; his method of composition, 17
Judeans, trilingualism of, 15
Judith, Book of, 5

koine, 8, 98
koine text, 46

Lamb of God, emphasized by Jn. to his disciples, 170
Lamed, as a sign of accusative, comfused with prepositional function, 114
Lazarus, death and resurrection, 157
Leaven, 41
Locusts, 79
Logos, in Jn. a mistranslation from the Aramaic, 169; in Greek and Christian thought, 167f
Lord of Flies, misreading of, 109
Luke, 1.5—2.52, composed in Aramaic (Moffat, Plummer); considered Semitic by Wellhauser, Nestle, Spitta; Hebrew (Torrey, Aytoun, composed in Gk. archaistically by Lk. 97. Luke, as translator, 19, 103, 114

ma'aseh bereshit, 165
Magi, 72

magistanes, 88
Magnificat, 97
manda' dehayye, 184
Mark, interpreter of Peter, 3
masah, 217
Matthew, Papias and, 4
Megillat Ta'anit, 7, 12, 16, 187
memra, 168
Merit, 52, 53
Messiah, 102, his function, 126
Misvocalization, 69, 75, 92, 164, 216
morus, 82

Nahorai, 103
Need for Aramaic to be translated into Greek, 23
Nehemiah, Book of, 10
Neighbor, 127
nomos, mistranslated as "law" by Paul, 216
Nuance, 57
nun, curtailed, 79

Obligation, man's religious, 54
Ordeal, 81
Oxyrhynchus Papyrus, 183

Palestine, 71
Peraea, 88
pascha, 10
Paul, see *nomos*
Pesach Sacrifice, 169
pe'il, 69; with dative of agent, 68; used for potential action, 98
Peshitta, 39, 201
Peter, 186, 202, 203
Pharisees, legal severities of, 42
Philo, 150
Pilate, character of, 150; wife of, 61
Planets, their influence, 72
Prayer, Hebrew, 97
Prologue, in Jn. coherent with the whole Fourth gospel, 170
Proto-Syriac, 20
Purification, by fire, 123

Question, misunderstood, 75
Quotation, unrecognized, 72

Revelations, Book of, Hebrew or Aramaic, 205f; questionable Hebraic reconstructions in, 205f.
Roots, confusion of, 93

Sabbath, episodes concerning, 120
Sacrifice, to be killed for leper, 44
saddik, 52
safra, 127
Samaria, woman of, 139
Samaritan, Aramaic and, 28
Satan, 153; "depths" of, 207
Schematism, 160
Seal, 144
Septuagint, Transliterations of Aramaic 9; Greek transliterations in NT, 9.
Shemoneh Esreh, 197
Simon Magus, 199
sofer, 127
Sorites, 183
Souls, not naked, 181
Spirit of God, as dove, 170
Syntax, 71, 72, 73, 74, 75, 76, 106, 120, 121, 123, 153, 170, 218; latitude in Semitic 90, 131; misconstrued in Gk. 129–137
Syria, Jews of 85; their dialect 22.
Syriac, see Proto-Syriac
sukmoros, 82

Talhin, 33, 36, 37, 40, 101, 118, 124, 125, 137, 143, 154, 158, 161, 216; See Wordplays.
Targum, of Job, 14
Tense, fluctuation in, 96, 146, 216
Tents, three, for new revelation, 175. See Transfiguration
Testimony, 143
Texts, discrepant Greek texts, 22, 56, 57, 60, 64, 69, 70, 82, 87, 106, 107
tme, not necessarily Samaritan, 21
Thomas, 147
Thyatira, 206f.

Tobit, Book of, 28, 31, 70
Torah, its violation, 131
Traditions, written, 22
Transliterations, in NT, 10
Translator, of Gk. Mt., his deficiencies, 33
Transfiguration, meaning of, 175
tribuni militum, 88
Typology, 175

Uzziah inscription, 21

Vocative, in Semitic, as reproduced in Greek, 112

Water and Spirit, 156

Waw adequaetionis, 149; *Waw* of consequence, 75
Wisdom, 48; in Hebrew and Greek thought, 167; its personification in Judaism and Hellenism, 168
Word of God, in Revelation, 209
Word plays, 76, 77, 79, 130, 157, 160; in Mt. 78; in Lk. 124–125; in Jn. 158–159
"World is a bridge," composed in Palestine, in Aramaic; figure used in Jewish literature, 190

Zacharias, Prayer of, 97
zakut 'abot, 52

Aramaic Words and Forms

II

אב 125
אבא 153
אבנא 125
אגוניסטא 94
אגר רוחא 105
אודי 128, 154
אודנא 69
אדרונא 69
אחד 77, 107, 128, 136
אחרינא 77
אכל 71
אל 186
אלף 124
אילפא 124
אמודי 26, 92

אמין 152
אמן 151, 158
אמר 69, 181
אמרא I 169, 210
אמרא II 169, 210
אמתא 112
אנא הוית 216
אנש 161
אסר 83
אפך 157
איקרא 117
אורחא 77, 78
אשמודי 28
ארמלתא 125
ארעא 71, 123

אשלמתא 96
אושענא 38
אתא 124
אתי 146, 157
אית 164
אתא I 51
אתא II 142
אתר 148

ב 99
בהל 101
בהלתא 101
בוע 85, 109
בועתא 56
בטל 58

INDEX

בטילאותא 93, 95, 101
בין 110, 121
ביעא 78, 125
בירא 47
בי (ת) 212
בי כנישתא 196
בי מדרשא 196
בי רבנן 196
ביתא 39, 159
בית חסדא 164
בית צלותא 196
בוכרא 173
בנא 66
בסמא 50
בסרא 170
בעא 60, 78, 95, 125
בעותא 85
בישא 77
בעל 176
בעל דבבא 109
בעל דינא 47
(בעת) ביעותא 56, 85
בר I 111, 125, 159
בר אלהא 126
בר אנשא 152
בר ביתא 216
בר הלכן 26
בר טבחא 26
בר נגרא 26
בר עילאה 126
בר ראבא 186
בר שלמותא 127
בר II 47, 92
ברם 68

גבא 50
גברא 125, 150
גבר הדיוט 27
גבר מלכא 27
גַּבְרָא 150
גברותא 207
גור 77, 176
גזם 71
גזרא 113, 157
גלילא 88
גמר 109
גמירא 98
גני 100
גנן 100, 175
גרא 105
גרבא 125
גרג 105

ד 132
דבק 200
דבר 124, 201, 202
דן 161
דין 27, 115, 148
דק 119
דלמא 155
דומיא 156
דמא 78
דמין 78
דמך 158
דועתא 119

היכנא 73
הימין (אמן) 59, 95, 125, 158, 161, 165
הכנא 73
הלך (דינא) 47
הלכא 47

ולא 130

זבן 159
זהמא 40
זע 51
זכות 52, 53
זלילותא 117
זמן 142
זימנא 164
זעירא 122

חב 213
חובא I 28, 76
חב (ב) 213
חובא II 28, 76
חבל 65, 165
חברא 79
חדא 77
חדא . . חדא 149
חדא (rejoice) 149, 161
חדיתאית 81
חר 141
חור I 119, 140, 206
חור II 55, 140
חורא 140
חזא 121, 141
חטף 131
חטיתא 159
חיא 161, 197, 198
דחיי (אע) 212
חיותא 88, 107, 108
חילא 173, 174, 186
חלא 66
חלם 61
חלף 78
חמם 39
חמירא 41
חמרא 79
חנק 58
חסר 208
חפי 78
חפר I 78, 125
חפר II 125
חוסנא 38
חרב I 48
חרב II 45
חורבא 46
חרד 60
חרש 90
חשוכא 37
חשיך 37
חשש 61

טבל 123
טבילותא 123
טב 122
טיבו 132
טליא 169
טלל 100

THE ARAMAIC ORIGIN OF THE FOUR GOSPELS

טמן 42f.
טמע 43, 79
טמר 43, 79
טנופתא 40
טעי 117
טעמא 80, 106
טשי 101
טרף 86, 87

(א) ידא 94, 95
יהוד 101
בר יהודי, יהודי 26
יוחנא (name) 79
יוחנא 79
יוחני (name) 79
ילוף 162
יומא 99
יסר 35, 83
ייסורא 35
יעד 216
יציפותא 101
יקירא 27
יקירתא 59
יקר 58
יתר 61, 74, 87
(מ) יתר 200
יתירותא 88

כחד 27
כלא 152
כוכבא 72
כינונא 171
כמנא 57
(ב) כן 67
כסי 99
כיסויא 99
כסף 27
כיפא 66, 117
כיפתא 77, 78, 125

ל = as 162
לבש 69
לחד 163

לחם 124
לחמא דמחרא 185

מ 133
מאנא 57, 182, 211
מאני זרע 182
מדנחה 72
מדינתא 101, 147
מחא 65, 124, 202
מחר 185
מיא 119, 156
מיין חיין 160
מית 158
מיתא 51
מיתותא 80
מועדא 151, 216
מכיך רוחא 62
מלא 53
מלאך 165, 207
מילחא 71
מלה 144
מוליא, מליא 145
מלך I 183
מלך II 183
מלל 90, 143
מלתא 105, 143, 165
מעברא 191
מפלתא 60
מפתח 136
מצד 107
מרא 158
ממרא 141
ממרמרנא 140
מרומא 37
מרח 200
מרי 141
מרר 199
משי 95
מתקלא 32, 217

נביא 181
נגד 114
נהוראי 102

נוחמא 108
נונא 78, 125
ניחא 184
נחשולא 89
נחת 201
נטר 84
נסיונא 81
נפש 37

סאתא 57
סבר 35, 160
סברתא 36, 118
סיבר 36, 160
סיברתא 161
סגי 74
(ס) שגיא 78
סגי (walk) 115
סופא 35
סחי 95
סיג 115
סם 125
סימתא 125
סימנא 55
סיפא I 137
סיפא II 137
סלק 155, 156
ספק 137
ספרא 136
סרח 70
סרי 70
סרק 39

עבד 99, 122, 153
עבד טב 75
עבד (happen) 163
עבדא 158, 159
עבר 27, 99, 153, 158
עבר עברה 216
עד 48
עק 84
עקתא 133
עידנא 216
עינא בישא 36

INDEX

עינא טבא 36
עלמא 159
עלמא דאתי 52
עומקא 207
עילא 143
על (ימא) 89
עלא 80
עמד 92, 122
עקרב 78, 125
ערבא 79
עריסא 57
עפורא 25
עפרא 25

פגר 173
פגרא 172
פגרותא 173
פוח 199
פטר 89, 176
פלג 68
פלגא (כאב) 67
פסחא 151
פקח 77, 128
פרס 40, 41, 155
פרש פרס 209
פריסתא 40
פרע 121
פורענא 116
פריע(ב) 116
פרתותא 78
פתאה 212
פתח 129, 200
פתר 129
פתורא 78

צבי 39, 78
צבע 78
ציד, צד 203
צלב 198
צליבא 199
צמח 102

קבורתא 161

קבל 154
קבל I (take) 64
קבל II (complain) 65
קבל מלכותא 179
קבל סהדותא 144
קם 26, 65, 83, 116, 148, 163, 165
קומא I 112
קומא II 112
קוצתא 81
קיל 30
קיסא 198
קלל 30, 151
קנטינר 193
קני I 51, 118
קני II 51
קנאה 63
קניא 51
קצא 173
קרב 78, 125, 161
קורבנא 43, 45, 77

רבא 126, 197
רבותא 34
רגלא 211
רגתא 88
רדף 90, 91, 200
רוח 51, 78
רחם 124
רחק 116
רים 146, 155
רישא (מד) 42, 120, 145
רמי 63, 125
רעי 47, 56
רעינא 54

שאל 58
שביט 72
שבת שבתא 187
שדי 63, 109, 151
שידא 109
שוא 53
שוא I (like) 55

שוא II (worth) 55
שוא I (place) 93
שוא II (compare) 93
שוא I (place) 103
שוא II (worth) 103
שג 94
שוח I 87
שוח II 87
שזג 95
שכב 158
שלא 58
שלותא 184, 217
שלט 122
שלם 36, 53, 96, 125, 147
שלמא 127
שלמותא 110
שמא 124
שמדי 28
שמדון שידא 28
שמם 60
שמע 124, 154
שמרי 28
שעמם 60
שפיר 117
שקר 164, 165
שקרא 213
שרי 63

תאנתא 82, 121
תבשילא 80
תגא 209, 210
תגרתא (גרא) 114
תגרותא (תגר) 114
תותא 82
תמה 60
תנינא 125
תנינא (ד) 91, 120
תקל 30
תקלא 31, 107
תקן 98, 118
תרעא I 25
תרעא II 25
תתא 82

# Greek Words and Forms

III

ἄβυσσος 92
ἀγαθός 130
ἄγγελος 207
ἅγιος 100
ἀγρεύω 107
ἀδικέω 207
αἴρω 136
αἰσχύνη 180
αἰτέω 95
αἰτία 80
αἰών 159
ἀκούω 104, 153
ἀκρασία 40
ἀληθής 158
ἄμμος 66
ἀνάστασις 148
ἀνίστημι 65
ἀνατολή 72, 102
ἀνάθεμα 117
ἄνθρωπος 27, 150, 151
ἀντιλέγω 140
ἄξιος 103
ἄνυδρος 39
ἀπέχω 74
ἄπιστος 125
ἁπλόος 36
ἀπο μιᾶς 58
ἀπολύω 89
ἀπορέω 84
ἀποτάσσομαι 89
ἀποθνῄσκω 57, 147
ἀποκτείνω 65
ἀποχωρίζω 208

ἅπτω 178
ἀργός 58
ἀρνέομαι 26, 27
ἁρπαγή 40
ἄρτος 171, 172
ἀρχή 145
ἀρχηγός 196, 197
ἀφαγίζω 71
ἄχρι καιροῦ 200

βαθύς 206
βαθύς 59
βάπτισμα 122
βασανίζω 34
βασιλεύω 182
βιάζω 131
βίβλος 208
βλέπω 118, 121
βοάω 10
βοή 10
βρῶμα 160
βρῶσις 71

γεύομαι 80
γνῶσις 136
γράφω 177

δένδρον 121
δευτερόπρωτος 120, 121
δεύτερος 91
δέχομαι 64, 104
διάνοια 53
διανοίγω 128, 200

διαπνέω 199
διαπραγματεύομαι 114
δίκαιος 61
δικαιόω 48, 127
δικαιοσύνη 52
διστάζω 67
διώγω 90
δόξα 37, 38, 154
δοῦλος 76
δουλόω 158
δῶρον 43
δράκων 210
δύναμις 173, 174, 186

ἐγείρω 83
εἰρήνη 110, 127
ἐκθαμβέομαι 133
ἐκλεκτός 48, 56
ἐκπλήσσω 60
ἔκστασις 55
ἐκχέω 151
ἑλίσσω 208
ἕλκυω 156
ἐμπνέω 199
ἐμπορία 114
ἐν 71
ἔνδυμα 180
ἐξηγέομαι 141
ἐξήγησις 141
ἐξανατέλλω 87
ἐξουσιάζω 121
ἐξυπνίζω 157
ἑορτή 151

INDEX

ἐπαγγέλλω 25
ἐπαισχύνομαι 29
ἐπάρατος 151
ἐπί 66
ἐπιθυμέω 88
ἐπιθυμία 87
ἐπιλαμβάνω 107
ἐπιούσιος 185
ἐπισκιάζω 100, 174
ἐργασία 114
ἔργον 48, 153, 182
ἑτοιμάζω 98
ἕτοιμος 159
εὐδοκέω 56
εὐεργέτης 121
ἔχω 156

ζάω 117
ζύμη 41

ἡδέως 85
ἡλικία 111
ἥκω 142

θάλασσα 89
θάνατος 80, 157
θεραπεία 211
θερίζω 149
θλίβω 178
θρόμβος 119

ἵστημι 25, 164
ἰσχυρός 207
ἰός 71
ἰῶτα 81

καινός 81
καιρός 159
κατισχύω 25
κακός 76
κάλαμος 50
καλέω 126
καταλαμβάνω 179
κτάομαι 117

κταρτίζω 98, 109
κατασκευάζω 98
κατασύρω 113
καταφρονέω 30
κέρας 81
κλάσμα 40
κλάω 217
κλείς 136
κλίνη 57
κοιμάω 157
κολλάω 200
κονιάω 55
κορβανᾶς 45
κοσμέω 39
κρατέω 128
κρεμάννυμι 198
κρίνω 161
κρίσις 59
κρυπτός 57
κρύπτω 43
κωφός 90

λέγω 69
λευκός 139
λίθος 117
λόγος 167
λοιπός 74, 87
λυπέω 133
λύπη 133

μαθητής 162
μακροθυμέω 104—5
μέγας 126
μένω 158
μεριμνάω 111
μετάνοια 103
μέτρον 143
μήτηρ 183
μόδιος 57
μοιχεύω 176
μόνος 162
μυρίος 34
μωραίνω 70

νηστεύω 186

ξύλον 198

ὀργυιά 112
ὁδός 47
οἶδα 121
οἰκονόμος 129
ὅμοιος 54
ὅρος 82
ὅτι 163
οὐκ 55
οὗτος 73

παγιδεύω 107
παραδίδωμι 96
παραιτέομαι 58
παρακαλέω 60
παράκλησις 108
παραλυτικός 68
πᾶς 52
πάσχω 61
πατάσσω 202
πατήρ 153
περικρύπτω 99
περιστερά 170
πέτρα 66
πετρώδης 87
πικρία 199
πιστεύω 151, 158
πιστός 95, 129
πλατεῖα 211
πλευρά 202
πληρόω 53
πλούσιος 60
πνεῦμα 89, 156, 183
ποιέω 75, 99, 163
ποίμνιον 112
πολύς 34
πόρνη 116, 153
πόρρωθεν 116
πραγματεύομαι 114
προσευχή 195
προσκυνέω 60

προσλαμβάνω 64, 121
πρῶτος 42, 88
πτωχός 62
πυγμή 93
πυκνός 93
πύλη 25

ῥήγνυμι 86
ῥῆμα 144, 197
ῥίπτω 63, 86

σάββατον 120, 121
σαλεύω 50
σαρόω 39
σατανᾶς 206, 207
σής 71
σκανδαλίζω 29
σκάνδαλον 29
σκηνόω 100
σκύλλω 63
σουδάριον 25
σπαράσσω 86
σπείρω 149
σπουδή 101
σταυρός 198
συκάμινος 82

συκῆ 82, 121
συγκλείω 107
συναγωγή 196
συντίθημι 75
συντηρέω 84
συσπαράσσω 86
σφραγίζω 142, 160
σχολάζω 39
σώζω 157
σῶμα 108
σωτηρία 198

τάφος 55
τέκνον 48
τέλος 136
τετράμενος 139
τίθημι 93
τολμάω 200
τόπος 39, 147
τόποι ἄνυδροι 39
τότε 66
τρόμος 55
τέκτων 26

υἱός 100, 109, 126, 127, 157

ὕψιστος 126
ὑπομένω 35
ὑπομονή 117, 118
ὑψόω 133, 146, 155

φεύγω 157
φιλέω 212
φημί 177
φοβέω 84
φόβος 55
φραγμός 115

χαρά 50, 55, 85
χάρις 132
χρόνος 164
χώρα 92

ψεῦδος 212
ψυχή 108, 117, 118

χολή 199

ὥρα 142
ὡσαννά 37

Hebrew Words and Idioms

IV

אגרוף 94
אחז 128
אכל 71
אל 186

אמר 141
ארך אפים 105

בא 51

בוש 144
בושש 144
בן עליה 126
בן עליון 126

INDEX

גט 144
גרה 105

דבר 80

הודה (ידה) 144, 154
היה 152
הלכה 47
הלכה (פסוקה) 48

חדש 81
חכה 118
חמס 131
חסד 132
חסר 208

יבל 51
יד 94, 95
יחל 118
יצר הטוב 54
יצר הרע 54, 153
יתרה 61

כף חובה 52
כשל 30

לבב 54
לפנים משורת הדין 48
לקח 179

מלאך 207
מנחה 44
מצה 172, 173
משא (נשא) 160
מרה 140

נבט 118, 119
נסיון 81
נשג 260
נפש 54, 108
נצר 84

ספר 141

עבד 122
עולם (ל) 187
עין טובה 36
עין רעה 36
עיסה 43
עמד 83, 165
ער 105

ערוה 80
עריסה 57

פקח 128
פשרה 48

צבא 174
צלוב 199
צר 84

קדח 80
קוה 118
קם 65
קוצו של יוד 81

ראשית (ב) 165
רב 197
רוח יי׳ 100
רחוב 212

שגגה 217
שכן 175
שמע 64

Other Words and Forms

I Arabic

'abara 193
faliǧ 68
ǧr 105
gantara 193
tagala 30

II Akkadian

elku 47
ataru 61
giṭṭu 144
zimanu, simanu 142, 159

III Latin

crastinum 185
filius magistri eorum 186
ganea 117
ganeo 117
ignorantia 184
medimnus 57
requies 183
super substantiali pane 185

Versions Cited

V

Greek Versions*:

I Septuagint

Genesis 4.12^{66}, 4.14^{66}, $6.5a^{66}$, 6.6^{66}, 27.33^{60}, 43.20^{145}
Deuteronomy 28.20^{60}
2 Kings 4.13^{60}
Isaiah 19.2^{66}
Ezekiel 26.16^{60}
Micah 6.11^{52}
Zechariah 12.4^{60}
Psalms 34.19^{62}, $72(73).13^{52}$
Proverbs 18.14^{62}

II Aquila

Is. 9.6^{186}
Ps. 80.10^{186}
Mic. 2.1^{186}

III Symmachus

Eccl. 3.1^{142}

Syriac Version:

Peshitta

Genesis 42.28^{60}
Leviticus 25.2^{187}

Jeremiah 51.10^{52}
Ezekiel 18.20^{52}
Psalms 40.16^{60}
2 Chronicles 19.7^{64}
Matthew 10.40^{64}, 15.30^{63}, 18.5^{64}
Luke 18.17^{64}

Aramaic Versions:

Onqelos

Genesis 2.4^{49}, $4.11^{64,179}$, 5.1^{49}, $14.24^{64,179}$, 15.6^{52}, 19.19^{132}, 20.13^{132}, 21.23^{132}, 24.65^{99}, 30.15^{67}, 30.33^{52}, 31.25^{200}, $41.45.50^{197}$, $42.11.31^{171}$, $42.19.33.34^{171}$, 43.12^{217}, $44.4.6.^{200}$, 46.20^{197}
Exodus 2.16^{197}, 13.2^{202}, 18.1^{197}, 34.6^{122}
Leviticus 4.2^{217}, 5.18^{217}
Numbers 15.28^{217}, 16.19^{67}, 20.12^{67}, 25.12^{67}
Deuteronomy 6.4^{155}, 6.5^{54}, 6.25^{52}, $9.4-6^{52}$, 13.15^{171}, 13.17^{212}, 17.4^{171}, 24.13^{52}, 28.28^{60}, 33.21^{52}

Targums of "Jonathan" to the Pentateuch and Prophets

Numbers 27.17^{64}, 31.18^{105}
Deuteronomy 6.4^{155}

*NB: The larger numerals refer to chapter and verse; the super linear smaller numerals to the pages in the text.

INDEX

Joshua 8.6.7[157]
Judges 5.21[202], 14.14[71]
1 Samuel 4.16.17[157]
1 Kings 11.29[99]
2 Kings 9.20[201]
Isaiah 3.7[99], 4.2[102], 11.5[102], 30.20[155], 44.15[60], 57.15[62], 66.2[62]
Jeremiah 33.15[102]
Jonah 3.6.7[99]

Targums to the Hagiographa

Job 18.9[107]
Canticles 7.5[114]
Lamentations 4.20[107]
Ecclesiastes 1.12[216]
Esther, Targum II 1.3[83], 3.14[81], 6.10[99], 8.13[122]
1 Chronicles 10.7[157], 19.1.15[157]

Josephus

Antiquities 1.1.1[10], 2.14.6[10], 3.6.6.[10], 3.10.6[10], 4.73.p.511 (Loeb Edition), 14.10.23[196], 15.7.10[176], 18.5.2[123], 20.11.2[215]
Wars 4.1.37[92], 4.7.3[88]

Apocrypha

Ben Sira ch. 14[168], 48.1—14[176], 50.25f.[28], *Greek Ezra* 17, *Judith* 5, *Tobit* 3.6[31], 3.13[31], *Wisdom* 9.1[168]

Pseudepigrapha

Enoch 9, 10, 61.10[174], 82.8[174]
Slavonic Book of Enoch 29.4f[155]

Patristic Writers

Barnabas, Letter of 7.11[178] [179]
Clement, First 40.1[207]
Clement *Stromata* III 13[178] [182], V 14.96.3[182-187]
Epiphanius *Haereses* 76.42.8[179]
Eusebius *Ecclesiastical History* 4.2-2.8[182]
Demonstratio Evangelica 10.8[186]
Gospel acc. to the Egyptans 180
Gospel acc. to the Hebrews 52, 182, 183
Gospel acc. to Thomas 190
Gospel (Coptic) acc. to Thomas 187, 190
Jerome *Against Pelagius* III, 2[52], Commentary on Isaiah 183, Commentary on John 183, Commentary on Matthew 185
Justin Martyr *Dialogue with Trypho* 47

Rabbinic Sources: Mishna (Tannaitic)

Abot 2.13.14[36], 3.15[59], 5.13[36]
Berakot 5.3[81], 9.5[54]
Eduyot 1.3[14], 8.4[11]
Ḥagigah 2.1[165]
Ḥullin 3.3[97]
Megillah 4.1[80]
Middot 2.5[196]
Nedarim 2.5[117]
Pesaḥim 10.1.2[133]
Sanhedrin 9.6[62]
Tamid 3.6[17]

Mekilta Yitro 5[48]
Sifre 1.7[110]

Babylonian Talmud

'Aboda Zara 8bf.^{165}, 16b$^{58\ 79}$, 37b^{11}
Baba Batra 20a^{46}, 25a^{191}, 83b^{217}, 98b^{43}
  ^{193}, 116a^{21}
Baba Mezia 30b$^{48\ 132}$, 33a^{171}, 61b^{43},
  83b^{14}, 84a^{216}, 86a^{27}
Baba Qamma 60b^{75}, 69a^{55}, 99a^{216}
Bekorot 5a^{14}, 8b^{70}
Berakot 2b^{196}, 3a$^{46\ 60}$, 6b^{21}, 15a^{53},
  22a^{196}, 27b^{52}, 34b^{126}, 37a^{18}. 44a^{185},
  45a^{183}, 45b^{48}, 47a^{14}, 59a.b.^{21}, 60b^{80}
Bezah 16a^{185}
'Erubin 13a^{208}, 54^{217}
Gittin 32b^{58}, 45a^{165}, 90a^{80}
Hullin 57a^{128}. 65a^{79}
Ketubot 13b$^{45\ 46}$, 27b^{45}, 97a^{216},
  101b^{181}, 106a^{155}
Menahot 29a^{81}, 29b^{217}, 90b^{44}
Mo'ed Qatan 9b^{217}
Niddah 66a^{173}
Pesahim 3b^{14}, 37a^{171}, 88a^{36}, 111b^{68}
Qiddushin 39b^{52}, 40b^{52}, 50a^{143}, 59a^{65},
  81a^{27}
Sanhedrin 6a^{48}, 39a^{123}, 65b^{128}, 90b^{181},
  95a^{86}, 97b^{126}. 113a^{21}
Shabbat 13a^{14}, 15a^{14}, 32a^{52} 133b^{76},
  145a^{45}, 152b^{21} 156a^{72}
Sotah 14a^{132}, 48b$^{14\ 185}$ 49b^{208}
Succah 45b^{126}
Ta'anit 21b^{105}
Yebamot 32b^{45}
Yoma 24b^{131}, 77a^{58}, 78b^{80}, 86b^{52}

Jerusalem (Palestinian) Talmud

'Aboda Zara II 14c^{40}, 41d^{41}
Berakot 2.5c^{115}, 4c^{53}, 7a^{53}
Kilayim IX 31a^{141}, 31b^{27}
Shabbat VIII 9c^{136}
Sotah 24b, 25a^{11}
Yebamot II 3d^{105}

Tosefta

Megillah 4(3).18^{180}
Sanhedrin 12.434^{115}
Sotah 13.4^{11}

Midrashim

Genesis Rabbah 16.6^{110}, 45^{131}, 96^{132}
Exodus Rabbah 6^{82}, 20^{153}
Numbers Rabbah 12^{89}
Qohelet Rabbah 10.14^{110}
Tanhuma Bereshit 13^{89}
Yalqut Shimoni on Josh. 1.4^{110}

Biblical Passages

VI
OT Passages

Genesis 2.1[174], 2.4[191], 3.7[77 128], 4.15[67], 32.23[218], 40.19[199]
Exodus 1.5[170], 6.6[67], 10.4[78], 11.8[60], 12.46[169]. 24.8[172], 32.1[144], 40.34[175]
Leviticus 4.2[80], 14.2–32[43], 14.25[44], 19.8[64], 19.17[80], 19.23[80], 20.17[64], 23.32[187], 24.11[38], 25.2[187], 26.34[187]
Numbers 3.23[206], 5.31[94], 9.12[169]. 12.13[106], 14.34[64], 16.3[94], 16.19[67], 17.10[140], 17.25[140], 18.32[64]
Deuteronomy 6.5[53 127], 16.16[68], 16.20[90], 24.1[80], 24.10[216], 29.17[199], 29.19[62], 31.27[140], 32.16[63], 32.17[109], 32.33[78], 32.39[106], 32.41[77]
Joshua 2.7[218], 7.19[154], 13.27[74]
Judges 3.10[100], 3.28[218], 5.28[144], 11.12[74], 11.29[100], 12.5[218], 14.6[100], 19.15[100]
I Samuel 10.6[100], 15.3[140], 16.7[69], 17.57[94], 19.24[51], 30.6[84]
II Samuel 17.11[89], 18.13[213], 23.21[94], 24.16.17[165]
I Kings 1.26[54], 3.9[54], 5.11[168], 8.37[80], 12.20[54], 14.29[74]
II Kings 3.11[93], 11.1[206], 23.30[51]
Isaiah 3.8[30], 5.25[94], 7.2[100], 13.10[174], 19.20[197], 21.4[92], 23.1[132], 24.22[46], 28.29[45], 34.4[174 208], 34.14[108], 41.4[165], 42.22[35], 44.15[60], 51.17[92], 56.11[108], 61.1–2[17 100], 63.13[30], 63.14[100]
Jeremiah 6.13[213], 8.8[213], 10.14[33], 15.19[59], 18.18[168], 23.5[102], 50.19[108]
Ezekiel 2.8[140], 2.9[206], 5.13[62], 8.1[202], 15.53[47], 20.8[140], 22.26[131], 33.20[179], 37.17[163] 38.19[62], 47.1–5[211 212]
Hosea 12.7[35], 14.2[30]
Micah 3.8[100]
Habakuk 2.3[35]
Zephaniah 3.4[130], 3.17[197]
Zechariah 3.8[102], 6.12[102], 8.19[187], 9.11[46]
Malachi 3.11[71], 3.18[121]
Psalms 10.3[54], 19.5[149], 22.1[186], 34.15[90], 35.13[187], 55.10[68], 55.24[92], 57.11[95], 60.5[92], 68.20[185], 69.11[187], 78.58[63] [82], 91.13[78], 107.4[174], 107.9[108], 109.24[30 133], 116.15[59], 118.26[38], 119.84[91], 139.20[141]
Proverbs 1.5[168], 3.13[167], 3.19[168], 4.5[167], 6.19[199]. 6.26[59], 8.22[167], 12.17[199], 14.5[191], 17.3[149], 17.24[53], 20.27[37], 21.21[91], 23.32[55], 24.23[168], 25.3[149], 26.15[43], 27.1[49], 27[108], 28.7[117]
Job 1.6[126], 2.1[126], 10.19[51], 21.32[51]
Esther 5.1[147]
Canticles 2.17[199], 4.6[199], 7.3[208]
Ecclesiastes 5.2[149], 5.17[147]
Daniel 2.37[38], 4.27[163], 4.37[38], 6.1[179], 6.8.9[26], 6.26[163], 8.2[147], 8.5[121], 8.16[212], 10.10[202], 11.11[141], 12.12[35]
Ezra 4.12[28], 4.23[101 163], 5.8[101], 8.21[187], 9.2.14[80]
Nehemiah Ch. 3[66], 3.34[28], 13.26[80]
I Chronicles 8.36[79], 21.21f.[165]
II Chronicles 9.5[147], 22.10[206], 25.1[79], 28.27[51]

NT Passages

Matthew
1   21^{197}
2   2^{72}, 11^{77}, 12^{77}, 9^{72}
3   9^{77}, 11^{123}, $15^{51\ 127}$, 16^{170}, 17^{56}
4   3^{77}, 10^{184}, 24^{68}
5   3^{61}, $8^{68\ 69}$, 13^{70}, 15^{57}, $18^{81\ 187}$, 22^{10}, 25^{47}, $28^{77\ 88}$, 29^{77}
6   13^{80}, 17^{186}, 19^{71}, 22^{36}, $24^{10\ 77}$, 25^{107}, 31^{107}
7   $9f.^{78}$, 17^{75}, 24^{66}, 27^{59}, 28^{120}
8   12^{46}, 22^{51}, 32^{57}
9   5^{83}, 14^{186}, 27^{200}, 36^{63}
10 5^{187}, 22^{118}, $27a,b,^{69}$, 33^{26}, 40^{64}
11 $7f.^{50}$, 10^{98}, $12^{130\ 131}$, 14^{64}, 15^{154}, 19^{48}, 24^{47}
12 11^{79}, 22^{135}, 33^{75}, 41^{65}, $43^{39\ 43}$, 45^{109}
13 $5^{25\ 87}$, 9^{154}, 20^{64}, 21^{178}, 28^{109}, 33^{43}, 40^{73}, 41^{31}, 52^{69}, 55^{26}, 57^{30}
14 13^{45}, 20^{41}, 23^{89}
15 5^{44}, 30^{63}
16 6^{41}, 12^{42}, 18^{25}, 22^{64}, 23^{10}, 28^{80}
17 $5^{56\ 100\ 174}$, $10f.^{71}$, 20^{82}, 21^{82}, 27^{31}
18 4^{29}, 5^{64}, 6^{30}, 10^{30}, 23^{27}, 24^{34}, 26^{60}, 29^{60}, 34^{34}, 35^{76}
19 3^{80}, $14f.^{30}$, 24^{60}
20 12^{78}, 16^{49}, 25^{122}, 28^{73}
21 6^{98}, 13^{196}, 32^{71}
22 2^{27}, $5^{58\ 114}$, 6^{65}, 13^{46}, 14^{49}, 15^{107}, 23^{161}, 28^{161}, $36f.^{53}$, 38^{54}, 39^{53}
23 2^{187}, 3^{187}, $4^{41\ 78}$, $23^{59\ 187}$, 25^{40}, 26^{40}, 27^{55}
24 5^{78}, 7^{148}, 9^{35}, $13^{35\ 118}$, 29^{174}, 32^{121}, $45f.^{66}$
25 $1f.^{66\ 77}$, 14^{67}, 18^{78}, 21^{50}, 23^{50}, 25^{25}, 30^{46}
26 9^{81}, 15^{25}, 17^{10}, 31^{202}, 37^{133}, 41^{80}, 45^{74}, 54^{73}
27 4^{73}, 5^{63}, $6^{10\ 78}$, 18^{62}, 19^{61}, 33^{10}, 57^{69}
28 $8^{55\ 85}$, $16f.^{67}$

Mark
1   6^{69}, 11^{56}, $21f.^{120}$, 22^{60}, 26^{87}
2   26^{73}
3   3^{83}, 17^{10}
4   5^{87}, 9^{154}, 16^{64}, 19^{87}, 21^{57}, 23^{154}, 30^{93}
5   2^{83}, 7^{83}, 10^{92}, 13^{57}, 33^{95}, 34^{95}
6   3^{26}, 6^{20}, 21^{88}, 32^{45}, 36^{89}, 41^{119}, 43^{41}, $45f.^{88}$, 48^{89}
7   3^{93}, 13^{95}, 16^{154}, 18^{73}, 34^{10}
8   8^{41}, $14-21^{41\ 160}$, 17^{137}, 32^{64}
9   1^{80}, $7^{56\ 100\ 174}$, $17f.^{89}$, 18^{86}, 25^{90}, 42^{29}
10 12^{176}, 13^{30}, 30^{90}, 42^{122}
11 2^{163}, 9^{37}, 10^{38}, 17^{196}, 18^{66}, $22f.^{82}$, 24^{95}, 38^{91}
12 1^{115}, 13^{107}, 26^{83}
13 8^{148}, $13^{35\ 118}$, $19^{178\ 184}$, 25^{174}, 28^{121}
14 11^{25}, $22^{171\ 172}$, 30^{91}, 33^{133}, 36^{10}, 38^{80}, 40^{133}, 41^{74}
15 10^{62}
16 $8^{55\ 85}$, 9^{109}, $9-20^{4}$

Luke
1   $5-2.52^{97\ 98}$, 15^{126}, 17^{98}, 24^{99}, 25^{99}, 31^{126}, 32^{126}, 33^{126}, $35^{99\ 126}$, 39^{101}, 52^{146}, 78^{102}, 79^{100}
2   48^{60}
3   ch.3^{98}, 8^{103}, $22^{56\ 126\ 170}$, 23^{103}, 38^{112}
4   1^{124}, $3^{105\ 124}$, 13^{200}, 31^{120}, 35^{86}, $36^{105\ 120}$, 42^{45}
5   3^{124}, 9^{66}, 33^{93}

INDEX

6   1^{120}, 6^{120}, 8^{83}, 20^{61}, 22^{90}, 23^{90} 24^{108}, 32^{132}, $40^{98\ 109}$, 47^{59}, 48^{66}, 49^{59}
7   $8^{135\ 154}$, 12^{124}, 27^{98}, 35^{48}
8   2^{109}, 6^{87}, 8^{124}, 13^{80}, 14^{88}, 16^{57}, 18^{118}, 28^{84}, 31^{92}, 33^{58}
9   10^{46}, 13^{160}, 26^{27}, 27^{80}, 33^{100}, 34^{100}, 35^{56}, 60^{51}
10 $1^{17\ 22}$, 6^{127}, 11^{200}, $15^{133\ 134}$, 16^{104}, 17^{19}, 20^{124}, 27^{63}, 29^{127}, 42^{134}
11 4^{80}, 5^{124}, 7^{107}, 8^{132}, $11^{11\ 78}$, 12^{78}, 14^{34}, 19^{109}, 21^{110}, $24f.^{39}$, 33^{57}, 39^{40}, $42^{27\ 125}$, 44^{55}, 46^{41}, 52^{136}
12 1^{42}, 3^{69}, 8^{128}, 9^{27}, 21^{125}, 22^{107}, 29^{107}, 32^{112}, 42^{129}, 43^{129}, 46^{125}, $49^{92\ 122}$, $50^{92\ 122}$, $50^{92\ 122}$, 58^{113}
13 1^{150}, 8^{130}, 9^{130}, $10f.^{120}$, 21^{43}, 25^{107}
14 1^{84}, 3^{120}, 5^{79}, 11^{146}, $18^{20\ 58}$, 21^{115}, 34^{70}
15 13^{117}, 30^{116}
16 3^{125}, 6^{115}, 9^{100}, $16f.^{130}$, 23^{109}
17 2^{29}, 6^{82}, 12^{116}, 14^{116}, 19^{197}
18 7^{104}, 8^{104}, 15^{30}, 17^{64}, 18^{130}, 19^{130}, 25^{108}, 31^{125}
19 9^{197}, 11^{169}, 12^{179}, 20^{25}, 30^{163}, 38^{37}, 46^{196}
20 20^{107}, 26^{107}
21 2^{125}, 5^{117}, 11^{148}, 12^{90}, $19^{35\ 117}$, 29^{121}, 30^{121}
22 5^{25}, 10^{125}, $15^{88\ 171}$, $22^{25\ 80}$, 34^{91}, 37^{136}, 40^{80}, 41^{33}, 44^{119}, 45^{133}, 46^{80}, 49^{202}
23 5^{88}, 15^{68}, 35^{125}
24 16^{128}, 27^{129}, 32^{128}, 35^{173}, 41^{85}

John

1   $1^{167\ 169\ 170\ 209}$, $2^{167\ 170\ 209}$, 3^{170}, 12^{180}, $14^{100\ 132\ 167\ 209}$, 16^{132}, 18^{141}, 19^{145}, 20^{144}, 22^{145}, 33^{144}, 34^{144}, 35^{170}, 36^{169}, $41^{10\ 170}$
2   4^{142}, 15^{150}, 16^{114}, $23-25^{151}$
3   5^{156}, 14^{146}, 17^{161}, $31-34^{142f.}$
4   $7f.^{139}$, 31^{159}, 35^{139}, $36f.^{148\ 161}$, 37^{149}
5   6^{164}, 16^{90}, 17^{145}, 19^{145}, 29^{148}, 46^{180}
6   12^{155}, 27^{160}, 46^{141}, 60^{154}
7   6^{159}, 8^{159}, 30^{142}, 33^{145}, 34^{145}, 38^{145}, 49^{141}
8   15^{161}, 25^{145}, $28^{144\ 146}$, $30-35^{158}$, $38-42^{152}$, 43^{155}, $44^{88\ 164}$, 48^{28}, 52^{80}, 58^{146}
9   8^{164}, 17^{163}, 24^{154}, 27^{162}
10 5^{157}
11 $11f.^{147\ 157}$, 16^{147}, 25^{161}, 40^{164}, 48^{147}, 54^{46}
12 16^{163}, 23^{142}, 24^{162}, 32^{155}, 34^{145}, 47^{161}, 48^{161}
13 $1^{142\ 152}$, 22^{119}, 38^{91}
14 30^{156}
15 20^{90}
16 6^{133}, 20^{133}, 21^{178}
17 1^{142}
19 5^{149}, 12^{140}, 13^{10}, 42^{161}
21 ch. $21^{4\ 215}$, 6^{156}, 12^{145}

Acts

1   14^{195}, 15^{22}, 26^{22}
2   4^{51}, 26^{118}, 36^{198}, 42^{173}, 46^{173}
3   15^{196}
4   10^{198}
5   12^{200}, 13^{200}, 20^{197}, $30^{198\ 198}$
6   $1f.^{19}$
8   23^{199}, 26^{201}
9   1^{199}
10 39^{198}
11 22^{19}
12 7^{202}
13 11^{200}, $29^{198\ 199}$
14 22^{178}
15 12^{141}, 31^{108}, 35^{4}
16 13^{196}, 16^{196}

17	3^{200}
20	7^{173}, 35^{177}
22	$16^{52\ 123}$
24	15^{118}

Revelations

2	24^{206}
5	2^{207}
6	6^{207}, 14^{208}, 15^{88}
12	12.9^{153}, 19^{29}
13	3^{205}, 11^{210}
19	$7^{209\ 210}$, 11^{209}, 12^{209}, $13^{209\ 210\ 211}$, $16^{209\ 211}$, 18^{210}
20	2^{29}
22	$1f.^{211}$, 2^{211}, 15^{212}

Romans 4.18^{118}, $8.24,^{36\ 118}$, 8.38^{174}, 11.35^{67}

I Corinthians 2.10^{207}, 11.24^{172}, $1.13-16^{52}$, $15.45-50^{111}$

II Corinthians 5.3^{181}, 6.22^{10}, 11.13^{153}

Galatians $3^{13\ 198}$, 3.28^{180}

Ephesians 1.21^{174}, 4.30^{144}

Philomen $3.4f.^{18}$

Hebrews $6^{11\ 36}$, 9.11^{111}

James 5.2^{71}, 5.14^{44}

I Peter 3.19^{25}

Index of Authors
VII

Albeck, Ch. 20
Albright, W. F. 4, 6, 7, 21
Alcalay, R. 37, 59, 81
Akbar, the Great 189
Aland, K. 48
Allen, W. C. 29, 31, 32, 46, 48, 58, 63, 72, 181, 185, 187
Aquila 186
Aquinas 167
Arndt, W. F.—F. W. Gingrich, 9, 32, 50, 71, 85, 92, 108, 117, 140, 147
Aytoun, R. A. 97, 179, 185, 196

Ben Sira 11
Ben Yehudah, E. 11, 13, 58, 91, 105
Bernard, J. H. 139, 142, 146, 147, 149, 152, 168
Black, M. 5, 33, 48, 66, 129
Blass, F.—Debrunner,A.-Funk, R. W., 9, 100
Blunt, A. W. F. 196
Bousset, W. 208
Brandon, S. G. F. 62

Brederek, E. 64
Büchler, A. 11
Burkitt, F. C. 57, 87, 88, 195
Burney, C. F. 4, 66, 90, 129, 131, 139, 141, 169

Cadbury, H. J. 36, 195
Cassanowicz, I. M. 33
Cassianus, J. 180
Charles, R. H. 5, 205f., 206, 207, 208, 209, 211
Chaucer, Geoffrey 217
Clay, G. H. 172
Colwell, E. C. 4
Conybeare, F. C. 89
Clement 180, 182
Conzelmann, H. 172
Cowley, A. E. 5, 159
Cumont, F. 181

Dalman, G. 20, 26, 38, 67, 73, 74, 83, 116
Davidson, I. 217

INDEX

Debrunner, A. See Blass, F.
Deissmann, A. 181
Dio Cassius 14
Driver, G. R. 5, 216
Dukes, L. 218

Ehrlich, A. B. 90, 91, 98, 131, 218
Elazar, the Great, 185
Epiphanius 179
Epstein, J. N. 20
Epstein, J. N.-Melamed, E. Z. 48
Eusebius 182, 186

Fathpur-Sikri 189
Federbush, S. 48, 216
Finegan, J. 177, 178, 179, 180, 182, 183, 186, 187
Finkelstein, L. 21
Foucart, G. 72
Foakes Jackson, F. J.-Lake, K. 108, 196, 197, 198, 201
Funk, R. W. see Blass, F.

Gamaliel, I., Epistles of 13
Gingrich, F. W; see Arndt, W. F.
Ginzberg, L. 42, 111, 145, 168, 181, 186
Goodspeed, E. J. 119, 146, 195, *et, passim*
Gordis, R. 33, 72, 102, 124
Grieve, A. J. 4
Grundmann, W. 174

Haberman, A. M. 217
Hadrian 14, 181
Harris, J. R. 4
Hava, J. G. 59
Hegesippus 182
Heinisch, P. 167
Hilgenfeld, A. 209
Hillel 185
Holmes, S. 167
Holtzmann, J. 208
Horst, J. 105
Huck A.-Lietzmann, H.-Cross, F. L. 34, 46, 131

Ibn Gabirol, Solomon 191
Ishmael, Rabbi 11

Jacoby, A. 102
Jaqut 217
Jastrow, M. passim
Jastrow Jr., M. 72
Jennings, W. 71, 101
Jeremias J. 172, 189, 191, 217
Jerome 108, 185
Josephus 17, 45
Joshua, Rabbi 191
Joshua b. Ḥananyah 70
Jülicher, A. 4
Justin Martyr 179

Klausner, J. 103
Knox, Ronald 120
Kosawski, Ch. 104
Krauss, S. 15, 193
Koster 177

Lachs, S. 47
Lagarde, de P. 178
Lake, K., see Foakes Jackson, 108
Lampe, G. W. H. 201
Lewysohn, L. 79
Levy, J. *passim*
Lieberman, S. 15, 114–115, 147
Loisy, A. 112, 168
Löw, I. 82

Manson, O. S. 168
Margolis, M. L. 10, 69, 78, 109, 168, 179, 216
Margoliouth, D. S. 190
Marsh, J. 65
Mary 101
Menahem ben Shelomoh 218
Merx, A. 181
Messiah ben Efrayim 102
Metzger, B. 48, 217
Meyer, A. 4, 91
Meyer, E. 167

Moffatt, J. 50, 97, 119, *et passim*
Montefiore, C. G. 39, 111, 113
Montgomery, J. A. 4, 68, 105, 106, 129, 139, 165
Moses ben Ezra 191
Moulton, J. H. 9, 73

Nestle, E. 48, 93, 97, 196, 217
Neubauer, A. 15
Nöldeke, T. 96, 130, 162, 164, 170, 216

Oepke, A. 181
Origen 183

Papias 3,4
Paul 111
Petrus Alfonsi 189
Pfeiffer, R. H. 28
Philo 111
Pick, B. 217
Plummer 46, 48, 105, 111, 117, 118, 119, 131
Pritchard, J. B. 93
Proksch, O. 100

Rabbinovicz R. 79
Rashi (Rabbi Solomon Izḥaqi) 44
Reckendorf, H. 33
Resch, A. 117
Robinson, J. Armitage 171
Ropes, J. H. 217

Sachs Senior 217
Salome 180, 181
Samuel, the Little 11
Schürer, E. 9, 88, 216
Schechter, S. 52
Schlatter, D. A. 4
Segal, M. H. 15, 206
Shammai 185
Siegfried, C. 167
Simon, the Just 12
Simon ben Yoḥai Rabbi 191

Smith, A. L. 216
Smith, G. A. 88, 201
Soith, V. A. 217
Spitta, F. 97, 209
Stählin, G. 31
Strack, H. L. 22
Strack, H. L.-Billerbeck, Paul 103, 185
Swete, H. B. 56, 62, 84, 87, 90, 92, 94, 208

Thackeray, H. St. J. 45
Theodor, J. 28
Theodor, J.—Albeck, Ch. 110
Theophrastus 45
Thompson, C. 46
Torrey, C. C. 4, 5, 6, 7, 36, 38, 38, 42, 66, 67, 91, 101, 103, 111, 129, 130, 195, 205, 206, 211, 216
Turner, N. 4, 5, 210
Tur-Sinai, N. H. 105

Valentius 180
Von Soden, H. 34, 217

Wellhausen, J. 4, 39, 97
Wensinck, A. J. 4
Wilcox, M. 195
Wilkgren, A. 48
Wright L. E. 177
Wright, W. 201
Würtheim, E. 81

Ya'aqob R. 191
Yadin, Yiga'el 14
Yehudah, Rabbi (mishnaic authority) 45
Yellin, D. 33 33
Yoḥanan I 12
Yoḥanan II 79

Zeitlin, S. 12, 38
Zimmermann, F. 10, 54, 120, 124, 125, 141
Zuckermandel, M. S. 11
Zwaan, de J. 4